Chapter 1

Applications for Everyone

In this increasingly complex world, a personal computer is most useful in organizing and simplifying the minutia of everyday life. In this chapter you will find an eclectic collection of applications for everyone, each designed to streamline daily life.

PERSONAL REFERENCE SOURCE

Reference information that is often referred to but too complex to memorize could be stored for instant retrieval. Possibilities are endless, but examples of charts, tables, and lists that have been stored in personal computers include

1. Calories and nutritional content of selected foods.
2. Appointment itinerary.
3. Important articles and books (stored by author, title, topic, and date).
4. Sports statistics, amateur or professional.
5. Product sources, specifications, and prices from various suppliers for comparison.
6. Names, addresses, and phone numbers.
7. Stock market data including name, symbol, shares, price, and historical data.
8. Recipes and shopping lists.
9. Postal and shipping rates, requirements, and regulations for the businessman.
10. Metric conversions and information.
11. Time differences and phone rates between cities.
12. Words commonly misspelled or misused (as a quick reference writer).
13. Ham Radio log of contacts, locations, and times.
14. Collection inventory, including name of item, age, values, and identifying information.
15. Private pilot flight planning data.
16. Household inventory for insurance and financial purposes.
17. Astronomical and astrological data.
18. Things to be done, ordered, or checked with times available and deadlines.
19. Fishing log.
20. Quotations by topic and source.

21. References from literature, the Bible, and so on.
22. Dates of birthdays, anniversaries, and other special occasions.
23. Automotive service information, especially for business car fleets.
24. Patient laboratory data over time, differential diagnoses, or drug for physicians.
25. Credit cards, with numbers to call in the event of theft.
26. Safety deposit box contents.
27. Physical contents, chemical data, formulae.
28. Emergency phone numbers.
29. Poison antidotes.
30. Computer software/hardware comparisons.
31. Cumulative weather data.
32. Abbreviations.
33. Wire information for the the connoisseur.
34. Horse racing statistics.
35. Anecdotal material for those obliged to make speeches.
36. Insurance policy inventory including coverage, cost, account numbers, and deductibles for house, car, health, and other kinds of insurance.

This list isn't exhaustive, and only a few of these applications may be of use to you, but it serves to illustrate the multiple possibilities primarily involving the storage of information. How would you store this information? Use the *Electronic Memorandum* program Listing 1-1, or the *Data Base Demonstration* program, Listing 1-12, for your own tailor-made application.

THE ELECTRONIC MEMORANDUM PROGRAM

In Listing 1-1 you will find a program that should be useful to everyone; think of it as a memory extension. The program allows you to store any type of information (household, business, financial) under a "keyword" for instant retrieval at a later date. For instance, if you had an appointment on a certain date, the pertinent information could be stored under the keyword "9/11/85;" on that date you would simply type "9/11/85" to receive a printout of all appointments or reminders stored under that keyword. Likewise, a remainder for an annual occasion could be entered under a keyword specifying only the month and day. Keywords may be dates or words such as "MARKS BIRTHDAY." Telephone numbers, business contacts, important dates, and many other bulletin-board type scraps of information could be stored so that they could not be forgotten or misplaced. This information could include the number and expiration date of your driver's license, the serial numbers of credit cards (and who to notify if they are lost), expense account information, information about insurance policies, warranty information on all appliances, names and addresses of dealers, magazine subscription dates, handy home repair tips (for example, the size of the air conditioner filter), lock combinations, special codes, the method of resetting a digital watch, Christmas gifts and to whom they were given, eyeglass prescription, and so on *ad infinitum*. Additionally, information may be stored under more than one keyword to ensure the ability to retrieve it.

This program is designed for use with floppy disks. It could be changed for use with a cassette, but this would be undesirable because of the amount of time needed to access the information. The program requires 6.3K of memory.

Listing 1-1: The Electronic Memorandum Program.

```
10 DEF SEG=&H40
20 POKE &H17,(PEEK(&H17) OR 64):REM SETS CAPS LOCK TOGGLE TO 'ON'
WITHOUT DISTURBING OTHER SETTINGS
30 DEF SEG:REM RETURNS SEGMENT POINTER TO BASIC DATA SEGMENT
40 PRINT "ELECTRONIC MEMORANDUM"
50 REM E$=FLAG TO INDICATE WHETHER DATA ID HAS BEEN USED
60 REM Z=ID NUMBER FOR ENTRY
```

```
70 REM M AND M$ USED TO COUNT ITEMS PRINTED TO SCREEN
80 CLEAR 3000:KEY OFF
90 CLS 'CLEAR SCREEN
100 PRINT "SELECT AN OPTION:"
110 PRINT "COMMAND","FUNCTION"
120 PRINT "INPUT","INPUT A NEW ITEM"
130 PRINT "CAT","GENERATE A CATALOG OF COMMON ENTRIES"
140 PRINT "FIND","FIND A PREVIOUSLY STORED ITEM"
150 PRINT "REDO","EDIT A PREVIOUSLY STORED ITEM"
160 PRINT "DEL","DELETE A PREVIOUSLY STORED ITEM"
170 PRINT "END","END THE PROGRAM"
180 INPUT A$
190 IF A$="INPUT" THEN 270
200 IF A$="CAT" THEN 660
210 IF A$="FIND" THEN 960
220 IF A$="REDO" THEN 460
230 IF A$="DEL" THEN 1140
240 IF A$="END" THEN CLOSE:END
250 PRINT "ILLEGAL COMMAND--PLEASE ENTER ONE OF THE FOLLOWING:"
260 GOTO 110
265 REM routine to input data
270 INPUT "ENTER A KEYWORD (MAY BE UP TO 20 LETTERS LONG)";B$
280 IF LEN (B$)>20 THEN 270
285 REM lines 290-310 are for verification of cata when inputting;
you may wish to delete these lines to save time when inputting
290 PRINT "IS THIS CORRECT (1=YES,2=NO):";B$
300 INPUT D
310 IF D><1 THEN 270
320 INPUT "ENTER THE DATA FOR THIS RECORD (MAY BE UP TO 105 LETTERS
LONG--DO NOT USE COMMAS  IN YOUR ENTRY)";C$
330 IF LEN(C$)>105 THEN 320
340 D$=LEFT$(B$,1)+".TXT"
350 CLOSE
360 OPEN "R",1,D$:Z=1        'OPENING RANDOM ACCESS FILE
370 FIELD #1,3 AS E$,20 AS F$,105 AS G$
380 GET #1,Z        'finding unused record number
390 IF E$="999" THEN Z=Z+1:IF Z=LOF(1)/128+1 THEN 400 ELSE 380
400 LSET F$=B$
410 LSET G$=C$
420 LSET E$="999"        'labelling this record number as used
430 PUT #1,Z        'STORING ENTRY
440 CLOSE
450 GOTO 90
455 REM routine to edit data
460 INPUT "ENTER THE KEYWORD FOR THE DATA TO BE EDITED";B$
470 D$=LEFT$(B$,1)+".TXT"
480 CLOSE:Z=1
490 OPEN"R",1,D$:IF LOF(1)=0 THEN PRINT "FILE END":CLOSE:GOTO 100
500 FIELD #1,3 AS E$,20 AS F$,105 AS G$
510 IF Z=LOF(1)/128+1 THEN PRINT "FILE END":CLOSE:GOTO 100
```

```
520 GET#1,Z
530 IF E$<>"999" THEN Z=Z+1:GOTO 500          'IF NO ENTRY GO ON
540 IF LEFT$(F$,LEN(B$))><B$ THEN Z=Z+1:GOTO 500          'IF NO MATCH
GO ON
550 CLS          'CLEAR SCREEN
560 PRINT "MEMORANDUM:"
570 PRINT G$:PRINT
580 INPUT "DO YOU WISH TO EDIT THIS ITEM (1=YES, 2=NO)";Y
590 IF Y<>1 THEN Z=Z+1:GOTO 500
600 INPUT "RE-ENTER ALL DATA:",C$
610 IF LEN (C$)>105 THEN PRINT "DATA TOO LONG--MUST BE LESS THAN
105 LETTERS."GOTO 600
620 LSET G$=C$:LSET F$=B$:LSET E$="999"
630 PUT #1,Z
640 INPUT "EDIT ANOTHER ITEM WITH THIS KEYWORD (1=YES, 2=NO)";Y
650 Z=Z+1:IF Y<>1 THEN CLOSE:GOTO 100 ELSE 500
655 REM routine to list catalog of entries
660 PRINT "SELECT: 1)LIST A CATALOG OF ALL ITEMS ON FILE"
670 INPUT "          2)LIST ALL ITEMS WITH A SPECIFIED KEYWORD";Y
680 ON Y GOTO 810,690
690 INPUT "ENTER THE KEYWORD";H$
700 D$=LEFT$(H$,1)+".TXT"
710 CLOSE:Z=1:M=1:PRINT:PRINT "ITEM #","ITEM"
720 OPEN "R",1,D$:IF LOF(1)=0 THEN PRINT "FILE END":CLOSE:GOTO 100
730 FIELD#1,3 AS E$,20 AS F$,105 AS G$
740 GET #1,Z
750 IF Z=LOF(1)/128+1 THEN PRINT "-------------------":PRINT:CLOSE:
GOTO 100
760 IF E$<>"999" THEN Z=Z+1:GOTO 730
770 PRINT Z,F$:M=M+1
780 IF INT(M/17)=M/17 THEN INPUT "MORE TO COME; PRESS ENTER WHEN
READY:",M$
790 Z=Z+1
800 GOTO 730
810 CLS          'CLEAR SCREEN
820 PRINT "RECORD #","KEYWORD"
830 X=65
840 J$=CHR$(X)
850 D$=J$+".TXT"
860 Z=1
870 CLOSE
880 OPEN "R",1,D$:IF LOF(1)=0 THEN X=X+1:IF X<=90 THEN GOTO 840
ELSE CLOSE:GOTO 100
890 FIELD #1,3 AS E$,20 AS F$,105 AS G$
900 IF Z=LOF(1)/128+1 THEN X=X+1:IF X<=90 THEN GOTO 840 ELSE
CLOSE:GOTO 100
910 GET #1,Z
920 IF E$<>"999" THEN Z=Z+1:GOTO 890
930 PRINT Z,F$
940 Z=Z+1
950 GOTO 890
```

```
960 CLS:REM routine to find selected data
970 INPUT "ENTER KEYWORD";B$
980 D$=LEFT$(B$,1)+".TXT"
990 CLOSE:Z=1
1000 OPEN "R",1,D$:IF LOF(1)=0 THEN PRINT "FILE END":CLOSE:GOTO 100
1010 IF Z=LOF(1)/128+1 THEN PRINT "FILE END":INPUT "PRESS ENTER TO
CONTINUE",M$: CLOSE:CLS:GOTO 100
1020 FIELD #1,3 AS E$,20 AS F$,105 AS G$
1030 GET #1,Z
1040 IF LEFT$(F$,LEN(B$))=B$ THEN 1080
1050 IF E$<>"999" THEN Z=Z+1:GOTO 1010
1060 Z=Z+1
1070 GOTO 1010
1080 PRINT "KEYWORD:";F$,"ITEM #:";Z
1090 PRINT G$
1100 PRINT
1110 Z=Z+1:M=M+1
1120 IF INT(M/5)=M/5 THEN INPUT "MORE TO COME; PRESS ENTER WHEN
READY",M$
1130 GOTO 1010
1140 CLS      'DELETE A RECORD
1150 INPUT "ENTER KEYWORD,RECORD NUMBER: ",B$,Z
1160 D$=LEFT$(B$,1)+".TXT"
1170 CLOSE
1180 OPEN "R",#1,D$      'OPENING RANDOM ACCESS FILE
1190 FIELD #1,3 AS E$,20 AS F$,105 AS G$      'DEFINE INPUT FIELD
1200 GET #1,Z
1210 IF LEFT$(F$,LEN(B$))><B$ THEN PRINT "KEYWORD AND ITEM NUMBER
DON'T MATCH":CLOSE:GOTO 100
1220 CLS      'CLEAR SCREEN
1230 PRINT "KEYWORD";F$
1240 PRINT G$
1250 PRINT
1260 INPUT "IF YOU WANT TO DELETE THIS RECORD TYPE '1'";Y
1270 IF Y><1 THEN CLOSE:GOTO 100
1280 FIELD #1,3 AS E$,20 AS F$,105 AS G$      'DEFINE OUTPUT FIELD
1290 LSET E$=""      'ERASING
1300 LSET G$=""      'INFORMATION
1310 LSET F$=""      'FROM THIS RECORD
1320 PUT #1,Z
1330 CLOSE
1340 GOTO 100
```

AN INDEX TO YOUR LIBRARY

How often do you remember reading an important article or chapter, yet you can't remember the name or date of the magazine or book? A personal computer can easily organize and cross-reference your books and articles for instant retrieval using only the name, subject, author, or other parameter to retrieve the entries you are interested in. With the wealth of personal computer magazines available, an index to pertinent articles will ease the difficulty of finding that special patch or program.

A program to accomplish indexing could store information regarding items as a continuous string of data, each string being composed of several "fields," and each field separated by a comma. An example of a string with fields describing a magazine article could be as follows:

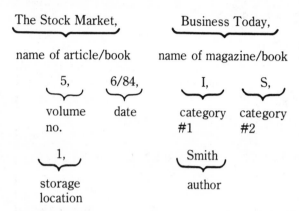

If data is formatted on disk in a manner similar to this example, *random access* disk commands will allow the computer to search through a selected field to find all entries with a given field. For example, the user could specify a search for all entries having an author named "Smith." The computer would then search through the entire disk file examining all the fields containing author's names (the last field in the above example) and printing all those with "Smith" as the author. The disk commands used for random access for the above format are shown in Listing 1-2.

Likewise, the computer could examine more than one field to limit the search to more specific entries. As an example, you could request a list of all articles published after 1980 concerning the stock market. The computer would search both the category and date fields for data meeting these

---

Listing 1-2: The Random Access Sample Routine.

```
10 KEY OFF:CLS:REM OPEN A FILE FOR RANDOM ACCESS ("R") USING
BUFFER #1 NAMED "FILE"
20 OPEN "R",1,"B:FILE"
30 REM FORMAT BUFFER #1 AS 30 LETTERS FOR THE NAME OF THE
ARTICLE/BOOK, 30 LETTERS FOR THE NAME OF MAGAZINE
40 REM TWO LETTERS FOR VOLUME NO., 5 LETTERS FOR DATE, 1 FOR
CATEGORY#1,1 FOR CATEGORY 2, 1 FOR STORAGE LOCATION
50 REM AND 10 FOR AUTHOR NAME
60 FIELD 1,30 AS NME$,30 AS MAG$,2 AS VOLUME$,5 AS DTE$,1 AS C1$,1
AS C2$,1 AS WHERE$,10 AS AUTHOR$
65 REM SET FILE COUNTER TO 1 TO BEGIN AT BEGINNING OF FILE
67 X=1:GOTO 120
70 REM IF REACH END OF FILE, THEN END SEARCH
80 IF EOF(1) THEN GOTO 500
90 REM INCREMENT FILE COUNTER
100 X=X+1
110 REM READ THE NEXT ENTRY INTO BUFFER #1
120 GET 1,X
130 REM IS THE AUTHOR "SMITH"? IF SO, PRINT OUT THAT ENTRY
140 IF AUTHOR$="SMITH" THEN PRINT NME$;MAG$;VOLUME$;DTE$;C1$;C2$;
WHERE$;AUTHOR$
150 REM INCREMENT  COUNTER
160 X=X+1:GOTO 80
500 CLOSE:REM CONTINUE PROGRAM FROM HERE...
```

requirements. A listing of all the information concerning each item would be outputted at the conclusion of the search. Floppy disks or high-speed random access cassettes are best-suited for this application.

WORD PROCESSING

Pencil and paper have never been the ideal servants of the mind. Paper refuses to accept instant changes at the whim of the writer. Instead, the writer must resort to erasing, inserting, cutting, and pasting.

But no longer are we restricted to pencil and paper. Word-processing programs can allow rearrangement of words at the touch of a finger; erasures are of the past. Correction fluid has likewise been replaced by the DELETE key. Word processors give you the ability to write spontaneously. Whereas most people try to edit their words before committing them to paper, the advent of word processors allows you to type as you think, and later rearrange words, sentences, and paragraphs in a painless fashion. Thus, the writer can make his ideas concrete by displaying them on the video screen and later concern himself with the grammatical aspects, before printing out a manuscript. Many writers feel that this enhances their creativity and makes writing easier and more enjoyable.

After your manuscript, letters, or documents are corrected on the video screen, you may assign various codes determining page widths, page lengths, page numbering, margins, and so on; the printer will reproduce the document perfectly, as you have specified. You can then edit the document and print it out again, without having to devote time and effort to retyping it. Additionally, this information can be stored on a floppy disk for later review and retrieval.

Anyone who writes professionally or composes a letter each day, should investigate the use of a word processor. Most are very easy to use and can be tremendous time, labor, and money savers. Many experts consider this application one of the most useful for personal computer owners. With most word processors you can:

- Block Move. This feature lets you move pieces of your text—from a word to several paragraphs—around like blocks. You can also delete a block at whatever point you designate, and the rest of the text will fill in the "hole." Or, conversely, you can add new blocks at any point. Think of a word processor as a word processor of writing, capable of slicing, chopping, and dicing the language with ease.
- Word Wrap. As you type on a word processor you can forget hitting the carriage return key at the end of each line, as the computer automatically puts as many words as possible on one line and then starts a new one. This, in computerese, is called *word wrap*.
- Search and Replace. You can instruct the word-processor program to search the entire text or a portion of it for the occurrence of a particular word or phrase. Suppose you would like to correct a misspelled name throughout a six page letter: just type in the name as you misspelled it and again as spelled correctly; the program will automatically correct this error throughout the text. The search command may also be used to rapidly locate a section in a large manuscript.
- Typeover. When you want to substitute one word or phrase for another, you can type your change right over the existing text, and the unwanted letters will vanish as the new ones appear to fill their places.
- Justify. Some programs will automatically adjust the spacing between words or letters so that each line can be printed out at the same length. This process is called *right justification*. Left justification simply means that the lines are aligned at the left margin as usual, although some programs can create special effects by aligning text only at the right margin or by centering all text.

These are the most basic features found on word processing programs. Many other special features come with certain word-processing packages. For example, a *mouse* can be used to position the cursor at any point on the screen to facilitate editing. An automatic directory program can check the spelling of each word you write against its vocabulary and make corrections. An automatic thesaurus program can, at your command, display five to ten synonyms for thousands of common English words. Other programs are designed to correct faulty grammar—for those who don't mind having a computerized English teacher—or allow you to design type fonts and integrate graphs and pictures with your text. Several typesetting firms will also accept word processor output directly via modem or floppy disk for instant, money-saving typesetting jobs.

LETTER WRITING

A specialized text editor, designed to edit and format your letters, could expedite the process considerably. For example, if you are writing a business letter, the address of the recipient could be stored when it is typed at the beginning of the letter and later recalled to print the envelope. If you are writing the same letter to several people, the body could be stored in the computer. You need type only the addresses and other personalized information, and this information would be integrated with the text to form a complete letter. Additionally, the editing features of a word processor facilitate the correction of mistakes while you are entering the body of the letter or the personalized information. A mailing list program can be integrated with such a program to automatically produce personalized letters. A program to prepare a personalized form letter is presented in Listing 1-3.

Listing 1-3: The Specialized Word-Processor Program

```
10 PRINT" SPECIALIZED WORD PROCESSOR--WRITES LETTERS"
20 CLEAR 5000
30 DIM A$(500)
40 PRINT "CHANGE LINES 490 - 530 TO PERSONALIZE PROGRAM":PRINT
50 LINE INPUT "ENTER THE DATE ",D$
60 INPUT "ENTER RECIPIENT'S NAME ",D1$
70 LINE INPUT "ENTER COMPANY NAME OR TITLE (PRESS ENTER IF NONE) ",C$
80 INPUT "ENTER STREET ADDRESS ",N1$
90 LINE INPUT "ENTER TOWN, STATE  ZIP ",T1$
100 INPUT "ENTER NAME FOR LETTER ADDRESS (E.G. DEAR ----) ",A1$
110 PRINT "ENTER SUCCESSIVE LINES FOR THE BODY.  IF YOU MAKE AN ERROR ON"
120 PRINT "A LINE AND WOULD LIKE TO CORRECT IT ENTER '#' AND THE NUMBER"
130 PRINT "OF THE LINE (E.G. #5) AS ANY OTHER LINE."
140 PRINT "TYPE 'END' TO PRINT OUT A COPY"
150 FOR X=1 TO 500
160 PRINT "#";X
170 LINE INPUT A$(X)
180 IF LEFT$(A$(X),1)="#" THEN 540
190 IF A$(X)="END" OR A$(X)="end" THEN 210
200 NEXT X:X=X-1
210 PRINT:INPUT "READY PRINTER TO OUTPUT LETTER";G$
220 LPRINT:LPRINT:LPRINT:LPRINT
230 LPRINT TAB(55) D$
240 READ N$,A$,T2$,A2$
250 LPRINT TAB(55) T2$
260 LPRINT TAB(55) A2$
270 LPRINT:LPRINT
280 LPRINT TAB(5) D1$
290 IF C$<>"" THEN LPRINT TAB(5)C$
300 LPRINT TAB(5) N1$
310 LPRINT TAB(5) T1$
```

```
320 LPRINT:LPRINT
330 LPRINT TAB(5) "Dear ";A1$;":"
340 LPRINT
350 FOR B=1 TO X-1
360 LPRINT TAB(5) A$(B)
370 NEXT B
380 C=23+B
390 LPRINT
400 LPRINT
410 LPRINT TAB(55) "Cordially,"
420 LPRINT
430 LPRINT
440 LPRINT TAB(55) N$
450 IF A$<>"X" THEN LPRINT TAB(55) A$
460 LPRINT:LPRINT:LPRINT:LPRINT:LPRINT:INPUT "PRINT ANOTHER COPY (Y/N)";A$:IF A$
="Y" OR A$="y" THEN RESTORE:GOTO 210
470 INPUT "START NEW LETTER (Y/N)";A$:IF A$<>"Y" AND A$<>"y" THEN END ELSE RESTO
RE:GOTO 50
480 REM ENTER YOUR ADDRESS HERE
490 DATA John Doe
500 DATA Citizen
510 REM: IF NO TITLE PUT 'X' IN PLACE OF CITIZEN IN LINE 500
520 DATA 321 Anystreet West
530 DATA New York  NY   10036
540 REM EDIT ROUTINE
550 Y=VAL(RIGHT$(A$(X),LEN(A$(X))-1))
560 INPUT "SELECT:1)RE-ENTER ENTIRE LINE, 2) EDIT ",A
570 ON A GOTO 580,600
580 LINE INPUT A$(Y)
590 X=X-1:GOTO 200
600 C=1
610 PRINT " USE SPACE BAR TO SEARCH THROUGH LINE"
620 PRINT " USE 'D' TO DELETE A CHARACTER"
630 PRINT " USE 'I' TO INSERT CHARACTERS; TYPE INSERTIONS AFTER '?' THEN PRESS R
ETURN"
640 PRINT " USE 'L' TO LIST A LINE NOW OR WHENEVER YOU WANT TO SEE THE RESULT OF
 EDITS"
650 PRINT " USE 'B' TO BACKSPACE AND 'ENTER' TO END"
660 PRINT "PRESS RETURN TO END EDIT"
670 FOR Q=1 TO 10000
680 Q$=INKEY$       'SEARCHES FOR KEYBOARD ENTRIES
690 IF Q$=" " THEN M=M+1:C=C+1:I$=MID$(A$(Y),M,1):PRINT I$;
700 IF Q$="L" OR Q$="l" THEN PRINT:PRINT A$(Y):C=1:M=0
710 IF Q$="I" OR Q$="i" THEN INPUT J$:A$(Y)=LEFT$(A$(Y),C-1)+J$+RIGHT$(A$(Y),LEN
(A$(Y))-C+1):IF J$=" " THEN 720
720 IF J$=" " THEN A$(Y)=LEFT$(A$(Y),C-1)+" "+RIGHT$(A$(Y),LEN(A$(Y))-C+1)
730 IF Q$="D" OR Q$="d" THEN A$(Y)=LEFT$(A$(Y),C-1)+RIGHT$(A$(Y),LEN(A$(Y))-C)
740 IF Q$="B" OR Q$="b" THEN C=C-1:PRINT CHR$(29)
750 IF Q$=CHR$(13) THEN PRINT CHR$(10)A$(Y):GOTO 590
760 NEXT Q
770 GOTO 600
```

CATEGORIZING INFORMATION

The purpose of the *subroutine* in Listing 1-4 is to categorize information stored in random access format on a floppy disk. Data is stored on disk with, for instance, a 10 character keyword preceding 240 characters of descriptive information (many random access disk systems have a string length limit of 255 total characters). The subroutine searches through the disk files to find and print all entries having a given keyword. This subroutine operates on the same principle as the *Electronic Memorandum* presented earlier in this chapter, but it is simplified for this application. Listing 1-5 is a simple categorizing program.

Why is a categorizer program useful? Businessmen, writers, and other professionals who need to categorize information for presentations, reports, outlines, or organizational purposes may find that a program incorporating this subroutine is helpful. A similar program was used in the preparation of this book. Many other applications, including categorizing income tax deductions, are possible.

Listing 1-4: The Categorizer Subroutine

```
10 REM CATEGORIZER SUBROUTINE
15 REM USES MICROSOFT DISK BASIC COMMANDS
20 REM INCORPORATE WITH A DATA BASE WHICH STORES INFORMATION
30 REM IN THE FORMAT OF (E.G.) 10 CHARACTERS FOR KEYWORDS
40 REM AND (E.G.) 240 CHARACTERS FOR DESCRIPTIVE INFO
50 REM IN ORDER TO USE THIS MANY CHARACTERS IN THE FIELD YOU MUST
CHANGE THE
60 REM DEFAULT SIZE OF THE BUFFER.  THIS IS DONE BY EXITING BASIC
(FIRST SAVE
70 REM THIS PROGRAM IF YOU HAVE NOT DONE SO) BY TYPING 'SYSTEM'
AND PRESSING
80 REM 'ENTER'.  NOW, AT THE DOS >A PROMPT, TYPE 'BASICA
[THE NAME OF THIS
90 REM PROGRAM]/S:250'
900 REM SELECT KEYWORD/CATEGORY TO SEARCH FOR
950 INPUT "ENTER KEYWORD/CATEGORY:",A$
1000 REM OPEN A FILE FOR RANDOM ACCESS("R") USING BUFFER #1 & FILE
NAMED "DATA"
1010 OPEN "R",1,"B:DATA",250:X=1:REM SET FILE COUNTER TO 1 TO BEGIN
AT BEGINNING OF FILE
1020 REM FORMAT BUFFER #1 AS 10 CHARACTERS FOR THE CATEGORY NAME
1030 REM AND 240 CHARACTERS FOR DESCRIPTIVE INFORMATION
1040 FIELD 1,10 AS CAT$,240 AS INFO$
1070 REM IF REACH END OF FILE, THEN END SEARCH
1080 IF EOF(1) THEN GOTO 2000
1090 REM INCREMENT FILE COUNTER
1100 X=X+1
1110 REM READ THE NEXT ENTRY INTO BUFFER #1
1120 GET 1,X
1125 REM IF THIS ITEM IS THE DESIRED CATEGORY, THEN PRINT OUT
1130 IF CAT$=A$ THEN PRINT INFO$
1140 REM INCREMENT COUNTER
1150 X=X+1:GOTO 1080
2000 CLOSE:REM CONTINUE PROGRAM HERE...
```

Listing 1-5. The Categorizer Program

```
10 REM CATEGORIZER PROGRAM FOR USE WITH DISK DRIVE
20 CLEAR 5000      'ADJUST ACCORDINGLY
30 DIM A$(1000)
40 INPUT "SELECT: 1) ENTER STRINGS, 2) CATEGORIZE, 3) END ",A:X=1
50 ON A GOTO 60,200,400
60 OPEN "A",1,"CATEGORY.DAT"      'OPEN SEQUENTIAL FILE FOR APPEND
70 PRINT "ENTER UP TO THREE LINES OF TEXT WITH KEYWORD AT THE BEGINNING"
80 LINE INPUT A$     'ACCEPTS STRINGS WITH EMBEDDED COMMAS
90 IF A$="END" THEN GOTO 120
100 PRINT #1,A$      'WRITES STRINGS WITH EMBEDDED COMMAS TO FILE
110 GOTO 80
120 CLOSE:GOTO 40
200 INPUT "ENTER KEYWORD ",B$
210 OPEN "I",1,"CATEGORY.DAT"      'OPEN SEQUENTIAL FILE FOR INPUT
220 WHILE EOF(1)=0      'CHECKING FOR END OF FILE
230    LINE INPUT #1,A$
240    IF B$=LEFT$(A$,LEN(B$)) THEN A$(X)=A$:X=X+1
250 WEND
260 CLOSE #1
270 INPUT "OUTPUT TO 1) PRINTER OR 2) DISPLAY";A
280 ON A GOTO 290,340
290 INPUT "READY PRINTER; PRESS ENTER TO CONTINUE",C$
300 FOR K=1 TO X-1
310    LPRINT A$(K)
320 NEXT
330 GOTO 40
340 CLS:FOR K=1 TO X-1
350    PRINT A$(K)
360    IF INT(K/17)=K/17 THEN INPUT "MORE TO COME; PRESS ENTER TO CONTINUE",C$:CL
S
370 NEXT
380 GOTO 40
400 END
```

A RECIPE INDEX AND CALCULATOR

A collection of your favorite recipes can be stored on your computer for rapid and selective retrieval. A list of the characteristics of each recipe could be included (for example, time required for preparation, hot or cold, number served, meal (dinner, lunch, or breakfast), expense, and calories). Using these characteristics, the computer could index recipes and print lists of recipes with a selected characteristic for a special occasion.

A recipe calculator could change the amounts of each ingredient so that the proper amount of the recipe will be made for a given number of people. A simple recipe calculator subroutine is presented in Listing 1-6. It can be used alone or can be incorporated in a recipe database program.

If the costs for various ingredients were stored in your computer, the cost of a given recipe could be instantaneously computed; allowance would also be made for the number of persons to be served. This type of program could be especially useful to those with a sideline or fulltime bakery or catering service, as the costs for any recipe for any number of people can be quickly estimated.

A sample field of information for one recipe is below:

MEATLOAF,   6,   1.5 lb.gr.beef*1cup
                             milk*.5cuponion* egg,

name of item	no. servings.	abbreviated ingredients
350 oven temp.	1.5 hr., bake time	Bill's favorite comments

A program to store information used in selecting and mixing *drinks* for instant retrieval could be created. Such a program could even store pictures of the size and shape glasses to use with each drink. The computer could also suggest an appropriate cheese to accompany a selected wine.

ITINERARY ASSISTANT

A list of appointments, deadlines, and various tasks could be stored in a computer and displayed in a specified format to assist you with your itinerary. The electronic memorandum program may be used for this task. Another format could be that of a calendar; each day-block would be filled with things to do. Is there something you must do periodically, but often forget? Program the computer to automatically remind you each time.

A program could also printout a *daily* appointment calendar of your custom design. It could include beginning and ending times, time intervals, and provisions for recording expenses, and comments. Incorporate the day-of-the-week program found in this chapter.

The professional may use a more sophisticated program for the purposes of time billing for clients. The computer can also be used as a medication reminder, signaling with an audible alarm, for those on complex therapeutic regimens.

Listing 1-6: The Recipe Calculator Program

```
10 REM RECIPE CALCULATOR
20 REM COULD BE IMPROVED TO CONVERT UNITS OF MEASUREMENT (E.G.
PINTS TO QUARTS)
30 INPUT "HOW MANY SERVINGS IS THE ORIGINAL RECIPE INTENDED FOR";
S1
40 INPUT "HOW MANY SERVINGS ARE TO BE PREPARED";S2
50 R=S2/S1
60 N=1
70 PRINT
80 PRINT "ENTER THE NAME OF EACH INGREDIENT, THE AMOUNT, THE
MEASURE (E.G. MILK,1,PINT).":PRINT
85 PRINT "USE DECIMAL NUMBERS FOR ALL AMOUNTS, SUCH AS '1.5
CUPS RATHER THAN 1 1/2 CUPS":PRINT
90 PRINT "ENTER 'END,1,1' WHEN FINISHED"
100 INPUT A$(N),B(N),C$(N)
110 IF A$(N)="END" OR A$(N)="end" THEN 130
120 N=N+1:GOTO 100
130 FOR X=1 TO N
135 IF A$(X)="END" THEN 160
140 PRINT A$(X),R*B(X),C$(X)
150 NEXT X
160 PRINT
165 INPUT "PRESS <ENTER> TO END ";EN$
170 END
```

PHONE TIMER

When you are making long distance phone calls, keeping track of the elapsed time can save you a considerable amount of money. Usually, the first one or three minutes is charged a flat rate, but for the remainder of the call the charges are updated by the minute. A countdown timer that makes use of a *timing loop*, for example FOR X = 1 to 500: NEXT X (which requires approximately 1 second), can display the amount of time remaining until the next charge. Also, a record could be kept of the number called and the cost for the call, for use with income-tax deductions or for comparison with telephone bill. The program in Listing 1-7 will time your calls and keep track of the charges.

Listing 1-7: The Telephone Call Timer Program

```
10 REM LONG DISTANCE TELEPHONE CALL TALLY
15 KEY OFF:CLS
20 INPUT "NEED TELEPHONE TIPS";A$
30 IF A$="YES" THEN 300
40 PRINT "TELEPHONE COST TALLY"
50 INPUT "IS THIS AN OPERATOR ASSISTED CALL";A$
60 IF A$="YES" THEN O=1 ELSE O=0
70 INPUT "ENTER INITIAL FLAT RATE";B
80 INPUT "ENTER CHARGE PER ADDITIONAL MINUTE";C
90 INPUT "ENTER DISCOUNT AS THE PERCENTAGE REMAINING TO BE PAID ",D
100 D=D*.01:IF D=0 THEN D=1
110 PRINT "TO BEGIN TIMING PRESS 'ENTER'"
120 PRINT "TO END TIMING PRESS SPACE BAR"
130 INPUT A$
135 CLS'CLEARS SCREEN
140 LOCATE 4,1:PRINT "ELAPSED MIN","CURRENT COST","SECONDS TO ADD
CHARGE";
150 S=60:B1=B*D
160 LOCATE 6,1:PRINT T,B1,S;
165 REM LINE 170 ACTS AS A TIMING LOOP; ADJUST TO YOUR BASIC
170 FOR X=1 TO 1050:NEXT:Q$=INKEY$:IF Q$<>"" THEN 230
180 S=S-1
190 IF S=0 THEN T=T+1:S=60:ELSE 160
200 IF (O=1) AND (T<3) THEN B1=B1+B*D:GOTO 160
210 B1=B1+C*D
220 Q$=INKEY$:IF Q$="" THEN GOTO 160
230 IF Q$=CHR$(32) THEN END
240 GOTO 180
300 PRINT "THE FLAT RATE FOR OPERATOR ASSISTED CALLS IS FOR THE
FIRST"
310 PRINT "3 MIN AND FOR THE FIRST MIN ON DIRECT-DIAL CALLS"
320 PRINT "DISCOUNT TIMES FOR CALLING ARE:"
330 PRINT "60%--8AM-5PM SUNDAY/8AM-11PM SATURDAY/11PM-8AM NIGHTLY
335 PRINT "PERCENT TO BE PAID = 40%."
340 PRINT "35%--8AM-11PM ON HOLIDAYS/5PM-11PM SUNDAY-FRIDAY"
342 PRINT "PERCENT TO BE PAID = 65%"
345 REM CHECK WITH YOUR LONG DISTANCE PROVIDER FOR CORRECT FIGURES
350 PRINT:GOTO 40
```

TELEPHONE FILE, DIALER, AND ANSWERING MACHINE

Listings of emergency and frequently used telephone numbers could be stored if the list is sufficiently long to warrant computer search capabilities.

The data strings used to store this information could be formatted as follows:

HOSPITAL,   AMBULANCE,
identifier   additional
                   related identifier
                   (to cross-reference)

643-1998 * 643-1997
tel. numbers

For those with a hardware bent, the addition of a pulse or tone dialing circuit for a modem with automatic dialing capability could allow a computer to search and then automatically dial a desired number. In connection with a burglar/security alarm system, the computer could be instructed to dial the police or fire departments and deliver a tape-recorded message. You could also construct a computer-controlled, programmable telephone answering machine with capabilities far exceeding those on the market.

GREETING CARD/INVITATION LIST

A mailing-list program could be used to address your Christmas greeting cards. If your list is large enough, the computer could sort zip codes, allowing you to send your cards under the bulk mail rate. (This would probably only be practical for businesses with large customer files.) Additionally, the computer could print a short "hello" note on the back of each card. The same idea could be applied to producing an invitation list for a party or meeting.

Similarly, a list of dates of birthdays and anniversaries could be stored and each month could remind you of the important dates for the upcoming month.

PERSONAL TIME MANAGEMENT SYSTEM

A personal time management system would assist you in planning the most effective schedule for completing a list of tasks. Input could include the description of each goal, the priority of that goal (using A, B, or C to represent categories of importance) and the deadline date. The program could use *PERT* Program Evaluation and Review Technique or *critical path* analysis to plan and output a schedule most evenly distributing the work load. PERT is described in numerous computer programming texts and PERT programs are available for many personal computers. Many people have found that they can accomplish much more if they make schedules and deadlines for themselves; PERT analysis will make that all more simple.

DECISION MAKER

Complex decision making may be facilitated through the use of the computer. In the program in Listing 1-8, the computer first requests you to enter a list of the factors involved in making a decision. Next, you are asked to rate the relative importance of each of these factors on a scale of ten. Finally, for each possible outcome to the decision, you are asked to rate the favorability of each factor on a scale of ten. This data is then analyzed, and the outcome with the highest "favorability" score for the most important factors is the one chosen as the final decision.

The most favorable decision will have the highest score, computed by summing the "rate of favorability" multiplied by the relative importance for each factor.

For example, if you had several locations in mind for building a home and could not come to a decision, you could form the following chart of factors for making the decision; these factors would be inputted to the decision-making program.

Shopping: are there adequate facilities nearby?

Churches: are they available and convenient?

Neighbors: are they likely to be compatible with your lifestyle?

Police and fire protection: are they adequate for the area?

Schools: are the schools your children will attend nearby?

Hospital: is there a medical center nearby?

Hazards: are there hazards such as oil tanks or streams that might overflow?

Recreation: are there suitable facilities within walking distance?

Traffic: are the streets quiet and safe?

Transportation: is public transportation available?

Lay of land and landscaping: is the land well-drained and not subject to erosion?

Water: is there an adequate pressure and is it drinkable?

Nuisances: are there nearby sources of excessive noise, smoke, soot, dust, or odors that will degrade your environment?

If this process is still too complex, try this program:

```
5   PRINT "THE DECISION IS:"
10   X = RND (0): IF X < .5 PRINT "NEGATIVE"
ELSE PRINT "AFFIRMATIVE"
```

If you need help in making a decision that many people have to make, at least once in a lifetime, you may want to use, the program in Listing 1-9, which determines the economic incentive for trading off a gas guzzling car for a new, more economical car sooner than you would if gas prices were not a factor.

Listing 1-8: The Universal Decision Making Program

```
10 PRINT "THE UNIVERSAL DECISION MAKING MACHINE"
15 CLEAR 5000:REM THIS COMMAND CLEARS STRING SPACE AND IS OPTIONAL WITH THE IBM
PC
20 DIM A$(100),B(100),C(100),D$(100)
30 INPUT "ENTER THE NUMBER OF FACTORS USED IN MAKING THE DECISION";NUM
40 PRINT "ENTER FACTORS AND RELATIVE IMPORTANCE ON SCALE OF TEN:"
50 FOR X=1 TO NUM
60    PRINT "#";X;" ";:INPUT A$(X),B(X)
70 NEXT X
80 INPUT "ENTER NUMBER OF POSSIBLE OUTCOMES ",X
90 PRINT "ENTER NAME OF EACH OUTCOME:"
100 FOR I=1 TO X
110    PRINT "#";I;" ";:INPUT D$(I)
120 NEXT I
130 PRINT "NOW, LET'S RANK EACH FACTOR FOR EACH POSSIBLE OUTCOME:"
140 FOR I=1 TO X
150    PRINT "FOR OUTCOME #";I;" ";D$(I);","
160    PRINT "RANK THESE FACTORS ON A SCALE OF TEN:"
170    FOR J=1 TO NUM
180     PRINT A$(J);:INPUT R
185     C(I)=C(I)+B(J)*R
190    NEXT J
200 PRINT
210 NEXT I
220 PRINT
230 PRINT "RANKINGS OF OUTCOMES ARE (HIGHEST RANKING=BEST DECISION):"
240 FOR I=1 TO X
250    PRINT D$(I),C(I)
260 NEXT I
270 END
```

```
10 REM SHOULD YOUR GAS GUZZLER GO?
20 REM DETERMINES THE ECONOMIC INCENTIVE IN TRADING OFF A
30 REM GAS GUZZLER FOR A MORE ECONOMICAL CAR
40 INPUT "ENTER NEW CAR'S M.P.G, CURRENT CAR'S M.P.G";R,M
50 INPUT "ENTER COST OF NEW CAR IN DOLLARS";C
60 INPUT "ENTER AVERAGE NO. OF MILES YOU DRIVE PER YEAR";D
70 INPUT "ENTER CURRENT PRICE PER GALLON OF GASOLINE";P
80 R=R/(R-M):Y=(C*R*M)/(D*P)
90 PRINT:PRINT "IF ";Y;" YEARS IS GREATER THAN THE NUMBER OF YEARS YOU"
100 PRINT "WERE PLANNING ON KEEPING YOUR CAR, YOU SHOULD STICK WITH"
110 PRINT "YOUR GAS GUZZLER FOR THE TIME YOU NORMALLY WOULD HAVE"
120 PRINT "KEPT IT.  OTHERWISE, YOU SHOULD TRADE IT IN NOW."
130 END
```

HEALTH

Your personal computer can even help you maintain your health. A listing of the caloric or nutrient content of various foods could be stored and subsequently referenced for determining the nutritive value of the food you eat. Additionally, data on the sugar or salt content of foods could be stored for the diabetic or person on a salt-free diet. Of course, such a program lends itself well to diet planning.

The "Nutritive Value of Foods," Home and Garden Bulletin No. 72, Agricultural Research Service, is an excellent source of nutritive values for all foods and is available from the superinten-dent of Documents, U.S. Govt. Printing Office, Washington, D.C. —Stock #001-000-03667-0. It lists the water, calorie, protein, fat, carbohydrate, mineral, and vitamin composition of all foods.

A low-calorie diet-planning program could compute the number of calories you use per day (on the basis of weight, sex, height, and activities). Of course, if you eat more calories than you use up in energy, you build up reserves in the form of fat. Thus, weight control is primarily based on calorie balance. The amount of weight you could lose by either reducing intake or increasing activities would be mathematically calculated. The following data should be helpful in writing a program to help you lose weight or maintain health through exercise.

A complete nutritional analysis program would allow you to input the types and amounts of foods you have eaten during the day, would compute the total intake of proteins, carbohydrate, fats, fiber, vitamins, and minerals, and would determine your average daily intake of each per day. Similarly, it would compute your average energy expenditure (see Table 1-1) and then subtract this from your average daily nutrient intake to determine your calorie balance and to compare your intake with the recommended daily allowances for your age, sex, and weight (see Table 1-2). Thus, areas for im-provement could be easily identified. A diet plan could then be determined to achieve these im-provements.

One hobbyist uses a computer to determine his pulse rate and lead him through an exercise ses-sion, acting as the coach and timer. Along similar lines, another hobbyist computes the aerobic points he earns in bicycling.

A general purpose data plotting subroutine could graph morning resting pulse on the X axis versus minutes run previous day on the y axis, miles run versus subjective feeling at end of day, or many other inputs to allow you to see where you've been and where you are going!

Listing 1-10 is a simple program that will help you calculate your pulse rate.

The beginning runner is often unsure how fast he should run. Pulse taking can be helpful to assure

Table 1-1. Energy Consumption Table.

Intensity of Exercise	Heart (Beats Minute)	Respiration (Breaths/Minute)	Energy Consumption (Calories/Hour)
maximum	200	50	1440
very	150	30	1008
heavy	140	25	864
fairly heavy	130	20	720
moderate	120	18	576
light	110	16	432
very light	100	14	288
resting	70	10	100

Table 1-2. Recommended Caloric Intake Table.

Mean heights and weights and recommended energy intake

Category	Age (years)	Weight (kg)	(lb)	Height (cm)	(in)	Energy needs (with range) (kcall)	(MJ)
Infants	0.0-0.5	2	13	60	24	kg × 115 (95-145)	kg × .48
	0.5-1.0	9	20	71	28	kg × 105 (80-135)	kg × .44
Children	1-3	13	29	90	35	1300 (900-1800)	5.5
	4-6	20	44	112	44	1700 (1300-2300)	7.1
	7-10	28	62	132	52	2400 (1650-3300)	10.1
Males	11-14	45	99	157	62	2700 (2000-3700)	11.3
	15-18	66	145	176	69	2800 (2100-3900)	11.8
	19-22	70	154	177	70	2900 (2500-3300)	12.2
	23-50	70	154	178	70	2700 (2300-3100)	11.3
	51-75	70	154	178	70	2400 (2000-2800)	10.1
	76+	70	154	178	70	2050 (1650-2450)	8.6
Females	11-14	46	101	157	62	2200 (1500-3000)	9.2
	15-18	55	120	163	64	2100 (1200-3000)	8.8
	19-22	55	120	163	64	2100 (1700-2500)	8.8
	23-50	55	120	163	64	2000 (1600-2400)	8.4
	51-75	55	120	163	64	1800 (1400-2200)	7.6
	76-	55	120	163	64	1600 (1200-2000)	6.7
Pregnancy						+ 300	
Lactation						+ 500	

One gram of Carbohydrate = 4 calories
One gram of Fat = 9 calories
One gram of Protein = calories

Listing 1-10: The Pulse Rate Program

```
10 REM CALCULATION OF PULSE RATE (BEATS/MIN)
15 INPUT "ENTER YOUR AGE ",AGE
18 INPUT "PRESS <ENTER> TO START";EN$
20 PRINT "PRESS ANY KEY FOR EACH BEAT":X=1:N=0
30 A$=INKEY$:IF X=3000 THEN 60        'CHANGE VALUE FOR YOUR
COMPUTER'S SPEED
```

```
40 IF A$="" THEN X=X+1:GOTO 30
50 N=N+1:GOTO 30
60 PRINT "THE NUMBER OF BEATS/MIN=";N*2
70 PRINT "TRAINING PULSE=";INT((.6)*(220-AGE))
```

beginners that they're doing the right amount of work—not too much or too little. First, determine your *base training pulse* using the formula [220-(your age)] × .65. Anyone who makes sure that his or her pulse does not rise above this value is in the safety zone where the heart is being strengthened rather than overtaxed.

SHORTHAND TRANSLATOR

You could develop a shorthand system that your computer could be programmed to understand and translate. The system could be similar to that used by court reporters, in which a single key represents a word or part of a word. In this manner, you could quickly commit your thoughts to paper, and the computer could quickly analyze the shorthand and print the English equivalent.

The basic stenographer's character and word assignment is given in Table 1-3.

In a like manner, a machine language program could translate a single keystroke into a full command. For instance, such a program could translate a CONTROL P or shifted P to the word PRINT, thereby facilitating the input of a program.

KITCHEN INVENTORY

A file of all food items on hand (pantry inventory) could be useful in determining whether or not a given recipe can be prepared. As each item is added or subtracted, the transaction would be entered into the computer. If a desired level of inventory is specified, the computer could automatically print out a shopping list of items that are below desired quantity levels. An inventory program of this type would be best suited for the gourmet cook who must have a wide variety of seasonings and other ingredients on hand. The inventory of a wine collection or food in the deep freezer may also be maintained.

RATING CALCULATIONS

An equation to determine a rating for a par-

Character	Word	Suffix	Character	Word	Suffix
A	and	able	V	very	ver
B	been	bility	W	with	ward
C	can	cial	X	experience	
D	down	day	Y	you	
E	even	ent	Z	the	zation
F	from	ful	0	zero	
G	good	ght	1	one	
H	have	hood	2	two	
I	into	ing	3	three	
J	just		4	four	
K	know		5	five	
L	like	less	6	six	
M	more	ment	7	seven	
N	not	ness	8	eight	
O	other	ous	9	nine	
P	people		!	hundred	
Q	quite			thousand	
R	right	rent	#	million	
S	said	self	$	dollar	
T	that	tion	%	percent	
U	united	ugh	c	cent	

Table 1-3. Basic Steno Character Assignment Chart.

ticular stock, car, horse, home, or any item of value could be computerized if it is referred to often or is complex. For example, the horse racing fan could use the following empirically derived equation to determine an objective rating for a particular horse:

$$Rating = (W + P/3 + S/6) \times 100/R + E/850$$
where W = the number of wins
P = the number of places
S = the number of shows
R = the number of races
E = the amount of earnings in dollars

Rating equations are empirically derived or are determined by finding the statistical correlation between a set of factors and the outcomes that the factors influence.

INVENTORY OF POSSESSIONS

A file of your personal property could be stored in computer format for insurance purposes or for determining your net worth. A database program could record the date of purchase, the place of purchase, the length of the warranty, description of item, price, serial number, and model number. For instance, you could set up a simple database for tracking possessions by using these four fields: date, store, item, and price. This information could be entered from sales receipts or from your checkbook. At the end of the year, the database could be printed and a backup disk or cassette put in safe keeping. This could save you $10,000 or more in the event of a major disaster, because you will have excellent documentation of what you've owned.

The computer may also be useful in comparing various insurance policies to determine which plan offers what you need at the lowest cost. Professionally prepared insurance-planning programs are available for a variety of personal computers.

The advantage to using a personal computer is that items may be easily added, deleted, or categorized, and a cassette or floppy disk copy of the inventory may be stored in a safe-deposit box. If you own a business, use this type of program to inventory your business equipment.

INDEX TO IMPORTANT LITERATURE

Your favorite lines of literature, passages from the Bible, quotations, scientific and business journal references, anecdotes, and other literary miscellanea could be collected, categorized, cross-referenced, and indexed for rapid retrieval. A specialized database program could be used for this purpose; see the database demonstration program at the end of this chapter. Sophisticated database programs are commercially available for searching the King James Bible for selected passages or references.

DAY OF THE WEEK CALCULATION

Calculation of the day of the week corresponding to a given date is useful to the businessman, vacation planners, historians, and others. For the sake of curiosity, some have found amazing congruencies between the days on which U.S. Presidents were born and other significant events in history.

To calculate the day of the week for a specific date in the twentieth century, either use the program in Listing 1-11 or use the following formula:

$$N = D+M+Y[(0.8(2M+1)] + [Y/4]$$
where D = day of the month
M = Month, where March is considered the first month, April the second, and February the twelfth
Y = Last two digits of the year
[ ] = The integer part of the result

Next, divide the sum N by 7. The remainder from the division gives the day of the week. Count 0 as Sunday, 1 as Monday, and so on.

Programs to calculate the date of Easter for forthcoming years have been written, and this remains an interesting programming challenge; hint—incorporate the above formula.

A simpler program could calculate the day of the year for a given date; the businessman may find such calculations useful.

FOOD STORE SHOPPING AID

Your programmable calculator can sum and

Listing 1-11: The Day of the Week Program

```
5 CLS
10 REM CALCULATION OF THE DAY OF THE WEEK CORRESPONDING TO A GIVEN DATE
20 REM APPLICABLE TO ANY DATE IN THE 20TH CENTURY
25 DEFINT A
30 INPUT "ENTER THE MONTH,DAY,YEAR (MM,DD,YY) ",M,D,Y
35 IF M=9 THEN M=M-5
40 IF M>2 THEN M=M-2 ELSE M=10+M:Y=Y-1
50 N=D+M+Y+INT(.8*(2*(M+1))+INT(Y/4))
60 A=(N/7-INT(N/7))*7.1
70 FOR X=0 TO 6
80 READ A$(X)
90 NEXT X
100 PRINT "THE DAY IS ";A$(A)
110 END
120 DATA SATURDAY,SUNDAY,MONDAY,TUESDAY,WEDNESDAY,THURSDAY,FRIDAY
```

categorize prices and types of items as they are removed from the shelf at the supermarket. Provision could be made for categorizing items into meat, groceries, produce, and taxable subdivisions. Additionally, there may be provisions for multiple entries, unit price calculations and comparisons, error correction, and a warning if a preset cash limit has been exceeded. Outputs could include total cost, tax, item count, and subtotals in each category.

COUPON FILE

For those who have the money-saving habit of collecting food coupons, a computerized list of your coupons could be helpful. Enter each coupon by its amount, brand name, product name, and location in your coupon folders or envelopes. Next, enter your shopping list. A computer search between your list and the available coupon list should yield a roster of coupons that may be used and where each one is.

Alternatively, the computer could store coupons by type of product, using, for instance these categories: restaurants, pasta products, drinks, cereals, snacks, meat, poultry, vegetables, fish, condiments, dairy products, baking items, pet food, cosmetics, paper goods, cleaning products, medicine, and miscellaneous. The shopper may call up the list of coupons within a category to select the coupons he is interested in and find out which brand name each one is filed under.

HOME PLANNING

An interesting program could be written to help a family design a house to fit their needs; the expense of a house certainly justifies an in-depth analysis of the design before construction is started. You could use video graphics to draw and transform basic house plans (preferably with a light pen).

Square footage could be calculated with the following guidelines in mind: the minimum square footage should equal the number of family members times 200; the desirable square footage should equal the number of family members times 300. An activity list such as the one below could be included to ensure that the family's activities will not conflict and that there will be provisions for all activities. The program could request the user to enter the activities that are to be done in each room and the times involved; conflicts could thus be analyzed, and the plans could be altered accordingly. The following activities could be included in the program:

Group Activities
1. Lounging—indoors and outdoors
2. Television watching
3. Listening to stereo, tapes, or radio
4. Playing a musical instrument
5. Meals
6. Children's play areas

Social Activities
1. Holding a meeting in the home
2. Children's/adult's games
3. Viewing movies/slides
4. Visiting with guests

Work Activities
1. Meal preparation and clean-up
2. Household business
3. Food preparation
4. Laundry
5. Ironing, sewing, or drying clothes
6. Workshop area

Private Areas
1. Study of reading areas
2. Grooming or dressing facilities

Traffic patterns and storage requirements could also be analyzed.

Storage requirements:
Bedrooms—minimum of 4′ × 6′ × 24″ closet
        space/person
Utility areas—about 36″ wide and 16″ deep
Kitchen—approximately 10 linear feet of base and
        wall cabinets

PRIVATE INFORMATION STOREHOUSE

Almost everyone has some private—financial information, diaries, or important numbers—that they would like to keep more securely than in a filing cabinet. A program could be written to store this information in coded form so that it could only be retrieved by someone with the proper password. Copies of such data could be stored in a safe-deposit box.

GENERAL PURPOSE CLOCK OR TIMER

If your computer is equipped with a real time clock, it could be used as an electronic timer or time controller for scientific research, sporting events, or other applications requiring a stopwatch. The capabilities that a computer has but a stopwatch doesn't include the automatic storage and printout of selected times and the automatic control of instruments or other devices that must be turned on or off at given times.

Even without a real time clock, your computer can still keep track of elapsed time for long distance telephone calls or act as a simple timer for applications in which accuracy is not a major factor. When they are not using their computers for more practical tasks, some hobbyists have transformed them into very expensive clocks, with graphic displays of hour and minute hands, digital displays, simulated sundials, or even sand timers. Digital watch circuits may be interfaced with computers to facilitate time keeping.

BLOOD ALCOHOL CONTENT

It would be a good idea to calculate your blood alcohol content after a few drinks, before attempting to drive. The formula used to calculate the percentage alcohol content in the blood is

$$C = \frac{OZ \cdot p \cdot 0.037}{W}$$

where C = blood alcohol content in % wt/vol
     OZ = ounces of drink consumed
      p = proof
     W = body weight (lbs)

The program in Listing 1-12 will automatically calculate your blood alcohol content.

Listing 1-12: The Blood Alcohol Content Program

```
10 REM BLOOD ALCOHOL CONTENT CALCULATOR
20 INPUT "ENTER THE NUMBER OF OZ. CONSUMED, THE PROOF OF THE
DRINK ",OZ,P
30 INPUT "ENTER YOUR WEIGHT IN POUNDS ",W
40 C=(OZ*P*.037)/W
50 PRINT "YOUR ESTIMATED BLOOD ALCOHOL CONTENT=";C
```

```
60 PRINT:PRINT
70 IF C<=.05 THEN PRINT "A LEVEL BELOW .05 IS NOT CONSIDERED AS
INTOXICATION."
80 IF C>.05 AND C<.1 THEN PRINT "A LEVEL BETWEEN .05 AND .1 IS
CONSIDERED BORDER LINE INTOXICATION."
90 IF C>=.1 THEN PRINT "A LEVEL GREATER THAN .1 IS CONCLUSIVE
INTOXICATION."
100 END
```

CARPENTERS' AND MECHANICS' HELPER

Your computer can expedite the numerous calculations required by carpenters and mechanics when they perform tasks such as changing the dimensions of a set of plans, converting anglo to metric measures or vice-versa, and estimating the amount of in many other situations building materials needed.

Some useful formulae include

Anglo/metric Conversions

$$
\begin{aligned}
1\ meter &= 39.37 \text{ inches} \\
&= 3.281 \text{ feet} \\
&= 1.0936 \text{ yards} \\
1 \text{ inch} &= 2.54 \text{ cm} \\
1 \text{ foot} &= 30.48 \text{ cm} \\
&= .3048 \\
1 \text{ yard} &= .9144 \text{ m} \\
1 \text{ mile} &= 1609 \text{ m} \\
&= 1.609 \text{ km}
\end{aligned}
$$

Wall paper estimator

$$ N = \frac{8640}{W \cdot (H + R)} \qquad P = \frac{S}{W \cdot N} $$

where N = the number of strips in one roll
W = the width of the paper
H = the height of the wall
R = the repeat length of the pattern
P = the number of double rolls needed
S = the width of the wall to be covered

Concrete block estimator

$$ N = \frac{H \cdot L \cdot 1.25}{125} $$

where N = the number of blocks
H = the height of the wall
L = the length of the wall

Concrete yardage estimator

$$ Y = \frac{L \cdot W \cdot W \cdot T}{324} $$

where Y = the volume of concrete in cubic yards
L = the length (ft.)
W = the width (ft.)
T = the thickness (in.)

CAR MAINTENANCE CALCULATIONS AND RECORD KEEPING

In addition to calculating and recording your car's miles per gallon, the computer could keep track of mileage statistics and signal you when a periodic check-up, overhaul, or oil change is necessary. For people having the privilege of deducting automotive expenses, the computer could keep tabs on amounts spent.

RAFFLE TICKET PRODUCER AND DRAWER

If your organization is sponsoring a raffle drawing, your computer could print out serialized raffle tickets and then draw the winning ticket based on a random number generator.

LIFE EXPECTANCY CALCULATOR

Listing 1-13 presents another program of interest to guests. Your life expectancy in years is calculated on the basis of life insurance studies. This program is interesting to run with data supplied for your present condition, and then run with data about yourself assuming you had kept your New Year's resolutions (stop smoking, lose weight, and so on). The difference in years is often surprising.

DATABASE DEMONSTRATION

Many of the program ideas described in this chapter can be implemented with a general purpose

Listing 1-13: The Life Expectancy Calculation Program

```
10 REM LIFE EXPECTANCY CALCULATOR
20 REM ESTIMATES HOW LONG YOU WILL LIVE
30 REM PROGRAM IS BASED ON SCIENTIFIC DATA
40 PRINT "LIFE EXPECTANCY CALCULATION FOR ADULTS 20-65 YRS. OF
AGE"
50 PRINT "TYPE '1' FOR YES, '2' FOR NO TO ANSWER QUESTIONS"
60 A=72
70 INPUT "ARE YOU MALE";B
80 IF B=1 THEN A=A-3 ELSE A=A+4
90 INPUT "DO YOU LIVE IN AN URBAN AREA (POPULATION >2 MILLION)";B
100 IF B=1 THEN A=A-2 ELSE INPUT "DO YOU LIVE IN A TOWN
(POPULATION<10,000)";B:IF B=1 THEN A=A+2
110 PRINT "IF YOU WORK BEHIND A DESK TYPE '1'"
120 INPUT "IF YOUR JOB REQUIRES REGULAR, HEAVY PHYSICAL LABOR
TYPE '2' ";B
130 IF B=1 THEN A=A-3 ELSE IF B=2 THEN A=A+3
140 PRINT "IF YOU EXERCISE STRENUOUSLY MORE THAN 5 1/2 ONE-HOUR
SESSIONS/WEEK"
150 INPUT "TYPE '1'.  IF YOU DO 2-3 TIMES/WEEK TYPE '2' ";B
160 IF B=1 THEN A=A+4 ELSE IF B=2 THEN A=A+2
170 INPUT "DO YOU LIVE WITH A SPOUSE OR FRIEND";B
180 IF B=1 THEN A=A+5 ELSE INPUT "HOW MANY DECADES HAVE YOU LIVED
WITHOUT OTHERS SINCE 25 YRS. OLD";B:A=A-B
190 INPUT "DO YOU SLEEP MORE THAN TEN HOURS. PER NIGHT";B
200 IF B=1 THEN A=A-4
210 PRINT "IF YOU ARE INTENSE, AGGRESSIVE, EASILY ANGERED TYPE
'1'"
220 INPUT "IF YOU ARE EASY-GOING, RELAXED, FOLLOWER TYPE '2' ";B
230 IF B=1 THEN A=A-3 ELSE IF B=2 THEN A=A+3
240 INPUT "IF YOU'RE HAPPY TYPE '1';UNHAPPY TYPE '2' ";B
250 IF B=1 THEN A=A+1 ELSE IF B=2 THEN A=A-2
260 INPUT "HAVE YOU HAD A SPEEDING TICKET WITHIN THE LAST YEAR";B
270 IF B=1 THEN A=A-1
280 INPUT "DO YOU EARN MORE THAN $50,000/YR";B
290 IF B=1 THEN A=A-2
300 INPUT "IF YOU'VE FINISHED COLLEGE TYPE '1';GRAD SCHOOL TYPE
'2' ";B
310 IF B=1 THEN A=A+1 ELSE IF B=1 THEN A=A+2
320 INPUT "IF YOU'RE 65 OR OVER AND STILL WORKING TYPE '1' ";B
330 IF B=1 THEN A=A+3
340 INPUT "IF ANY OF YOUR GRANDPARENTS HAVE LIVED TO 85 TYPE '1'
";B
350 IF B=1 THEN A=A+2:INPUT "DID ALL 4 LIVE TO BE 80";B:IF B=1
THEN A=A+6
```

```
360 INPUT "DID EITHER OF YOUR PARENTS DIE OF STROKE/HEART ATTACK
BEFORE 50";B
370 IF B=1 THEN A=A-4
380 PRINT "HAVE ANY OF YOUR PARENTS OR BROTHERS/SISTERS UNDER 50
HAD A"
390 INPUT "HEART CONDITION, CANCER, OR CHILDHOOD DIABETES";B
400 IF B=1 THEN A=A-3
410 PRINT "IF YOU SMOKE:  >2 PACKS/DAY TYPE '1',1-2 PACKS /DAY
TYPE '2'"
420 INPUT "1/2-1 PACK/DAY TYPE '3' ";B; OTHERWISE TYPE '4'"
430 IF B=1 THEN A=A-8 ELSE IF B=2 THEN A=A-6 ELSE IF B=3 THEN
A=A-3
440 INPUT "DO YOU DRINK THE EQUIVALENT OF 1/4 BOTTLE LIQUOR/DAY";B
450 IF B=1 THEN A=A-1
460 PRINT "IF YOU ARE OVERWEIGHT BY >50 LBS. TYPE '1', 30-50 LBS.
TYPE '2'"
470 INPUT "10-30 LBS. TYPE '3' ";B; OTHERWISE TYPE '4'
480 IF B=1 THEN A=A-8 ELSE IF B=2 THEN A=A-4 ELSE IF B=3 THEN
A=A-2
490 PRINT "IF YOU'RE MALE AND HAVE AN ANNUAL CHECK-UP TYPE '1'
AND IF"
500 INPUT "FEMALE TYPE '1' IF YOU SEE A GYNECOLOGIST ANNUALLY ";B
510 IF B=1 THEN A=A+2
520 PRINT "IF YOU'RE BETWEEN 30-40 TYPE '1', 40-50 TYPE '2',
50-60 TYPE"
530 INPUT "'3',>70 TYPE '4' ";B
540 A=A+B+1
550 PRINT ""
560 PRINT "YOUR LIFE EXPECTANCY IS ";A;"YEARS."
570 END
```

database computer program. This type of program should be able to store information pertaining to many items on a cassette tape or floppy disk and retrieve selected information.

The usual method of storing data on a cassette or disk involves the use of one string of information containing several *fields* of separate data. A field is an item of data. For example, a string containing five fields might look like this:

Boolean Algebra*Byte Magazine*25*Schwartz*
Feb 1978

The first field signifies the title of the item (in this case a magazine article); all of the strings to be stored would be formatted in the same way, with the title of the item in the first field. Also, a limit is usually set on the length of any field (so that the data

will fit neatly on a cassette or disk). If the information in one field does not contain enough characters to fill the allocated space, extra spaces are added. The longer the fields, the fewer records the disk or cassette can hold. You'll learn to make fields as short as possible when you are dealing with a large data base.

The second field in the example above contains the name of the source of the item. The third, fourth, and fifth fields contain the page number, author, and issue date respectively. An adequate database program should be able to search through many such strings and output those that contain items you want. For example, you can store an index to your library on a database system and subsequently obtain a listing of all the references pertaining to the stock market and written after a specific date. You would simply instruct the computer to search for all items that contain *stock market* in a certain field and a date later than the date specified in another field. Because the position of each field in all strings is fixed, the computer can search through a string (using the MID$ command, for example) to the beginning of the proper field:

specific information can easily be accessed in this manner.

The variety of commands available in a database management program are summarized in lines 1790-1850 in the program in Listing 1-14 and may be summoned to the screen by typing HELP in response to COMMAND?

Listing 1-14: The Database Program

```
100 REM DATA BASE DEMONSTRATION PROGRAM
110 REM MAY BE USED TO MAINTAIN MAILING LISTS, COLLECTIONS
120 REM INVENTORY, ETC.
130 REM THE COMMAND 'HELP' PROVIDES INSTRUCTIONS
140 CLS      'CLEARS SCREEN
150 REM INITIALIZED FOR UP TO 200 RECORDS WITH 30 FIELDS EACH
160 CLEAR 6000
170 REM ALTER THESE DIM STATEMENTS TO ALLOW FOR MORE RECORDS
180 DIM M$(200),D$(200)
190 DIM P$(30),C$(31),F(31)
200 INPUT "SELECT: 1)BEGIN ANEW, 2)LOAD OLD DATA FILE";V
210 CLS
220 IF V=2 THEN 1640
230 F1$="      ":C$="":P$(0)="BUFFER EMPTY":N=0
240 PRINT:PRINT
250 PRINT "INPUT FIELD NAME, FIELD TYPE (A=ALPHA, N=NUMERIC)"
260 REM
270 FOR I=1 TO 30
280    PRINT I;") ";
290    E$="":INPUT E$,RS$
300    IF E$="" THEN GOTO 380
310    IF (RS$<>"A") AND (RS$<>"N") THEN 320 ELSE 330
320    PRINT "INCORRECT SYNTAX, PLEASE RE-ENTER":GOTO 290
330    E$=LEFT$(E$+F1$,4)+","+RS$
340    GOSUB 2190      'ROUTINE TO THROW OUT EXTRANEOUS SPACES
350    P$(I)=E$
360 NEXT I
370 GOTO 390
380 P$(I)="END"
390 PRINT:PRINT "THE RECORDS AND FIELDS ENTERED WERE:"
400 FOR I=1 TO 10
410    IF LEFT$(P$(I),3)="END" THEN GOTO 440
420    PRINT I;": ";P$(I)
430 NEXT I
440 PRINT:GOTO 460
450 PRINT "INCORRECT SYNTAX, PLEASE RE-ENTER YOUR COMMAND"
460 INPUT "COMMAND";E$
470 N1=0:PRINT
480 RESTORE
490 READ Z$,T
```

```
500 IF Z$="##" THEN 450
510 IF LEFT$(Z$,3)<>LEFT$(E$,3) THEN 490
520 ON T GOSUB 560,850,850,850,1840,3040,1050,980,2870,850,2320
530 GOTO 460
540 DATA ADD,1,LIST,2,CHANGE,3,LABELS,4,HELP,5,END,6,SEARCH,7
550 DATA SUM,8,SAVE,9,RUBOUT,10,SORT,11,##,-1
560 REM ADD RECORD ROUTINE
570 PRINT "BEGIN ADDING RECORDS.  TYPE 'END'WHEN FINISHED."
580 N=N+1:N1=N1+1:E$=""
590 PRINT N;") ";
600 FOR I=1 TO 30
610    IF LEFT$(P$(I),3)="END" THEN GOTO 730
620    PRINT TAB(7)P$(I);": ";
630    RS$=" ":INPUT RS$
640    REM
650    IF RS$="" THEN RS$=" "        'ADD A SPACE
660    IF RS$="END" THEN 800
670    IF MID$(P$(I),6,1)<>"N" THEN 700
680    IF ASC (RS$)>43 AND ASC(RS$)<58 THEN 700
690    PRINT "THIS IS A NUMERIC FIELD--ENTER NUMBERS ONLY":GOTO 620
700    REM
710    IF LEN (E$)+LEN (RS$)>245 THEN GOTO 760 ELSE E$=E$+CHR$(126)+RS$
720 NEXT I
730 P$=STR$(N)
740 E$=P$+E$+CHR$(126)
750 GOTO 770
760 PRINT "YOU HAVE EXCEEDED THE ALLOWED RECORD LENGTH, PLEASE RE-ENTER":GOTO
590
770 M$(N)=E$
780 PRINT
790 GOTO 580
800 REM END OF ADDITION TO RECORDS
810 N=N-1:N1=N1-1
820 PRINT "YOU ADDED";N1;"RECORDS"
830 RETURN
840 REM ROUTINE TO LIST RECORDS
850 GOSUB 1930:REM DETERMINE RECORD RANGE TO LIST
860 IF T=10 THEN 1160
870 IF T<>4 THEN 1070
880 INPUT "WOULD YOU LIKE TO TEST LABEL ALIGNMENT";Z$
890 IF Z$="NO" THEN INPUT "PRESS ENTER WHEN YOU ARE READY TO PRINT DATA ";EN$:
GOTO 1070
900 INPUT "ALIGN PRINTOUT AND PRESS 'ENTER' WHEN READY";W9%
910 FOR I=1 TO 2
920    FOR J=1 TO 5
930      LPRINT "XXXXXXXXXXXXXXXXXXXXXXXXX"
940    NEXT J
950 LPRINT:NEXT I
960 GOTO 1070
970 INPUT "PRESS ENTER WHEN YOU ARE READY TO PRINT THE DATA ";EN$:GOTO 1070
980 REM ROUTINE TO SEARCH RECORDS AND PERFORM SUMMATIONS
990 INPUT "ENTER THE NUMBER OF THE FIELD TO BE SUMMED";SM%
```

```
1000 IF MID$(P$(SM%),6,1)="N" THEN 1030
1010 PRINT "INCORRECT TYPE OF FIELD, PLEASE RE-ENTER"
1020 GOTO 990
1030 INPUT "DO YOU WANT TO SUM OVER ALL RECORDS? (Y/N)";S1$
1040 IF S1$<>"Y" THEN 1050 ELSE S%=0:GOTO 1060
1050 INPUT "ENTER THE FIELD NUMBER AND EXPRESSION TO BE COMPARED";S%,S$
1060 T1=1:SM=0:T2=N
1070 FOR I=T1 TO T2
1080   RS$=M$(I)
1090   E$=LEFT$(RS$,5)
1100   T3=VAL(E$)
1110   E$=RS$
1120 RS$=CHR$(126)
1130 GOSUB 2750        'ROUTINE TO PARSE STRING
1140 GOTO 1220
1150 REM RUBOUT COMMAND ROUTINE
1160 FD=T2-T1+1
1170 FOR I=T2+1 TO N+1
1180 M$(I-FD)=M$(I)
1190 NEXT I
1200 N=N-FD
1210 RETURN
1220 IF T<=4 THEN 1300
1230 IF S%=0 THEN 1250       'SUM THE RECORDS
1240 IF C$(S%)<>S$ THEN 1600       'GO TO SEARCH ROUTINE
1250 IF T=7 THEN 1400
1260 PRINT "(";I;")";
1270 T3=VAL(C$(SM%))
1280 SM=SM+T3
1290 GOTO 1600
1300 ON T-1 GOTO 1400,1400,1310
1310 REM ROUTINE TO PRINT LABELS
1320 FOR J=1 TO 5
1330   IF C$(J)="END" THEN 1360
1340   LPRINT C$(J)
1350 NEXT J
1360 LPRINT
1370 GOTO 1600
1380 REM
1390 PRINT "YOU HAVE EXCEEDED THE ALLOWED RECORD LENGTH, PLEASE RE-ENTER"
1400 PRINT I;") "
1410 FOR J=1 TO 10
1420   IF LEFT$(P$(J),3)="END" THEN GOTO 1500
1430   PRINT P$(J);": ";C$(J)
1440   IF T<>3 THEN 1480
1450   INPUT RS$
1460   IF RS$="-" THEN GOTO 1480
1470   C$(J)=RS$
1480 NEXT J
1490 REM
1500 IF T<>3 THEN 1600
1510   P$=C$(0)        'ROUTINE TO ADD A CHANGED RECORD
```

```
1520    PRINT P$
1530    E$=P$+CHR$(126)
1540    FOR J=1 TO 10
1550      IF LEN (E$)+LEN(C$(J))>245 THEN GOTO 1390
1560      E$=E$+C$(J)+CHR$(126)
1570      IF P$(J)="END" THEN 1590
1580    NEXT J
1590    M$(I)=E$
1600 NEXT I
1610 IF T<>8 THEN 1630
1620 PRINT "THE SUM OF RECORD";P$(SM%);"=";SM
1630 RETURN
1640 REM LOAD DATA FILE FROM DISK
1650 CLOSE:J=-1
1660 INPUT "ENTER FILE NAME";F$
1670 OPEN "I",1,F$
1680 INPUT #1,E$
1690 J=J+1:INPUT #1,E$
1700 IF E$="EOF" THEN 1730
1710 M$(J)=E$
1720 GOTO 1690
1730 E$=M$(0)
1740 RS$=CHR$(126)
1750 GOSUB 2740
1760 FOR I=1 TO 30
1770    P$(I)=C$(I)
1780    IF LEFT$(P$(I),3)="END" THEN 1810
1790 NEXT I
1800 I=I-1
1810 N=VAL(C$(I+1))
1820 CLOSE
1830 GOTO 460
1840 REM HELP SEQUENCE
1850 PRINT "COMMANDS AVAILABLE:"
1860 PRINT "ADD:ADDS RECORDS TO THE FILE":PRINT "CHANGE:CHANGES RECORDS IN FILE:
1870 PRINT "RUBOUT: DELETES A RECORDS FROM THE FILE":PRINT "LIST:LISTS ALL OR
CERTAIN RECORDS"
1880 PRINT "LABELS: LINE PRINTS CONTENTS OF THE FILE":PRINT "SAVE: SAVES DATA
ON DISK"
1890 PRINT "SORT:SORTS RECORDS INTO ALPHANUMERIC ORDER BY A SPECIFIED FIELD":
PRINT "SUM:SUMS A SPE
1900 PRINT "SEARCH: FINDS A RECORD CONTAINING A SPECIFIED FIELD"
1910 PRINT "HELP: BRINGS YOU HERE":PRINT "END:ENDS THE PROGRAM"
1920 RETURN
1930 REM DETERMINE THE RANGE
1940 IF N=0 THEN PRINT "EMPTY FILE"
1950 IF N=0 THEN 460
1960 PRINT "ENTER MODE:A(ALL),O(ONE),R(RANGE)"
1970 INPUT E$
1980 IF E$<>"A" THEN 2010
1990 T2=N:T1=1
2000 GOTO 2150
```

```
2010 IF E$<>"O" THEN 2060
2020 INPUT "ENTER NUMBER OF RECORD";T1
2030 IF T1>N THEN 2160
2040 T2=T1
2050 GOTO 2150
2060 IF E$="R" THEN 2090
2070 PRINT "IMPROPER SYNTAX, PLEASE RE-ENTER"
2080 GOTO 1960
2090 PRINT "INPUT THE LOWER BOUND"
2100 INPUT T1
2110 IF T1<1 THEN T1=1
2120 IF T1>N THEN GOSUB 2160
2130 INPUT "INPUT THE UPPER BOUND";T2
2140 IF T2>N THEN 2160
2150 RETURN
2160 PRINT "THERE ARE ONLY";N; "RECORDS IN THIS FILE"
2170 GOTO 1960
2180 REM
2190 REM ELIMINATE EXTRANEOUS SPACES FROM STRINGS
2200 T1=LEN(E$):C$=" ":IF T1=0 THEN 2300
2210 FOR T2=2 TO T1
2220    IF MID$(E$,T2-1,1)<>C$ THEN 2250
2230    E$=MID$(E$,2,T1-1)
2240 NEXT T2
2250 T1=LEN(E$)
2260 IF T1=0 THEN 2300
2270 IF RIGHT$(E$,1)<>C$ THEN 2300
2280 E$=LEFT$(E$,T1-1)
2290 GOTO 2270
2300 RETURN
2310 PRINT "PLEASE RE-ENTER DATA"
2320 INPUT "INPUT THE FIELD NUMBER TO BE SORTED";S%
2330 PRINT "THE FIELD NAME IS:";P$(S%)
2340 T2=N
2350 T1=1
2360 FOR I=T1 TO T2
2370    E$=M$(I)
2380    RS$=CHR$(126)
2390    GOSUB 2740
2400    D$(I)=C$(S%)
2410 NEXT I
2420 IF MID$(P$(S%),6,1)<>"A" THEN 2450
2430 SR%=1
2440 GOTO 2490
2450 IF MID$(P$(S%),6,1)="N" THEN 2480
2460 PRINT "ERROR: THE WRONG FIELD TYPE WAS ENTERED"
2470 GOTO 460
2480 SR%=2
2490 REM SORT ROUTINE
2500 M=N
2510 M=INT(M/2)
2520 IF M=0 THEN 2730
```

```
2530 J=1
2540 K=N-M
2550 I=J
2560 L=I+M
2570 IF SR%=2 THEN 2600
2580 IF D$(I)<D$(L) THEN 2700
2590 GOTO 2610
2600 IF VAL(D$(I))<VAL (D$(L)) THEN 2700
2610 E$=D$(I)
2620 D$(I)=D$(L)
2630 D$(L)=E$
2640 E$=M$(I)
2650 M$(I)=M$(L)
2660 M$(L)=E$
2670 I=I-M
2680 IF I<1 THEN 2700
2690 GOTO 2560
2700 J=J+1
2710 IF J>K THEN 2510
2720 GOTO 2550
2730 GOTO 460
2740 REM
2750 REM STRING PARSING ROUTINE
2760 K=-1
2770 FOR J2=1 TO LEN(E$)
2780 IF RS$=MID$(E$,J2,1) THEN 2810
2790 NEXT J2
2800 RETURN
2810 M%=J2-1
2820 K=K+1
2830 C$(K)=MID$(E$,1,M%)
2840 E$=MID$(E$,J2+1)
2850 J2=0
2860 GOTO 2770
2870 REM ROUTINE TO SAVE DATA
2880 INPUT "INPUT A NAME FOR FILE BEING SAVED";F$
2890 OPEN "O",1,F$
2900 PRINT #1,CHR$(34)+F$+CHR$(34):E$="00000"
2910 FOR I=1 TO 10
2920 E$=E$+CHR$(126)+P$(I)
2930 RS$=LEFT$(P$(I),3)
2940 IF RS$="END" THEN 2960
2950 NEXT I
2960 E$=E$+CHR$(126)+STR$(N)+CHR$(126)
2970 PRINT #1,CHR$(34)+E$+CHR$(34)
2980 FOR J=1 TO N
2990    PRINT #1,CHR$(34)+M$(J)+CHR$(34)
3000 NEXT J
3010 PRINT #1,"EOF"
3020 CLOSE 1
3030 RETURN
3040 END
```

Table 1-4. Uses for Database Management System.

BUSINESS USES	EDUCATIONAL USES	HOME & HOBBY USES
Customer filing	Student records	Personal records
Prospect lists	Grade records	Check lists
Master files for . . .	Teacher lists	Club rosters
Gen. Ledger	School lists	Telephone directories
Accts. Receiv.	Program design	Recipes files
Accts. Payable	Tuition data	Medical information
Payroll Records	Enrollment data	Property records
Personal data	Property/equipment	Appliance warranties
Telephone logs	Athletic schedules	Insurance records
Telephone lists	Player assignment	Christmas lists/gifts
Hotel/travel data	Games schedules	Appointments
Reservations	Player statistics	Articles indexes
Property control	Mailing lists	Tax records/data
Library catalogues	Test scores	Expenses
Inventory	Menus	Book ownership
Key Employee data	Diet selections	Utility records
Advertising data	Inventory	Deposit files
Source files	Seating charts	Due dates
Sales leads	Cataloguing	Travel records
Mail lists	Laboratory data	Meal planning
Private records	Inspection data	Mortgage data
Corp. records	Experimental data	Auto records
Directories	Attendance data	Crop yields
Billing information	Course description	Source files
Delivery schedules	Purchase orders	Magazine Article index
Routes	Requisitions	Estimate files
Territories	Vacation records	Investments
Quotations	Budgets	Plus all the Business &
Applintments	Maintenance data	Educational overlaps
Conventions	Locker assignment	
Workshop data	Field trips	
Assets lists	Vehicle records	
Marketing data	Tenure records	
Insurance data	Parking assignment	
Pricing schedules	Violation records	
Formulas	Meeting schedules	
Production data	Facility schedules	
Processes		
Cross referencing		
Commission records		
General filing		

Database programs are perhaps the most useful personal computer programs because of their wide application. In what applications could you use a database? The list in Table 1-4 names a number of the thousands of types of information that may be stored, indexed, organized, or cross-referenced by a database program. Many of these applications are discussed in more detail throughout the book.

Sophisticated database programs are commercially available, but the following database demonstration program should be adequate for most home uses. Unlike most commercial programs, which rely upon machine language commands for added speed, this program is written in BASIC for easy modification. It is designed for use with floppy disks.

Chapter 2

Business and Financial Applications

Personal computers have greatly altered the business world by permitting rapid calculation of numerous "What if . .?" questions involving financial formulas, in addition to providing accounting functions. Likewise, the homeowner will find the personal computer useful in analyzing loans, budgets, and investments. Calculations that were previously open to error and time-consuming can now be accomplished with ease and permit better decision making.

FINANCES AND INVESTMENTS

A growing number of investors are using their personal computers to help them manage their stock and bond portfolios, analyze trends in the financial markets, and investigate individual stocks and decide when to buy or sell. A personal computer connected to a database can sort out enormous quantities of market and company statistics for an investor; and within seconds the results may be projected on the screen as charts, tables, or graphs, enabling an investor to evaluate a buying

opportunity—or a must-sell situation—quickly and probably more accurately than if the calculations were done by hand. The personal computer can sometimes make your life as an investor more rewarding, and often much easier. Additionally, the cost of investment programs may be counted as a business expense for tax purposes, as can part or all of the cost of your computer.

STOCKS, BONDS, AND SECURITIES

The personal computer has come to the aid of the individual investor in three areas: portfolio management, technical and fundamental analysis; and database access. Making investment decisions or recommendations requires accurate technical analysis of large amounts of data on a timely basis. Compiling information in standard formats concerning stock performance or company finances, doing statistical computations to update individual stock files, tracking moving averages, and maintaining complete records of one or a number of portfolios are all tasks ideally suited to the personal computer. Professional brokers as well as individuals have witnessed the significant impact that the personal computer can have on the analytical functions on which they base their recommendations. With the advent of the bull market of the early 1980s and the rise of the discount broker, professional software packages have become available to help investors at home make the investment decisions that used to be made by their full-service brokerages.

Portfolio Management

Portfolio management programs are really just electronic notebooks. They keep a complete record of the stocks you own and show how well you're doing at the game. They are especially useful at tax time; their compilations of your losses, gains, dividends, brokerage commissions, and more make it easy to account to Uncle Sam for your Wall Street activity.

The limitations on most packages involve the number of stock characteristics maintained or computed for each stock. Most packages will allow for a virtually unlimited number of stock records (letting you track your own portfolio as well as that of several financial advisors), as long as you are willing to maintain them on a number of disks.

The simplest individual portfolio management programs provide a means of recording the basic information on stocks in your own portfolio or on any other stocks you wish to track for comparison. When you choose to update—on a daily, weekly, or other periodic basis—the program will automatically perform certain calculations, such as present value of the issues, or long- and short-term gains and losses (as if you sold the stock on that date). It can automatically remind you of a stock that will go long-term within 30 days or maintain other information such as dates and number of shares purchased, total number of shares owned, dividends, growth rate, and percentage appreciation or depreciation. The following analysis factors may be computed for the entire portfolio: sum of cost prices, sum of current value, sum and percentage difference between cost and current price, percentage return on a cost basis, and percentage return on the

current value. A report may be automatically prepared for attachment to IRS forms, and the portfolio information may be printed in a variety of formats for ready reference.

More advanced portfolio management packages allow hundreds of open tax lots in a system that matches your transactions against open positions to let you make investment decisions that minimize your tax liability. You can track stocks, options, bonds, treasuries, and mutual funds; the system can accommodate buy, sell, short sell, and buy-to-cover transactions. Return on investment for each stock and the entire portfolio may be computed as well as the total net earnings. Sophisticated programmers could make use of Sharpe's method (or another method) in determining the proportion of funds that should be allocated to each security in a portfolio to maximize returns.

Technical and Fundamental Analysis

Fundamental analysis assumes that the price fluctuations of stocks are based on the basic financial health of the economy and the performance of the individual company. Thus, fundamental analysts look at such factors as earnings, sales, assets, and liabilities and use these to predict future price movements.

Technical analysts argue that these factors affect stock prices only over the long run. Short-term fluctuations, they maintain, are governed by psychological conditions in the market itself, not external factors. Therefore, they believe the study of the past market behavior can determine the way to profits in the future. There are many different theories that promote various indicators as the key to future price movement. Some of the major indicators are the relationship between price and volume, market averages, and new highs versus lows.

Both fundamental and technical anlysis call for extensive number crunching and are well suited for being handled by computers, although fundamental analysis involves the capacity of most personal computers. In fact, almost all of the analysis programs available on the personal computer market do technical analysis. In technical analysis, computers can be especially useful in charting various relationships between individual stock prices and trading volumes. A personal computer can turn a pile of statistics that might take several hours to plot by hand into a chart within seconds. In this chapter I will discuss some popular means of technical and fundamental analysis. Interested readers are referred to popular manuals on investment analysis, statistics, and these publications on computer-assisted stock analysis for further information:

*L.R. Schmeltz, *Playing the Stock and Bond Markets With Your Personal Computer*, TAB BOOKS Inc., Blue Ridge Summit, PA 17214.
*Leslie E. Sparks, *Investment Analysis With Your Microcomputer*, TAB BOOKS Inc., Blue Ridge Summit, PA 17214.
The Microcomputer Investor, The MicroComputer Investors Association, 902 Anderson Dr., Fredricksburg, VA 22401.
Computerized Investing on the Stock Market from Investment Software Concepts, P.O. Box 27, Bronxville, NY 10708.
*Woodwell, Donald, *Automating Your Financial Portfolio: An Investor's Guide to Personal Computers*, Dow-Jones-Irwin, 1818 Ridge Rd., Homewood, IL 60430.

With a microcomputer at your disposal, you can now develop and test a market theory without countless, error-prone manual calculations! A "paper portfolio," or collection of stocks to track that are not actually owned, was once too time and effort consuming for the individual investor to experiment with. When you experiment each "buy and sell" decision can be based on actual market performance and serve as a "lesson learned" in developing your own trading strategies.

Moving Averages

Moving averages provide a measure of the movement of a stock relative to itself (in price, dividend, or volume), a composite summary of a key factor (for example, the average price of a stock group), and a ratio of two or more key factors (for example, P/E ratios). The moving average is often most useful in predicting the buy versus sell position of a stock in regard to its past trend. If the current stock price drops below the moving average, a sell position would be taken and vice-versa for a buy position. The program in Listing 2-1 computes the moving average for a stock or other security given a set of successive daily prices and the length of the span over which the average is to be computed.

Listing 2-1: The Moving Average Calculator Program

```
5 KEY OFF:CLS
10 REM MOVING AVERAGE CALCULATOR
20 PRINT "ENTER PRICE VALUES SUCCESSIVELY, '9999' TO END"
30 DIM A(200),B(200):X=0
40 X=X+1:PRINT "#";X;:INPUT A(X)
50 IF A(X)=9999 THEN X=X-1:GOTO 60 ELSE 40
60 INPUT "ENTER SPAN LENGTH";C
70 E=(1+C)/2:D=1:G=C
80 F=0:FOR I=D TO G
90 F=A(I)+F:NEXT
100 G=G+1:B(E)=INT(.5+F/C):E=E+1:D=D+1
110 IF G<1+X THEN 80
140 PRINT "  WEEK #      WEEKLY PRICE AVE.      MOVING AVE"
150 A$="  ####          ####                ####"
160 FOR I=1 TO X:PRINT USING A$;I,A(I),B(I)
170 NEXT I
180 INPUT "TYPE '1' TO CHOOSE NEW SPAN";ZZ
```

```
190 IF ZZ<>1 THEN END
200 FOR I=1 TO X:B(I)=0:NEXT I
210 GOTO 60
```

Price/Volume Trace

In this analysis technique, the daily stock price and volume data are considered as (x, y) data points. Probability rules may be developed as clues to the immediate future performance of the stock price as it relates to volume.

Rate of Change

The rate of change is a measure that involves price fluctuations of a stock to itself and may be used to compare stocks in terms of price, sales, or earnings. On this basis you can find the stock with the best potential to increase in price in the immediate future, barring any information or indication that the current stock trend will change or reverse. It is computed as follows:

$$\% \text{ Rate of Change} = \frac{\dfrac{\text{Ending-Starting Price}}{\text{Starting Price}}}{\text{No. of trading days}} * 100$$

This value may be determined for daily, weekly, monthly, yearly or other periods by alternating the denominator.

Change Distribution

This analysis technique compares the distributional change of individual stocks within a group to the average change of the group for a given time period. This provides a probabilistic measure of the rate of change in either relative or absolute terms.

The stock distribution, like a normal distribution, is described by the factors of price average and standard deviation; the standard deviation usually increases as the length of time considered increases and as the market rate of change increases. By knowing the typical stock price distributions for different market index rates of change, the probability of success in short-term trading is increased; the investor is equipped with the probability dis-tribution of the price change.

Price Indexes

Price indices are indicators of the central drift of a set of stocks or the market as a whole. These include the Dow Jones, New York Stock Exhange, American Stock Exchange, Standard & Poor index, and other indices. They can be best applied to determine a consensus of individual stock trends within a given stock category. An indicator that is well suited for computation on your personal computer would use the formula

$$\text{INDEX} = \overset{\text{all stocks}}{\Sigma} \frac{x_n y_n}{y}$$

where x_n = stock price
y_n = number of shares traded at x_n
y = total shares traded

The moving average and indexing concepts may be used as powerful decision-making tools in determining whether the investor should be anticipating a trading decision, trading, or investigating other investments.

Ratio Relationships

The use of ratios is popular in business and finance because they afford a means of comparison of two or more factors that influence investment decisions. A well-known example is the price/earnings (P/E) ratio used in measuring the potential of a stock. Others include the ratio of sales growth, the ratio of consecutive period earnings, the yearly high stock price versus the low price, and the relative strength of a stock versus the market index. The personal computer may be used in automatically calculating many of the popular ratios and in forecasting changes of ratios through the use of statistical regression. For instance, the future price of a stock may be computed given current value per share, projected earnings, and projected percent change in the P/E ratio using this simple formula:

$$V_p = \frac{V_c\,E_p^{\,2}}{E_c^{\,2}}$$

where V_c = current value per share
E_p = projected earnings
C = projected percent change of P/E ratio
E_c = current earnings
V_p = projected value per share

Note that all projected values must be for the same length of time.

Trend Line Analysis

Trend-line analysis is a major statistical computation in financial analysis and is accomplished by using the method of *linear least squares* fitting of data. Suppose you obtained a set of data listing the value of one stock over a period of time. If these values were plotted versus the Dow Jones Index the result could appear as shown in Fig. 2-1.

A trend line analysis would determine the equation of the line that best fits or describes the data, telling you how one variable is related to another. This equation, in the form of $y = a + bx$, provides a means to estimate the value of a variable (y) given the value of the other variable (x). The values of a

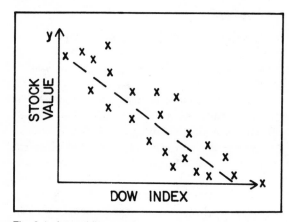

Fig. 2-1. A trend line graph.

and b are determined using these regression equations:

$$b = \frac{n\Sigma XY - \Sigma X \Sigma Y}{n \Sigma X^2 - (\Sigma X)^2}$$

$$a = \frac{1}{n}(\Sigma Y - b\Sigma X)$$

where   n = no. of (x,y) pairs
X = individual x values
Y = individual y values
b = slope of line
a = y axis intercept

As described in the chapter concerning mathematical and statistical applications, the standard error may be calculated for a regression line to determine how well it describes the data.

The technique of multiple linear regression is used by investors in determining the influence of more than one variable ($x_1 - x_n$) on another variable (y). The total variation in y may often be better explained through the use of multiple x variables ($y = a + b_1 x_1 + b_2 x_2 + \ldots b_n x_n$), allowing more precise prediction than is possible through the simple linear regression discussed above. For instance, one investor using microcomputer techniques has developed a four-variable regression equation describing the stock market average:

$$\log V = a + b \log E + c \log G - d \log R$$

where V = Value of the average
E = Earnings of the average
G = Growth rate of the average's earning
R = Yield of quality long-term bonds

In this example, the variables (E, G, R) are regressed on V. The constants a, b, c, d are determined and used in predicting future values of V based on past relationships to E, G, and R. Multiple linear regression is also computed using the least squares method. For more information on the least squares method, to a textbook of statistics.

Investors using multiple linear regression

techniques have developed modeling equations that reflect the influence of a wide variety of factors, with high correlations, on stock and security prices, earnings, and P/E ratios. These include

- The current month's interest yield of the Moody's AAA Bond Index.
- The ratio of pretax corporate profits for the preceding twelve months to pretax corporate profits adjusted for inventory profits for the same period.
- The ratio of current dollar gross national product for the preceding twelve months to current dollar gross national product for twelve months ending one quarter into the future.
- The average yield on taxable U.S. Government 3-5 year issues for the preceding six months.
- The average year-to-year percentage gain of the Consumer Price Index.
- The equity of the S&P 400 one year previous divided by the earnings of the S&P 400 for the latest twelve months.
- The relative consistency of divided growth for ten years, in terms of the ratio of the correlation of the stock's dividend growth with time to that of the S&P Industrial Stock Average's dividend growth.
- The relative consistency of earnings growth for ten years, computed as above.
- The relative profit margin for the latest report twelve months.
- The relative rate of earnings growth for the previous ten years on a per-share basis.
- The relative size measured by net income for the latest twelve months.
- The relative return on equity, as earnings less dividends divided by equity at the beginning of the twelve-month period.
- The relative five-year earnings-per-share least-squares growth rate.
- The relative prospective return on equity in the year for which earnings are being estimated.
- The relative prospective earnings growth for the next quarter.
- The relative reinvestment rate in the latest year.
- The relative prospective earnings growth for the next two quarters.

- The relative dividend payout ratio for the latest twelve months.
- The relative earnings growth for the latest twelve months.

Of course, many other variables could be used at the investors discretion, including DJIA, specific industrial indicators, GNP, employment statistics, disposable personal income statistics, indices of industrial production, bank deposits, money supply, interest rates, inventory levels, accounts receivable/payable, and railroad freight usage. With a large selection of apparently useful variables to employ, you can now build a multiple regression equation on your personal computer, seeking both the highest possible correlation and confidence level and the least interaction among variables chosen. The variables may be regressed against individual stock performance, group stock performance, and market indices or other securities. Those variables that are generally most useful include measures of preceding and following interest rates, inflation, economic activity (for example GNP), industry health, and rates of change.

Database Searching

With the advent of databases available to the individual investor at low rates, a personal computer can be instructed to search for stocks fulfilling any combination of investment criteria. If, for example, you are a conservative investor, you could have a program hunt for companies whose shares have a P/E ratio of 5 or less and annual yields of 10% or more—both of which can signify undervalued companies.

Financial Ratio Analysis

Financial ratio analysis is an ideal, simple method of determining how well a particular company has performed in relation to other companies in its industry or in relation to its own past performance and of predicting future performance. Described below are several popular financial ratios that can be determined using figures from corporate annual reports and a simple BASIC program that does the necessary divisions and tabulations or comparisons with figures concerning other corporations. Over the years, security analysts, brokers, and investors have found that financial statements become more meaningful when ratios between various values on the income and balance sheets are computed. These ratios may be divided into four categories, as shown below:

Liquidity Ratios
Current ratio
Quick ratio
Inventory to working capital

Leverage Ratios
Debt to total assets
Times interest earned
Current liabilities to net worth
Fixed assets to net worth
Debt to equity

Activity Ratios
Cash velocity
Inventory turnover
Fixed assets turnover
Average collection period
Total assets turnover

Profitability Ratios
Net operating margin
Net income margin
Return on assets
Return on net worth

Liquidity ratios are designed to measure a firm's ability to meet its obligations as they mature and relate to the amount of cash and assets convertible into cash in the near future.

Leverage ratios measures the financing provided by owners as compared with the financing provided by the firm's creditors. Creditors look at the owner-supplied funds to provide them with a margin of safety, but by raising funds through debt, the owners are able to maintain control of the firm with a small investment. The return of the owners is magnified when the firm earns more on the borrowed funds than it pays in interest.

Activity ratios determine how effectively the firm utilizes the resources available.

Profitability ratios demonstrate the result of the policies and decisions of the firm's management. Both operating margins and new profits are calculated to distinguish between the results of operating policies and the results of financial policies.

The input data needed for computation of these ratios is usually found in the financial statements of a company and includes

Cash: all cash on hand plus cash in the company's bank accounts. Any cash in certificates of deposit or other short-term deposits should be included.

Marketable securities: investments in obligations that are readily marketable and can be converted into cash on short notice.

Receivables (beginning): receivables should be net of any reserve for doubtful accounts and be fully collectible within one year. Beginning receivables are those that were due to the company at the beginning of the operating year.

Receivables (ending): those receivables due to the company at the end of the operating year.

Inventory (beginning): inventory that is on hand at the beginning of the operating year.

Inventory (ending): inventory that is on hand at the end of the operating year.

Current assets: the total of cash, marketable securities, receivables, inventories, and other assets of the company that are expected to be converted into cash in the normal course of business within the current operating year.

Fixed assets: assets such as land, buildings, leasehold improvements, equipment, fixtures, furnishings, vehicles and other assets with lives longer than one year that are used in the operations of the company.

Total assets: the total of all assets of the company, including current assets, fixed assets, and other assets.

Current liabilities: debts of the company that must be paid within one year, usually consisting of trade accounts payable, payroll taxes withheld, accrued expenses, and that portion of long-term debt coming due within one year.

Total liabilities: the total of all the debt of the company, including current as well as noncurrent liabilities.

Net worth: (also called owner's equity or stockholders' equity) the difference between total assets and total liabilities.

Sales: the total revenues earned by the company during the year, net of all sales discounts and returns.

Gross operating profit: found by subtracting cost of sales from sales. It represents the difference between the sales price of all items sold and the cost of the items sold.

Interest charges: the total amount of interest that has been paid by the company on its indebtedness.

Profit before income taxes: the net income of the company for the year after all expenses have been considered. It is commonly referred to as the "bottom line."

Current ratio. This ratio is computed by dividing current liabilities into current assets. This ratio is the generally accepted measure of the ability to satisfy short-term obligations and indicates the extent to which the claims of short-term creditors can be covered by assets that can be expected to be converted to cash in a period corresponding to the time obligations become due.

Quick ratio. This ratio is computed by deducting inventories from current assets and divid-

ing the remainder by current liabilities. This is a measure of the ability to pay short-term obligations without relying on the sale of inventories and is a better guide to short-term liquidity than the current ratio.

Inventory to working capital. This ratio demonstrates the proportion of working capital tied up in inventory and is used to find the possible loss to the company resulting from a decline in inventory values; a low ratio is desirable.

Debt to total assets. This ratio measures the company's obligations to creditors in relation to all the funds provided to the company; the lower the ratio, the greater the protection from losses being incurred by creditors in the event of liquidation. Generally, the maximum debt ratio should be 50%.

Times interest earned. This ratio is determined by dividing earnings before interest and taxes by interest expense. This measures the extent to which earnings could fall before the company is unable to pay annual interest costs; the lower the ratio, the more difficulty the company will have in raising additional funds. A manufacturing company should cover interest more than four times and public utilities should cover interest about three times.

Current liabilities to net worth. This ratio determines the amount of funds supplied by owners compared to funds provided by current debt; if the owners have not put enough funds into the company, long-term creditors will be less willing to provide funds, and the company will have to utilize short-term financing to a great extent, resulting in greater time before current bills are paid. Lower ratios are favorable.

Fixed assets to net worth. This ratio indicates the extent to which owner's funds are invested in assets with little turnover. Higher ratios will result for industries that are capital intensive versus companies that are labor intensive.

Debt to equity. This ratio demonstrates the relation between total debt of the firm and funds provided by the owners; the lower the ratio, the greater the protection against creditor's losses in the event of liquidation. Owners may desire a high ratio because this will magnify earnings and prevent possible dilution of control of the company if additional equity must be raised.

Cash velocity ratio. This ratio is computed by dividing cash and cash equivalents into sales. This ratio indicates the number of times cash has turned over within the year; a high cash velocity indicates cash is being used effectively.

Inventory turnover. This ratio is computed by dividing the cost of sales by inventory. This ratio indicates the liquidity of inventory; a high inventory turnover shows that inventories are being held to a minimum, and a low ratio may indicate obsolete or slow-moving stock.

Fixed assets turnover. This ratio is computed by dividing sales by fixed assets. This measures the utilization of fixed assets; a low ratio may indicate the plant isn't being utilized as effectively as possible, unless the company is labor-intensive.

Average collection period. This ratio is computed by dividing accounts receivable by average daily sales. This represents the average time period after making a sale before cash is received, indicating the effectiveness of credit and collection policies; these may need to be strengthened if this ratio is on the increase.

Total assets turnover. This ratio is computed by dividing sales by total assets. This shows the effectiveness of the firm in utilizing resources to generate sales; a high ratio may indicate over-utilization of assets, and a low ratio may indicate an excessive investment or idle assets.

Gross operating margins. This ratio is computed by dividing gross operating profit by sales. This ratio determines how far unit selling prices may decline without resulting in a loss from the sale of units and how products are priced in relation to their cost.

Net operating margin. This ratio is computed by dividing profit before taxes by sales. This shows the amount each sales dollar provides to the continuing operation of the firm before consideration of income taxes.

Net income margins. This ratio is determined by dividing net profits after taxes by sales. A lower ratio indicates selling prices are relatively low and total costs are relatively high; thus, a small percentage drop in sales may result in losses. This ratio indicates the profitability after taking into account all income taxes and expenses and measures the return on sales.

Return on assets ratio. This ratio is computed by dividing net profits after taxes by total assets. This measures rate of return on total resources.

Return on net worth ratio. This ratio is computed by dividing net profit after taxes by net worth. This ratio is indicative of the company's earning on the investment of shareholders. A high or increasing value is favorable, although a very high value may indicate intense competition. Additionally, temporary inventory profits may be the result of increasing commodity prices. A high value could also be caused by general prosperity or a declining position.

Combined coverage. Combined coverage is computed by dividing annual interest and debt costs plus preferred dividends into the adjusted operating profit after taxes and before interest. A combined coverage of four is considered acceptable for an industrial company; a coverage of three times the combined requirements would make a utility stock high-grade.

Dividend payout. The dividend payout is the percentage of earnings on common stock that are paid out as dividends. Industrial companies average about 55%, utilities 70%, and growth companies less than 55%.

Book value per share. The book value per share is determined by adding the stated or par value of the common stock to the additional paid-in capital and retained earnings accounts and dividing by the number of common shares. The book value would be lower for companies in which preferred stock is entitled to share in additional paid-in capital. The book value is not as important an indicator as earnings and prospects for industrial companies. However, the book value of stock for financial institutions and utilities is important in anlysis.

Additional Investment Applications

On the following pages you will find ten more ways in which you can use your microcomputer as a tool for making profitable financial decisions.

Company growth rates. The program in Listing 2-2 may be used to calculate company growth rates using historical financial data:

Earnings per share estimation. A historical balance sheet and income data could be used to estimate future earnings for a given stock; future estimations may be made with trend-line analysis.

Listing 2-2: The Growth Rate Calculator Program

```
100 REM CALCULATION OF THE GROWTH RATE
110 A=0
120 INPUT "ENTER THE NUMBER OF DATA POINTS ";Z(0)
130 PRINT "ENTER DATA POINTS SUCCESSIVELY"
140 FOR B=1 TO Z(0)
150    INPUT Z(B)
160 NEXT B
170 FOR B=1 TO Z(0)
180    IF Z(B)=<0 THEN PRINT "DATA LESS THAN ZERO NOT ALLOWED":GOTO 110
190 A=A+LOG(Z(B))
200 NEXT B
210 A=(1/Z(0))*A
220 Z6=0:Z7=0
230 FOR B=1 TO Z(0)
240 Z6=Z6+(LOG(Z(B))-A)*(B-(Z(0)/2))
250 Z7=Z7+((B-(Z(0)/2))^2)
260 NEXT B
270 V=Z6/Z7
280 PRINT "THE GROWTH RATE IS ";INT((100*V)+.5);"%"
290 PRINT
300 END
```

The intrinsic value of a stock. This value is calculated with this formula:

$$I = \frac{TC \cdot AMT}{CS}$$

Where I = intrinsic value
TC = total corporation capital
AMT = price per share
CS = amount in dollars of capital stock

A stock valuation program. A program of this type could find current and future values of a stock and the rate of return before and after taxes. Commissions would be considered in all calculations.

Brokerage commissions. Commissions could be calculated on standard and odd lots, as well as for stocks selling below one dollar per share.

An options valuation program. Using the Black-Scholes or another economic model, an options valuation program could determine the optimum hedge ratio and spread of any options. When selling partially covered calls or when selling puts and shortening stock, an options writing program could be used to find the maximum profit and upper and lower break-even points.

A program of this type is presented in Listing 2-3. The purpose of this program is to assist the investor in planning the most profitable stock-option buy and sell strategy. The strategy used by the program involves the selling of options against stock bought; this is usually considered the least risky strategy and it is often the most profitable one. For example, you could buy 100 shares of stock to use as collateral for each call option sold. A call option, which is sold at a premium, allows the purchaser the right to buy the stock at a certain price (called the strike point), no matter what the true stock price becomes. However, the option is valid only for a certain length of time, known as the life of the option. This computer program will request information pertaining to the stock and will calculate the value of the stock and return on investment (ROI) over a range of 40% to 160% of the current value. Using this data, the investor should be able to decide the probability that a certain buy and sell strategy will be profitable. In the final analysis, the program uses a set of financial formulas to recommend a specific buy-sell strategy and then prints an itemized listing of all costs, brokerage fees, proceeds and returns. To make the best use of this program, it is suggested that you study references concerning stock-option strategies.

Listing 2-3: The Stock Option Analysis Program

```
10 REM STOCK OPTION ANALYSIS PROGRAM
20 KEY OFF:CLS
30 DIM D(12),A$(20),B(10),F(12),K$(12)
40 FOR D4=1 TO 12
50    READ D(D4):F(D4)=D4:READ K$(D4)
60 NEXT D4
70 INPUT "ENTER THE NUMERICAL MONTH, DAY, YEAR ",M1,D9,Y1
80 INPUT "IS THE STOCK TO BE BOUGHT ON MARGIN (1=YES,2=NO)";M
90 INPUT "ENTER THE % MARGIN RATE ",M2
100 IF M=1 THEN D5=.5 ELSE D5=1
110 INPUT "ENTER THE NAME OF THE STOCK OR ID, THE DIVIDEND IN $'S PER SHARE PER
QUARTER ",D6$,D7
120 INPUT "ENTER THE NUMBER OF SHARES TO BE PURCHASED (MULTIPLE OF 100 SHARES) "
,D8
130 INPUT "ENTER THE PRICE PER SHARE ";P9
140 INPUT "SELECT MARKET 1)NYSE, 2)OTC ",E
150 INPUT "ENTER THE EXPIRATION MONTH (E.G. 1=JANUARY, 2=FEBRUARY...) ",E2
160 INPUT "ENTER THE STRIKE PRICE ",E3
170 INPUT "ENTER THE COST PER OPTION (MULTIPLY PRICE BY 100) ",E4
180 E5=D8/100
190 INPUT "ENTER THE JANUARY, APRIL, JULY, OCTOBER, PREMIUMS ",B(1),B(4),B(7),B(
10)
195 C4=100:C3=100
200 FOR C8=1 TO 10 STEP 3
210    IF B(C8)=0 THEN 590
220    C9=B(C8)
230    A4=C8*30.4225
240    A8=A4+A7-((M1-1)*30.4225)-D9
250    C=P9*C3
260    FOR A9=1 TO 2
270       C4=A9*C4
280       D=C4*C9
290       B4=D*.034+.017*C
300       B5=B4+C-D
310       B6=B5*.085*A8/365
320       D1=B6+B5
325 INPUT "MORE--PRESS ENTER ",A$:CLS
```

```
330     PRINT "MONTH OF CALL";C8
340     PRINT "INITIAL INVESTMENT";B5
350     PRINT "TOTAL INVESTMENT ";D1
360     PRINT "EFFECTIVE WRITING RATIO";A9
370     PRINT
380     PRINT "STOCK PRICE      RETURN          ROI           ROI/YR"
390     FOR D2=-4 TO 6
400       A1=(1-(.1*D2))*C
410       IF A1/C3>(.25+E3) THEN 460
420       B9=0
430       B7=A1-D1
440       GOTO 480
450       D1=(1-A9)*A1+D1
460       B7=C3*E3-D1-100*(A9-1)*E3
470       B9=(((A1/C3+1)-(1.068*C9))*100)/(1.068*C9)
480       B8=B7/D1*100
490       C2=A1/C3
500       D3=B8/(A8/365)
510       PRINT C2,B7,B8,D3
520     NEXT D2
530   NEXT A9
590 NEXT C8
600 IF A8>180 THEN PRINT "LONG TERM"
610 PRINT
620 E6=INT(E5*E3*100)
630 E7=INT(E4*E5)
640 E8=Y1*365
650 E9=D9+D(M1)+E8
660 F=E8+20+D(E2)
670 F1=F-E9:IF F1<0 THEN F1=F1+365
680 F2=INT((F1/90)+.5)
690 F3=INT(F2*D7*D8)
700 F5=INT(P9*D8)
710 F6=INT(D5*F5)
770 GOSUB 1150
780 G1=G2:F9=E6:G=D8/100:GOSUB 1150
820 G3=G2:F9=E7:G=E5:F8=3
830 GOSUB 1150
860 GOSUB 1150
870 G4=G2
880 G5=F7-E7-F3+G3+G4+G1
900 IF D5=1 THEN G6=0 ELSE G6=INT(((M2/100)*G5)*F1/365)
910 G7=G6+G3+F7+G4+G1+F6
920 G8=F4-G7
930 G9=F6-F3-E7+G6+G3+G1+G4
940 H=INT((G8*1000)/G9)/10
950 H2=INT((((G7-F3-E7)*100)/D8)/100
960 H1=INT(3650*H/F1)/10
970 INPUT "PRESS ENTER TO CONTINUE ",A$:PRINT
980 PRINT "COVERED WRITE:";D6$;" DATE (MMDDYY):";M1;D9;Y1
990 PRINT "HEDGE STRATEGY:"
1000 PRINT "BUY";D8;"SHARES.(PRICE=$";P9;")"
```

```
1010 PRINT "SELL";E5; " ";K$(E2);E3; " 'S ($";E4;"APIECE)"
1020 INPUT "PRESS ENTER TO CONTINUE ",A$
1030 CLS:PRINT "EXPENSES:"
1040 PRINT "  IMMEDIATE      $";F6
1045 PRINT "  LOAN (50%)     $";F7
1050 PRINT "  BROKER'S FEES $"
1055 PRINT "      OPTION     $";G4
1060 PRINT "      IN         $";G1
1065 PRINT "      OUT        $";G3
1070 PRINT "  MARGIN COST    $";G6
1080 PRINT "TOTAL           $";G7
1100 PRINT "INCOME:":PRINT " STOCK $";E6
1105 PRINT "  OPTION      $";E7
1110 PRINT "  DIVIDENDS   $";F3
1115 PRINT "TOTAL         $";F4
1120 PRINT "TOTAL         $";F4
1125 PRINT:PRINT "THE RETURN ON YOUR MONEY IS";H;"% ($";G8;" ON $";INT(G9);")"
1130 PRINT "FOR";F1;" DAYS,";H1;"% ANNUALLY."
1140 PRINT "THE BREAK-EVEN POINT IS A PRICE OF $";(INT(H2*10))/10:END
1150 G2=((9.000001E-03*F9)+22)+(6*G)
1160 ON F8 GOTO 1180,1190,1200
1170 IF G2<25 THEN G2=25
1175 RETURN
1180 G2=INT(.7*G2):RETURN
1190 G2=21*G:RETURN
1200 G2=INT(.82*G2):RETURN
1300 DATA 0,JANUARY,31,FEBRUARY,59,MARCH,90,APRIL,120,MAY,151,JUNE,182,JULY,212,
AUGUST,243,SEPTEMBER,272,OCTOBER,304,NOVEMBER,334,DECEMBER
```

Computation of short-term insolvency.
In this "Z-Score" computation based on an American Institute of Certified Public Accountants timesharing program, the short-term liquidity trend score indicates whether a company is likely to face financial difficulties in the near future.

$$Z = .012*((G-L)/I) + .014*(W/I) + .033*((P+E)/I) + .006*(W/M) + .999*(S/I)$$

where G = current
L = current liabilities
I = total assets
W = net worth
P = profit before income taxes
E = interest changes
M = total liabilities
S = sales
Z = "Z score"

Stock alpha and beta. In this approach to analysis, the investor compares movement of a stock over a period of time with movement of a market average. This can be best measured by comparing the percent change in a given stock's price with the percent change in the market as a whole over several large recent market fluctuations and deriving a result in the form y=a+bx where y=percent change in a stock's price given x as the percent change in the market level. The constant a is called *alpha* and is a measure of the stock's absolute continuing movement; high positive alphas are always attractive in stocks. The coefficient b is called the stock's *beta* and is a measure of the riskiness of a given stock. High betas should produce good relative performance in a bull market, but relatively poor performance in a declining market. Beta's may be calculated separately as a function of such factors as size of the company involved, its

44

capital structure (for example, its debt/equity ratio), return on equity, earnings consistency, and so forth. You may experiment with multiple linear regression in determining the relationship between beta's and these or other variables. In general, the greater the beta, the cheaper the stock should seem to be and the greater the appreciation potential. A risk versus benefit analysis may be conducted, with, for example, betas charted versus potential appreciation based on present discounted value of the price of the stock.

Equations used to independently determine stock betas are as follows and are well-suited for incorporation into a portfolio analysis program:

Stock Beta

$$\text{Beta} = \frac{\left(\begin{array}{c}\text{Covariance of market and}\\ \text{stock risk premiums}\end{array}\right)}{\text{Variance of market risk premium}}$$

$$\text{Variance} = \underset{\text{time}}{\Sigma}\ (\text{market risk premium-ave. market risk premium})^2$$

$$\text{Convariance} = \frac{\underset{\text{time}}{\Sigma}\ (\text{SRP-ave. SPR})*}{(\text{MRP-ave. MRP})}$$

SRP = stock risk premium
MRP = market risk premium

$$\text{risk premium} = \begin{array}{l}(\text{rate of return})-\\ (\text{risk free rate of return})\end{array}$$

$$\text{risk free rate of return} = \frac{1}{12\bullet(\text{annual rate of a 3 month T-bill})}$$

$$\text{rate of return} = \frac{\begin{array}{l}(\text{price at month end + dividend})-\\ (\text{price at month start})\end{array}}{\text{price at month start}}$$

For market statistics use the *Standard & Poors 500 Stock Index.*

Portfolio Beta

$$\underset{\text{portfolio}}{\text{Beta}} = \underset{\text{portfolio}}{\Sigma}\ \begin{array}{l}(\text{stock beta})\bullet\\ (\% \text{ of market value})\end{array}$$

$$\% \text{ market value} = \frac{\text{market value of a stock}}{\text{total market value}}$$

market value of a stock = current price × no. of shares

Inflation rate effect. An oversimplified but often useful method of forecasting the effect of a given inflation rate on the stock market is as follows. First, assume that the cost of money is constant at three percent. Add to this value a one-percent constant that will be assumed to be the risk factor for owning stocks instead of bonds. To this sum add the current inflation rate. Divide this final sum into 100; the result is the average stock market multiple of earnings. Now, multiply this result by the sum of the estimated yearly earnings of the thirty Dow Jones Industrial stocks. If the sum of the estimated earnings is not known, a simple computer program could determine earnings for the industrial stocks from the newspaper listings of price and price/earnings ratios (earnings=price/price-earnings ratio); a method of determining future earnings growth would have to be employed. The final product calculated is a projected Dow Jones industrial stock average.

The calculations would be as follows, assuming an inflation rate of five percent and estimated Dow industrial stock earnings of $110:

$$\frac{100}{(3\% + 1\% + 5\%)} \bullet 110. = 1222.$$

Calculation of the future value of an investment. You can use the program in Listing 2-4 to calculate how much an investment will be worth in the future.

Investment analysis using interest rate formulas. The set of interest rate formulae outlined below may be used to assess and compare the values of investments with respect to time and money, considering that money today is inherently

```
Listing 2-4: The Future Value Program


100 REM CALCULATION OF THE FUTURE VALUE OF AN INVESTMENT
110 CLS       'CLEAR SCREEN
120 DEFDBL F,D,E,B,C,A
130 INPUT "ENTER THE CONSUMER PRICE INDEX FOR PREVIOUS YEAR ",F
140 INPUT "ENTER THE CONSUMER PRICE INDEX FOR CURRENT YEAR ",E
150 INPUT "ENTER THE PRESENT VALUE OF THE INVESTMENT (OR PRODUCT/SALARY) ",C
160 INPUT "ENTER THE NUMBER OF PERIODS TO BE CALCULATED ",B
170 A=(100*(E-F)/F)/100
180 D=INT((C*(A+1)²B)*100+.5)/100
190 PRINT
200 PRINT "THE FUTURE VALUE IS: $";D
210 PRINT
220 END
```

worth more than the same money tomorrow. In an investment, money passes from and to the investor in the form of borrowed money, loaned money, dividends received, installment loan payments made, and so on; these are called *cash flows*. The resulting profit or loss can be measured as an interest rate, the rate being absolute throughout the whole period of investment or applying only to a specific time interval. A $30 profit on a $100 investment four years ago is a 30% profit in absolute terms, but when it is measured at an annual rate (using the equations below), the profit comes to 6.8%.

The interest equations below may be divided into two sets: equations 1, 4, 7, and 9 are used to measure investments in which transactions occur only twice—once at the beginning and once at the end of the investment period. The other eight equations apply to problems in which constant dollar transactions occur at regular intervals. An installment loan is a good example of this kind of problem. If you borrow $4000 to buy a car and pay off the loan over 36 months at 12% interest, equation 11 may be used to compute the amount for each payment ($132.86).

It is important to note that there is no formula for solving for interest rates directly in the second set of equations, because *i* cannot be isolated on one side of the equation. The only method to solve for interest rates in this situation is to use a "brute-force" approach in which the computer tries values for *i* and solves for *F* or *P* until the right answer is found. The value for *i* would be successively approximated.

The formulae in Table 2-1 will be used throughout this chapter in discussing loans, mortgages, annuities, and real estate evaluation. The uses are as varied as the diversity of investments. The personal computer becomes useful in answering "what if?" questions involving changes in interest rates, time periods, and other variables with these equations or useful in solving equations 5 and 6 in Table 2-1, which require an iterative approach.

Financial databases. The easiest way to enter information into stock-market programs is over the telephone. Various database services supply detailed financial information—both current and historical—which can be retrieved by any computer through a telephone modem. On-line services offer most, if not all, of the securities you are likely to be interested in. For instance, one of the popular personal computer networks (CompuServe) offers the following financial information for instant retrieval:

• Figures on more than 9,000 securities, updated throughout each trading day—no need to wait for day-old stock values in the newspaper.
• Detailed descriptive and financial information on thousands of major publicly-held companies.

This table shows the appropriate formulae to use given three input parameters and a required output parameter.

GIVEN														
no. of uniform periods	(n)	x	x	x	x	x	x							
interest rate per period	(i)	x	x	x					x	x	x			
present value	(P)	x			x	x			x	x				
future value	(F)		x		x		x	x						
uniform payments	(R)			x		x	x		x	x				

REQUIRED											
n									1	2	3
i						4	5	6			
P				7	8						
F		9	10								
R	11	12									

1. $n = \dfrac{\log \frac{F}{P}}{\log(1+i)}$

2. $n = \dfrac{\log \frac{1}{1-iP/R}}{\log(1+i)}$

3. $n = \dfrac{\log 1 + \frac{iF}{R}}{\log(1+i)}$

4. $i = \sqrt[n]{\dfrac{F}{P}} - 1$

5. $i = \dfrac{R}{P}(1 - [1-i]^{-n})$

6. $i = \dfrac{R}{F}([1+i]^{n} - 1)$

7. $P = \dfrac{F}{(1+i)^{n}}$

8. $P = R\dfrac{1 + (1+i)^{-n}}{i}$

9. $F = P(1+i)^{n}$

10. $F = R\dfrac{(1+i)^{n} - 1}{i}$

11. $R = P\dfrac{i}{1 - (1+i)^{-n}}$

12. $R = F\dfrac{i}{(1+i)^{n} - 1}$

Table 2-1. Look-up Table of Financial Formulae.

- Current and historical information on more than 40,000 stocks, bonds, and options.
- Continually updated information on prices and basic news stories incorporating market commentary and statistics.
- Specialized reports on commodities, today's economy, and implications for the future.
- Financial commentary from the nation's leading news publications.

Alternatively, companies such as Standard & Poor offer market statistic updates sent periodically on floppy disk. The S&P package costs about $500 per year and provides monthly updates of some 100 types of basic financial data, ranging from sales to assets, for about 1,500 publicly traded companies.

Other databases specialize in business information and can supply text of leading industry newsletters, with extensive search and indexing capabilities. The NewsNet Network, 945 Haverford Road, Bryn Mawr, PA 19010, for instance, provides full text of over 125 business newsletters in the following areas:

advertising and marketing
aerospace
automobile industry
behavioral sciences and social services
corporate communications

47

education
electronics and computers
energy
entertainment and leisure
environment
farming and food
finance, accounting, and taxes
general business management
government regulations and law
international affairs
investments
labor
metals and mining
office automation
politics
publishing and broadcasting
real estate
politics
telecommunications
transportation

Interest calculations. The microcomputer can be used to calculate simple, compound and true interest. A program could be written to calculate the exact number of days between two dates, and number of months, days, and years in the interest period: leap years would be accounted for. The following formula would be used:

$$i = \frac{cpd}{100 \ 360}$$

where i = interest on the capital
c = capital, invested or borrowed
p = rate of interest
d = number of days

Compound interest can also be calculated. Given three of the four variables F, P, i, and n, the fourth may be solved for using equations 1, 4, 7, or 9 in Table 2-1.

The true interest is calculated as follows:

$$R = \frac{24F_c}{m \ I_m \ (m + 1)}$$

where R = the true interest rate
F_c = finance charge
m = number of months
I_m = monthly installment

The BASIC program in Listing 2-5 computes the true annual interest rate. An ideal application involves evaluation of installment loans.

Listing 2-5: The True Annual Interest Rate Program

```
5 KEY OFF
10 REM TRUE ANNUAL INTEREST RATE COMPUTATION
20 REM FOR USE WITH INSTALLMENT LOANS
25 CLS       'CLEAR SCREEN
30 INPUT "ENTER THE AMOUNT OF THE LOAN (WITHOUT INTEREST) ",B
40 INPUT "ENTER THE AMOUNT OF EACH PAYMENT ",A
50 INPUT "ENTER THE TOTAL NUMBER OF PAYMENTS ",C
60 INPUT "ENTER THE NUMBER OF PAYMENTS PER YEAR ",D
70 PRINT:PRINT
80 IF C=1 THEN 680
90 IF C*A>=B THEN 150
100 PRINT:PRINT
110 PRINT "THE PAYMENTS SUM TO LESS THAN THE AMOUNT OWED ";
130 PRINT
135 INPUT "TYPE ENTER WHEN READY ",A$
140 GOTO 10
```

```
150 E=0:F=100
160 GOSUB 260
170 IF A=G THEN 360
180 IF A>G THEN 220 ELSE E=E-F:GOTO 230
220 E=E+F
230 F=F/2
240 IF F<.0001 THEN 360
250 GOTO 160
260 H=E/(100*D)
270 J=H+1
280 IF C*J<=75 THEN 310
290 G=B*H
300 RETURN
310 IF G>1 THEN G=B*J^C*H/(J^C-1) ELSE G=B/C
320 RETURN
360 E=.01 *INT(.05+100*E)
370 IF E<199.5 THEN 430
380 PRINT
390 PRINT "THE INTEREST RATE IS TOO HIGH, RE-ENTER ";
420 GOTO 10
430 PRINT:PRINT "TRUE ANNUAL INTEREST RATE=";E;"%"
440 PRINT:PRINT
450 CLEAR:INPUT "PRESS ENTER WHEN READY; TYPE 'QUIT' TO END: ",A$
460 IF A$="QUIT" THEN END ELSE GOTO 10
680 E=(A/B-1)*D
690 E=100*E
700 GOTO 360
```

Minimum investment for withdrawals.
This formula may be used to determine the minimum investment required to allow regular withdrawals of a given amount over a given time period, assuming compounded interest with each withdrawal and an ending balance of $0. A retiree might use this formula to compute the amount to invest in a savings account at 6 percent interest to provide monthly withdrawals of $100.00 for 10 years.

$$P = \frac{R \cdot N}{i} \left(1 - \frac{1}{(1 + i/N)^{NY}} \right)$$

where P = initial investment
       R = amount of regular withdrawal
       i = nominal interest rate
       N = number of withdrawals per year
       Y = number of years

Mortgages

The computer can be very useful to the home buyer in simplifying the many financial options available. You can use your computer to determine mortgage payments based on the interest rates available, the length of the life of the mortgage, and the amount. With recent swings in interest rates, knowing what you will be paying at any given interest can be very important; a difference of a half or one percent can be substantial. This information is also important in budget planning—in determining how much of the family income must be allocated to mortgage or loan payments. You can do a "What if?" analysis; that is, if interest rates are predicted to decline by 3% next year, is it best to buy or wait? With your microcomputer and the financial formulae outlined in Table 2-1, the financial ramifications of home buying or other investments can be easily determined.

It may be worth your while to analyze a

mortgage agreement on your computer before signing any contracts. A yearly amortization program could calculate a schedule of payments, the annual debt service, the mortgage constant, the remaining balance, the payment to principal, the payment to interest, the accumulated principal, and the accumulate interest for each year. A general amortization program could solve for the following additional factors: the number of payments to reach a certain balance, the payment amount, the annual percentage rate, and the principal amount. Listing 2-6 is a sample mortgage schedule program.

Special programs could calculate the above values for wraparound mortgages and determine the price and yield of discounted mortgages.

Loans

An amortization schedule for a loan as well as the time required for repayment can be calculated by the loan amortization program in Listing 2-7.

Here is a sample run showing how this program functions.

Listing 2-6: The Mortgage Schedule Program

```
100 REM MORTGAGE SCHEDULE CALCULATION
110 REM BASED ON MONTHLY PAYMENT
120 DIM A(3),B(3)
130 B$="##     $######.##     $######.##     $######.##     $######.##"
140 INPUT "ENTER THE NUMBER OF YEARS OF THE MORTGAGE ",X
150 INPUT "ENTER THE YEARLY INTEREST RATE ",X1
160 INPUT "ENTER THE AMOUNT OF THE MORTGAGE ",B
170 B1=12*X
180 X1=X1/1200
190 B2=B*X1/(1-(1/(1+X1))^B1)
200 T=0
210 B(2)=0:B(1)=0:B3=B2*B1-B:A(2)=0:A(3)=B:A(1)=0
220 PRINT USING "MONTHLY PAYMENT IS $####.##";B2
230 PRINT
240 PRINT "YEAR PRINCIPAL PAID  PRINCIPAL LEFT   INTEREST PAID   TOTAL PAID"
250 FOR I=1 TO X
260   FOR J=1 TO 12
270     T=T+B2
280     B(1)=A(3)*X1
290     A(1)=B2-B(1)
300     A(2)=A(2)+A(1)
310     A(3)=A(3)-A(1)
320     B(2)=B(2)+B(1)
330     B(3)=B(3)-B(1)
340   NEXT J
350   PRINT USING B$;I,A(2),A(3),B(2),T
360 NEXT I
370 PRINT
380 END
```

LOAN AMORTIZATION SCHEDULE

PRINCIPAL=$4800.00
#OF PERIODS=12
INTEREST RATE=5.6%

PAYMENT NUMBER	REMAINING PRINCIPAL	MONTHLY PAYMENT	PRINCIPAL PAYMENT	INTEREST PAYMENT
1	4410.16	412.24	389.84	22.40
2	4018.51	412.24	391.66	20.58
3	3625.02	412.24	393.48	18.75
4	3229.70	412.24	395.32	16.92
5	2832.54	412.24	397.16	15.07
6	2433.52	412.24	399.02	13.22
7	2032.64	412.24	400.88	11.36
8	1629.89	412.24	402.75	9.49
9	1225.26	412.24	404.63	7.61
10	818.74	412.24	406.52	5.72
11	410.32	412.24	408.42	3.82
12	0.00	412.24	410.32	1.91
OVERALL TOTALS		$4946.84	$4800.00	$146.84

Listing 2-7: The Loan Amortization Program

```
10 REM LOAN AMORTIZATION CALCULATOR
20 CLS      'CLEAR SCREEN
30 PRINT "LOANS":PRINT
40 PRINT "SELECT: 1)PAYMENT AMOUNT CALCULATION"
50 INPUT "          2)TIME OF PAYMENT CALCULATION ",A
60 ON A GOTO 70,2000
65 GOTO 40
70 INPUT "ENTER THE AMOUNT OF THE LOAN ",AM
80 INPUT "ENTER THE NUMBER OF PAYMENTS (YRS. *12 USUALLY) ",N
90 INPUT "ENTER THE ANNUAL INTEREST RATE ",I
100 B=I/1200
110 C=N
120 INPUT "ENTER THE MONTH OF THE FIRST PAYMENT (1-12) ",M
130 INPUT "ENTER THE YEAR OF THE FIRST PAYMENT ";Y
140 D=1:FOR X=1 TO C
150    D=(1+B)*D
160 NEXT X
170 D=1/D:F=B/(1-D)*AM
180 G=F:GOSUB 5000
190 F=G
200 H=Y:J=1:L=AM:K=M-1:E=0:P=0
210 CLS
220 PRINT "AMORTIZATION TABLE"
230 PRINT "MONTHLY PAYMENT: $";F
```

```
240 PRINT "AMOUNT OF LOAN: $";TAB(18)AM;TAB(28)"INTEREST RATE=";I;
260 IF S=0 THEN PRINT:GOTO 280
270 PRINT "TERM+";TAB(55)N;TAB(59)"MONTHS"
280 PRINT "NO.";
290 PRINT TAB(8)"DATE";TAB(19)"INTEREST";TAB(33)"PRINCIPAL";TAB(50)
"BALANCE"
300 FOR X=J TO J+9
310    K=K+1
320    IF K=13 THEN K=1:H=H+1
330    A2=L*B:G=A2
340    GOSUB 5000
350    A2=G:S=F-A2:G=S
360    GOSUB 5000
370    S=G
380    L=L-S:G=L
390    GOSUB 5000
400    L=G:P=A2+P:E=S+E
410    PRINT J;TAB(6)K;"-";H;TAB(19)A2;TAB(33)S;TAB(49)L
420    IF J=C-1 THEN 600
430    J=J+1
440 NEXT X
450 G=P
460 GOSUB 5000
470 P=G
480 PRINT "TOTAL INTEREST TO DATE $";P;"TOTAL PRINCIPAL TO DATE
$";E
490 INPUT "PRESS ENTER TO SEE NEXT PAGE ",A1
500 GOTO 210
600 A2=B*L
610 G=A2:GOSUB 5000
620 A2=G:S=L:A3=F:F=S+A2:K=K+1
630 IF K=12 THEN K=1:H=H+1
640 L=L-S:J=J+1:E=S+E:P=P+A2
650 PRINT J;TAB(6)K;"-";TAB(19)A2;TAB(33)S;TAB(49)L
660 PRINT "TOTAL INTEREST TO DATE=$";P
670 PRINT "TOTAL PRINCIPAL TO DATE=";E
680 PRINT "FINAL PAYMENT=$";F
690 G=F:GOSUB 5000
700 F=G:F=A3
710 INPUT "CONTINUE OR END (C/E)";A4$
720 IF A4$="C" THEN GOTO 30 ELSE END
2000 CLS
2010 INPUT "ENTER THE AMOUNT BORROWED ",B1
2020 INPUT "ENTER THE INTEREST RATE/YR. ",B2
2030 INPUT "ENTER THE MONTHLY PAYMENT ",E
2040 INPUT "ENTER THE MONTH PAYMENTS BEGIN (1-12) ",M
2050 INPUT "ENTER THE YEAR OF THE BEGINNING PAYMENT ",Y
2060 B3=B1*B2/1200-E*(12-M)
2070 IF B3<=0 THEN 2130
2080 PRINT:PRINT:PRINT:PRINT
2090 PRINT "THE MINIMUM PAYMENT=$";B1*B2/1200
2100 GOTO 2010
```

```
2130 B=1-B2/1200*B1/E
2140 X=B:GOSUB 4000
2150 B=R
2160 F=1+B2/1200
2170 X=F:GOSUB 4000
2180 F=R
2190 J=-(B/F)
2200 PRINT
2210 IF B3=0 THEN PRINT "PAYMENTS COVER INTEREST ONLY ":GOTO 2230
2220 PRINT "NO. OF MONTHS FOR PAYMENTS=";J
2230 H=INT(J/12):N=J-H*12
2240 IF N>1 THEN N=N+1
2250 N=INT(N):C=12*H+N
2260 IF N>11 THEN H=H+1:N=N-12
2270 IF B3=0 THEN S=0:GOTO 2290
2280 PRINT "=";H;"YEARS+ ";N;" MONTHS TO PAY LOAN"
2290 PRINT:PRINT:PRINT
2300 INPUT "PRESS ENTER TO CONTINUE",A$
2310 J=N:B=B2/1200:F=E:N=N+12*H:AM=B1:R=B2
2320 F=F/B3
2325 F=E:I=B2
2330 GOTO 180
2340 GOTO 180
2350 AM=(X-1)/(X+1)
2360 C=AM*AM*AM
2370 R=2*(AM+1/3*C+1/5*AM*AM*C+A/7*C*C*AM+1/9*C*C*C+1/11*C*C*C*AM
*AM)
4000 AM=(X-1)/(X+1)
4010 C=AM*AM*AM
4020 R=2*(AM+1/3*C+1/5*AM*AM*C+1/7*C*C*AM+1/9*C*C*C+1/11*C*C*C*AM
*AM)
4030 RETURN
5000 G=INT((G-INT(G))*100+.50001)/100+INT(G)
5010 RETURN
```

Loan with points. *Points* are a percentage of the value of a loan that is paid at the start of the loan period. Theoretically, the seller pays the points, but in practice it does not matter who pays—the price of the house increases with the addition of points.

One point represents one percent of the mortgage value. It must be paid at the beginning of the loan. The important question to consider is how does the addition of points affect the annual percentage rate actually being paid for the loan? The program in Listing 2-8 will calculate this value given the number of points, amount of the loan, years, and annual percentage rate of the loan. It outputs the value for monthly payments and true annual percentage rate.

Listing 2-8: The Loan with Points Program

```
10 REM LOAN WITH POINTS
20 INPUT "ENTER LOAN AMOUNT, NUMBER OF POINTS";L,P
30 INPUT "ENTER ANNUAL PERCENTAGE RATE, YEARS";A,Y
```

```
40 P=P*.01:A=.01*A/12:Y=Y*12
50 R=L*((A*(A+1)^Y)/((A+1)^Y-1))
60 PRINT "MONTHLY PAYMENT--$";R
70 FOR D=1 TO 100
75 REM ^   MEANS TO RAISE TO A POWER
80 F=.001*D+A:X=(1-P)*L*((F*(1+F)^Y)/((1+F)^Y-1))
90 IF X>R THEN 110
100 NEXT D:PRINT "PROGRAM UNABLE TO CALCULATE VALUE":END
110 PRINT "ACTUAL ANNUAL PERCENTAGE RATE=";F*1200;"%":END
```

Direct reduction loan. The payment, present value, or number of time periods for a reduction loan may be calculated by using equations 2, 8 and 11 in Table 2-1.

Additional loan formulae. Here are some more formulae that you will find useful when you are dealing with loans.

• Principal on a loan

$$P = \frac{R \cdot N}{i} \cdot \left(1 - \frac{1}{(1 + i/N)^{N \cdot Y}}\right)$$

where P = principal
      R = regular payment
      i = annual interest rate
      N = number of payments per year
      Y = number of years

• Regular payment on a loan

$$R = \frac{i \cdot P/N}{1 - \left(\frac{i}{N} + 1\right)^{-N \cdot Y}}$$

where R = regular payment
      i = annual interest rate
      P = principal
      N = number of payments per year
      Y = number of years

• Term of a loan

$$Y = -\frac{\log\left(1 - \frac{P \cdot i}{N \cdot R}\right)}{\log\left(1 + \frac{i}{N}\right)} \cdot \frac{1}{N}$$

where Y = term of payment in years
      P = principal
      i = annual interest rate
      N = number of payments per year
      R = amount of payments

Depreciation Calculations

Standard, composite, and excess depreciations may be calculated with the following methods:

1) Straight line depreciation

$$D = PV/n$$
$$B_k = PV - kD$$

2) Sum-of-the-years-digits depreciation

$$B_k = \frac{S + (n-k)\,D_k}{2} \qquad D_k = \frac{2\,(n-k+1)\,PV}{n\,(n+1)}$$

3) Variable rate declining balance depreciation

$$D_k = PV \frac{R}{n} (1 - R/n)^{k-1}$$

$$B_k = PV\,(1 - R/n)^k$$

In each of the above depreciation formulas,

PV = original value of asset (less salvage value)
 n = lifetime number of periods of asset
 B_k = book value at time period K
 D = each year's depreciation
 k = the number of the time period (that is, 1, 2, 3, . . . n)
 S = salvage value
 R = depreciation rate
 D_k = depreciation at time period k

The program in Listing 2-9 can be used to compare depreciation methods.

Here are some sample results from the depreciation program.

YEAR NO.	STRAIGHT LINE	DOUBLE DECL.	SUM OF DIGITS
1	$ 1250.00	$ 2750.00	$ 2000.00
2	$ 1250.00	$ 1375.00	$ 1500.00
3	$ 1250.00	$ 687.50	$ 1000.00
4	$ 1250.00	$ 343.75	$ 500.00

The actual depreciation rate for an investment is computed with the formula.

$$\text{depreciation rate} = 1 - \left(\frac{\text{resale price}}{\text{original price}}\right)^{1/\text{age}}$$

and may be used to answer queries such as "If a car was bought for $9000 and sold three years later for $5100, what was the depreciation rate?"

The *salvage value* of an item at the end of a given year may be calculated with the formula

$$S = P(1 - i)^Y$$

where S = salvage value
P = original price
i = depreciation rate
Y = age in years

Annuities

Given the values of the required variables as input data, an annuity program could calculate the remaining variable in any of the following situations:

- Sinking funds—a sinking fund is an annuity in which a future value is accumulated by making equal payments at equal intervals at a certain interest rate. The value can be computed using equation 10 in Table 2-1.
- Annuity due—the future or present value can be calculated using equations 8 and 10 in Table 2-1.
- Ordinary annuity—This value may or may not include a balloon payment. Again, use equations 2, 8, and 11 in Table 2-1.

Bonds and Warrants

A useful, simple program could be written to determine the value of both short and long term warrants. Given present value, coupon interest, yield to maturity, and maturity value or the number of periods (three values out of the four), a computer program can compute the remaining term. Taxes, commissions, and current yield could also be determined. The formula used to calculate the present value (cost) of a bond with annual coupons is as follows:

$$\text{Price} = \left[\left(\frac{1 - (1 + i/c)^{-n}}{ic}\right)^{(1000 \ Cr/2)}\right] + (1 + i/c)^{-n} (1000)$$

55

where i = discount rate as %

       n = number of years to maturity multiplied by 2

      Cr = coupon rate of bond

      c = number of compounding periods per year

The formula used to calculate the bond yield of an annual coupon is as follows:

$$j = \frac{Fg - \dfrac{(B.V.)_1 - (B.V.)_n}{n}}{\dfrac{(B.V.)_1 + (B.V.)_n}{2}}$$

where j = nominal yield rate

$(B.V.)_1$ = original bond value

$(B.V.)_n$ = bond at n years

    F = face value

    g = nominal dividend rate

    n = number of years

PERSONAL ACCOUNTING

There are a number of ways in which your personal computer can help you manage your personal finances more effectively. The computer can help you deal with everything from credit card payments to income tax calculations.

Personal Accounts Receivable/Payable

A personal AP/AR program similar to a business AP/AR program could manage a large portion of your financial affairs. The program could include these features:

1. A checking and savings account management program to enable you to maintain the current balance of your checking and savings accounts. Interest credits could be calculated and added. A file of each check (with its number, purpose, notes, amount, and payee) could be stored for later income tax preparation. Specialized reports could be generated from this check file including a check register for a specified time period, the distribution of expenditures, and statements of selected accounts. The ideal pro-gram would request all information concerning each check written, store this information, and print the check itself.

2. A budgeting program to keep you up to date on expenditures in various areas so that income can be allocated appropriately. A plan for family spending could take the following format:

Set-asides	
Emergencies and future goals	_____
Seasonal expenses	_____
Debt payments	_____
Regular monthly expenses	_____
Rent or mortgage payment	_____
Utilities	_____
Installment payments	_____
Other	_____
Total	_____
Day to day expenses	
Food and beverages	_____
Household maintenance	_____
Furnishings, equipment	_____
Clothing	_____
Personal	_____
Transportation	_____
Medical care	_____
Recreation, education	_____
Gifts, contributions	_____
Total	_____
Total of all expenses	_____

Alternatively, you could take realistic estimates for the upcoming year and enter these figures. A program could use this information in computing the percentage of gross income that each item requires. As a rule of thumb, housing should cost no more than one fourth of your gross income. (This is an example of one of the budgeting principles discussed in most references concerning family budget preparation.) The home computer removes the drudgery of manual calculations for those determined to stick to a well-planned budget.

On command, a budget program could print month-to-date figures and an end-of-month comparison of budget versus actual expenses. It can also show the amount of cash needed to meet

Table 2-2. A Portion of a Personal Budget Sheet in Spreadsheet Form.

EXPENSE	JAN	FEB	MAR	APR	MAY	JUN	JUL	AUG
			ACTUAL FOR JOE SMITH OCT. 8, 1982					
RENT	650	0	0	0	0	0	0	0
FOOD	323	361	357	371	290	251	410	356
CLOTHES	154	0	54	0	0	0	0	68
UTILITIES	57	56	50	59	62	51	53	59
CREDIT CARD INTEREST	0	0	0	0	0	0	0	0
ENTERTAINMENT	143	100	58	13	24	45	125	54
GASOLINE	100	110	90	100	100	100	95	90
MORTGAGE INTEREST	0	0	0	0	0	0	0	0
MISCELLANEOUS EXPENSE	28	0	44	0	98	0	0	48
CAR EXPENSES	990	0	0	0	0	0	0	0
TOTAL EXPENSE	2445	627	653	543	574	447	683	675
NET INCOME	105	1623	1597	2091	1676	1803	1863	1825

budgeted expenses for the rest of the month. It could also maintain tax records, keep a running balance of cash on hand, keep an inventory of your possessions, and even help in planning weekly menus.

Table 2-2 shows a portion of a personal budget report that indicates where the money has been and will be spent in spreadsheet fashion. Such spreadsheets, besides being a personal planning benefit, are often useful when securing a personal loan.

3. A financial behavior determination program to help you analyze your expenditures and summarize your spending in various areas (the categories of the budget above) that would be useful in preparing a budget plan.

According to the experts at the U.S. Dept. of Labor, a family of four should typically allocate its spending as follows:

Housing	24%
Food	24%
Transportation	15%
Clothing, personal care	13%
Taxes	13%
Medical	7%
All other	4%

Families differ, but how do your own expenses correspond to these percentages?

4. A file of unfulfilled contracts, mail orders, and so on for which you have sent checks and yet have received no reply. As replies are received, the appropriate accounts are removed from the file.

Daily Interest Passbook Savings Account

You can use the BASIC program in Listing 2-10 to maintain a savings account. The program has

Listing 2-10: The Daily Interest Savings Program

```
10 PRINT "DAILY INTEREST PASSBOOK SAVINGS COMPUTATION":PRINT
20 PRINT "ENTER DEPOSITS AS POSITIVE NUMBERS, DEDUCTIONS AS NEGATIVE NUMBERS;"
30 INPUT "PRESS ENTER TO BEGIN: ",A$
40 CLS        'CLEAR SCREEN
50 INPUT "ENTER THE ANNUAL INTEREST IN PERCENT ",F
60 E=F/360000!
```

```
70 INPUT "SELECT: 1) USE ACTUAL DAYS IN MONTH 2) USE 30 DAYS FOR MONTH ",D
80 G=0
90 INPUT "ENTER THE STARTING DATE NUMERICALLY AS MONTH,DAY ",A,B
100 INPUT "ENTER THE STARTING BALANCE ",C
110 IF D=1 THEN INPUT "IS THIS A LEAP YEAR (1=YES,2=NO)";H:GOSUB 390 ELSE GOSUB
180
120 J=K:PRINT
130 PRINT "  #     DATE     WITHDRAWAL   DEPOSIT   BALANCE      INTEREST"
140 PRINT K;A;",";B;TAB(38);C
150 INPUT "ENTER MONTH, DAY, AMOUNT: ";A,B,L
160 IF D=2 THEN GOSUB 180 ELSE GOSUB 390
170 GOTO 250
180 M=B
190 IF (A=2) OR (A=4) OR (A=6) OR (A=9) OR (A=11) THEN 200 ELSE 230
200 IF (A=2) AND (B=28) THEN INPUT "IS THIS A LEAP YEAR (1=YES,2=NO)";N:IF N=1 T
HEN RETURN ELSE 220
210 IF B>27 THEN B=31
220 IF B=30 THEN B=31
230 K=B+(A-1)*30
240 RETURN
250 O=K
260 IF J=K THEN 300
270 FOR P=J TO K-1
280 G=G+G*E+C*E
290 NEXT P
300 C=C+L
310 G=(INT((G-INT(G))*100+.5001))/100+INT(G)
320 PRINT K;A;",";M;
330 IF L<0 THEN PRINT TAB(13)L;:GOTO 350
340 PRINT TAB(24)L;
350 PRINT TAB(38)C;
360 PRINT TAB(50)G
370 J=0
380 GOTO 150
390 ON A GOTO 400,410,420,430,440,450,460,470,480,490,500,510
400 K=B:GOTO 520
410 K=B+31:GOTO 520
420 K=B+N+59:GOTO 520
430 K=B+N+90:GOTO 520
440 K=B+N+120:GOTO 520
450 K=B+N+151:GOTO 520
460 K=B+N+181:GOTO 520
470 K=B+N+212:GOTO 520
480 K=B+N+243:GOTO 520
490 K=B+N+273:GOTO 520
500 K=B+N+304:GOTO 520
510 K=B+N+334
520 M=B:RETURN
```

provisions for interest, withdrawals, and deposits.

Income Tax

Preparation of income tax forms is a task that lends itself well to computers because computers are great organizers and calculators, and they can save you time and money. Tax preparation programs range from simple arithmetic calculators to complete personal accounting programs. In the most popular approach, the computer requests answers to such questions as, "What are your federal withholding taxes?" You proceed to answer all the possible questions necessary to prepare a 1040 tax form (approximately 50), but unfortunately you must first do considerable accounting and calculating to answer some of the questions. The program completes the simple arithmetic for filling in the 1040 form and prints the proper values in the boxes on the form.

A more complex approach would involve the periodic storage of all elements of your finances on cassette or floppy disk (for example, each week you could store the names, addresses, purposes, numbers, and amounts of all checks written or cashed.) At years' end, the computer would search and group all relevant data and do all of the necessary calculations. In this latter approach, a complete summary of all deductions, income, and so on could be printed categorically. References to the filed location of the original checks, bills, and receipts could be included for proof of the transactions. A warning could also be issued in the event that your deductions exceed ten percent of your income (a tax audit would be likely). Provisions could be made to compare the taxes you would pay if you filed jointly with your spouse to what you would pay if you filed as an individual.

A tax planning program can help cut your tax liability in the years to come. Investment decisions, personal financial decisions, and business decisions with tax consequences can all be analyzed in planning a tax strategy. In a divorce, for example, the arrangement of a settlement can result in substantially less tax depending upon how the money is allocated between property settlement, alimony, and child support. A tax planning program can be used to quickly answer "what if?" questions during the negotiation of a settlement. The ease of changing inputs and having the program recalculate the entire return can be a tremendous time saver. Additionally, complex calculations such as income averaging on Form G can be done automatically, perhaps yielding a bigger refund for those who previously would not have attempted the calculations manually. A tax planning program in the form of a spreadsheet allows the simultaneous consideration of multiple cases covering different facts and years. The spreadsheet can include graphical representations showing the impact of adding or subtracting income, deductions, or credits, and varying tax computations over a several-year period—including regular tax, alternative minimum tax, add-on minimum tax, income averaging, and the consideration of limitations on the use of credits. For instance, you could consider the possibility of a second income versus staying at home by having your computer program figure the after-tax results of that extra income, which is often discouraging. As another example, assume that you own a business and want to know if you should pay your wife a salary. Depending upon your income level, this may or may not be advantageous; a tax planning program could determine the best option for your income bracket.

A recurring question among investors is "What are the sources of tax-free income whose yields are equal to or greater than yields provided by taxable investments?" Should you invest in tax-free bonds and other tax-free securities or place your money in a fully taxable bond, savings account, or treasury bill? (Remember, however, that you may wish to consider other factors, such as liquidity of assets.) The two formulas necessary to compute taxable and tax-free yields are given below. A simple BASIC program could compute these for a given situation and determine which alternative offers the better investment.

taxable yield=tax-free yield/(1−federal tax bracket)
tax-free yield=taxable yield*(1−federal tax bracket)

For instance, if you are in the 35% federal income bracket, have invested in a money-market account at 8%, and are offered the opportunity to invest in a tax-free fund yielding 6.2%, which is the better investment? Using the second equation above, you find that the tax-free fund would be a better investment at 6.2% versus 5.2% after taxes for the money-market account. A more sophisticated program could print a table of yields given the known tax-free or taxable yield starting value and the increment, and the starting value of the tax bracket and the increment. Investors in some states are allowed tax exemptions for qualifying tax-free investments. In this situation, simply add the exempted state tax rate to the federal tax rate when entering your tax bracket value.

Home Banking

You may soon be able to do your banking from home with a personal computer. Many banks are conducting pilot home-banking studies and are beginning to sell such services to depositors. These include the major banks listed below:

Central Trade Bank of Memphis, Memphis, TN

Citibank, New York, NY

First Tennessee Bank, Knoxville, TN

Huntington National Bank, Columbus, OH

Shawmut Bank of Boston, Boston ,MA

With most of these services, a customer dials the bank's central computer or uses one of the timesharing networks, such as CompuServe, through his modem. After providing a secret password, the customer can, for instance, ask for a list of recent deposits and pay bills directly by transferring money from his account to those of his creditors. Banks charge from $5 to $15 per month for this service.

Retirement Planner

The formulas given below, translated into BASIC statements, will calculate how much initial capital you need to financially survive a given number of retirement years at a given standard of living. Inflation and return on invested capital are accounted for. By using a BASIC program, you could quickly determine the effect of changes on these and other variables. You can use this information in deciding whether or not you can afford to retire.

$$S = (EXP(I*N))*(T+(F*(1-EXP(-J*N))/J)-(E*(EXP((I-J)*N)-1)/(I-J)))$$

$$T = (E*((EXP(I-J)*N)-1)/(I-J))-((F*(1-EXP(-J*N)))/J),\ \text{for I not equal to J}$$

$$T = (N*E)-(F*((1-EXP(-J*N))/J)),\ \text{for I equal to J}$$

where N = number of years after retirement for which financial survival is planned
  S = Investment capital remaining after N years
  T = Initial capital
  F = Annual fixed (after tax) income
  E = Initial excess living expense
  I = Annual average inflation rate
  J = Annual after-tax return on investment

MONEY-MAKING APPLICATIONS

There are many ways to use your microcomputer to make money; you might consider starting a part-time or full-time business based on one of the following ideas.

Stock Market

One "hobbyist" is deriving his income from his stock prediction newsletter that is composed of market predictions determined using "twelve confidential indicators" on his home computer. In similar fashion, you could experiment with mathematical analysis of the stock market using the statistical methods outlined earlier in this chapter. A personal computer could also serve to maintain stock portfolios and organize or correlate market predictions and stock recommendations to ease decision making. With the proliferation of financial databases available through the use of a modem, information on stock prices, market performance, and so on could be entered automatically to a stock analysis program designed to scan the entire market, stocks of a given industry group, or particular stocks. Financial data bases may also be scanned to provide historical data or the latest news reports on selected corporations.

The home computer is certainly useful in mathematical analysis and data storage for other forms of financial investment, including stock options and commodities. An options analysis program was presented earlier in this chapter and should serve as a good starting point for newcomers in computer application to the options market. Again, use of financial databases accessable via modems permits the automatic input of data to your analysis program. The commodities trader will probably find the personal computer to be a boon in organizing and obtaining information in the fast moving and volatile commodities market and in allowing trading from the home for the first time.

Services

The home computer owner is in the position to offer the following services.

Mailing lists. A mailing list of people in your area could be used by local firms with direct mail campaigns. The mailing list could be compiled from area phone books, association directories, and so on, entered into your computer, and stored permanently on floppy disks. The list may be printed on adhesive labels and sold to local businesses. The advantage of being a local business serves to eliminate competition from large mailing list brokers in other cities.

Resumes. People in all metropolitan areas can use a resume preparation service to write, type, and mail resumes to potential employers. A computer word-processing system could automate this business almost entirely.

Typesetting, indexing, and editing. All businesses and organizations can use a printing preparation enterprise for typesetting and editing promotional material. Small computers interfaced to IBM composers, executive typewriters, DIABLO proportional printers, laser printers, or conventional typesetting equipment can produce excellent justified and camera-ready material for printing. The cost savings of using a computer will allow the entrepreneur to offer lower prices for such services and ensure greater accuracy. Additionally, an indexing service using a simple computer program to create book or magazine indexes could provide a valuable service to small publishing firms.

Home swap and rental locator services. The practice of swapping one's home with other people during vacation time is becoming popular. A service that used a computer to categorize homes available and homes wanted could profit by publishing a newsletter of listings.

A rental locator service categorizes homes and apartments for rent from classified newspaper ads or other sources. In metropolitan areas, where finding an ideal home to rent is a difficult task, a service to match people with the right living conditions at the right price would be useful. In a similar manner, a service company could match people with cars for sale by the owners.

One entrepreneur has developed a computerized bartering service for matching needs and services of those in high income tax brackets for the purpose of mutual tax write-offs. He charges a small fee for successful bartering arrangements.

Finder's fees. A *finder's fee* is a sum of money paid to someone who finds something wanted by another person who is willing to offer an award for it, be it business opportunities, products, or rare items. Usually, finder's fees are expressed as a percentage of the amount of money involved in purchasing the item to be found. A few organizations publish newsletters listing finder's fee opportunities. A hobbyist could computerize hundreds of listings for future reference and could correlate the need of buyers with the offerings of sellers.

Telephone answering message service and newspaper clippings service. Telephone answering services of sufficient size can use a small computer to increase efficiency and lower costs. A newspaper clipping service, which clips articles of interest to paying clients, could use a computer to keep track of the varied categories to search for.

Computer dating service. Popular a few years ago, computer dating services could make a return appearance, especially in metropolitan areas.

Sports predictions and gambling. An enterprising hobbyist uses his computer to predict college football scores. The information produced is sold as "CLYDE the computer" sports forecasts to television stations for use on local news broadcasts. Other entrepreneurs have used computer predictions of sporting events to publish flyers that are sold at dog and horse races. It would be silly to deny that personal computers have also found widespread application in illegal gambling circles for the analysis of point spreads and historical performance, and for bookkeeping!

Employment agency. The computer could be useful to an employment agency in matching the right people with the right jobs. The use of the computer may also serve to increase business in itself.

Small business systems and software. Many hobbyists have turned personal computers into a profitable sideline business by selling packaged computer systems with accounting, word processing, and spreadsheet software to small business and offering technical support and training. You could also create personalized programs including databases and mailing lists on a freelance basis for firms with small computers.

Collection service. A word-processing computer system could automatically output personalized collection letters, which theoretically generate greater response. Thus, a low-cost collection service charging a flat rate or a percentage of the money collected would be an excellent sideline business for the computer hobbyist.

Word Processing. A word-processing service can be employed by businesses to prepare typewritten personalized sales letters. Such a business would be almost totally automated by a small computer.

Bowling league bookkeeping. A few hobbyists have sideline businesses that calculate bowling league scores and handicaps for ten to thirty cents per player per week. This cost is usually less than the costs for hiring a person to do the bookkeeping.

Supermarket comparison service. A hobbyist turned businessman uses his personal computer to collect and compare price data for popular foods at local supermarkets and sells a listing of the most economical stores to shoppers.

Personalized books. Children's books containing a child's name, address, and other personalized information can be printed by a small computer economically. Studies show that children prefer reading personalized books over any other type of book, and there is a considerable demand for them. An enterprising hobbyist could develop a large-scale business along these lines. Perhaps a humorous personalized book could be sold for adults as well.

Educational programs. You could form a distributorship to bring educational computer materials to schools, bookstores, and other institutions. The market for educational computer programs is also growing. Popular tutorials could be developed concerning electronics, higher mathematics, business and investments, computers, and an unlimited variety of other topics.

Real Estate

Possible applications for personal computers in real estate include the following:

Residential purchase analysis. A useful program could calculate the total monthly payment, income tax deductions, and equity build-up resulting from the purchase of a home. An own versus rent analysis could also be useful.

General real estate investment analysis. By considering such factors as inflation and interest rates, mortgages, cash flow in percent growth return, taxable income (tax shelter), and financial feasibility can be calculated. Income property reports and closing statements may also be generated.

Rental property management. A program designed for management of rental properties could store the following types of information for each property or client: receipts, disbursements, gross income, calculated profit and loss, calculated return on investment, and calculated net income.

Appraisal tabulator program. A program designed for the appraiser could organize and tabulate variables and could determine an appraisal.

Real estate evaluation. The program in Listing 2-11 is designed for use by a potential investor in evaluating a piece of real estate, preferably an apartment building. The program estimates the total monthly income, annual rate of return, and tax deductions based on such input data as cost, down payment on mortgage, estimated overhead costs, and income.

First, here's a sample run that will show you what information the program will request and what kind of results it will produce.

```
ENTER THE PURCHASE PRICE OF THE REAL
    ESTATE? 75000
ENTER THE MORTGAGE INTEREST (%) ?
    9.75
ENTER THE MORTGAGE DOWN PAYMENT
    AS A % OF PURCHASE COST? 10
ENTER THE NUMBER OF YEARS IN THE
    LOAN TERM? 25
ENTER THE CLOSING COST (% OF PUR-
    CHASE PRICE)? 2
ENTER MISCELLANEOUS INITIAL EX-
    PENSES AS ONE SUM? 100
ENTER THE ESTIMATED INCOME PER
    MONTH FROM THE PROPERTY? 1125
ENTER THE REAL ESTATE TAX FOR ONE
    YEAR? 1300
ENTER THE ESTIMATED OVERHEAD COSTS
    (MAINT., UTILITIES, INSUR., ETC.)? 525
FOR TAX DEDUCTION PURPOSES, ENTER
    THE EST. PROPERTY VALUE? 15000
ENTER YOUR TAX BRACKET AS A% OF
    YOUR INCOME? 40
IS THE BUILDING ON THE PROPERTY NEW
    OR USED ("N" OR "U")? N

TAX AND CASH FLOW ANALYSIS

MONTHLY EXPENSES $525.00
MONTHLY TAXES $108.33
MONTHLY MORTGAGE $601.52
MONTHLY INCOME $1125.00

MONTHLY CASH FLOW $109.85-

TAX HEDGE:

EXPENSES (YR. #1) $7650.00
DEPRECIATION (YR. #1) $6000.00
DEDUCTIBLE INTEREST $6581.25
REAL ESTATE TAX (YEARLY) $1300.00

TOTAL: (YR. #) $21531.30
TOTAL INCOME (YR. #1) $13500.00
NET DEDUCTION (YR. #1) )8031.25
TAX ADVANTAGE (YR. #1) $3212.50

RETURN ON INVESTMENT 18%
```

Listing 2-11: The Real Estate Evaluation Program

```
10 REM REAL ESTATE PURCHASE EVALUATION PROGRAM
20 REM DETERMINES TAX ADVANTAGE AND CASH FLOW OF
30 REM A PROSPECTIVE PURCHASE
40 INPUT "ENTER THE PURCHASE PRICE OF THE REAL ESTATE ",A
50 INPUT "ENTER MORTGAGE INTEREST (%) ",B
55 INPUT "ENTER MORTGAGE DOWN PAYMENT AS A % OF PURCHASE COST ",C
60 B=B/100:C=C/100
70 INPUT "ENTER NUMBER OF YEARS IN THE LOAN TERM ",D
80 INPUT "ENTER THE CLOSING COST (% OF PURCHASE PRICE) ",E
90 E=E/100
100 INPUT "ENTER MISCELLANEOUS INITIAL EXPENSES AS ONE SUM ",G
110 INPUT "ENTER THE ESTIMATED INCOME PER MONTH FROM THE PROPERTY ",J
120 INPUT "ENTER THE REAL ESTATE TAX FOR ONE YEAR ",K
130 INPUT "ENTER THE EST. OVERHEAD COSTS (MAINT.,UTILITIES, INSUR.,ETC.) ",L
```

63

```basic
132 INPUT "FOR TAX DEDUCTION PURPOSES, ENTER THE EST. PROPERTY VALUE ",M
134 INPUT "ENTER YOUR TAX BRACKET AS A % OF YOUR INCOME ",R7
136 C$=" **$##,###.##-"
138 INPUT "IS THE BUILDING ON THE PROPERTY NEW OR USED ('N' OR 'U')";B$
140 X=B/12+1
150 Y=X^(12*D)*(X-1)/(X^(12*D)-1)*(A-C*A)
160 N=L+K/12+Y
170 P=(A-C*A)*B
180 IF B$="N" THEN Q=2 ELSE Q=1.25
190 R=L+E*(A-C*A)/12
200 R1=(A-M)/20*Q
210 R2=K+R1+P+12*R-12*J
220 R3=R7/100*R2
230 R4=G+E*A+C*A-12*(J-N)
240 R5=INT(100*((J-N)*12+R3)/R4)
260 PRINT "TAX AND CASH FLOW ANALYSIS:"
270 PRINT "MONTHLY EXPENSES    ";
280 PRINT USING C$;L
290 PRINT "MONTHLY TAXES     ";
300 PRINT USING C$;K/12
310 PRINT "MONTHLY MORTGAGE    ";
320 PRINT USING C$;Y
330 PRINT "MONTHLY INCOME    ";
340 PRINT USING C$;J
350 PRINT MONTHLY CASH FLOW    ";
360 PRINT USING C$;J-N
370 PRINT:PRINT
380 PRINT "TAX HEDGE:"
390 PRINT "EXPENSES (YR. #1)    ";
400 PRINT USING C$;12*R
410 PRINT "DEPRECIATION (YR. #1)    ";
420 PRINT USING C$;R1
430 PRINT "DEDUCTABLE INTEREST (YR. #1)    ";
440 PRINT USING C$;P
450 PRINT "REAL ESTATE TAX (YEARLY) ";
460 PRINT USING C$;K
470 PRINT:PRINT "TOTAL:YR. #1)    ";
480 PRINT USING C$;K+P+R1+R*12
490 PRINT "TOTAL INCOME (YR. #1(    ";
500 PRINT USING C$;J*12
510 PRINT "NET DEDUCTION (YR. #1)    ";
520 PRINT USING C$;R2
530 PRINT "TAX ADVANTAGE (YR. #1)    ";
540 PRINT USING C$;R3
550 PRINT:PRINT "RETURN ON INVESTMENT";
560 PRINT R5;"%"
570 PRINT:PRINT:END
```

Curve fit. A program to fit such data as land prices or construction cost per square foot to a curve may be used to make more accurate forecasts, bids, and estimates.

Internal rate of return and cash flows. One purpose of an internal rate of return and cash flow programs such as the one in Listing 2-12 would be to calculate the net present value of a series of cash flows. In general, an investment, V_o, is made in some enterprise that is expected to bring periodic cash flows $C_1, C_2 \ldots C_n$. Given a discount rate, i, the program will compute the net present value at period k, NPV_k for each cash flow. A negative value for NPV_k indicates that the enterprise has not been profitable. A positive value for NPV_k indicates that the enterprise has been profitable to the extent that a rate of return, i, on the original investment has been exceeded.

$$NPV_k = -V_o + \sum_{j=1}^{k} \frac{C_j}{(1+i)^j}$$

Listing 2-12: The Internal Rate of Return Program

```
150 REM HOME PURCHASE INTERNAL RATE OF RETURN
160 DIM Y(10)
170 INPUT "ENTER CURRENT COST OF HOUSE";HS
180 INPUT "ENTER % RISE";PH
190 PH=PH/100
260 INPUT "ENTER MORTGAGE INTEREST RATE";MR
270 MR=MR/100
290 INPUT "ENTER MORTGAGE DURATION IN YEARS";NY
310 INPUT "ENTER DOWN PAYMENT";DP
320 INPUT "ENTER RATE THAT COULD BE EARNED ON DOWN PAYMENT";IR
330 IR=IR/100
360 INPUT "ENTER CURRENT INCOME TAX RATE";TR
370 TR=TR/100
380 INPUT "ENTER % RISE";PT
400 PT=PT/100
410 INPUT "ENTER TRANSACTION COSTS TO BUYER IN %";BC
420 BC=BC/100
450 INPUT "ENTER TRANSACTION COSTS TO SELLER IN %";SC
460 SC=SC/100
470 INPUT "ENTER REAL ESTATE TAXES TODAY";RE
500 INPUT "ENTER % RISE";PR
510 PR=PR/100
530 INPUT "ENTER UTILITY AND MAINTENANCE COSTS";HM
550 INPUT "ENTER % RISE";PM
560 PM=PM/100
580 INPUT "ENTER APARTMENT RENT TODAY";AR
590 INPUT "ENTER % RISE";PA
600 PA=PA/100
630 INPUT "ENTER APARTMENT UTILITIES";AU
650 INPUT "ENTER % RISE";PU
660 PU=PU/100
670 P1=(HS-DP)/((1-(1+MR)^-NY)/MR)
680 PRINT "YRS      INTERNAL RATE OF RETURN"
720 FOR I=1 TO 10
730 Y(0)=-DP-BC*HS
```

```
740 B1=HS-DP
750 FOR J=1 TO I
760 Y(J)=-(DP*TR)
770 Y(J)=Y(J)-P1
780 T1=TR+PT*(J-1)
790 Y(J)=Y(J)-RE*(1+PR)^(J-1)
800 Y(J)=Y(J)-HM*(1²PM)^(J-1)
810 Y(J)=Y(J)+AR*(1+PA)^(J-1)
820 Y(J)=Y(J)+AU*(1+PU)^(J-1)
830 Y(J)=Y(J)+((RE*(1+PR)^(J-1))+(B1*MR))*(TR+PT*(J-1))
840 B1=B1-(P1-(B1*MR))
850 NEXT
860 Y(I)=Y(I)+HS*(1+PH)^I-B1-HS*(1+PH)^I*SC
900 HIGH=1:LOW=-1
920 MEAN=(HIGH+LOW)/2
930 PV=0
940 FOR J=0 TO I
950 PV=PV+Y(J)/(1+MEAN)^J
960 NEXT
970 IF (.05>PV) AND (-.05<PV) THEN 1000
980 IF PV>0 THEN LOW=MEAN ELSE HIGH=MEAN
990 GOTO 920
1000 A$="##      ###.#%"
1010 PRINT USING A$;I,MEAN*100
1020 NEXT
```

BUSINESS DECISION MAKING

The following computer applications can help you make the decisions that will optimize the way you run your business.

Spreadsheets

Most people have seen or worked with the traditional accounting ledger spreadsheet or worksheet. Typically there are descriptions along the left edge, month designations across the top of each column, and room for a totals column on the right. For budget preparation, each line could represent a budget category and have budgeted monthly amounts across the page. Each line and each month's column are totaled. A change to a single number involves replacing a figure with a new one, and reading the affected column and row. This is a tedious procedure prone to error. Hence, you can understand the tremendous benefits of a totally electronic spreadsheet.

A spreadsheet program is a super calculator that provides you with a giant electronic grid that functions analogously to the traditional spreadsheet, as described above. When you change the values of numbers in the grid, the program automatically calculates what effect, if any, there is on all the other numbers. The spreadsheet can provide answers within seconds to all sorts of financial "what ifs." For example, to qualify for the mortgage you want, how much income must you have? Or how would your portfolio value change with a half-point advance in a stock?

The electronic spreadsheet may be as large as 2,048 rows long by 256 columns high, depending on the program. Formulas, equations, and algorithms may be input to provide comparisons, ratios, totals, and other information.

Who uses a spreadsheet program? Anyone who works with numbers might find a use for such a program. Obviously accounting is a primary area of application, but scientists, engineers, managers, executives, and members of almost any discipline use spreadsheets. How useful a spreadsheet is in a particular situation depends on the degree to which it increases productivity. Frequently, a spreadsheet user will get important answers that previously were not cost effective to obtain. Anyone who needs more accurate and speedier calculations is a potential spreadsheet user.

Spreadsheet programs are being used in an endless variety of applications. Some use it for solving simple or complex equations, others for normal calculator functions, and others as a complete decision support tool. Specific uses include financial modeling, budgeting, doing cash flow analysis, planning, making projections, making business plans, creating sales reports, doing what-if analysis, pricing, making cost estimates, tax planning, improving time management, performing chemical formulation, doing regression analysis, and analyzing structural design. Anything that can be done using a calculator can be done more easily and more extensively through the use of a spreadsheet program.

Other Decision Making Computer Applications

In addition to making the electronic spreadsheet available as a decision-making tool, the microcomputer enables you to use programs to guide you in making decisions in the following areas.

Long and short term financing requirements. A commercially available long term financing requirement calculation program could compute the cost of capital for various forms of funding (for example, common stocks, preferred stocks, and bonds,), select the cheapest form, and determine the amount needed to support operating plans. A short term financing requirement calculation program could compute the amount and timing of short term financing based on sales forecasts, inventory purchases, and collection and payment policies.

Breakeven analysis. Programs can be used to compute breakeven points for projects or products based on fixed and variable costs and selling prices; learning curves may also be applied.

To breakeven the following must hold true

$$P K = FC + (VC \cdot Q)$$

where   P = sales price of each unit
       K = quantity of units sold
     FC = fixed costs over the period in question
    VC = variable costs per unit produced
     Q = no. of units produced

Inventory Control. The generalized inventory model known as the *economic order quantity* (EOQ) is an important part of the management of inventory. The formulae below may be used to compute the EOQ, the minimum inventory costs for a specified time period, and the number of times to order replacement stock during a period.

$$EOQ = \sqrt{\frac{2KL}{M}} + S$$

$$C_{min} = \sqrt{2KLM}$$

$$N = \frac{L}{EOQ}$$

where EOQ = the economic order quantity in units
      C_{min} = the minimum inventory costs for the time period
      N   = the number of times replacement stock should be ordered during the period
      K   = the cost of placing and receiving each order
      L   = the total number of units used during the period
      M   = the cost of carrying one unit in inventory for the time period
      S   = the "safety" quantity of stock to be held in inventory, to minimize the risks or losses involved in running out of a crucial part or item.

Reorder timing. Programs can be used to

compute the reorder point based on inventory carrying costs, stockout costs, and demand variation.

Facility scheduling. Programs can be used to compute job shop performance (average turnaround time, percent late, and so on) based on a variety of scheduling rules (for example, first in-first out, or most over-due items first) and on job processing times.

Demand forecasting. Programs can be used to compute a forecast of future demand by exponentially smoothing past demand.

Market and media research. Programs can perform many aspects of this kind of research, including questionnaire analysis.

Purchasing. Program can analyze vendors (for example, order-filling speed, and previous complaints) to select the best over-all vendors.

Bid preparation and job pricing. The salesman or contractor would find a bid preparation program useful in calculating variable sales prices, keeping running totals, and figuring mark-ups or mark-downs. Preparation on the computer typically requires one fifth to one tenth the time required by manual methods and frees time for profit-making.

GENERAL BUSINESS CALCULATIONS AND BUSINESS ACCOUNTING SYSTEMS

The computer can be used to keep track of accounts receivable, to prepare aged trial balances, monthly statements, follow-up sales letters, and collection letters, and to provide on-line account status inquiry handling.

Writing a Small Business Accounting System

The following is an outline of a small business accounting system designed for use on a small computer with a printer and floppy disks. The program is intended for use by an individual proprietorship or a small partnership. For such a business, tax returns are prepared (either form 1040 schedule C or form 1065), bookkeeping is done, and balance sheets are produced by the system described for management and banking purposes. Advantages of computerizing this information include savings in time and improved error detection.

The most desirable bookkeeping system is called the *double entry* system; each transaction is entered into two different accounts, and thus, the system is self-checking. With the double entry system, each transaction is first recorded as money coming from some account and then recorded as money going to some account. Debits, abbreviated as DR for computer use, represent an addition to your account or to an expense; credits, abbreviated CR represent a subtraction from an account or from an expense. To determine whether or not the bookkeeping has been done correctly, find out whether or not the debits always equal the credits. For example, if you paid a bill for $50 and received a check for $100 for services performed, the bookkeeping entries would be as follows:

a. Debit (subtract from what you owe) accounts payable for $50.
b. Credit (subtract from what you have) cash on hand for $50.
c. Debit (add to what you have) cash on hand for $100.
d. Credit (add to revenue) income or revenue for $100.

The continual up-keep of the status of each account for a business is the purpose of the bookkeeping program. An example of the account files along with a suggested computer abbreviation for each is listed here:

EXPENSES (debit to add, credit to subtract)

Return and allowances	RTN	(goods returned for refund)
Depreciation	DEP	(for equipment owned)
Business taxes	TAX	
Rent	RNT	
Repairs	RPR	
Bad debts	BDB	(for the charge-off accounting method)
Professional fees	PRF	
Amortization	AMT	(charge partial costs of organiza-

tion expense, research / development, etc.)

Fuel	FUL	
Telephone	PON	
Electricity	PWR	
Salaries and wages	SAL	(does not include wages included in cost of goods sold)
Interest	INT	(interest paid, only)
Labor/production costs	LAB	
Purchases	PUR	
Insurance	INS	
Pension/profit sharing	PEN	
Depletion	DPL	(used for such assets as mines/oil fields)
Materials/supplies	MAT	
Cost of goods sold	CGS	(includes: purchases, materials/ supplies, labor/ production costs, other costs)

ASSETS (debit to add, credit to subtract)

Cash	CSH	(usually checking acct. balances)
Receivable	RBL	(amounts owed by customers on accounts)
Inventory	INV	
Prepaid expenses	PPD	
Supplies	SUP	
Equipment	EQT	
Investments	IVS	
Miscellaneous	ETC	

LIABILITIES AND EQUITY

Payables	PBL	(amounts owed on an account)
Notes	NOT	(borrowed money)
Long term payables	LTP	
Proprietor	PRP	(amount invested in business and net income)
Drawing	DRW	(amount from which owner may use money for personal expenses)

REVENUES (credit to add, debit to subtract)

Gross receipts	RCP
Other revenue	REV

The IRS requires reports in the following areas: depreciation, business taxes, repairs, and amortization.

The various reports that may be generated by the system include the balance sheet; a sample balance sheet is listed below:

ASSETS		LIABILITIES	
Equipment	5000.	Notes	2000.
Receivables	500.	Payables	3500.
Cash	3000.	Total	5500.
Total	8500.		

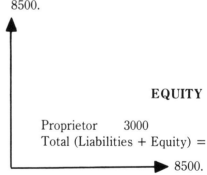

EQUITY

Proprietor   3000
Total (Liabilities + Equity) = 8500.

Assets represent what the businessman has, liabilities represent the amounts owed, and equities are amounts contributed or earned by the owners.

Another report that is a necessary part of a small business accounting system is termed the *income statement*. It displays the income and expense of the business during a certain length of time (a period); it may be used to fill out tax forms 1040C or 1065. To generate this report, total income is computed and total expenses are subtracted from this figure. Income for accounts may be stated on an accrual basis, which is to say that future expenses or revenues are included if the exact amount is known and certain (for example, the amounts customers owe may be stated on an accrual basis). Business owners may prefer to prepare a tax return report on a cash basis in which the only revenue considered is to be cash in and the only expenses considered are cash out. To prepare such a report, you must eliminate payables, receivables, prepaid expenses, and supplies not yet part of the cost of goods sold; the revenue and expense accounts should be adjusted to reflect this change.

Another necessary report is the *ledger* of which may be two types: summary and detailed. The detailed ledger is a complete listing of each account transaction (name, amount, and so on) that has been input within a certain period of time (usually done on a weekly or monthly basis). The balances up to the time of the beginning of the report have been stored from prior ledgers and are read into the computer. Thus, a report listing each transaction and the remaining balance in each account is generated. The summary ledger report only lists the remaining balances after adding and subtracting all transactions for a given period of time.

The balance sheet is the final report necessary on a small accounting system. The sum of the liabilities is subtracted from the sum of the assets to determine the balance or net profit for the business owner. This balance is credited to the proprietor (PRP) account, and thus, the assets plus the net income will balance (equal) with the liabilities.

Additional functions of the accounting system could include forecasting income using trend-line analysis of previous balance sheets, forecasting other accounts using previous records, preparing amortization schedules, determining depreciation amounts and budgeting cash based on forecasted cash on hand and cash payable.

The accounting system flowchart is shown in Fig. 2-2.

ADDITIONAL APPLICATIONS FOR THE SMALL BUSINESS PERSON OR THE PROFESSIONAL

The small business person or professional could use his or her microcomputer for the following additional purposes.

Order processing. The computer could be used for order editing, freight cost computation, credit checks, stock availability checks, and order status checks. A billing/invoicing calculation program could provide the following information: net total, total tax, total tax plus freight, total profit, percent of net profit, total value of back-ordered items, total discount amount, total gross amount, and total cost amount.

Sales. The computer could prepare a breakdown of sales volume and profitability by product, customer, or salesman. Sales order processing software could print packing slips, deduct sold merchandise from inventory, verify orders, process returned goods, accumulate back orders, enter cash receipts, print invoices, print sales and credit journals, and maintain a customer master file.

General accounting. General accounting functions include cost record keeping, budgeting, daily exception recordkeeping, and the issuing of profit and loss statements.

Mailing list. One of the prime assets of a small business is its mailing list, representing customers who are likely to be repeat purchasers. The personal computer simplifies mailing list maintenance and is capable of sorting names according to a variety of characteristics, depending upon how much information is stored by the program in addition to names and addresses. Consider the following promotional or money-saving activities that can easily be accomplished through the use of a full-featured mailing list program:

- Sort list by zip for bulk mail savings.
- Sort list alphabetically and printout as a customer reference.
- Mail pieces to residents of a certain town or zip for a special local promotion.
- Mailings to customers having an upcoming birthday.

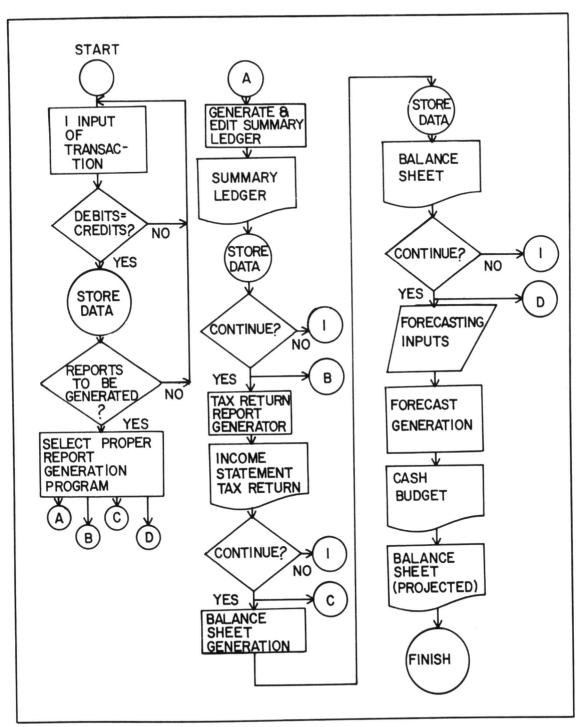

Fig. 2-2. A flowchart for an accounting system program.

- Mailings to all women announcing a special sale on dresses.
- Mailings to only the most active customers for a special "favored customer".

The ability of a mailing list program to sort customers by these and other criteria requires that special codes be input along with names and addresses. The coding used and its extent are at the user's discretion.

Customer file management. By functioning in a manner similar to the way a mailing list program functions, a customer file management program could keep track of customers in a way that is useful to the business. The data stored could include customer name, address, phone, occupation, credit limit, current balance, brand preference, total purchases, sales representative, and date of last order. The business manager could then obtain lists of customers according to

- Outstanding balance of 30+ days, for collection purposes.
- Brand preference, for research and promotional purposes.
- Sales representatives.
- Those who have not ordered within the last year, for consideration of removal from the active list or for a followup campaign.

A mailing list program could be combined with a customer maintenance program to provide a powerful tool—an accurate profile of your customer base, useful reports for the sales staff, and a means for select mail promotion.

Payroll. A complete payroll calculation program would include the following features: timecard hours computation, check writing, and provisions for commissions, bonuses, piecework salaries, incentives. W-2 forms, and payroll summaries could also be outputted.

Inventory. A complete inventory management program should be able to output the following reports: detailed inventory, inventory status, on-order, order exception, analysis by cost, list for use in physical inventory, period to date, year to date, minimum quantity search, and inventory projections. The following file update functions should also be provided: place and order, cancel an order, add a new inventory form, delete an existing inventory item, initial a new period or year. The inventory program could also print purchase orders or reminders.

Contract preparation. A word-processing system could print personalized contract forms. Cost estimation functions could also be integrated into the contract preparation program.

General business calculations. Consider the use of your personal computer or programmable calculator in performing the following general business computations, which may previously have been too awkward or time consuming when done by manual methods: cash flow, breakeven point, government withholding calculations, selling price from cost and gross profit prorating, unit price comparisons, order quantity for optimum price break, moving average, seasonal average, cyclical analysis, histogram generation, worse-case analysis, universal rate of return, summation of ledger columns, optimum markup or markdown, net present value, choice between debt and equity, lease versus buy determinations, funds statement preparation, perpetual sales quantity, and gross sales revenue.

Capital equipment investment analysis. The simple BASIC program in Listing 2-13 computes the maximum purchase price for a piece of equipment based upon estimated profits.

Listing 2-13: The Capital Equipment Investment Analysis Program

```
100 REM CAPITAL EQUIPMENT INVESTMENT ANALYSIS
110 REM DETERMINES THE MAXIMUM PURCHASE PRICE FOR EQUIPMENT
120 REM BASED UPON ESTIMATED PROFITS
130 INPUT "ENTER THE EST. NO. OF YEARS OF EQUIPMENT LIFE ",N
```

```
140 INPUT "ENTER THE INTEREST RATE ",I
150 FOR X=1 TO N
160    PRINT "ENTER THE PROJECTED EARNINGS FOR YEAR: ";X
170    INPUT R(X)
180 NEXT X
190 FOR X=1 TO N
200 Q=Q+R(X)/I^X
210 NEXT X
220 PRINT "THE RECOMMENDED PURCHASE PRICE IS: $";Q
230 END
```

Professional Practice Management

Professionals with large practices should consider using a personal computer system in

- Maintaining appointments
- Billing and collection
- Generating appointment reminders
- Accessing reference libraries and data resources for journal articles, diagnoses, case laws, standards, rules and regulations, codes, and drug information.
- Correspondence and document preparation
- Telecommunication with laboratories for diagnostic tests.
- Insurance form preparation or transmission.

Business Letters

Professionally prepared files of business letters are available for popular personal computers to save you time and enable you to produce better letters. Typically over 1000 letters are available for review, modification, and output with the use of a word processing program.

The new U.S. Post Office E•COM (electronic computer-originated first class mail) system permits the transmission of business letters via modem to the E•COM network; the letter will be printed and mailed for delivery the next day anywhere in the U.S. The current rate is $0.26 each. The system may be used for anyone with a modem and a personal computer upon payment of a $50.00 annual accounting fee.

Sales Device

The small computer may be used as a sales device in several ways. Now that telephone dialing interfaces are available, you can use the computer to call every possible telephone number in an exchange or from a customer file and deliver a tape-recorded retail sales message to anyone who answers. At expositions or retail sales outlets, a computer with a video display can continually list sales information. Crude question-answering capabilities could also be provided.

Use of the computer as a customer advisor can increase sales traffic as well. For example, a garden supply shop could provide customers with access to a computer programmed to answer gardening questions about specific plants (for example, questions about growing seasons and nutrient requirements), amount and type of fertilizer for a certain size lawn and type of grass, and possibly output a complete garden plan. A wine shop computer could recommend a type of wine to accompany a given meal, the glass and temperature to use, and the comparative prices of wines. The cosmetics department of a store could use the computer to suggest brand name cosmetics to use in achieving a certain complexion. A swimming pool maintenance company advertises that it offers a free computer analysis of anyone's swimming pool water. From water samples, the computer determines the type and amount of chemicals necessary to maintain a specific pool; these chemicals are then sold to the pool owner.

The Calculation of the Number of Days Between Two Dates

Businesspeople often need to know how much time (usually in terms of days) there is between two

```
10 REM DAYS BETWEEN TWO DATES CALCULATION (IN SAME YEAR)
20 DIM M(12)
30 FOR X=1 TO 12
40 READ M(X)
50 NEXT X
60 PRINT "IS THIS A LEAP YEAR 1=YES,2=NO";
70 INPUT A
80 IF A=1 THEN M(2)=29
90 INPUT "INPUT  THE FIRST DATE NUMERICALLY IN THIS FORM: DAY, MONTH ",D1,M1
110 INPUT "INPUT THE SECOND DATE IN THE SAME FORM ",D2,M2
125 IF M1=M2 THEN DA=D2-D1:GOTO 200
130 EM=M(M1)-D1
140 IF MA+1=M2 THEN 190
150 FOR X=M1+1 TO M2-1
160    DA=DA+M(X)
170 NEXT X
190 DA=DA+EM+D2
200 PRINT "THE NUMBER OF DAYS=";DA
210 END
220 DATA 31,28,31,30,31,30,31,31,30,31,30,31
```

given dates. A program, such as the one in Listing 2-14 stores the number of days in each month and could serve to calculate this value. Additionally, time conversions between seconds, minutes, hours, days, weeks, months, and years could be performed.

Time Calculations

Calculation of the difference in hours or days between two given times is another business application. The results can be used in determining hours worked for payroll purposes or in figuring accumulated interest. The program in Listing 2-15 calculates the difference between two times.

Time differences between major cities or time zones could be calculated by a program. A world map could also be displayed on a video screen with the appropriate times in major cities continuously

Listing 2-15: The Time Difference Program

```
10 KEY OFF:CLS
20 PRINT "TIME DIFFERENCE CALCULATION
30 PRINT "COMPUTE DIFFERENCE IN HOURS, MINUTES, AND SECONDS
40 PRINT "INPUT THE FIRST TIME IN 24.HR. CLOCK FORMAT--"
50 PRINT "HOURS, MINUTES, SECONDS."
60 INPUT H1,M1,S1
70 PRINT "INPUT FINAL TIME IN 24. HR. FORMAT."
80 INPUT H2,M2,S2
90 NH=H2-H1
100 NM=M2-M1:IF NM<0 THEN NH=NH-1:NM=60+NM
```

```
110 NS=S2-S1:IF NS<0 THEN NM=NM-1:NS=60+NS
120 PRINT "THE DIFFERENCE IN H,M,S IS:";NH;NM;NS
130 PRINT
140 END
```

updated. This application may be useful to those making long distance calls or flying into other time zones.

The Calculation of Reference Tables

Any mathematical function may be expressed as a table of values corresponding to the factors in the equation. Businesspeople who need to calculate the value of a particular function could produce a table listing values at specified intervals for easy reference. For example, a portion of a chart used in converting British pounds to American dollars is reproduced here. Note that the dollar equivalents are found in the interior of the chart.

hundredths of pounds

pounds	.00	.10	.20	.30	.40	.50	.60	.70	.80	.90
1	1.90	2.09	2.28	2.47	2.66	2.85	3.04	3.23	3.42	3.61
2	3.80	3.99	4.18	4.37	4.56	4.75	4.94	5.13	5.32	5.51
3	5.70	5.89	6.08	6.27	6.46	6.65	6.84	7.03	7.22	7.41
4	7.60	7.79	7.98	8.17	8.36	8.55	8.74	8.99	9.12	9.31

The conversion rate for this chart is 1.90 dollars per British pound. As an example of its use, the number of dollars that are equivalent to 4.90 pounds is given by the chart as 9.31. The BASIC program used to print the chart is shown in Listing 2-16 and can be used as a model for similar programs designed to calculate reference tables.

Your computer can be a time saver by computing and outputting tables concerning areas such as

- Stock commissions.
- Values of an investment or savings account over periods of time.
- Unit prices after certain quantity purchases.
- Break-even values for various prices and sales of a product.
- UPS/USPS rates to various cities for various weights.

THE COMPUTER AND THE PROFESSIONS

In this section a variety of ways in which the

Listing 2-16: The Reference Table Program

```
10 KEY OFF:CLS
20 PRINT " CONVERT DOLLARS TO FOREIGN CURRENCY"
25 INPUT "ENTER NAME OF FOREIGN CURRENCY TO BE CONVERTED:",B$
30 INPUT "ENTER DOLLAR VALUE OF ONE UNIT OF DESIRED FOREIGN CURRENCY (I.E., 1.9
FOR BRIT- ISH POUND) ",A
40 INPUT "PRESS ENTER TO PRINT CHART. FOR A HARD COPY, PRESS CTRL-PRTSC WHEN CHA
RT IS     DONE.",A$
50 A$="##.##  "
55 CLS
60 PRINT TAB((80-LEN(B$))/2)B$:PRINT
70 PRINT "$      .00     .10     .20     .30     .40     .50     .60     .70     .80
. 90
80 FOR X=1 TO 10
90   PRINT USING "$$# ";X;
100   FOR B=0 TO 1 STEP .1
110     PRINT USING A$;A*(X+B),
```

```
120    NEXT B
130    PRINT
140 NEXT X
150 END
```

personal computer or programmable calculator can be used in the professions and in many blue collar occupations are listed. This short listing is far from complete; uses of calculators and computers are so diverse that these descriptions can only be suggestive of a few of the many applications.

Accountants and tax specialists: All aspects of work

Advertising:
Client fees
Composition and printing costs
Production (film and TV) costs
Space and time buying
Statistics in market research

Agriculture:
Yields per acre
Livestock growth and feeding
Livestock food supplements
Crop mix and rotation
Fertilizer ratios

Appraisers:
Comparative values
Quantities
Summations

Architects:
Strength of materials
Loads, stresses, and strains
Geometrical configurations

Artists and designers:
Supplies and materials
Scale reductions and expansions
Client fees by hours worked

Attorneys:
Terms of contracts
Tax calculations
Bankruptcy dispositions

Auto salesmen:
Optional equipment costs
Discounts and prices
Used car allowances

Auto service and repair:
Towing and road service costs
Costs of materials and labor
Estimates

Banking:
Interest, assets, annuities, insurance
Foreign exchange
Collateral
Trust and pensions

Broadcasting:
Program scheduling
Advertising rates
Station logs

Building contractor:
Measuring land sites
Amounts and costs of roofing, flooring, siding, etc.
Electrical loads and needs
Figuring gutters, windows, screen sizes
Water pressures, plumbing
Work schedules and transportation

Building maintenance:
Supplies and power
Waste disposal

Buyer:
Comparative costs among suppliers
Shipping charges
Foreign size conversions
Cost relative to markup at retail
Profit potential

Chemists and lab technicians:
Quantitative measurements

76

Construction trades:
Composition of solutions and compounds

Rates of reactions

Volumetric and gravimetric analysis

Calculations of materials, labor time, charges, and so on by bricklayers, masons, carpenters, plasterers, plumbers, etc.

Dieticians:
Food quantities and costs

Nutritional and caloric values

Educators—teachers:
Grading homework and examination papers

Classroom games and instructions in arithmetic, English, etc.

Employment counselors:
Working conditions, wages, and salaries

Fringe benefits

Labor supply and openings

Engineers:
All phases of construction, including plant location studies, tax rates, labor and transportation charges, loads, amounts and costs of raw materials, excavation needs, fill, wood, wire and cement forms, steel reinforcement, strength of materials, electrical loads, chemical reactions, etc.

Geologists:
Land measurements

Chemical analysis and assays

Mineral depletion rates

Hotel and inn keepers:
Supplies and labor

Occupancy rates

Concession profits and activity

Group discounts and catering

Independent businesses:
Balance sheet, profit and loss statements

Purchases, returns, and allowances

Cost of materials, labor, services, loans

Figuring profit on investment and costs of expansion

Itemizing for tax deductions

Depreciation schedules

Insurance salesman:
Premiums, dividends on policies

Annuities

Alternative insurance packages

Proper levels of coverage

Interior decorating:
Amounts and costs of fabrics, rugs, carpeting, drapes, wallpaper, etc.

Discounts for quantity

Shipping times and charges

Jewelers:
Pricing and costs

Composition of precious metals

Gem weights and sizes

Landscape architects and contractors:
Land areas, planting and fertilization schedules

Land fill

Manufacturer's representative:
Cost of items less discounts

Shipping and insurance costs

Invoices prepared for suppliers and clients

Market research:
Statistics of opinion and

	field testing		Inventory control
	Extent and nature of competition	Real estate:	Distribution costs
Medical, dental, and other health services:	Prescribing or utilizing medications, anesthetics, prosthetic devices, etc.		Discounts
			Market and appraised value
			Development costs
	Operational costs of services		Taxes, insurance, water, and heating costs,
			Closing fees
	Supplies inventories and costs	Restaurants:	Commissions
Pattern makers:	Geometric configurations		Food and liquor costs and prices
	Measurements and conversions		Tips
		Renting and leasing:	Interest charges and cash flow
	Alternative designs		Inventory and usage rates
Personnel administration:	Absenteeism rates, efficiency	Sales, door to door:	Travel and other expenses
	Vacations, illness rates		
	Wage rate compliances and comparisons		Statements to suppliers
			Commissions
	Employee benefits	Sales, retail:	Taxes and commissions
	Hirings and severances		Inventory and turnover
Pharmacists:	Pharmaceutical measurements		Pricing—markups and markdowns
	Supplies inventory and costs	Secretaries:	Petty cash, travel expenses
	Pricing		Postage costs
Photographers:	Composition of solutions		Budget, production, sales reports
	Supplies comparisons		
	Pricing		Employer's personal finances
	Exposure times and shutter speeds		Correspondence and memo verification
Pilots:	Passenger and freight loads	Security analysts:	Profits, expenses, P/E ratios working capital, depreciation, growth rates, dividends, etc.
	Fuel consumption and capacities		
	Navigation		
Printers:	Paper stocks		Technical and fundamental analyses
	Scheduling printing runs		
Psychologists:	Psychological testing	Securities salesmen:	Margin costs and availability
	Statistics of experiments		
Publishing:	Composition and printing costs		Dividend and interest yields
	Postage and shipping costs		Commissions earned

Surveyors: Growth rates, price changes, balanced portfolios

Welfare availability versus family needs

Family budgeting

Land measurements

Travel agents: Discounts on fares, tours, hotels

Commissions earned

Distances and costs per distance

Converting foreign currencies, kilometer distances, etc.

Billing airlines, steamship lines, bus companies, tours, hotels, etc.

Trucking and shipping: Load capacities by weight and volume

Typographers: Distances, time schedules, costs

Equipment inventory and maintenance

License fees and taxes

Printers' measurements

Plates and etchings

Waiters and waitresses: Tips

Totaling checks

Wholesalers and manufacturers   Labor and overhead

Loss on discounting customers' interest-bearing notes

Interest on account balances

Recording payments, promissory notes, partial payments

Consignments and returns

Shipping costs and taxes

Chapter 3

Mathematical and Statistical Applications

One of the biggest assets of the computer is its ability to perform complicated and tedious mathematical calculations with unerring diligence. Your personal computer may be programmed to emulate a simple adding machine or a complex scientific business calculator. It can perform statistical computations of use to those involved with businesses, investments, questionnaire analysis, the sciences, and other fields.

THE COMPUTER AS A SOPHISTICATED CALCULATOR

A program could be written to emulate the functions of an ordinary or an RPN calculator. The computer could be used as a simple business or scientific calculator for a variety of purposes. Additionally, functions not provided on an ordinary calculator could easily be included (for example, the ability to solve quadratic equations).

RPN Calculator

RPN stands for Reverse Polish Notation and is a system of representing mathematical equations.

Some of the advanced scientific calculators use the RPN system because fewer keystrokes are required to do complex calculations with an RPN system than with the regular system. The RPN system is often easier to use after you have gained familiarity with it. The purpose of the program in Listing 3-1 is to emulate an RPN calculator, providing about 50 mathematical functions. This program is thus composed of 50 subroutines, identified by REM statements, that may be used as subroutines in other BASIC programs that require functions not provided by your version of BASIC.

In the RPN system there are no parentheses and no = (equals) key. Only two numbers are worked with at one time. A sample calculation would proceed as follows:

Step	Input	Display	Comments
①	2.5	2.5	Enter first number
		0	
		0	These are the four registers
		0	

Step	Input	Display	Comments	function	description
(2)	4	4	Enter second number	*	multiplication
		2.5	as new numbers are	+	addition
		0	input, preceding inputs	/	division
		0	are shifted through the	−	subtraction
			registers.	^	powers (e.g., x ^ y
					stands for X^y and x ^ .5
(3)	*	10	* stands for multiplica-	√	stands for $\sqrt{x}$)
		4	tion. The answer to	INV	inverse (e.g., 1/x)
		2.5	2.5 × 4 was calculated	C	clear display/registers
		0	and put in the first po-	SIN	compute the sine of x
			sition in the display.	ASIN	compute the arcsine of x
				COS	compute the cosine of x
(4)	10	10	enter third number	ACOS	compute the arccosine of
		10			x
		4		TAN	compute the tangent of x
		2.5		ATAN	compute the arctangent of x
				SEC	compute the secant of x
(5)	5	5	enter fourth number	ASEC	compute the arcsecant of
		10			x
		10		COT	compute the cotangent of
		4			x
				ACOT	compute the arccotangent
(6)	/	2	/ stands for division.		of x
		5	The following calcula-	CSC	compute the cosecant of
		5	tion was performed,		x
		10	and the answer was	ACSC	compute the arccosecant
		10	stored in the first dis-		of x
			play position:	PI	place the value of π in
			10/5 = 2		the register
				E	compute the exponential
(7)	+	12	The + sign instructed		of x (i.e., e^x)
		2	that the two preceding	LOG	compute the logarithm
		5	results were to be		of x
		10	added: 10+2=12; the	MEM+	add a number to the
			answer was stored in		memory register
			the first position. The	MEM−	delete a number from the
			two preceding results		memory register
			were added because no	%	change x to a percentage
			new numbers were in-		value
			put for the computa-	N!	compute the factorial of x
			tion.	SD	compute the standard
					deviation for a set of
					scores

The functions available in this program are listed and described below:

function	description
HYP	compute the value for the hypotenuse of a triangle

function	description	function	description
	given the two sides	#SIN	cotangent of x
SIDE	compute the value for a side of a triangle given the hypotenuse and another side		inverse hyperbolic sine of x
DEG	change x from radians to degrees	#COS	inverse hyperbolic cosine of x
RAD	change x from degrees to radians	#TAN	inverse hyperbolic tangent of x
POLR	compute polar coordinates given rectangular coordinates	#SEC	inverse hyperbolic cosecant of x
		#CSC	inverse hyperbolic cotangent of x
RECT	compute rectangular coordinates given polar coordinates	#COT	inverse hyperbolic secant of x
MET	compute metric conversions—a subprogram	SZ	switch the z registers
		RZ	rotate the z registers
HSIN	compute the hyperbolic sine of x	QUAD	compute solutions to quadratic equations with the quadratic equation
HCOS	compute the hyperbolic cosine of x	?	put computer in monitor mode so that ordinary calculations may be made in the form PRINT 5*1.6. Type CONT in some BASICs to continue with the program
HTAN	compute the hyperbolic tangent of x		
HSEC	compute the hyperbolic secant of x		
HCSC	compute the hyperbolic cosecant of x		
HCOT	compute the hyperbolic		

Listing 3-1: The RPN Calculator Program

```
10 CLS:KEY OFF
20 REM RPN CALCULATOR
30 REM (C) 1978 MARK R.SAWUSCH--MAY NOT BE SOLD
40 DIM A(100),M$(21),D$(50),K(25)
50 L=2
60 DEFDBL B,A,X,C,Z
70 PRINT "MAXI-CAL"
80 G=1:F=1
90 FOR D=1 TO 50:READ D$(D):NEXT
100 PRINT"* + / MIN ^ INV C SIN ASIN COS ACOS TAN ATAN SEC ASEC COT ACOT CSC ACS
C PI E LOG MEM+ MEM- % N! SD HYP SIDE DEG RAD POLR RECT MET HSIN HCOS HTAN HSEC
HCSC HCOT #SIN #COS #TAN #SEC #CSC #COT SZ RZ QUAD ?"
110 PRINT "EACH COMMAND/FUNCTION IN LINE 60 MUST CONTAIN 4 LETTERS AND/OR SPACES
 FOR PROP- ER OPERATION.  FOR EXPLANATIONS OF THE COMMANDS, SEE THE TEXT IN THE
BOOK ACCOMPANYING THIS SOFTWARE."
120 D=1
```

```
130 REM ASK FOR COMMAND/VALUES
140 REM
150 INPUT "COMMAND";C$
160 O=0
170 IF VAL(C$)=0 THEN GOTO 230        'IS IT A LETTER OR A NUMBER?
180 A(G)=VAL(C$):A(G)=CDBL(A(G)):X=A(G):IF F(1)=2 THEN F(2)=2 ELSE F(1)=2
190 L=G
200 IF G=1 THEN G=2 ELSE G=1
210 GOTO 2200
220 GOTO 150
230 A(G)=L1:IF F(1)=1 THEN F(2)=1 ELSE F(1)=1
240 REM SEARCH TO FIND THE COMMAND
250 FOR I=1 TO 50
260   IF C$=D$(I) THEN 290
270 NEXT I
280 PRINT "ILLEGAL FUNCTION ":PRINT:GOTO 150
290 IF I<=44 THEN 310
300 IF I>=45 THEN I=I-44:GOTO 320
310 ON I GOTO 340,370,400,430,460,480,500,520,550,580,610,640,670,700,730,760,79
0,820,850,880,910,940,970,1040,1090,1120,1160,1320,1350,1370,1400,1430,1480,1490
,1750,1780,1810,1840,1870,1900,1930,1960,1990,2020
320 ON I GOTO 2050,2080,2100,2110,2120,2160
330 REM CALCULATE *
340 IF F(1)=F(2) AND F(1)=1 THEN X=Z1*Z4 ELSE X=Z1*Z2
350 GOTO 2200
360 REM CALCULATE +
370 IF F(1)=F(2) AND F(1)=1 THEN X=Z1+Z4 ELSE X=Z1+Z2
380 GOTO 2200
390 REM CALCULATE /
400 IF F(1)=F(2) AND F(1)=1 THEN X=Z4/Z1 ELSE X=Z2/Z1
410 GOTO 2200
420 REM CALCULATE -
430 IF F(1)=F(2) AND F(1)=1 THEN X=X4-X1 ELSE X=Z2-Z1
440 GOTO 2200
450 REM CALCULATE POWERS
460 X=Z2^Z1:GOTO 2200
470 REM CALCULATE INVERSES
480 Z1=1/Z1:GOTO 2210
490 REM CLEAR REGISTERS
500 Z1=0:Z2=0:Z3=0:Z4=0:GOTO 2210
510 REM CALCULATE SIN
520 A(L)=SIN(A(L)*.0174533)
530 GOTO 2190
540 REM CALCULATE ARC SIN
550 A(L)=ATN(A(L)/SQR(-A(L)*A(L)+1))*57.29578
560 GOTO 2190
570 REM CALCULATE COSINE
580 A(L)=COS(A(L)*.0174533)
590 GOTO 2190
600 REM CALCULATE ARC COSINE
610 A(L)=(-ATN(A(L)/SQR(-A(L)*A(L)+1))+1.5708)*57.29578
```

```
620 GOTO 2190
630 REM CALCULATE TANGENT
640 A(L)=TAN(A(L)*.0174533)
650 GOTO 2190
660 REM CALCULATE ARC TANGENT
670 A(L)=ATN(A(L))*57.29578
680 GOTO 2190
690 REM CALCULATE SECANT
700 A(L)=1/COS(A(L)*.0174533)
710 GOTO 2190
720 REM CALCULATE ARC SECANT
730 A(L)=(ATN(SQR(A(L)*A(L)-1))+(SGN(A(L)-1)*1.5708))*57.29578
740 GOTO 2190
750 REM CALCULATE COTANGENT
760 A(L)=1/TAN(A(L)*.0174533)
770 GOTO 2190
780 REM CALCULATE ARC COTANGENT
790 A(L)=(-ATN(A(L)+1.5708))*57.29578
800 GOTO 2190
810 REM CALCULATE COSECANT
820 A(L)=1/SIN(A(L)*.0174533)
830 GOTO 2190
840 REM CALCULATE ARC COSECANT
850 A(L)=(ATN(1/SQR(A(L)*A(L)-1))+(SGN(A(L)-1)*1.5708))*57.29578
860 GOTO 2190
870 REM VALUE FOR PI
880 Z1=3.141592654#:GOTO 2210
890 GOTO 2190
900 REM CALCULATE NATURAL LOGARITHM
910 A(L)=EXP(A(L))
920 GOTO 2190
930 REM CALCULATE LOG. _THM
940 A(L)=LOG(A(L))
950 GOTO 2190
960 REM MEMORY ADDITION
970 DD=DD+1
980 INPUT "WHICH REGISTER";D
990 IF D=1 THEN M$(DD)=STR$(Z1) ELSE IF D=2 THEN M$(DD)=STR$(Z2) ELSE IF D=3 THE
N M$(DD)=STR$(Z3) ELSE M$(DD)=STR$(Z4)
1000 INPUT "DESCRIPTION:",C$
1010 M$(DD)=M$(DD)+" "+C$
1020 GOTO 150
1030 REM MEMORY LISTING
1040 FOR D=1 TO DD
1050 PRINT M$(D)
1060 NEXT D
1070 GOTO 150
1080 REM CONV. FOR %
1090 A(L)=A(L)*.01
1100 GOTO 2190
1110 REM COMPUTE FACTORIAL
1120 FOR YY=1 TO A(L)
```

```
1130 A(L)=A(L)*(A(L)-YY)
1140 NEXT YY:GOTO 2190
1150 REM STATISTICS
1160 PRINT "IN STATISTICAL MODE "
1170 PRINT
1180 PRINT "ENTER VALUES SEPARATELY AND ENTER 9999 WHEN DONE"
1190 B=0:C=0:D=1
1200 INPUT K(D)
1210 IF K(D)=9999 THEN 1240
1220 B=B+K(D):C=C+K(D)^2:D=D+1
1230 GOTO 1200
1240 PRINT "SCORES:":FOR H%=1 TO D-1
1250 PRINT K(H%);
1260 NEXT H%:PRINT
1270 PRINT "SUM OF SCORES","NUMBER OF SCORES"
1280 PRINT B,D-1
1290 PRINT B/(D-1),C-(B/(D-1))^2
1300 PRINT "STANDARD DEVIATION=";SQR(C-(B/(D-1))^2)
1310 REM COMPUTE HYPOTENUSE
1320 X=SQR(Z1^2+Z2^2)
1330 GOTO 2200
1340 REM COMPUTE SIDE OF TRIANGLE
1350 X=SQR(ABS(Z1 2-Z2 2)):GOTO 2200
1360 REM CONV. TO DEGREES
1370 A(L)=A(L)*57.2957791#
1380 GOTO 2190
1390 REM CONV. TO RADIANS
1400 A(L)=.017453292#*A(L)
1410 GOTO 2190
1420 REM RECT. TO POLAR CONV.
1430 Z1=SQR(Z1*Z1+Z2*Z2)
1440 A=Z2/Z1
1450 Z2=(ATN(A/SQR(-A*A+1)))*57.29578
1460 GOTO 2210
1470 REM POLAR TO RECT. CONV.
1480 B=Z1*SIN(Z2*.0174533):Z2=Z1*COS(Z2*.0174533):Z1=B:GOTO 2210
1490 A(G)=Z1:PRINT "M E N U:"
1500 PRINT "USE THE NEGATIVE OF THE MENU # TO CONVERT VICE-VERSA)"
1510 PRINT "1) FEET TO METERS"
1520 PRINT "2) INCHES TO CENTIMETERS"
1530 PRINT "3) MILES TO KILOMETERS"
1540 PRINT "4) GALLONS TO LITERS"
1550 PRINT "5) FARENHEIGHT TO CENTIGRADE"
1560 PRINT "6) POUNDS TO KILOGRAMS"
1570 PRINT "7) END CONVERSIONS"
1580 INPUT "SELECT:",H
1590 IF H<0 THEN GOTO 1610
1600 ON H GOTO 1620,1640,1660,1680,1700,1720,140
1610 ON -H GOTO 1630,1650,1670,1690,1710,1730
1620 X=.33047851#*A(G):GOTO 2270
1630 X=A(G)*3.281:GOTO 2270
1640 X=A(G)*2.54:GOTO 2270
```

```
1650 X=A(G)*.3937:GOTO 2270
1660 X=A(G)*1.609:GOTO 2270
1670 X=A(G)*.6215:GOTO 2270
1680 X=3.7853*A(G):GOTO 2270
1690 X=.2642*A(G):GOTO 2270
1700 X=.5555555*(A(G)-32):GOTO 2270
1710 X=1.8*A(G)+32:GOTO 2270
1720 X=.4536*A(G):GOTO 2270
1730 X=2.2046*A(G):GOTO 2270
1740 REM COMPUTE HYPERBOLIC SINE
1750 A(L)=(EXP(A(L))-EXP(-A(L)))/2
1760 GOTO 2190
1770 REM COMPUTE HYPERBOLIC COSINE
1780 A(L)=(EXP(A(L))+EXP(-A(L)))/2
1790 GOTO 2190
1800 REM COMPUTE HYPERBOLIC TANGENT
1810 A(L)=-EXP(-A(L))/EXP(A(L))+EXP(-A(L))*2+1
1820 GOTO 2190
1830 REM COMPUTE HYPERBOLIC SECANT
1840 A(L)=2/(EXP(A(L))+EXP(-A(L)))
1850 GOTO 2190
1860 REM COMPUTE HYPERBOLIC COSECANT
1870 A(L)=2/(EXP(A(L))-EXP(-A(L)))
1880 GOTO 2190
1890 REM COMPUTE HYPERBOLIC COTANGENT
1900 A(L)=EXP(-A(L))/(EXP(A(L))-EXP(-A(L)))*2+1
1910 GOTO 2190
1920 REM COMPUTE INV. HYPERBOLIC SINE
1930 A(L)=LOG(A(L)+SQR(A(L)*A(L)+1))
1940 GOTO 2190
1950 REM COMPUTE INV. HYPERBOLIC COSINE
1960 A(L)=LOG(A(L)+SQR(A(L)*A(L)-1))
1970 GOTO 2190
1980 REM COMPUTE INV. HYPERBOLIC TANGENT
1990 A(L)=LOG((1+A(L))/(1-A(L)))/2
2000 GOTO 2190
2010 REM COMPUTE INV. HYPERBOLIC SECANT
2020 A(L)=LOG((SQR(-A(L)*A(L)+1)+1)/A(L))
2030 GOTO 2190
2040 REM COMPUTE INV. HYPERBOLIC COSECANT
2050 A(L)=LOG((SGN(A(L))*SQR(A(L)*A(L)+1)+1)/A(L))
2060 GOTO 2190
2070 REM COMPUTE INV. HYPERBOLIC COTANGENT
2080 A(L)=LOG((A(L)+1)/(A(L)-1))/2
2090 GOTO 2190
2100 B=Z2:Z2=Z1:Z1=B:GOTO 2210
2110 B=Z4:Z4=Z3:Z2=Z1:Z1=B:GOTO 2210
2120 B=-Z2*Z2+SQR(Z2*Z2-4*Z3*Z1)/2*Z3
2130 Z1=-Z2*Z2-SQR(Z2*Z2-4*Z3*Z1)/2*Z3
2140 Z2=B
2150 GOTO 2210
2160 PRINT "ENTERING MONITOR MODE; PRESS <F5> TO CONTINUE PROGRAM"
```

```
2170 STOP
2180 GOTO 150
2190 Z1=A(L):GOTO 2210
2200 Z4=Z3:Z3=Z2:Z2=Z1:Z1=X
2210 PRINT "Z1:";Z1
2220 PRINT "Z2:";Z2
2230 PRINT "Z3:";Z3
2240 PRINT "Z4:";Z4
2250 PRINT:PRINT
2260 GOTO 140
2270 PRINT "=";X:PRINT:PRINT:GOTO 1490
2280 DATA *,+,/,MIN,^,INV,C,SIN,ASIN,COS,ACOS,TAN,ATAN,SEC,ASEC,COT,ACOT,CSC,ACS
C,PI,E,LOG,MEM+,MEM-,%,N!,SD,HYP,SIDE,DEG,RAD,POLR,RECT,MET,HSIN,HCOS,HTAN,HSEC,
HCSC,HCOT,#SIN,#COS,#TAN,#SEC,#CSC,#COT,SZ,RZ,QUAD,?
```

STATISTICS

The microcomputer is well-suited for dealing with statistics. Basic statistics for one or two variables—the mean, variance, and standard deviation may be found for a set of observations on one variable. For paired variable sets, the above statistics could be determined for each, and the covariance and correlation coefficient calculated.

Mean $\quad \bar{x} = \dfrac{\Sigma x}{n}$

Variance $\quad \sigma^2_x = \dfrac{\Sigma(\text{deviation from true mean})^2}{n}$

$$= \dfrac{\Sigma(x - \mu)^2}{n}$$

Standard deviation $\sigma_x = \sqrt{\text{variance}}$

$$r = \dfrac{\Sigma XY - nXY}{\sqrt{(\Sigma X^2 - n\bar{X}^2)(\Sigma Y^2 - n\bar{Y}^2)}}$$

Means and moments. For grouped or ungrouped data, the arithmetic, geometric, and harmonic means may be determined; the second, third, and fourth moments about the mean and the coefficients of skewness and kurtosis may also be calculated.

One and two way analysis of variance. The mean and variance for two treatment groups and for the entire sample may be calculated, and an F statistic can be applied to the differences between populations.

Contingency table analysis. The chi-square statistic may be used to test independence between row and column classifications of a contingency table.

Linear regression. A set of observations may be fit to a straight line by linear regression; the coefficient of determination, the standard error of y on x, and the standard error for the coefficients may also be computed. Multiple linear regression fits, and polynomial regression could also be performed.

For the linear equation y = a + bx.

$$b = \dfrac{\Sigma XY - n\bar{X}\,\bar{Y}}{\Sigma X^2 - n\bar{X}^2}$$

$$a = \bar{Y} - b\bar{X}$$

where $\bar{X} = (\Sigma X)/n, \bar{Y} = (\Sigma Y)/n$

Survey analysis. The following statistical parameters could be calculated by a complete survey analysis program: multivariate analysis, regression analysis, time-series analysis, variance determination, factor analysis, descriptions, and tabulations.

Generation of frequency tables. For a large sample, a sorting program could output a standard or relative frequency table.

Hypothesis testing. A useful program could determine confidence intervals for a given sample, which may then be used in testing hypotheses. Statistical hypothesis testing is used to answer such questions as, "A businessman claimed that 20% of the public prefer his products; if 100 people were asked their opinion, what percentage would have to respond negatively for this claim to be refutable?

Statistical Distributions. The approximations for normal and student's t-distributions given below are designed for easy translation into BASIC program statements and have wide applications in statistical analysis.

• Normal Distribution

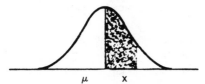

Standard Normal Distribution

$$u = \frac{(x - \mu)}{\sigma x}$$

probability of x falling in the shaded area above =
$$1 - r(a_1 t + a_2 t^2 + a_3 t^3) + \epsilon(x)$$

where: $a_1 = 0.4361836$
$a_2 = -0.1201676$
$a_3 = 0.9372980$
$r = (e^{-x^2/2})(2\pi)^{-\frac{1}{2}}$
$t = (1 + 0.3326x)^{-1}$
$|\epsilon(x)| < 10^{-5}$

• Student's t-distribution

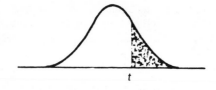

Student's t-distribution

area of right-tail $= \frac{1}{4}(1 + a_1 x + a_2 x^2 + a_3 x^3 + a_4 x^4)^{-4} + \epsilon(x)$

where: $a_1 = 0.196854$
$a_2 = 0.115194$
$a_3 = 0.000344$
$a_4 = 0.019527$
$t =$ t-value
$d =$ no. degrees of freedom

$x = (t^{2/3}(1 - 2/9d) - 7/9)(2/9 + t^{2/3} \cdot 2/9d)^{-\frac{1}{2}}$
$|\epsilon(x)| < 2.5 \cdot 10^{-4}$

Similar approximations, available in statistical handbooks and the U.S. Bureau of Standards manuals of computer approximations, may be used to compute Chi-Square and F distributions.

Statistical Analysis

The statistical analysis program in Listing 3-2 has a wide range of applications in business, stock analysis, and the sciences. The program consists of six subprograms including statistics with one variable, statistics with two variables, area under a curve computation, and exponential smoothing calculations.

The first subprogram, statistics with one variable, is used to find basic descriptions for a set of data (that is the mean and the standard deviation). The second subprogram determines the linear regression for a set of (x,y) pairs. For example, the relationship between the price of a stock (x) to the Dow Jones Industrial Average (y) could be determined by inputting corresponding pairs of values. The third subprogram computes the area under a normal curve between two points. A normal curve is used to describe many phenomena; it is pictured and mathematically described above. The area under the curve is equal to one; the average of a set of data (x) is the point at which the curve peaks. If two values on the x axis are picked, the area under the curve between these two points is equal to the probability of a value being between those points; this subprogram computes the area, or probability, between two given points. The fourth subprogram computes the cumulative binomial probability for the occurrence of a given value. The fifth subprogram plots data described in subprogram one in simple bargraph format. This section could be improved to plot data on an x, y axis or to create a labeled histogram. The sixth subprogram exponentially smooths a set of data. Data values are entered, and an exponential function is used to predict future values. This smoothing constant should be adjusted so that the output error is minimized.

Listing 3-2: The Statistical Analysis Program

```
5 CLS
10 CLEAR 2000
20 PRINT "STATISTICAL ANALYSIS PROGRAM"
30 PRINT "FOR BUSINESS AND STOCK ANALYSIS"
40 DIM X(105),A(105),Y(105)
50 DIM Q(100,2),S(3,2)
60 PRINT "MENU:"
70 PRINT "1) STATISTICS FOR 1 VARIABLE"
80 PRINT "2) STATISTICS FOR 2 VARIABLES"
90 PRINT "3) AREA UNDER A CURVE COMPUTATION"
100 PRINT "4) CUMULATIVE BINOMIAL PROBABILITY CALCULATION"
110 PRINT "5) PLOT DATA"
120 PRINT "6) EXPONENTIAL SMOOTHING PROGRAM"
130 PRINT "7) END"
140 INPUT A:ON A GOTO 160,1010,710,1800,1960,2060,2370
150 GOTO 60
160 REM ONE VARIABLE CALCULATIONS
170 PRINT "ENTER SUCCESSIVE VALUES SEPARATELY, '9999' TO END"
180 D=1:C=0:B=0:E=0
190 INPUT A(D)
200 GOTO 230
210 INPUT A(D)
220 IF A(D)=9999 THEN 270
230 B=B+A(D)
240 C=C+A(D)*A(D)
250 D=D+1
260 GOTO 210
270 D=D-1:M=B/D
280 CLS
290 PRINT "NO. SCORES","SUM OF SCORES"
300 PRINT D,B
310 PRINT
320 FOR H=1 TO D
330 G=G+A(H)-M
340 SG=SG+(A(H)-M)*(A(H)-M)
350 NEXT H
360 SG=SG/(D-1):SG=SQR(SG)
370 PRINT "MEAN","VARIANCE","MEAN AVERAGE DEVIATION"
380 PRINT M,SG^2,SG,G
390 PRINT:PRINT "PROBABLE ERROR","COEFFICIENT OF VARIATION"
400 PRINT .6745*SG,,D/M
410 PRINT
```

```
420 PRINT "STANDARD ERROR FOR THE MEAN=";SQR(SG*SG/D)
430 PRINT
440 FOR I=1 TO D-1
450   FOR J=1 TO D-1
460     X=A(J):Y=A(J+1)
470     IF A(J)<=A(J+1) THEN 490
480     A(J)=Y:A(J+1)=X
490 NEXT J,I
500 INPUT "PRESS ENTER TO CONTINUE ",A$:CLS
510 PRINT "# MEASURE FREQ REL FREQ DEV FROM AVE DEV SQUARED STD
DEV"
520 J9=0
530 FOR J8=1 TO D
540   H=1
550   FR=1
560   J=1
570   IF A(J8)=A(J8+J) THEN FR=FR+1 ELSE 600
580   J=J+1
590   GOTO 570
600   J9=J9+1
610   A2$="## ####.### ######.##### ####.#### #######.### #####.
#####"
620   PRINT USING A2$;J9;A(J8);FR;FR*1/D;M-A(J8);(M-A(J8))*(M-A(J8)
);(A(J8)-M)/S G
630   IF FR>1 THEN J8=J8+FR-1
640   RM=RM+FR*A(J8)*A(J8)
650 NEXT J8
660 PRINT "HIGHEST SCORE","LOWEST SCORE"
670 PRINT A(D),A(1)
680 PRINT "ROOT MEAN SQUARE-";SQR(RM)
690 PRINT "THUS X=";M;" PLUS/MINUS";SG/SQR(D)
700 INPUT "TYPE ENTER TO CONTINUE";A$:GOTO 60
710 REM AREA UNDER NORMAL CURVE
720 PRINT "ENTER THE STANDARD Z VALUE ",BE
730 INPUT BE
740 PRINT
750 PRINT "X VALUE","AREA TO LEFT","AREA TO RIGHT"
760 A=BE
770 C=0:E=1:H=BE:D=0:G=BE*BE:F=.398942*EXP(-.5*G)
780 J=H/E
790 C=C+J:IF J/C<.000001 THEN 850
800 L=1:E=1:D=D+1:H=G*H
810 FOR K=1 TO D
820   E=E+2:L=L*E
830 NEXT K
840 E=L:GOTO 780
850 M=F*C+.5:N=1-M
860 PRINT A,M,N
870 GOTO 990
880 BE=BE/1.14142:O=BE*BE:P=EXP(-O)*.56419/BE:O=.5*O
890 P1=O*O:M=O*P:P2=0:P3=0
900 P5=1:P4=1
```

```
910  P2=P2+2
920  IF P3=P THEN 950 ELSE P3=P
930  P=P5:P4=0*P4*(P2-1)+P5:M=P2*M*P1*(P2+1)
940  GOTO 910
950  P6=P*.5:Q=1-P6
960  PRINT A,Q,P6
970  BE=A+10
980  GOTO 760
990  PRINT
1000 GOTO 60
1010 D=1:PRINT "REGRESSION AND CORRELATION ANALYSIS":PRINT
1020 PRINT "ENTER X,Y VALUES AS PAIRS SEPARATED BY COMMAS"
1030 PRINT "ENTER 9999,9999 WHEN DONE"
1040 INPUT X(D),Y(D)
1050 IF X(D)=9999 AND Y(D)=9999 THEN 1100
1060 Q9=Q9+X(D):R9=R9+Y(D)
1070 Q8=Q8+X(D)*X(D):R8=R8+Y(D)*Y(D)
1080 R6=R6+X(D)*Y(D):D=D+1
1090 GOTO 1040
1100 D=D-1:N=D:Q7=Q9/D:R7=R9/D
1110 A9=Q8-Q9*Q7:A8=R8-R9*R7
1120 B9=R6-Q9*R7:B8=B9/A9:B7=R7-B8*G7
1130 A7=A8-B8*B9:A6=A7/(D-2)
1140 FOR I=1 TO N
1150    B(I)=Y(I):A(I)=X(I)
1160 NEXT I
1170 GOSUB 1640
1180 PRINT
1190 PRINT "AVE. OF X","AVE. OF Y"
1200 PRINT A1,A2
1210 PRINT "STD. DEV X","STD DEV Y"
1220 PRINT D1,D2
1230 PRINT "CORRELATION COEFFICIENT X-Y:";C9
1240 PRINT:A9=A2
1250 INPUT "PRESS ENTER WHEN READY ";Z9$
1260 PRINT "THE FOLLOWING EQUATIONS EXPRESS THE X,Y RELATIONSHIPS"
1270 PRINT:PRINT "EQUATION 1"
1280 PRINT "Y=";S9;"X+";I9
1290 PRINT "% ACCURACY OF Y VARIANCE DESCRIPTION=";P9
1300 PRINT "Y-INTERCEPT=";I9
1310 PRINT "SLOPE=";S9
1320 PRINT "F-RATIO=";S9/(A6/(D-2))
1330 PRINT
1340 FOR I=1 TO D
1350    IF X(I)<=0 THEN 1420
1360    A(I)=LOG(X(I))
1370 NEXT I
1380 GOSUB 1640
1390 PRINT:PRINT "EQUATION 2"
1400 PRINT "Y=";S9;"*LOG X+";I9
1410 PRINT "% ACCURACY OF DESCRIPTION";P9:PRINT
1420 FOR I=1 TO N
```

```
1430    A(I)=X(I):IF Y(I)<=0 THEN 1540
1440 B(I)=LOG(Y(I))
1450 NEXT I
1460 GOSUB 1640
1470 GOSUB 1730
1480 PRINT
1490 INPUT "PRESS ENTER WHEN READY ",Z9$
1500 PRINT "EQUATION 3"
1510 PRINT "LOG Y=";S9;"*X+";I9:PRINT "OR"
1520 PRINT "Y=";EXP(S9);"^X+";EXP(I9)
1530 PRINT "% ACCURACY OF DESCRIPTION";P9
1540 FOR I=1 TO N
1550    IF A(I)<=0 THEN 1780 ELSE A(I)=LOG(X(I))
1560 NEXT I
1570 GOSUB 1640
1580 GOSUB 1730
1590 PRINT "EQUATION 4"
1600 PRINT "LOG Y=";S9;"*LOG X+";I9:PRINT "OR"
1610 PRINT "Y=";EXP(I9);"*X^";S9
1620 PRINT "% ACCURACY DESCRIPTION";P9
1630 GOTO 1780
1640 S1=0:S2=0:S3=0:S4=0:S5=0:FOR I=1 TO N
1650    S1=S1+A(I):S2=S2+B(I):S3=S3+A(I)*A(I)
1660    S4=S4+B(I)*B(I):S5=S5+A(I)*B(I)
1670 NEXT I
1680 A1=S1/N:A2=S2/N:V1=(S3-(D*(A1*A1)))/(N-1)
1690 V2=(S4-(D*(A2*A2)))/(N-1):D1=SQR(V1)
1700 D2=SQR(ABS(V2)):DO=N*S3-S1*S1:I9=((S2*S3)-(S1*S5))/DO
1710 S9=((N*S5)-(S1*S2))/DO:P9=((S9*S9)*V1)/V2:C9=SQR(P9)
1720 P9=100*P9:RETURN
1730 S7=0:S8=0
1740 FOR I=1 TO N
1750    E=EXP(I9+S9*A(I)):S8=S8+(Y(I)-E)^2:S7=S7+(Y(I)-A9)^2
1760 NEXT I
1770 P9=100*(1-S8/S7):RETURN
1780 INPUT "PRESS ENTER WHEN READY ",Z9$
1790 GOTO 60
1800 REM CUMULATIVE BINOMIAL PROBABILITIES
1810 F=0
1820 INPUT "ENTER THE # SUCCESSES, # TRIALS (F(Y,N,P)),PROB
SUCCESS/TRIAL";Y,N,P
1830 S1=1:FOR I=1 TO N
1840 S1=S1*I:NEXT I
1850 FOR X=0 TO Y
1860    S2=1:S3=1
1870    FOR I=1 TO X
1880    S2=S2*I:NEXT I
1890    FOR I=1 TO N-X
1900    S3=S3*I:NEXT I
1910    F=F+S1/(S2*S3)*P^X*(1-P)^(N-X)
1920 NEXT X
1930 PRINT "THE CUMULATIVE BINOMIAL PROBABILITY=";F
```

```
1940 PRINT "FOR F(Y;N,,P) WHERE Y=";Y;", N=";N;", P=";P
1950 GOTO 60
1960 CLS
1970 PRINT "---------------------------------------------------"
1980 DX=55/A(D)
1990 FOR X=D TO 1 STEP -1
2000    IF A(X)=A(X-1) THEN GOTO 2030
2010    A$="####.##":PRINT USING A$;A(X);:PRINT "I";
2020    PRINT STRING$(DX*A(X),"+")
2030 NEXT X
2040 PRINT "---------------------------------------------------"
2050 GOTO 60
2060 REM EXPONENTIAL SMOOTHING
2070 DEFDBL Q,S
2080 GOSUB 2120
2090 GOSUB 2160
2100 GOSUB 2270
2110 GOTO 60
2120 INPUT "ENTER SMOOTHING CONSTANT(0-1)";A
2130 INPUT "ENTER PREDICTION PERIOD LENGTH ",T
2140 INPUT "ENTER THE FIRST DATA SET (9999 TO END)",Q(1,1):Q(2,2)
=Q(1,1)
2150 S(1,0)=Q(1,1):S(2,0)=Q(1,1):S(3,0)=Q(1,1):N=2:RETURN
2160 REM
2170 PRINT N;:INPUT Q(N,1)
2180 IF Q(N,1)=9999 THEN 2260
2190 S(1,1)=A*Q(N,1)+(1-A)*S(1,0):S(2,1)=(1-A)*S(2,0)+S(1,1)*A
2200 S(3,1)=(1-A)*S(3,0)+S(2,1)*A:P1=6*(1-A)*(1-A)+(6-5*A)*A*T+
(A*T)*(A*T)
2210 P2=S(1,1)/(2*(1-A)*(1-A)):P3=6*(1-A)*(1-A)+2*(5-4*A)*A*T+2*
(A*T)*(A*T)
2220 P4=S(2,1)/(2*(1-A)*(1-A))
2230 P5=2*(1-A)^2+(4-3*A)*A*T+(A*T)^2:P6=S(3,1)/(2*(1-A)*(1-A))
2240 Q(N+1,2)=P1*P2-P3*P4+P5*P6:S(1,0)=S(1,1):S(2,0)=S(2,1)
2250 S(3,0)=S(3,1):N=N+1:GOTO 2170
2260 RETURN
2270 PRINT:PRINT "PERIOD OBSERVATION PREDICTION ERROR"
2280 PRINT 1;Q(1,1)
2290    A$="####.##"
2300 FOR J=2 TO N-1
2310    PRINT USING A$;J;Q(J,1);Q(J,2);Q(J,2)-Q(J,1)
2320    IF J/12<>INT(J/12) THEN 2350
2330 PRINT:INPUT "PRESS ENTER TO CONTINUE ",A$
2340 CLS:PRINT "PERIOD OBSERVATION PREDICTION ERROR"
2350 NEXT J
2360 GOTO 60
2370 END
```

MATHEMATICS

Personal computers can be called upon to perform all of the following:

• Solution of quadratic and cubic equations: given the coefficients of either a quadratic or cubic equation, a program could solve for both real and complex roots; equations of degrees could also be solved for.

- Roots of f(x): a program could find the roots of a user-defined function using the bisection method or Newton's method.
- Vector operations: given two vectors in two dimensions, a program could calculate their magnitudes, the angle between them, and their dot and cross products.

The program in Listing 3-3 calculates the sum of two vectors.

- Triangle solution: for a triangle with three known "variables," the lengths of the sides, the angles between sides, and the area could be computed.
- Curve solution: the arc length, central angle, radius, chord length, and tangent length for a curve could be calculated given two known parts; the area enclosed by these parts could also be calculated.
- Arithmetic, geometric, and harmonic progressions: a table of elements for the above three progressions could be generated. The element and the sum of the first n elements could also be determined.
- Factors of integers, GCD, LCM: the prime factors of an integer, the greatest common divisor (GCD), and the least common multiple (LCM) of two integers could be determined.

- Function value table: a useful program could print the values for a user-defined function over a specified interval.
- Prime number table: a table of prime numbers or a test for primes in a specified interval could be generated.
- Partial sums and products: the partial sum or product of a user-defined function could be computed.
- Interpolation between known values: Lagrange polynomial interpolation, or the Newton divided difference method may be performed to interpolate values of a function.
- Gaussian integration: the integral of a user-defined function can be determined by Gaussian quadrature.
- Solutions of differential equations: first-order differential equations may be solved by a program using the Runge Kutta method; a step size may be determined to yield results within a specific error tolerance.
- Polynomial arithmetic: addition, subtraction, multiplication, and division of polynomials may be accomplished.
- Polynomial evaluation: a polynomial $(P_x) = a_0 + a_1 x + a_2 x^2 + \ldots + a_n x^n$ may be evaluated at a point x with complex coefficients. The program in Listing 3-4 evaluates a polynomial expression

---

Listing 3-3: The Vector Addition Program

```
10 REM VECTOR ADDITION
20 INPUT "INPUT THE DATA FOR THE FIRST VECTOR IN THIS FORM: MAGNITUDE,ANGLE ",M1
,A1
30 X1=M1*COS(A1)
40 Y1=M1*SIN(A1)
50 INPUT "INPUT THE DATA FOR THE SECOND VECTOR IN THE SAME FORMAT. ",M2,A2
60 X2=M2*COS(AS)
70 Y2=M2*SIN(A2)
80 X=X1+X2:Y=Y1+Y2
90 A=ATN(Y/X)
100 M=SQR(X*X+Y*Y)
110 PRINT "NEW VECTOR MAGNITUDE=";M;"UNITS"
120 PRINT "AT AN ANGLE OF ";A;"DEGREES."
130 PRINT "(X,Y,) COORDINATE AT ENDPOINT=(";X;",";Y;")."
140 PRINT
150 END
```

Listing 3-4: The Polynomial Evaluation Program

```
100 REM POLYNOMIAL EVALUATION PROGRAM
110 REM COMPUTES VALUE AT A GIVEN PT. & 1ST AND 2ND DERIVATIVES
120 DIM B(50),Z(509),C(50,2)
130 LET E=0
140 PRINT "ENTER THE DEGREE OF THE POLYNOMIAL";
150 INPUT X
160 PRINT "ENTER THE COEFFICIENTS SEPARATELY";
170 FOR D=0 TO X
180    INPUT B(D)
190 NEXT D
200 PRINT "ENTER THE NO. OF VALUES TO BE EVALUATED"
210 INPUT N:N1=N
220 PRINT "ENTER THE POINTS SEPARATELY";
230 FOR D=1 TO N
240    INPUT Z(D)
250 NEXT D
260 GOSUB 340
270 GOSUB 450
280 E=E+1
290 GOSUB 340
300 GOSUB 450
310 E=E+1
320 GOSUB 340
330 GOTO 500
340 FOR F=1 TO N1
350    N=Z(F)
360    GOSUB 400
370    C(F,E)=H
380 NEXT F
390 RETURN
400 H=0
410 FOR D=0 TO X
420    H=B(D)+N*H
430 NEXT D
440 RETURN
450 FOR D=0 TO X
460    B(D)=(X-D)*B(D)
470 NEXT D
480 X=X-1
490 RETURN
500 PRINT
510 PRINT   "PT OF EVAL.","EVAL.","DER1","DER2"
520 PRINT
530 FOR F=1 TO N1
540    PRINT Z(F),C(F,0),C(F,1),C(F,2)
550 NEXT F
560 PRINT
570 END
```

at a given point and determines the first and second deviatives.

- Polynomial root finding: Barstow's method is well suited for computer evaluation of quadric factors for polynomials of degree n.
- Complex arithmetic: addition, subtraction, multiplication, division, squares, inverses, and so on may be performed using complex numbers.
- Complex trigonometric functions: common trigonometric functions may be evaluated using complex numbers.
- Base conversions: a useful program could transform numbers of any real base to another base.
- Graphing calculations: the intervals to use for proportional axes given the minimum/maximum values and number of major divisions could be calculated and used for plotting data manually or with a plotter/printer. Additionally, conversion routines between radians, quadrants, revolutions, and degrees could be provided.
- Coordinate conversion between rectangular and polar equivalents may be computed with these formulae:

$$r = \sqrt{x^2 + y^2}$$
$$A = \text{arctangent } (y/x)$$
$$x = r \cdot \text{cosine } (A)$$
$$y = r \cdot \text{sine } (A)$$

where: x = abscissa $\Big\}$ Cartesian coordinates
$\quad\quad\; y$ = ordinate

$\quad\quad\; r$ = magnitude of ray $\Big\}$ Polar coordinates
$\quad\quad\; A$ = angle (in degrees)

The Solution of Simultaneous Equation

The small computer can be used to find the solution to a set of simultaneous equations. This mathematical operation has applications in many areas including business and science. An example of two equations to be solved simultaneously follows:

$$5X = 4Y + 24$$
$$2.5Y = 6X - 4$$

If the equations are solved simultaneously, a value will be found for X and Y such that both equations will be correct. The number of simultaneous equations that can be solved by the program in Listing 3-5 is limited only by the available memory in the computer.

Integral Evaluation

Among the many methods used for computer evaluation of integrals is Simpson's Rule:

$$\int_a f(x)dx \sim h/3[f(a)+4f(a+h)+2f(a+2h)+4f \\ (a+3h)+ \ldots +2f(a+(n-2)h)+4f \\ (a+(n-1)h)+f(b)]$$

where $h = \dfrac{b-a}{n}$ and n = number of iterations

(as n increases, accuracy increases)

The trapezoidal approximation is another algorithm used with computers.

Listing 3-5: The Dimultaneous Equation Solver Program

```
100 REM SIMULTANEOUS EQUATION SOLVER
110 REM NO. OF VARIABLES=NO. OF EQNS.
120 REM THERE MUST BE MORE THAN 1 EQN.
130 REM THE ARRAYS MAY BE REDIMENTIONED TO
140 REM ACCOMMODATE ANY NO. OF EQUATIONS
150 REM LIMITED ONLY BY AVAILABLE MEMORY
160 DIM M(30,30),P(30),L(30)
170 INPUT "ENTER NO. OF VARIABLES ",Z
180 FOR E=1 TO Z:FOR D=1 TO Z
```

```
190     PRINT "EQUATION #";E;", VARIABLE #";D;
200     INPUT M(E,D)
210   NEXT D:PRINT "CONSTANT FOR EQN #";E;
220 INPUT L(E):NEXT E
230 FOR E=1 TO Z-1
240   L=ABS(M(E,E)):B=E
250   FOR D=E+1 TO Z
260     IF ABS(M(D,E))<L THEN 280
270     B=D:L=ABS(M(D,E))
280   NEXT D
290   IF L=0 THEN 550
300   IF B=E THEN 390
310   FOR D=1 TO Z
320     G=M(B,D)
330     M(B,D)=M(E,D)
340     M(E,D)=G
350   NEXT D
360   V=L(B)
370   L(B)=L(E)
380   L(E)=V
390   FOR D=E+1 TO Z
400     T=M(D,E)/M(E,E)
410     FOR C=E+1 TO Z
420       M(D,C)=M(D,C)-T*M(E,C)
430     NEXT C
440     L(D)=L(D)-T*L(E)
450   NEXT D
460 NEXT E
470 IF M(Z,Z)=0 THEN 550
480 E=Z-1:P(Z)=L(Z)/M(Z,Z)
490 U=0:FOR D=E+1 TO Z
500   U=U+M(E,D)*P(D)
510 NEXT D
520 P(E)=(L(E)-U)/M(E,E)
530 E=E-1:IF E>0 THEN 490
540 GOTO 570
550 PRINT:PRINT "EQNS ARE UNSOLVABLE"
560 GOTO 610
570 PRINT:PRINT
580 FOR E=1 TO Z
590   PRINT "VARIABLE #";E;"=";P(E)
600 NEXT E:PRINT
610 INPUT "TRY AGAIN (1=YES,2=NO)";N
620 PRINT:PRINT
630 IF N=1 THEN PRINT:GOTO 170 ELSE END
```

Plotting Mathematical Functions

With a little ingenuity, the TAB function may be used to produce crude plots of trigonometric and other functions. Try this "one-liner"

```
10   FOR X=0 TO 6.28 STEP .25:PRINT
TAB (SIN(X)*30+30);"*":NEXT X
```

The plotter program. The program in Listing 3-6 is a general purpose plotting routine designed for use with a printer. Three types of plots may be made: two-dimensional, three-dimensional, and simultaneous plots. Lines 40-80 explain how functions to be plotted are to be entered into the program.

Listing 3-6: The Plotter Program

```
10 REM PLOTTER
20 REM PLOT FUNCTIONS IN 2D,3D OR SIMULTANEOUSLY
30 REM ROTATE OUTPUT 90 DEGREES FOR ACTUAL PLOT
40 PRINT "IF THE FUNCTIONS DEFINED IN LINES 690,710,730 ARE TO"
50 PRINT "BE CHANGED, STOP THE PROGRAM AND ENTER FUNCTIONS IN THIS FORMAT:"
60 PRINT "FUNCT. #1- 690 Y=SIN(X) (Y IN TERMS OF X)"
70 PRINT "FUNCT. #2- 710 Y1=COS(X) (Y1 IN TERMS OF X)(Y1 IN TERMS OF X- FOR SIMU
L. PLOT"
80 PRINT "FUNCT. #3- 730 Z=EXP(Z) (Z IN TERMS OF Z- FOR 3D PLOTS"
90 PRINT
100 PRINT
110 PRINT
120 PRINT "SELECT: 1) 2D PLOT, 2),3D PLOT, 3) END"
130 INPUT A
140 ON A GOTO 160,420,150
150 END
160 PRINT "SELECT: 1)PLOT 1 FUNCTION, 2)PLOT 2 FUNCTIONS SIMULTANEOUSLY"
170 INPUT A
180 F1=A
190 PRINT "ENTER MIN. X VALUE, MAX. X VALUE, X INCREMENT (SEPARATED BY
COMMAS)";
200 INPUT E,F,D
210 PRINT "ENTER MIN. Y VALUE, MAX. Y VALUE";
220 INPUT H,G
230 Y1=40/(G-H)
240 PRINT "Y MIN:";H;" Y MAX:";G;" INCREMENT:";Y1
250 PRINT
260 PRINT TAB(5)H;TAB(56);G
270 FOR B=1 TO 58
280    PRINT "+";
290 NEXT B
300 PRINT
310 A$="####.##"
320 FOR X=E TO F STEP D
330    PRINT USING A$;X;:PRINT ":";
340    GOSUB 690
350    IF F1=1 THEN 390
360    GOSUB 710
370    IF Y>Y1 THEN PRINT  TAB(9+(INT(10*Y1*Y1)))"*";TAB(9+(INT(10*Y*Y1)))"#" ELS
E PRINT TAB(9+(INT(10*Y*Y1)));"#";TAB(9+(INT(10*Y1*Y1)))"*"
380 GOTO 400
390 PRINT TAB(9+INT(10*Y*Y1));"*"
400 NEXT X
410 GOTO 120
```

```
420 REM 3D PLOT ROUTINE
430 A$="*"
440 E=5
450 V=25
460 G=.707106
470 C=961
480 PRINT "ENTER X INCREMENT";
490 INPUT IN
500 FOR X=-31 TO 31 STEP IN
510    A=0
520    B=1
530    D1=E*INT(SQR(C-X*X)/E)
540    FOR Y=D1 TO -D1 STEP -E
550       Z=SQR(X*X+Y*Y)
560       GOSUB 730
570       Z=INT(V+Z-G*Y)
580       IF A$="*" THEN A$="+" ELSE A$="*"
590       IF Z<=A THEN GOTO 650
600       A=Z
610       IF Z=F THEN IF A$="*" THEN A$="+" ELSE A$="*"
620       PRINT TAB(Z)A$;
630       IF B=0 THEN LET F=Z
640       B=0
650    NEXT Y
660    PRINT ""
670 NEXT X
680 GOTO 120
690 Y=ABS(SIN(X))
700 RETURN
710 Y1=ABS(COS(X))
720 RETURN
730 Z=30*(EXP(-Z*Z/100)):RETURN
740 RETURN
```

Determining the Equation of a Line

The program in Listing 3-7 accepts (x, y) data points and uses linear regression to determine the equation of the line that best fits (describes) the data. Applications are numerous. For instance, if you were on a weight-loss plan and inputted values for your weight versus amount of exercise or calorie intake, the program could find the equation of a line that best fits this data. Thus, you could input a value for one variable (for example, calorie intake) and receive a corresponding value (for example, weight) for the other variable. Other areas that could be analyzed include stock price versus Dow Index, miles traveled versus gallons used, distance versus time, and heating costs versus outside temperature. This program uses the *least squares* method of linear regression.

Solving for Corresponding Values

Given two points of a line linear interpolation can be used to solve for y values corresponding to a given x value. Although this method is not as accurate as the least squares linear regression method, it can be used in situations in which the correlation coefficient is high.

$$y = y_1 + \frac{(y_2 - y_1) \cdot (x - x_1)}{(x_2 - x_1)}$$

Listing 3-7: The Line Equation Calculator Program

```
1 REM LINE EQUATION CALCULATOR
2 REM MAY BE USED TO DESCRIBE A SET OF DATA
3 REM AND DETERMINE A CORRESPONDING POINT FOR
4 REM ANY ENTERED POINT
5 CLS        'CLEAR SCREEN
10 INPUT "ENTER A NAME FOR THE FIRST SET OF DATA ",A$
20 INPUT "ENTER A NAME FOR THE SECOND SET OF DATA ",B$
72 PRINT "ENTER X,Y PAIRS SUCCESSIVELY, SEPARATED BY COMMAS"
75 PRINT "ENTER 0,0 TO END"
76 N=1
80 INPUT X,Y
90 IF (X=0) AND (Y=0) THEN 200
110 N=N+1
120 PRINT "SET NO.:";N
130 A=A+X
140 B=B+X*X
150 C=C+Y*Y
160 D=D+Y
170 E=E+X*Y
180 GOTO 80
190 N=N-1:M=(E*N-D*A)/(B*N/A*A)
200 N=N-1:M=(E*N-D*A)/(B*N/A*A)
210 V=(D*B-E*A)/(B*N-A*A)
220 CLS
230 PRINT "Y=";M;"X+";V
240 PRINT "ENTER A VALUE FOR ";A$;" TO RECEIVE A CORRESPONDING"
250 PRINT "VALUE FOR ";B$
260 INPUT "ENTER 9999 IF YOU WANT VICE-VERSA ",A
270 IF A=9999 THEN GOTO 350
280 PRINT
290 PRINT "Y=";M*A+V
300 GOTO 240
350 REM
390 CLS
400 PRINT:PRINT "X=";-1/M;"*Y+";V/M
419 PRINT "ENTER A VALUE FOR ";B$;" TO RECEIVE A CORRESPONDING"
429 PRINT "VALUE FOR ";A$
439 PRINT "ENTER 9999 FOR VICE-VERSA "
449 INPUT A
460 IF A=9999 THEN 350
470 PRINT "THE VALUE FOR X=";(A-V)/M
480 PRINT
490 GOTO 419
```

where: x_1, y_1 = coordinates of first point on the line

x_2, y_2 = coordinates of second point on the line

x = absicissa of point to be interpolated

y = ordinate of the point on the line with x

Computer Calculus

Long perceived as merely number crunchers, computers are now moving into the realm of elegant mathematics. Computer algebra programs are now available for personal computers. These programs can manipulate abstract symbolic mathematical expressions and have the ability to do virtually everything taught in the first two years of university mathematics. They can factor polynomials, simplify expressions, differentiate functions, solve equations, expand functions into a Taylor series, invert matrices, and even integrate functions, as a coup de grace. An outgrowth of the MACSYMA program developed on large mainframe computers, muMath is a rewritten version capable of running on virtually any Z80 or 8080 microcomputer. A simplified version (called Picomath) has also been written in BASIC to run on just about any personal computer. Both programs are marketed by the Microsoft Corporation, 10700 Northup Way, Bellevue, WA 98004, and should be seriously considered for purchase by professionals who must have reliable solutions to mathematical problems and by students of mathematics. Examples of symbolic computer algebra produced by the muMath program appear below, and demonstrate that their programs are approaching true artificial intelligence capabilities:

Factor $x^{25} + 1$:

$$(x - 1) (x^4 - x^3 + x^2 - x + 1)(x^{20} - x^{15} + x^{10} - x^5 + 1)$$

Integrate $\dfrac{2x}{x^3 + 1}$:

$$2 \frac{\log\ (x^2 - x + 1)}{6} - \frac{\log\ (abs(x + a))}{3}$$

$$\frac{atan\ \left(\dfrac{2x - 1}{\sqrt{3}}\right)}{\sqrt{3}}$$

Expand $\displaystyle\prod_{n\ =\ 1}^{\infty} (1 - x^n)^{24}$

$$x - 24x^2 + 252x^3 - 1472x^4 + 4730x^5 + \ldots$$

Determinant of $\begin{bmatrix} x^3 & x^2 & x & 1 \\ y^3 & y^2 & y & 1 \\ z^3 & z^2 & z & 1 \\ w^3 & w^2 & w & 1 \end{bmatrix}$

$$- (k{-}w)\ (y{-}w)\ (y{-}x)\ (z{-}w)\ (z{-}x)\ (z{-}y)$$

Calculate 30!
265252859812191058636308480000000000

MATHEMATICAL RECREATIONS AND PROGRAMMING CHALLENGES

Interesting mathematical problems and ideas to implement on your computer include the following.

Using probability to forecast the outcome of a sporting event. For example, an equation expressing the probability that a stronger team will win in a seven game series is

$$p^4 + 4p^4q + 10p^3q^2\ x + 10p^2q^2(1{-}x)p$$

where p = probability that stronger team will win ($\geq$.5)

q = probability that weaker team will win (=1−p)

x = conditional probability particular to a sport for example, for basketball this value has been calculated to be = .408)

For further information see *Mathematics Magazine,* Sept.-Oct. 1975, pp. 187-192.

The program in Listing 3-8 can help in predicting the outcome of the World Series (or other seven-game series) if you can estimate (that is, guess) the probability of a given team winning each of the seven games based upon such factors as game location, opposing pitchers, and other rational or irrational hunches. For further discussion consult "The World Series Competition," Journal of the *American Statistical Association* 47, Sept. 1952, pp. 335-80.

Listing 3-8: The World Series Predictor Program

```
10 REM WORLD SERIES PREDICTOR
20 RANDOMIZE(VAL(RIGHT$(DATE$,2)))
25 DIM P(20),F(20),T(20),G(20)
30 PRINT "ENTER THE GAME PROBABILITIES FOR ALL SEVEN GAMES"
40 PRINT "IN DECIMAL FORM (E.G. USE .40 FOR 40%)"
50 REM THE USER MUST DETERMINE INDIVIDUAL GAME PROBABILITIES
55 REM (NATIONAL VS. AMERICAN LEAGUE)
60 REM ON THE BASIS OF PITCHERS, HUNCHES, WHERE PLAYED, ETC.
65 REM PROGRAM DETERMINES OUTCOME OF A 1000 GAME SERIES TO
66 REM PREDICT THE SERIES OUTCOME
70 FOR X=1 TO 7:INPUT P(X):NEXT X
74 PRINT "WAIT WHILE I PLAY 1000 GAMES"
75 PRINT
80 N=0:A=0:FOR X=1 TO 7:IF RND<P(X) THEN 100
90 A=A+1:IF A=4 THEN 140 ELSE 110
100 N=N+1:IF N=4 THEN 170
110 NEXT X
140 A1=A1+1:G(N+A)=G(N+A)+1:GOTO 190
170 N1=N1+1:F(N+A)=F(N+A)+1
190 T(N+A)=T(N+A)+1
200 IF N1+A1<1000 THEN 80
210 PRINT "SERIES #","TOTAL","NATIONAL","AMERICAN"
220 FOR X=4 TO 7:PRINT X,T(X),F(X),G(X)
230 NEXT X:PRINT ,"_____","_____","_____"
240 PRINT "TOTALS:","1000",N1,A1:PRINT
245 PRINT "SIMULATED 1000 GAME SERIES RESULTS ABOVE":PRINT
250 PRINT "AVE. LENGTH OF SERIES IS ";(4*T(4)+5*T(5)+6*T(6)+7*T(7))/1000
260 END
```

Solving mathematical puzzles. Puzzles such as the following can probably be solved with the use of brute-force, trial and error computer techniques only—if they can be solved at all:

- Find three distinct right triangles with the following properties:

    A. Are pythagorean (all three sides are integers)

    B. The perimeters of the three triangles are equivalent

    C. The areas of the triangles are in arithmetic progression

- Find the smallest solution in positive integers x and y of $x^2 - n \cdot y^2 = 1$ where n = 61

- Find how many ways the integer 10,000 can be expressed as a sum of distinct positive integers (ignoring permutations).

- Find the minimum value of the gamma function. gamma $(n)=(n-1)!$

    for an integer n in the range $1< n <2$.

Puzzles that are simpler to solve include such popular logic games as

- Instant Insanity™ blocks: five blocks with different colors on each side must be arranged so that all five blocks in a row have the same colors on each side. The computer could determine all possible solutions. (7,962,624 possible combinations exist and there are 192 solutions.)

- The High I.Q. Game consists of a board in the shape of a cross with markers in every hole except the center hole. The player jumps markers with adjacent markers as in checkers and then removes the one jumped over. Markers may not be moved unless a jump is possible. The object of the game is to jump all the markers on the board, leaving only one final marker; this is difficult to accomplish. The computer could determine the strategy for winning the game and the number of different ways possible to win (is there only one method?). A mathematical analysis of this game appeared in *The Journal of Recreational Mathematics,* Vol. 5, No. 2, 1972 pp. 133-. The triangular version was discussed in *The Mathematics Teacher,* January 1979, pp. 53-.

Computing Pi, e, solutions for high-degree equations, and mathematical oddities. Many mathematicians take delight in computing values for irrational expressions, determining equations for special mathematical circumstances, and discovering unusual properties of specific numbers. The computer is, of course, useful in such computations.

Calculation of the value of Pi to any number of decimal places can be accomplished by the BASIC program in Listing 3-9.

Pi can be calculated using this successive approximation:

$$\pi = 4 - 4/3 + 4/5 - 4/7 + 4/9 - 4/11 + \ldots$$

Similarly, the value of the natural log e may be calculated using this successive approximation:

$$e^x = 1 + x + \frac{x^2}{2!} + \frac{x^3}{3!} + \frac{x^4}{4!} + \ldots$$

Programs to compute a Fibonacci Sequence are also popular. The sequence is created by adding each previous term to the term before that:

1, 1, 2, 3, 5, 8, 13 . . .

Sunflower and daisy florets, pinecones, pineapples, the shells of some mollusks, and even patterns of paving stones and the mating habits of bees and rabbits exhibit properties given by the Fibonacci Sequence. For instance, the seeds of sunflowers and daisies form a pattern of two sets of spirals, one clockwise and the other counterclockwise. The numbers of spirals in the two sets are usually consecutive Fibonacci numbers (for example 34 and 55).

Playing games. Interesting mathematical games for your computer include the following:

- The four color map problem: a recreation that has interested mathematicians for many years is to prove that only four colors are needed to copy any map in such a manner that no bordering countries

---

Listing 3-9: The Pi Calculation Program

```
1 REM PI CALCULATION PROGRAM
2 REM DEMONSTRATES ITERATIVE TECHNIQUES (REQUIRES 30,000
3 REM LOOPS TO CALCULATE TO FIVE DECIMAL PLACES.)
5 DEFINT D
10 S=0:V=-1:R=1
11 FOR D=1 TO 10000
20    L=10000
30    T=2*R-1
40    V=-1*V
50    S=S+V/T
60    N=N+1:R=R+1
70    L=L+10000:IF L>110000! GOTO 30
80    PRINT N,4*S
90 NEXT D
100 END
```

are of the same color. The proof was accomplished by a large-scale, brute-force computer program.

A game based on this fact could involve two players who attempt to force each other to color two bordering countries the same color. In each turn, a player would choose any color to apply to any country on a map with random boundaries. Proper logic will ensure that one player will lose. The computer could serve as one of the opponents.

- Magic squares game: the magic squares game pits the computer against a human in an attempt to complete a magic square while blocking an opponent. A magic square is composed of smaller squares, each with a separate number inside. The numbers in the smaller squares in horizontal, vertical, and diagonal rows sum to the same amount. Opposing players could attempt to complete a magic square in opposing directions.
- Maze games: maze games involve a randomly generated maze and a computer controlled mouse that learns to find its way through the maze.
- Exacto: this game for young people involves two five-digit numbers that have been randomly selected by the computer. Players are instructed to transform the first number into the second through multiplication, division, addition, or subtraction of any other number within a specified range. The computer would keep track of all computations at each stage. The players are scored according to speed or number of operations required to finish.
- Euclid: in this game (p,q) represents a pair of positive numbers such that p is greater than q; A and B signify the two players. Players alternate turns. Each turn consists of replacing the larger of the two numbers given to a player by any positive number obtained by subtracting a positive multiple of the smaller number from the larger number. (All numbers are integers). The first player to obtain zero for the (new) smaller number is declared the winner.

A sample game is shown below; (51,30) is the starting pair of numbers.

A:(30,21) B:(21,9) A:(9,3) B:(3,0)   B wins

or the game could have been

A:(30,21) B:(21,9) A: (12, 9) B:(9,3)
A:(3,9)   A wins

- The Two Move Game: in the first half of this game, the two players secretly enter four non-negative numbers totaling the same number into the cells of a 2 by 2 matrix:

$$x1 \quad x2 \quad y1 \quad y2$$
$$x3 \quad x4 \quad y3 \quad y4$$

The entries are then exposed and a third 2 by 2 matrix is developed in which the entries are $x_i y_i$. This final matrix is then analyzed by the first player who chooses a column and tries to maximize. The second player then chooses a row and tries to maximize. The player with the greatest variation wins. A mathematical strategy exists to win this game; can you find it?

- Sim: the game of Sim involves a gameboard like this:

```
           x       x
       x               x
           x       x
```

The players take alternate turns drawing lines between two points. The first player to draw an equilateral triangle or square loses. A mathematical strategy exists to win this game.
- Life: this popular computer recreation was devised by John Conway, a mathematician at Cambridge University. It simulates an ecological system and illustrates the rise, fall, and changes of a society of living organisms as they interact with their environment and each other. The game begins with a small population of organisms; as time progresses (measured in terms of generations), the population experiences one of three fates: it dies out due to over or underpopulation, it becomes stable, or it oscillates in a repeating

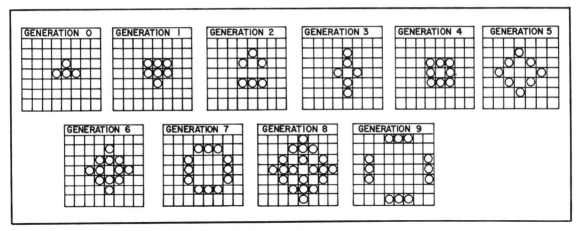

Fig. 3-1. The course of a Life population through nine generations.

pattern. Each member of the population has one of three fates during each generation. It can die from "starvation," give birth to another organism, or survive in a stable form.

The game board is a grid of arbitrary size, often larger than 20 × 20. Each square on the grid may be occupied by one organism or empty. Thus, each organism always has eight surrounding squares. It will die if it touches fewer than two or more than three occupied squares. If three occupied squares touch an empty square, a new occupant is born to fill that square. Births and deaths are evaluated simultaneously.

When the game of Life is written in machine language, it will progress at speeds faster than one generation per second and can create a fascinating display of computer graphics. The course of a population through the first few generations is shown in Fig. 3-1.

Computing probabilities. You could use your computer to calculate the following probabilities.

- Poker Probabilities: you could compute the probability that m * n cards held by a defender in a bridge hand will be split m and n, or the probabilities for obtaining a certain hand in poker after certain cards have been played.
- Birthdays: in a classroom of 24 students, how many would you estimate have the same birthday? The chances are slightly better than even

that 2 or more students will have birthdays on the same date, counter to our intuition! For a given number of people, x, the percent chance that 2 or more will have the same birthday is given by

$$\% \text{ chance} = 100 - 100 \cdot \left(\frac{365-x}{365}\right)$$

Write a BASIC program to calculate the percent chance of coincident birthdays for any input of x, the number of people in the group considered.

- An Apocalyptic Possibility: an equation expressing the probability of an accidental nuclear missile launch by the United States or the Soviet Union falsely triggering World War III is as follows:

$$PA = 1-(1-P)^{(N(U+S)}$$

where PA=Probability of the Apocalypse (for percent chance, multiply PA•100)
U=total number of strategic missiles in the U.S. arsenal (2000 est.)
S=Total number of strategic missiles in the Soviet arsenal (2300 est.)
P=Probability of accidental launching of a nuclear missile by either side during a 24-hr. period (1F-8 estimated)

N=Number of days under consideration (20 years=7,300 days)

Write a BASIC program to consider different values for U, S, P, and N.

Calculating useful information. You can use your computer to figure out practical information such as the following:

- Easter: a program to calculate the date of Easter for any year would make use of the fact that Easter falls on the first Sunday following the arbitrary Paschal Full Moon, which does not necessarily coincide with a real or astronomical moon. The Paschal Full Moon is calculated by adding 1 to the remainder obtained by dividing the year by 19 and applying the information given in Table 3-1.

    Thus, for the year 2000, the key is 6, or April 18. A program to calculate the day of the week (see the Business and Financial Applications chapter) could then indicate that April 18, 2000 is a Tuesday. Note: If the Paschal Full Moon falls on a Sunday, Easter is the following Sunday. The earliest Easter can fall is March 23rd and the latest is April 25th.

- Horizons: the distance to the horizon in miles is approximately $= \sqrt{1.5h}$, where h = elevation above sea level in feet. Write a BASIC program to draw a mountain and print the miles to the horizon for viewers located at 100 foot intervals.

    Creating artistic patterns. You can use

Table 3-1. The Paschal Full Moon Date.

1-Apr 14	6-Apr 18	11-Mar 25	16-Mar 30
2-Apr 3	7-Apr 8	12-Apr 13	17-Apr 17
3-Mar 23	8-Mar 28	13-Apr 2	18-Apr 7
4-Apr 11	9-Apr 16	14-Mar 22	19-Mar 27
5-Mar 31	10-Apr 5	15-Apr 10	

your microcomputer to generate interesting, artistic patterns such as *Pascal's art.* As described in the December 1966 issue of *Scientific American,* Pascal's triangle may be used to generate artistic geometric patterns. A sample Pascal triangle is shown below; each number in the successive rows is generated by adding the two numbers above and to the immediate left and right of the number in question.

```
        1
       1 1
      1 2 1
     1 3 3 1
    1 4 6 4 1
  1 5 10 10 5 1
```

To write a BASIC program to generate patterns using the triangle you could, for instance, represent all odd numbers by an X and all even numbers by a space. Print the results on a line printer; a variety of interesting geometrical patterns involving triangles will be formed.

Chapter 4

Technical and Scientific Applications

Personal computers, rather than their large-scale counterparts, are increasingly being used by technicians and scientists for problem solving. They offer the advantages of ease of use, low cost, and greater portability. Although many large scale scientific problems are best left to supercomputers, the personal computer has become an asset in its own right in all types of laboratories.

In this chapter I will examine the ways personal computers have been put to scientific and technical use. The personal computer can help to rid the professional or amateur scientist of the mathematical drudgery that is so much a part of the discovery process. It can rapidly and accurately solve problems, many of which would not have previously been undertaken because of their sheer magnitude.

Many of these applications are specialized; the purpose of this chapter is to touch upon just a few of the most commonly used scientific applications, provide sources for further information, and demonstrate some solutions in BASIC. Due to space restrictions, formulas and in-depth coverage of each application is impossible, but this information should be readily available in standard reference manuals.

WEATHER FORECASTING

Forecasting the weather is usually thought to be a task for large computers only. However, local weather forecasting can be accomplished with surprising accuracy by taking note of wind direction and barometric changes. A chart in use by local weather bureaus has been based upon these two parameters and could easily be computerized. This data could be input automatically by the use of electronic barometers and wind direction instruments.

Wind change		Barometric condition	Forecast code
From	*To*		
S	SW	7	L
S	SE	3	E
		4	F

Wind change		Barometric condition	Forecast code
From	*To*		
		9	M
NE	SE	3	G
		4	H
		5	J
		6	K
		9	M
N	E	3	I
		4	A
		9	N
to the West		8	O
NW	SW	1	C
		2	B
		3	D
		7	L

If a forecast is not listed for the proper barometric condition, enumerated below, other factors must be used to provide the forecast.

Barometric Conditions
(IN INCHES Hg)

1. 30.1 or more and steady
2. 30.1-30.2 rising rapidly
3. 30.1 or more falling slowly
4. 30.1 or more falling rapidly
5. 30.0 or less falling slowly
6. 30.0 or less falling rapidly
7. 30.0 or less rising slowly
8. 29.8 or less rising rapidly
9. 29.8 or less falling rapidly

A rapid change is considered to be over .06 inches per hour. 3 inches Hg = 760 mm Hg.

Forecasts

A. Summer rain probable/12-24 hours. Winter rain or snow, increasing wind; bad weather often sets in when barometer begins to fall and winds set in from the N.E.
B. Fair, followed within two days by rain.
C. Continued fair, no decided temperature change.
D. Fair for two days with slowly rising temperatures.
E. Rain within 24 hours.
F. Wind increasing, rain within 24 hours.
G. Rain within 12-18 hours.
H. Wind increasing, rain within 12 hours.
I. Summer light winds, rain may not fall for several days. Winter rain within 24 hours.
J. Rain will continue for 1 to 2 days.
K. Rain, with high wind, followed within 36 hours by clearing, and in winter by colder temperatures.
L. Clearing within a few hours, fair for several days.
M. Severe storm imminent, followed within 24 hours by clearing, and in winter by colder temperatures.
N. Severe northeast gale and heavy precipitation, in winter, heavy snow followed by a cold wave.
O. Clearing and colder.

A cloud chart with forecasts included is also useful. The forecast data for the various types of clouds could be stored and a comparison made between this forecast and a forecast from the above chart.

Other suggestions for applying a personal computer to weather calculations include the following.

1. Pressure/height conversions to allow an anaeroid barometer to serve as an altimeter.
2. Dew point temperature and relative humidity from wet and dry bulb readings.
3. Normal maximum, mean, and minimum temperature degrees days for a given date and location.
4. Estimates of cloud base heights from dew point and surface temperature observations.
5. Almanac data for a given time and date (for example, declination of the sun, distance of the sun from the earth, phase of the moon, and positions of the planets) stored for ready access.
6. Analysis and display of hourly weather data

derived from a phone line connected with a weather data channel.

7. Temperature humidity index and relative humidity calculations. The program in Listing 4-1 determines the effective temperature given the relative humidity and the actual temperature.

8. Wind chill factor calculations. To calculate the wind chill factor, use the following formula:

$$H = (.14 + .47 V) (36.5\text{-}T)$$

where H = chill in calories lost per square centimeter of skin per second

V = wind velocity (m/sec.)

T = Temperature (°C)

The program in Listing 4-2 converts dry bulb temperature in °F and wind speed in mph to apparent wind chill temperature.

THE SUNDIAL DESIGN PROGRAM

Use the program in Listing 4-3 to compute the correct angles to use in constructing a sundial for your latitude.

The style should be set so that it lies in a north south direction as shown in Fig. 4-1. The top edge points to the North star, equal to the latitude in degrees above the horizon. The program gives you the angles to use in graduating the scale for each hour.

ENERGY EFFICIENCY COMPUTATION

You can use your small computer to make the following studies.

• A computerized statistical comparison between the water temperature in a solar energy system and the outside temperature, the angle of the sun, and so on could serve to evaluate the efficiency of a home solar energy system. Analog to digital

Listing 4-3: The Sundial Design Program

```
100 PRINT "SUNDIAL DESIGN PROGRAM"
110 PRINT "COMPUTES NECESSARY ANGLES FOR YOUR LATITUDE"
120 PRINT "ENTER YOUR LATITUDE";
130 INPUT A
140 PRINT "CUT OUT A STYLE SUCH THAT THE UPPER EDGE MAKES AN ANGLE"
150 PRINT "OF ";A;" DEGREES WITH THE BASE."
160 S=SIN(A)
170 X=1
180 FOR B=15 TO 90 STEP 15
190    T=TAN(B)
200    C=S*T
210    X=X+1
220    PRINT "AT ";X;" O'CLOCK, THE ANGLE SHOULD BE";ATN(C)*57.29578
230    REM IN STATEMENT 220 THE CONSTANT 57.29578 IS USED TO CONVERT
240    REM FROM RADIANS TO DEGREES.
250 NEXT B
260 END
```

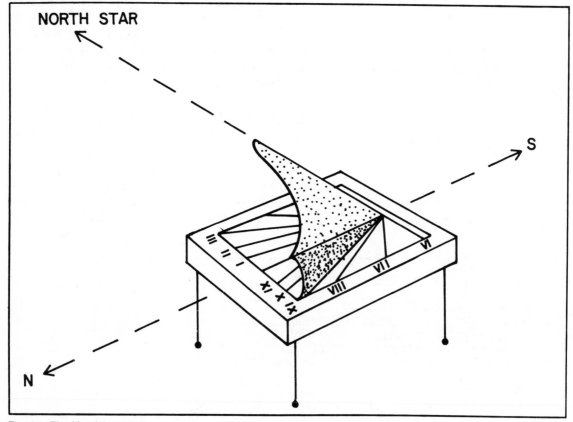

Fig. 4-1. The Moorish sundial.

converters could be used to gather the information automatically.

- Those of you considering the installation of a solar system might want to do another statistical analysis of the heating requirements for your home based on Btu/hr times the number of hours that your furnace operates during the heating season. The size of a solar system necessary to heat your house can then be calculated using this data and the manufacturer's efficiency data.

In the central U.S. on June 21, the maximum solar energy striking the earth is 290 Btu/square foot (approximately 15 hours in the day). On December 21, the solar energy is a maximum of 220 Btu/square foot (approximately 9 hours in the day). Thus, you can compute average values for the variables in the formula below.

$$\text{Solar collector Btu output} = \frac{B*h*s*m*}{2}$$

where B = Btu/sq ft $\quad s$ = sq.ft of collector
$\quad\quad\quad h$ = hrs/day $\quad m$ = max. efficiency

Keep in mind that it takes 500 Btu to heat water at ground temperature (40°F) to 100°F and that the desired water temperature for home use is 120°F.

- The answer to "How much fuel can be saved by turning the thermostat down from 70°F to 60°F at night?" may be determined using this equation:

$$A = \frac{.0625\ (n-1)W}{Z}$$

Where A = amount of heat (Btu)
$\quad\quad\quad W$ = the normal heat loss/hr. (Btu)
$\quad\quad\quad n$ = the number of hours of discontinued heating

z = the number of hours from the beginning of reheating until the house is at an acceptable temperature

- To find the heat loss of your home, use the formula

$$H = \frac{kA(t-t^1)T}{d}$$

where H = heat transmission (Btu)
$\quad\quad\quad K$ = coefficient of thermal conduction (Values for the type of construction used in your home may be found in builder's manuals)
$\quad\quad\quad A$ = exposed area
$\quad\quad (t-t^1)$ = temperature difference between inside and outside (°F)
$\quad\quad\quad T$ = duration of exposure (hours)
$\quad\quad\quad d$ = thickness of walls (inches)

- To calculate fuel requirements use the formula

$$C = \frac{H(t_a - t_b)N \times S \times q}{100{,}000 \times (t_i - t_o)}$$

where C = fuel cost
$\quad\quad\quad H$ = heat loss/hr.
$\quad\quad\quad t_o$ = outside temperature
$\quad\quad\quad t_i$ = inside temperature
$\quad\quad\quad t_a$ = average inside temperature
$\quad\quad\quad t_b$ = average outside temperature
$\quad\quad\quad N$ = number of hours of heating required
$\quad\quad\quad S$ = number of units of fuel
$\quad\quad\quad q$ = cost per unit of fuel

The program in Listing 4-4 calculates estimated costs for heating your home with gas, oil, and electricity. Be sure to enter your heat loss in British thermal units, not degrees.

Listing 4-4: The House Heating Program

```
10 CLS:KEY OFF
100 PRINT "HOUSE HEATING EVALUATION PROGRAM"
110 PRINT "THE PURPOSE OF THIS PROGRAM IS TO COMPUTE THE"
120 PRINT "RELATIVE EFFICIENCY OF HEATING A HOME WITH"
130 PRINT "ELECTRICITY, NATURAL GAS, OR OIL.  IT WILL BE"
140 PRINT "NECESSARY TO CONTACT YOUR LOCAL DISTRIBUTORS OF"
```

```
150 PRINT "THE ABOVE FUELS TO MAKE A COST COMPARISON."
160 PRINT "THERE ARE OTHER FACTORS TO CONSIDER WHEN EVALUATING"
170 PRINT "THE COST FOR HEATING (I.E. THE AMOUNT OF INSULATION"
180 PRINT " YOU HAVE), BUT THE RATIOS BETWEEN DIFFERENT"
190 PRINT "FUELS SHOULD BE CONSISTENT."
195 PRINT "USE THE COST EFFICIENCIES THE PROGRAM OUTPUTS ALONG WITH"
196 PRINT "THE COST OF THE HEATING SYSTEM TO DETERMINE WHICH YOU"
197 PRINT "SHOULD CHOOSE."
200 INPUT "ENTER ESTIMATED HEAT LOSS PER HOUR ",H
205 REM THIS MAY BE APPROXIMATED USING FORMULA ON PAGE 136 OR WITH BUILDERS
MANUALS
210 PRINT "IF YOU KNOW THE EFFICIENCY OF THE OIL BURNING SYSTEM"
220 PRINT "PLEASE ENTER THE VALUE, ";
230 INPUT "OTHERWISE ENTER '0' ",B
240 IF B=0 THEN B=.8 ELSE B=B*.01
250 INPUT "ENTER THE AVE. NO. OF MONTHS OF COLD SEASON PER YEAR ",C
260 C=C*720
270 INPUT "AT WHAT TEMPERATURE WILL YOU SET THE THERMOSTAT";D
280 INPUT "WHAT IS THE AVERAGE WINTER TEMPERATURE";E
290 REM COMPUTE HEAT LOSS PER HOUR
300 X=((D-E)/70)*((H*C)/(140000!*B))
310 PRINT "WHAT IS THE AVE. PRICE OF OIL IN YOUR AREA PER GALLON-"
320 INPUT "IF NOT KNOWN TYPE '0'",F
330 IF F=0 THEN F=.5
340 PRINT "YOU WILL REQUIRE AN ESTIMATED ";X;" GALLONS OF OIL--COST=";X*F
350 INPUT "ENTER THE COST PER KILOWATT HR. IN YOUR AREA IN DOLLARS";G
360 PRINT "ELECTRICITY TO RUN THE OIL PUMP MAY COST UP TO ";206*G;"DOLLARS"
370 PRINT "IF YOU KNOW THE EFFICIENCY OF THE NATURAL GAS HEATER PLEASE "
380 INPUT "ENTER, OTHERWISE ENTER '0' ",B
390 IF B=0 THEN B=.8 ELSE B=B*.01
400 Y=((D-E)/70)*((H*C)/(100000!*B))
410 INPUT "WHAT IS THE COST PER THERM IN YOUR AREA ",I
420 PRINT "YOU WILL REQUIRE AN ESTIMATED ";Y;"THERMS TO HEAT/COST=$";I*Y
430 Z=((D-E)/70)*(H*C)/3405
440 PRINT "AND AN ESTIMATED";Z;"KWH WILL BE REQUIRED TO HEAT WITH"
450 PRINT "ELECTRICITY--COST=$";Z*G
460 PRINT "SUMMARY:"
470 PRINT "MEDIUM","AMOUNT","COST"
480 PRINT "OIL",X,X*F
490 PRINT "NATURAL GAS",Y,I*Y
500 PRINT "ELECTRICITY",Z,Z*G
510 PRINT "REMEMBER THAT THESE VALUES ARE ONLY ESTIMATES"
520 PRINT "AND WILL DIFFER ACCORDING TO THE INSULATION, BUILDING"
530 PRINT "MATERIAL, FURNISHINGS, AND CLIMATE."
540 PRINT "THE VALUES GIVEN ARE MOST USEFUL IN DETERMINING THE"
550 PRINT "MOST INEXPENSIVE METHOD OF HEATING FOR YOUR HOME."
560 PRINT "THUS, THE PROCUREMENT COSTS FOR THE VARIOUS SYSTEMS"
570 PRINT "SHOULD BE ANALYZED ALONG WITH THE ABOVE COSTS TO"
580 PRINT "ARRIVE AT A FINAL FIGURE."
590 REM A COMPLETE PROGRAM COULD BE WRITTEN WITHOUT MUCH DIFFICULTY
600 REM TO CONSIDER THE ABOVE FACTORS...
```

Listing 4-5: The Air Conditioning Program

```
1 CLS:KEY OFF
10 PRINT "AIR CONDITIONING REQUIREMENT CALCULATION"
20 PRINT "DETERMINES THE BTU RATING FOR AN AIR COND./HEATER FOR YOU HOME"
30 INPUT "ENTER THE ESTIMATED TOTAL SQUARE FEET OF EXTERIOR WALL AREA FOR YOUR
HOUSE ",W
40 INPUT "ENTER THE ESTIMATED TOTAL GLASS AREA FOR YOUR HOUSE ",G
50 INPUT "ENTER THE ESTIMATED TOTAL AREA WITHIN THE ROOF CROSS-SECTION ",R
60 INPUT "ENTER THE NUMBER OF OCCUPANTS ",N
70 BTU=W*5+G*35+R*12+N*100+2000
80 PRINT "THE ESTIMATED BTU NECESSARY TO AIR CONDITION YOUR HOME=";BTU
90 PRINT
100 END
```

- To calculate the Btu rating for an air conditioner for your home, use the program in Listing 4-5.

- Use the simple program in Listing 4-6 to track the yearly cost of operation for electrical appliances and determine where cuts in electric bills would best be made.

- You can use additional formulas available in building manuals to compute the savings of installing insulation or the area of a solar collector necessary to heat a house of certain dimensions and construction.

TECHNICAL AND SCIENTIFIC CALCULATIONS

The computer can be used to perform calculations needed by those involved in many fields from navigation to chemistry.

Aviation

The private or business pilot will find the following calculations useful. Some are designed for portable programmable calculators so that programs may be used while in flight.

1. Flight plan with wind allowances: calculation of the heading, speed, fuel, ETA, and so on for a trip of multiple legs could be done.
2. Long-range flight plan: calculations could be done for great circle routes and could include distance, time, fuel, source.

Listing 4-6: The Electric Cost Analysis Program

```
10 REM ELECTRIC COST ANALYSIS
20 INPUT "ENTER COST PER K.W.H. IN $";C
30 INPUT "FOR NEXT APPLIANCE, SELECT 1)WATTS, 2)VOLTS + AMPS";X
40 ON X GOTO 50,70
50 INPUT "WATTS";W
60 GOTO 90
70 INPUT "VOLTS, AMPS";V,A
80 W=V*A
90 INPUT "ENTER APPROXIMATE NO. HOURS PER DAY THIS APPLIANCE IS USED";H
100 KWH=(H*360*W)/1000
110 PRINT "THIS APPLIANCE USES APPROXIMATELY ";KWH;" KILOWATT HOURS"
120 PRINT "PER YEAR, AT AN ANNUAL COST OF $";KWH*C
130 PRINT:GOTO 30
```

3. Atmosphere, speed, temperature and altitude: from pressure altitude, a program could calculate the speed of sound, temperature, pressure and density relative to standard sea level.
4. Prediction of freezing level and lowest usable flight level.
5. Wind components and average vector: crosswind and tail or head wind components of a single wind vector could be calculated.
6. Dead reckoning of position.
7. Great circle flying navigation.
8. Course correction to fly correct path.
9. Rhumbline navigation.
10. Unit conversions: length, volume, weight, English and metric temperature conversions.

$$°F = (9/5) (°C+32°)$$
$$°C = (5/9) (°F-32°)$$

Several BASIC programs and additional information on aviation calculations may be found in *Computers for Sea and Sky* by Steven J. Rogowski, Creative Computing Press, Morristown, N.J. 07960.

Marine Navigation

Some of the following applications are designed for use with programmable calculators as well as pocket or lap computers so that they can be used aboard a small vessel.

1. Time-speed-distance with current sailing: a useful program could solve time-speed-distance equations and could consider the current in determining the proper course to steer and the speed through the water necessary to reach a given destination in a specified length of time.
2. Distance short of, beyond, or to a horizon: a program could calculate the distance to the apparent horizon as well as the distance to and visibility of an object of known height.
3. Velocity, VMG, and current vectors: given two of the following, 1) drift and set of the current, 2) speed and course through the water, 3) speed and course made good, a program could calculate the unknown value.

4. Running fix from two objects: a program could calculate a fix of a vessel from bearings of two objects.
5. Planet location. A program could estimate the altitude and azimuth of the four navigational planets. The GMT (Greenwich mean time) of twilight could also be calculated or manually inputted.
6. Rhumbline and great circle navigation calculation.
7. Sight reduction calculation.
8. Length conversions. (for example, nautical miles to statute miles)
9. Vector addition.
10. Estimated time of arrival.
11. Conversion of compass points to degrees.
12. Area navigation by VOR (very-high-frequency omnirange)
13. Rhumbline navigation.
14. Dead reckoning of position.
15. Great circle computations.
16. Distance from VOR/OMNI.
17. Course correction.
18. Distance by two bearings.
19. Conversions between knots, miles, statute-miles, kilometers.
20. Speed computation given distance covered and time.

Many of the above navigation calculations are explained in *Computers for Sea and Sky*, by Steven J. Rogowski, Creative Computing Press, Morristown, N.J. 07960.

The program in Listing 4-7 computes the distance in nautical miles and bearing between two points on earth. Enter starting and ending latitudes and longitudes as decimal degrees.

Medical Calculations

Doctors, nurses, technicians and other medical personnel may find the following calculations useful.

1. Conversions of weight, length, and volume to other units, or English to metric conversion.
2. Lung diffusion calculations.
3. Blood acid-base status determination.

Listing 4-7: The Great Circle Navigation Program

```
10 REM GREAT CIRCLE NAVIGATION CALCULATIONS
20 REM ENTER SOUTHERN LATITUDES AND EASTERN LONGITUDES AS NEGATIVE NUMBERS
30 INPUT "ENTER LATITUDE AND LONGITUDE OF STARTING POINT";U,W
40 INPUT "ENTER LATITUDE AND LONGITUDE OF ENDING POINT";Z,R
50 PRINT:M=1.745329E-02
60 A=SIN(U*M)*SIN(Z*M)+COS(U*M)*COS(Z*M)*COS((R-W)*M)
70 D=60*(-ATN(A/SQR(-A*A+1))+1.5708)*57.29579
80 C=(SIN(Z*M)-(SIN(U*M)*COS(D/60*M)))/(SIN(D/60*M)*COS(U*M))
90 H=(-ATN(C/SQR(-C*C+1))+1.5708)*57.29579
100 F=SIN(R-W)
110 IF F>=0 THEN H=360-H
120 PRINT "THE DISTANCE IS ";D;" NAUTICAL MILES AT A BEARING OF ";INT(H);" DEGR
EES."
```

4. Beer's law calculation.
5. Protein electrophoresis: given integration counts of a number of protein fractions, the percentage of each may be found.
6. Body surface area estimation.
7. Oxygen saturation and content. Oxygen content and saturation in the blood may be found given pO_2, pCO_2, pH, and body temperature.

Publications containing computer programs and applications of use to the health professional include

Computer in Biology and Medicine
Computers in Medicine
Medical Computer Journal 42 East High St., East Hampton, CT 06424
Physicians Microcomputer Report P.O. Box 6483, Lawrenceville, NJ 08648

Surveying Calculations

Those involved in surveying could utilize the following calculations.

1. Azimuth/bearing traverse: given reference coordinates, leg length, azimuth or bearing, and quadrant, the endpoint coordinates, departure, latitude, and total distance may be computed.
2. Slope reduction determinations.
3. Point of intersection calculation.

Chemistry

Chemists and chemistry students may find the following calculations useful.

1. Calculation of requirements to produce a given solution. The program in Listing 4-8 will do the calculations for you.

Listing 4-8: The Stock Solution Computation Program

```
10 REM STOCK SOLUTION COMPUTATION
20 REM COMPUTES THE AMOUNT OF STOCK SOLUTION AND WATER NECESSARY TO
30 REM PRODUCE A GIVEN SOLUTION
40 PRINT "ENTER THESE VALUES: CONCENTRATION OF WORKING SOLUTION, CONCENTRATION O
F"
50 INPUT "STOCK SOLUTION, TOTAL AMOUNT OF SOLUTION. ",PW,PS,QT
60 OS=(PW*QT)/PS
70 W=QT-OS
80 PRINT "THE QUANTITY OF STOCK SOLUTION=";OS
90 PRINT "THE QUANTITY OF WATER TO ADD=";W
100 PRINT:PRINT
110 END
```

2. Calculations of the following parameters, given adequate inputs: pH, molality, total atomic weights, gas density and pressure, electron energies, gravimetric factors, liquid pressure, degree of saturation, gram equivalent weight, normality, percent composition, mole fraction, mole percent, and ionic strength dilution factor.
3. Plotting/simulation of reaction rates, electron distribution, and so on.

Physics

Those involved with physics will also find the computer's capacity for performing calculations useful. Potential uses include the following.
1. Plotting of potential energy functions, lab data, and so on.
2. Conversions of units.
3. Solutions to elementary equations: velocity, acceleration, momentum, work, power, etc.
4. Statistical analysis and data compilation.

An article discussing the use of personal computers to physicists appeared in *Physics Today,* December 1983, pp. 25-28. The author states "it is very likely that most calculations in physics will be performed by the home computer in the future," because of the benefit of independence from large computer organizations, bureaucracies, and economic constraints. He describes a Monte Carlo simulation that ran for about a week on his personal computer and estimated that the same job would have cost $2000 if run on his university CPU.

General Purpose Experimental Applications

Scientists in many fields can use their home computers to perform the following types of calculations.
1. Statistical analysis of data: useful statistical applications include curve fitting and plotting, Chi-square tests, analysis of variance and standard deviation, solutions to equations, and correlation coefficients.
2. Calculation of tables for a specific application: functions that are commonly referred to, yet do not have reference tables, could be calculated for a number of values, and the results displayed in table form for easy reference.

In addition to using computers for calculations, scientists can interface microcomputers to lab instrumentation and develop automatic data log and aquisition systems. They can also develop voice input interfaces that could accept data called out by a lab technician too busy to manually record data.

ENGINEERING APPLICATIONS

Professionals and hobbyists will have use for computer programs in the following engineering fields.

Electrical Engineering

Computers can help those who deal with electricity by performing calculations and analyses, and by facilitating design work.

Active high- and low-pass filter design. High- and low-pass filters may be designed for given center frequency, gain, and Q values for the resistors and capacitors in the infinite-gain multiple-feedback circuit. Listing 4-9 shows a program that performs these functions.

This program may be modified and extended for use in designing simple filters by the use of the

Listing 4-9: The Low-Pass Filter Design Program

```
100 PRINT "LOW PASS FILTER DESIGN PROGRAM"
110 PRINT "SHUNT M-DERIVED FILTER"
120 INPUT "ENTER THE CUTOFF FREQUENCY ",F1
130 INPUT "ENTER THE FREQUENCY OF REMOTE CUTOFF ",F2
140 INPUT "ENTER THE TERMINATING RESISTANCE ",R
150 L=SQR(1-(F1*F1/(F2*F2)))*R/(3.14159*F1)
```

```
160 C1=(1-(SQR(1-(F1*F1/(F2*F2))))-2)/(4*3.14159*SQR(1-F1*F1/(F2*F2))*F1*R)
170 C2=SQR(1-(F1*F1/(F2*F2)))/(3.14159*R*F2)
180 PRINT "THE VALUE FOR L=";L
190 PRINT "THE VALUE FOR C1=";C1
200 PRINT "THE VALUE FOR C2=";C2
```

schematics and formula in Fig. 4-2.

Active bandpass filter design. Second-order active bandpass filters may be designed using a multiple-feedback network. Both high-Q and low-Q circuits could be designed. Standard values may be selected for easy implementation.

Chebyshev and Butterworth filter design. Chebyshev and Butterworth low-pass filters may be designed for specified filter order, termination resistance, and corner frequency.

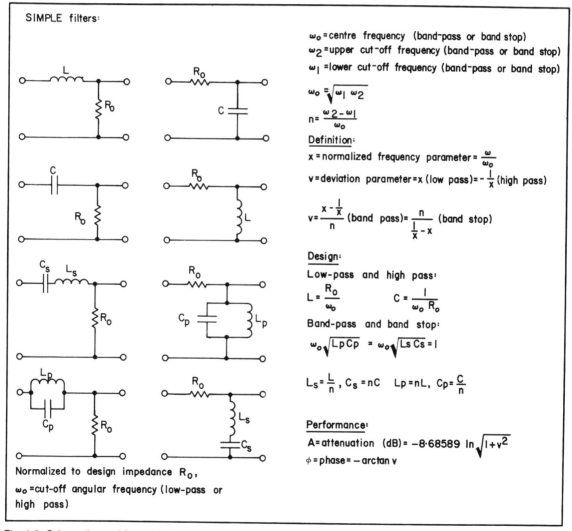

SIMPLE filters:

ω_o = centre frequency (band-pass or band stop)
ω_2 = upper cut-off frequency (band-pass or band stop)
ω_1 = lower cut-off frequency (band-pass or band stop)

$$\omega_o = \sqrt{\omega_1 \omega_2}$$

$$n = \frac{\omega_2 - \omega_1}{\omega_o}$$

Definition:

x = normalized frequency parameter = $\frac{\omega}{\omega_o}$

v = deviation parameter = x (low pass) = $-\frac{1}{x}$ (high pass)

$$v = \frac{x - \frac{1}{x}}{n} \text{ (band pass)} = \frac{n}{\frac{1}{x} - x} \text{ (band stop)}$$

Design:

Low-pass and high pass:

$$L = \frac{R_o}{\omega_o} \qquad C = \frac{1}{\omega_o R_o}$$

Band-pass and band stop:

$$\omega_o \sqrt{L_p C_p} = \omega_o \sqrt{L_s C_s} = 1$$

$$L_s = \frac{L}{n}, \quad C_s = nC \quad L_p = nL, \quad C_p = \frac{C}{n}$$

Performance:

A = attenuation (dB) = $-8.68589 \ln \sqrt{1+v^2}$

ϕ = phase = $-\arctan v$

Normalized to design impedance R_o,

ω_o = cut-off angular frequency (low-pass or high pass)

Fig. 4-2. Schematics and formulae for simple filters.

Resonant circuits. The impedance and resonant frequency could be calculated by a program for series or parallel resonant circuits whose component values are specified.

Attenuators. Component values for T and Pi impedance matching circuits may be found for specified input/output impedances and desired loss. Minimum-loss pad matching may be performed for given impedances.

T to Pi transformations. T(Pi) networks may be transformed to Pi(T) networks having the same characteristics. A T network design program is shown in Listing 4-10.

Ladder network analysis. The input impedance for a ladder network could be calculated; the network may be composed of any combination of resistors, capacitors, and inductors.

Coil properties. The inductance or number of turns for a single or multilayer coil may be found given wire diameter and dimensions of the coil. The inductance of two parallel, round wires, one forming a return circuit is given by

$$L = .0041 \left[2.303 \log_{10} (2\ D/d - D/1) \right]$$

where L = inductance (μH)

D = distance in cm. between centers of wires

d = diameter of wire (cm)

l = length of conductor (cm)

Listing 4-10: The Network Design Program

```
10 CLS:KEY OFF
100 PRINT "T-NETWORK DESIGN PROGRAM"
105 PRINT "PROVIDES A GRAPHIC REPRESENTATION OF THE CIRCUIT"
110 INPUT "ENTER THE RESISTANCE OF THE CIRCUIT WITH OUTPUT TERMINALS UNLOADED ",
RI
120 INPUT "ENTER THE OUTPUT RESISTANCE WITH THE INPUT TERMINALS UNLOADED ",RO
130 INPUT "ENTER THE RESISTANCE WITH THE OUTPUT TERMINALS SHORTCIRCUITED ",RN
140 A=-1
150 B=RO+1
160 C=RO*RN-RI
170 Q1=(-B+SQR(B*B-4*A*C))/(2*A)
180 Q2=(-B-SQR(B*B-4*A*C))/(2*A)
190 IF Q1>=0 THEN R3=Q1 ELSE R3=Q2
200 R2=RO-R3
210 R1=RI-R3
220 PRINT:PRINT:PRINT
230 PRINT "T-NETWORK CIRCUIT"
240 PRINT:PRINT "          R1          R2                 "
250 PRINT "---------     -----     ---------------"
260 FOR X=1 TO 3
270 PRINT "!               !          !                   "
280 NEXT X
290 PRINT "R-IN-------------------     ---------------R OUT"
300 PRINT "---------------------     --------------------";R3;"OHM"
310 PRINT "---------------------------"
320 FOR X=1 TO 3
330 PRINT "!               !          !"
340 NEXT X:PRINT "------------------------------------------------"
350 PRINT:PRINT
360 END
```

Power transformer design. Core weight may be calculated for a specified power requirement. For a specified core, area flux density, and frequency, the number of primary and secondary turns is found. A BASIC program to design power transformers may be found in *Electronic Design News*, October 27, 1983, p. 346.

Rectifier circuits. Full-wave or half-wave rectifier circuits may be evaluated for given component values, input voltage, and frequency. The dc output voltage and peak-to-peak ripple may also be calculated.

S and Y parameter transformations. A set of S(Y) parameters expressed as magnitudes and angles may be transformed to a set of Y(S) parameters.

Phase-locked loops. Natural frequency, damping factor, and loop noise bandwidth may be found for either passive or active phase-locked loops. Loop gain and component values for the circuits are required for input.

Transistor amplifier design. Collector current and sensitivity factors can be computed for transistor circuits for specified current gain, supply voltage, and resistor values.

Fourier series. Fourier coefficients may be computed for discrete values for a periodic function. Sine and cosine coefficients may be found and could be used to calculate new values of the function.

Reactive L-Network impedance matching. Networks that will match any two complex impedances may be determined.

Bilateral design, stability factor, maximum gain, and optimum matching. A program could compute the maximum gain available and the load and source reflection coefficients that yield the maximum gain.

Frequency conversion program. A BASIC program to interconvert velocity, period, wavelength, and frequency values could make use of these commonly-used formulas:

$$T = 1/f$$
$$\omega = 2\pi f$$
$$\lambda = v/f$$

$$f = 1/T$$
$$f = \omega/2\pi$$
$$f = v/\lambda$$

where T = period
   f = frequency
   ω = radian frequency
   λ = wavelength
   V = propagation velocity

Similarly, frequency and reactance conversions may be accomplished with these formulae:

$$X_c = \frac{1}{2\pi fC} = \frac{1}{\omega C}$$

$$X_L = 2\pi fL = \omega L$$

$$C = \frac{1}{2\pi fX_c} = \frac{1}{\omega X_c}$$

$$L = \frac{X_L}{2\pi f} = \frac{X_L}{\omega}$$

$$f = \frac{1}{2\pi CX_c}$$

$$f = \frac{X_L}{2\pi L}$$

555 timer circuit design. Given the frequency duty cycle and either the timing capacitor or resistor, a program could calculate the other timing component, charge time, discharge time, and period of the commonly used 555 stable multivibrator circuit.

Resonance calculations. Resonant frequency of inductance-capacitance circuit is given by:

$$fr = \frac{L - R_L^2 C}{2\pi\sqrt{LC\ (L - Rc^2 C)}}$$

where $L = 1/(4\pi^2 f^2 C)$

$C = 1/(4\pi^2 f_r^2 L)$

R_L = series resistance of inductor

R_C = effective series resistance of capacitor

f_r = resonant frequency

Antenna-design. A given frequency could be inputted to a program that would calculate the antenna dimensions for a dipole, Yagi, or cubical quad antenna. The program in Listing 4-11 can be used to calculate the dimensions for a yagi antenna to receive television, radio, or amateur radio broadcasts; the antenna is designed for a specific frequency. Such an antenna can often receive signals from distances not previously approached. If the mathematical specifications of the antenna design are unclear, refer to an electronic manual for a picture. Construction of the antenna is not difficult and should cost no more than twenty dollars.

Listing 4-11: The Yagi Antenna Design Program

```
10 PRINT "YAGI ANTENNA DESIGN PROGRAM"
20 INPUT "INPUT THE FREQUENCY FOR WHICH THE ANTENNA IS TO BE DESIGNED IN
MEGAHERTZ ",F
30 PRINT:PRINT
40 PRINT "FOR";F;"MEGAHERTZ THE LENGTHS OF THE ELEMENT ARE:"
50 PRINT "ELEMENT NUMBER","LENGTH IN INCHES"
51 A=466.667/F:D=A*.05*A:B=11.52*A
53 W=6*A:X=4.32*A:E=11.28*A
55 Y=4.8*A:G=3.6*A:L=4.8*A
57 C=11.4*A:Z=11.46*A
59 R=5*W+X+G+Y+L+.333
60 PRINT "1",D
70 PRINT "2",B
80 PRINT "3",C
90 PRINT "4",E
100 PRINT "5",E
110 PRINT "6",A
120 PRINT "7",Z
130 PRINT "8",E
140 PRINT "9",E
150 PRINT "10",E
160 INPUT "PRESS 'ENTER' TO CONTINUE ",A$
165 PRINT:PRINT
170 PRINT "ELEMENT SPACING:"
180 PRINT "ELEMENT NUMBER:","SPACING IN INCHES:"
190 PRINT "1-2",L
200 PRINT "2-3",X
210 PRINT "3-4",W
220 PRINT "4-5",W
230 PRINT "5-6",W
240 PRINT "6-7",Y
250 PRINT "7-8",Y
260 PRINT "8-9",W
270 PRINT "9-10",W
280 PRINT "THE BOOM IS";C;"INCHES LONG (";C/12;"FEET LONG)"
290 END
```

Decibel conversion and voltage to dBm conversion. Voltage ratio in Decibels is given by

$$N_{dB} = 20 \log_{10} (E_{OUT}/E_{IN})$$

where E_{OUT} = output voltage
E_{IN} = input voltage

Such computations would be helpful to the serious audiophile. Also of interest to the audiophile would be a formula used to compute the inductance of a straight wound speaker wire:

$$L = .0021[2.303 \log_{10} (41/d) - .75]$$

where L = inductance (μH)
d = diameter of wire (cm)
l = length of conductor (cm)

Evaluation routine for a program of Boolean function. AND, OR, NOT, and the other logic statements could be evaluated as a program; the circuit status at each step would be outputted.

Ohm's law calculation. A computer can be used to determine the unknown value.

$$E = IR$$

where R = resistance (ohms)
E = voltage
I = current

Resistor or capacitor color codes. An ideal program for the novice in electronics would output the value for a resistor or capacitor given the color from a component.

Inductance Bridge calculation. Given this design,

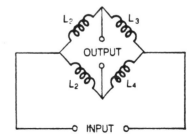

if any three values are known the fourth may be calculated:

$$L_1 = L_2 L_3 / L_2$$
$$L_2 = L_1 L_4 / L_3$$
$$L_3 = L_1 L_4 / L_2$$
$$L_4 = L_2 L_3 / L_1$$

RL Equivalent Impedance Calculation. The program in Listing 4-12 will calculate equivalent impedances.

A/C voltage divider calculation. The program in Listing 4-13 will calculate the modules and phase of the angular frequencies you enter.

Logic circuit analysis. The purpose of the program in Listing 4-14 is to simulate the operation of a simple logic circuit. The circuitry (gates and connecting lines or *nodes*) is described to the computer along with the input states to the circuit (on

---

Listing 4-12: The RL Equivalent Impedance Program

```
100 PRINT "RL EQUIVALENT IMPEDANCE"
110 PRINT "ANSWERS A QUESTION SUCH AS 'WHAT IS THE EQUIVALENT IMPEDANCE OF A"
120 PRINT "300 OHM RESISTOR AND A 30 MILLIHENRY INDUCTOR AT A FREQUENCY OF"
130 PRINT "2000 HERTZ?'"
140 INPUT "ENTER RESISTANCE IN OHMS ",R
150 INPUT "ENTER INDUCTANCE IN MILLIHENRIES ",IND
160 INPUT "ENTER FREQUENCY ",FREQ
170 EQU=(2*3.141582*FREQ*IND*.001)*(1/(SIN(ATN((2*3.141592*FREQ*IND*.001)/R))))
180 PRINT "THE EQUIVALENT IMPEDANCE=";EQU
```

and off are represented as 1 and 0 respectively). Next, the program determines what the resultant states of nodes will be throughout the circuit following all logic "decisions." Essentially, this program allows you to design and test a logic circuit without breadboarding it.

The program recognizes the following gates: AND, OR, INV, NAND, exclusive OR (abbreviated XOR), and exclusive NOR (abbreviated XNOR); up to 64 gates and 255 nodes may be used in one circuit. To begin, the program will allow you to input a circuit; answer 1 for a new circuit to the first question. Next, the program will request a *label* for the first gate, which may be any gate in the circuit. This label is simply a distinguishing number (any number) you want for the gate. Now, input the gate type AND, OR, etc.), and then input the identifying nodes connected to the gate (first the output node and then the input nodes). For example, to describe the illustrated circuit, the following sequence could be used:

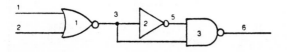

SELECT: 1) NEW CIRCUIT   2) OLD CIRCUIT ?1

ENTER THE LABEL?1
ENTER THE GATE? NOR

ENTER THE NODE?3
ENTER THE NODE?1
ENTER THE NODE?2
ENTER THE NODE?0

(0 is used here to mean go to next gate)

ENTER THE LABEL?2
ENTER THE GATE?INV
ENTER THE NODE?5
ENTER THE NODE?5
ENTER THE NODE?3
ENTER THE NODE?0

ENTER THE LABEL?3
ENTER THE GATE?NAND
ENTER THE NODE?6
ENTER THE NODE?5
ENTER THE NODE?3
ENTER THE NODE?0

Remember to enter the output node for each gate first, followed by the input nodes.

After describing the circuit, the logic states of various nodes will be described. Simply type the number of the node and its initial state (1 or 0). Usually, only the input nodes are described.

Finally, the program analyzes the operation of the circuit, outputting the state of each node after the circuit has been completed. The circuit is analyzed according to standard logic tables. In this

122

Listing 4-14: The Logic Circuit Analysis Program

```
1 CLS:KEY OFF
10 PRINT "LOGIC CIRCUIT ANALYSIS PROGRAM"
30 DIM F(3000)
40 FOR X=1 TO 8
50   READ X(X)
60 NEXT X:READ A1,A2
65 A(9)=25
70 B$="AND OR  INV NANDNOR XOR XNOR"
80 PRINT
90 PRINT "SELECT: 1)ENTER A CIRCUIT"
100 PRINT "          2)ENTER SPECIFIED STATES FOR NODES"
110 PRINT "          3)ANALYZE CIRCUIT OPERATION"
120 PRINT "          4)OUTPUT THE STATES OF NODES"
130 INPUT "          5)OUTPUT THE CIRCUIT";A3
140 ON A3 GOTO 150,350,500,1300,1500
150 INPUT "SELECT: 1)NEW CIRCUIT, 2)OLD CIRCUIT ",X
155 IF X=2 THEN 190
160 FOR A4=8 TO 511
170   F(A2+A4)=0
180 NEXT A4
190 PRINT
200 INPUT "ENTER THE LABEL ",A5:A5=8*A5
205 IF A5<=0 THEN 80
210 FOR A4=0 TO 7
220   F(A5+A4+A2)=0
230 NEXT A4:A6=0
240 INPUT "ENTER THE GATE ",W$
250 IF W$="REDO" THEN 190
260 IF W$="AND" THEN A6=1
261 IF W$="OR" THEN A6=2
262 IF W$="INV" THEN A6=3
263 IF W$="NAND" THEN A6=4
264 IF W$="NOR" THEN A6=5
265 IF W$="XOR" THEN A6=6
266 IF W$="XNOR" THEN A6=7
270 IF A6=0 THEN 240
300 F(A2+A5)=A6:A5=A5+1
310 INPUT "ENTER THE NODE ",A6
320 IF A6<>0 THEN 300 ELSE 200
350 INPUT "SELECT: 1)REDO OR BEGIN 2)CONTINUE ",X
360 IF X=2 THEN 400
370 PRINT:FOR A4=1 TO 255
380   F(A1+A4)=255
390 NEXT A4
400 INPUT "ENTER THE NODE ",A6
405 IF A6<=0 THEN 80
410 INPUT "ENTER THE STATE ",A7
420 F(A1+A6)=A7
```

```
430 GOTO 400
500 A8=0
520 A8=A8+1:PRINT "NO.";A8
525 A9=0
530 FOR A4=1 TO 63
540   A6=F(A4*8+A2)
545   IF A6=0 THEN 950
550   ON A6 GOTO 600,650,700,750,800,850,900
600   B=0:GOSUB 1180
610   GOTO 920
650   B=1:GOSUB 1180
660   GOTO 920
700   B1=F(A1+F(A2+2+8*A4))
710   GOSUB 980
720   GOTO 920
750   B=0:GOSUB 1180
760   GOSUB 980
770   GOTO 920
800   B=1:GOSUB 1180
810   GOSUB 980
820   GOTO 920
850   GOSUB 1110
860   GOTO 920
900   GOSUB 1110
910   GOSUB 980
920   IF B1=F(A1+F(8*A4+1+A2)) THEN 950
930   A9=1
940   F(A1+F(A2+8*A4+1))=B1
950 NEXT A4
960 IF A9=1 THEN 520
970 GOTO 80
980 IF B1>1 THEN 1000
990 B1=1-B1:RETURN
1000 B1=257-B1:RETURN
1110 B2=F(A1+F(8*A4+2+A2))
1120 B3=F(A1+F(8*A4+3+A2))
1130 IF B2<>0 AND B<>0 THEN 1140 ELSE B1=B2+B3:RETURN
1140 IF B2-1<>0 AND B3-1<>0 THEN 1150 ELSE B1=B3*B2:GOSUB 980
1145 RETURN
1150 B1=1
1160 IF B3=B2 THEN B1=0
1170 RETURN
1180 B1=1-B
1190 FOR B4=2 TO 7
1200   B2=F(8*A4+B4+A2)
1210   IF B2=0 THEN 1260
1220   B5=F(B2+A1)
1230   IF B5<>B THEN 1240 ELSE B1=B:RETURN
1240   IF B1+B5<>257 THEN 1250 ELSE B1=B:RETURN
1250   IF B5=1-B THEN 1260 ELSE B1=B5
1260 NEXT B4
```

```
1270 RETURN
1300 A9=1
1310 FOR A4=1 TO 255
1320    IF F(A4+A1)>1 THEN 1400
1330    PRINT A4;": ";F(A4+A1)
1400 NEXT A4
1410 PRINT
1420 GOTO 90
1500 FOR A4=1 TO 63
1510    A6=F(8*A4+A2)
1520    IF A6=0 THEN 1700
1530    PRINT A4;TAB(4);
1540    A9=10:PRINT MID$(B$,A6*4-3,4);
1550    FOR B4=1 TO 7
1560       A6=F(8*A4+A2+B4)
1570       IF A6=0 THEN 1610
1580       PRINT TAB(A9);A6;
1590       A9=4+A9
1600    NEXT B4
1610    PRINT
1700 NEXT A4
1710 GOTO 90
2000 DATA 1,4,6,9,13,16,19,23
2001 DATA 768,1025
```

manner, the professional or hobbyist can test circuit operation without breadboarding.

Additional applications for electrical engineers. The following list includes a number of other areas in which the microcomputer can make the lives of those who work with electricity easier.

- Transistor configuration conversion
- Resistive attenuator design
- Smith chart conversions
- Phase shift oscillator design
- Dc bias analysis
- Waveform limits determination
- Plotting of waveforms
- Plate resistance/transconductance calculations
- Gauss calculations
- Reactance chart calculations
- Design of controlled rectifier circuits
- Integrated circuit current-source design
- Solution of resistive networks
- Rf amplifier analysis
- Bipolar junction transistor analysis
- Complex matrix calculations as used in electrical engineering
- Wheatstone bridge design

Civil Engineering

Civil engineers will find small computers useful for performing the following functions.
- Moment of inertia calculation
- Vector statics
- Section properties
- Stress on an element or beam
- Static equilibrium about a point

Chemical Engineering

Chemical engineers can use small computers, for the following:
- Ideal gas equation of state
- Conservation of energy calculations
- Heat exchanger analysis
- Curve fitting
- Hydrocarbon combustion calculations

Machine Design

Machine designers can use computers to do the following:
- Constant acceleration calculations, relation to time and velocity.
- Kinetic energy determination
- Critical shaft speed calculation
- Cam design functions
- Gear and spring calculations/design
- RPM/torque/power computation
- Tachometer/dwell meter calculation: your oscilloscope can be converted into a tachometer and dwell meter in conjunction with your computer. The following information must be input to the computer to determine engine RPM and dwell angle:
  a. Number of cylinders in the engine
  b. Interval in milliseconds for open ignition points
  c. Interval in milliseconds for closed ignition points

Factors a and b are determined using the oscilloscope. (RPM may also be calculated using the factors of tire diameter, gear ratio, and vehicle speed.)

$$\text{ignition pulse frequency} = \frac{\text{RPM} \times \text{No. Cylinders}}{120}$$

Chapter 5

Educational Applications

One of the most important uses for a personal computer is certainly education. The acronym *CAI*, which stands for Computer Assisted Instruction, is often used. Not only can the computer serve as a drill and practice machine for teaching subjects ranging from the alphabet to Schrodinger wave equations, but it can teach the fundamentals of computer programming and prepare the learner for a career and for the computerized future.

Needless to say, we all have memories of learning addition and subtraction, repeating spelling words until we spelled them correctly, and memorizing dates of important historical events. Most of us considered this to be one of the boring essentials of elementary education, and our attention span was accordingly short.

With the addition of the computer to education, this is no longer the case. Although the subject matter has not changed, the method of drill and practice has become much more entertaining with the computer. Countless studies have shown that computerized education makes learning more interesting and is more effective. The task of learning

school subjects has become colorful, individualized, and in some cases exciting. The students have instant feedback from the computer so that they know whether their answers are right or wrong and can build from that point; this kind of immediate feedback has been shown to be an effective learning tool.

Computer programs designed for drill and practice are usually capable of providing questions at various levels of difficulty. With simple multiplication, for example, problems with single digit, double digit, or even triple digit (or more) multiplication can be provided. In this way, the student learns his basic multiplication tables before tackling 472×952. The computer can either randomly generate these problems or choose them from a large collection stored in memory. As the student masters a certain number of problems at the beginning level, he can advance at his own pace to succeeding levels. If he encounters difficulty at a particular level, the computer provides more of the same kinds of problems or offers help. The computer can even be programmed to remember what level a student has achieved and can begin from that point the next time he uses the program.

Each time the student answers a question, the computer informs him whether the answer is right or wrong. If the answer is correct, the student can be awarded with a picture of a smiling face, a colorful, animated display, or an encouraging message. If the student responds incorrectly, the computer offers a gentle correction, which may be humorous to keep the learning experience enjoyable rather than painful.

Computer drill and practice systems have been applied to every educational area from preschool to college level. Some programs make use of computer graphics for those situations in which "a picture is worth a thousand words." Newer systems make use of random-access video disc players in which short video segments can be selected by the computer.

Certainly one of the best ways to learn about computer operation and programming is to purchase a personal computer. Not only can a child learn how to program computers to do simple (or even complex!) tasks, but he can also learn how to think logically and how to draw conclusions based on fact and analysis rather than on guesswork or emotions. To be able to define and analyze a problem, and develop a set of computer instructions to solve it is a considerable accomplishment and is certainly applicable in many areas other than computer programming. Children and adults also need to become familiar with computer operation, capabilities, and programming in preparation for our increasingly computerized world.

Caveat emptor. Software publishers have discovered that there's no surer way to a parent's pocketbook than to sell the notion that using a personal computer will improve a child's mind. If you intend to purchase a "professionally" prepared program, ask for a demonstration before spending that $30. Beware of flimflam floppies, snakeoil, and superhype. You may want to consult *Software Reports*, which evaluates 382 educational programs in 20 subject areas in terms of content, ease of use, entertainment, and other criteria. It's available from many computer stores and by mail from Allen-

bach Industries, 2101 Las Palmas Dr., Carlsbad, CA 92008. Additionally, many of the popular home computing magazines carry regular reviews of educational software.

APPLICATION IDEAS

The educational uses for personal computers are unlimited; a few of the possible ways of using the computer to instruct yourself, your children, or your friends include the following. You may wish to incorporate these ideas in programs that you can sell to others.

• Create a program describing how to program computers in BASIC or another language such as assembly language or FORTRAN, etc. with step-by-step examples.

• Create a story building program for youngsters in which the computer randomly selects individual story parts and combines them to produce a different story each time. Questions could be asked to test reading comprehension, grammar, and writing skills. For example, the program could produce a personalized story for a child using his or her name. Occasionally, questions such as this should be displayed:

Johnny, should I write the next sentence as

    1. "Johnny and I went to the park."
or
    2. "I and Johnny went to the park."

If the child answers correctly, the computer reply could be "O.K., that's correct," and a wrong answer could be explained—"No that's wrong. The person who is talking should place the "I" last, after the names of other people."

• Create an I.Q. builder program to familiarize people with the types of questions and problem solving methods used on tests such as the Scholastic Aptitude test, Civil Service tests, and the American College Assessment test. Research has shown that familiarization with the tests can improve performance considerably. Sample questions are readily available in test-preparation books.

- Create a future-potential evaluation program designed to quiz high school or college students about their talents, interests, and abilities. The program could direct them toward promising occupational careers based upon this information.
- Computerize psychological questionnaires, which are often found in popular magazines and books for recreational and education use. Tests particulary suited for computerization are those requiring tedious calculation to analyze. For instance, this quiz is designed to test your "happiness quotient" and could be easily computerized:

Answer each question as true or false.
  1. My work is usually fulfilling or interesting.
  2. I have a good ability to relax.
  3. I can enjoy happiness in little things easily.
  4. I seldom envy other people.
  5. My moods have great fluctuation.
  6. I have a great desire to change either my location, family situation, or job.
  7. I usually sleep well and don't feel tired in the morning.
  8. I periodically "blow my top" without knowing the real reason.
  9. I am usually a pessimistic person.
  10. I cannot have happiness without others being around me.

Scoring:

Start with zero, add one point for each true answer to questions 1, 2, 3, 4, 7 and add one point for each false answer to questions 5, 6, 8, 9, 10. Multiply the total by 10 to determine percentage happiness (average score is approximately 50).

An ambitious programmer could program the computer to print out an analysis of the subject based on his answers. Such a program would make use of stock phrases to be used for many possible combinations of answers and could read like this:

If you don't derive much pleasure from little things or if you regularly lose your temper (3 and 8), you should give some attention to your attitudes. Is your social situation the cause of the trouble (6) or is it your job situation (1)? Often, the simple recognition of this difficulty will serve to clear up the situation. The person who is truly happy can find happiness while alone (10) and isn't envious (4). The moody person (5 and 9) can often benefit from the advice of a counselor.

- Create a spelling program that would allow you to input and store words. Words would be randomly selected and flash on the screen from .1 to 10 seconds. The player must then type in the word from memory.

COMPUTER ASSISTED INSTRUCTION

Computer assisted instruction (CAI) refers to the use of a computer as a teaching device. Graphics, text, or questions can be presented on the screen. The simple program presented is designed to ask a question of any subject, wait for a response in Listing 5-1, determine whether or not the answer was correct, and keep track of progress. Two incorrect answers are allowed before the correct answer is given; change line 100 if this is not desired.

Sample data for a quiz about computers could be as follows:

300 DATA IS YOUR COMPUTER CONSIDERED A MICROCOMPUTER OR A MINICOMPUTER, MICROCOMPUTER

310 DATA WHAT DOES CPU STAND FOR, CENTRAL PROCESSING UNIT

The question comes first in the DATA statements and is immediately followed by a comma and the answer.

Listing 5-1: General CAI Program

```
1 PRINT "GENERAL COMPUTER-ASSISTED INSTRUCTION PROGRAM--QUESTIONS AND ANSWERS"
```

```
2 PRINT "ARE CONTAINED IN THE DATA STATEMENTS."
3 PRINT "CAI- TO STOP AT ANY POINT TYPE 'STOP' AS AN ANSWER"
5 CLEAR 1000     'adjust to your requirements
8 Y=0:Z=0:N=3      'N=THE NUMBER OF QUESTIONS IN THE DATA STATEMENTS
10 INPUT "PRESS ENTER TO BEGIN",A$:CLS:KEY OFF
15 FOR A=0 TO N-1:Y=1
20 READ A$,B$
30 PRINT A$
40 INPUT C$:IF C$="STOP" THEN 150
50 IF C$=B$ THEN 140 ELSE 100
60 GOTO 150
100 IF Y=2 THEN 130
110 PRINT "INCORRECT ANSWER...PLEASE TRY AGAIN":Y=Y+1
120 GOTO 40
130 PRINT "THE ANSWER WAS:":PRINT B$:Z=Z+1
140 NEXT A
150 PRINT "YOU ANSWERED";A-Z;"OR";(A-Z)/N*100;"% QUESTIONS CORRECTLY"
160 PRINT "AND";Z;" QUESTIONS WERE ANSWERED INCORRECTLY "
180 INPUT "TRY AGAIN";A$
190 IF A$="YES" THEN 5
210 DATA SAMPLE QUESTION,SAMPLE ANSWER
300 DATA IS YOUR COMPUTER CONSIDERED A MICROCOMPUTER OR MINI COMPUTER,
MICROCOMPUTER
310 DATA WHAT DOES CPU STAND FOR, CENTRAL PROCESSING UNIT
999 END
```

COMPUTER TUTOR

You can use your computer to assist you in the memorization of lists, vocabulary words, and other types of abstract information. For instance, the computer could quiz you in flashcard fashion from a list of vocabulary words, displaying each randomly-selected word individually. Once you have glanced at a word, and attempted to recite the definition to yourself (or to the computer), press the enter or return key. The definition could be automatically displayed afterwards at this point. If you did not know the correct definition, you could type "w" (wrong) to indicate this mistake, and the word and definition could be stored for review. If you were right, you would simply press the enter or return key and the next word would be displayed. Additionally, the number and percentage of correct answers could be maintained.

The high school or college student should find computerized quizzes helpful in memorizing such information as

1. Historical names, dates, and places — presidents, authors, inventors . . .
2. Parts and functions of the anatomy
3. Mathematical or chemical formulae
4. Verses in literature
5. Spellings or definitions of difficult words
6. Trigonometric identities
7. Geography — states, capitals, countries
8. Technical and scientific terminology
9. Anglo/metric unit conversions

EDUCATIONAL SIMULATIONS

Because of the ability of the computer to perform calculations rapidly, they are well-suited to be used for educational and mathematical simulations. Simulations for educating young people include the following:

The Manhattan Indian Problem. This simulation teaches the principle of compounded interest. As the story goes, the new world settlers paid the Indians $24 for the entire island of Manhattan in 1626. Today, this property is worth millions of dollars. But, what would have happened if the settlers had deposited the $24 in a savings account at 6% interest compounded daily? How much would that account be worth today? A computer generated chart listing the value of the account after each decade would serve to illustrate the geometrical growth rate involved and the surprising answer to the Manhattan Indian Problem. Use the formula $A_1 = A(1+r)^n$ where A_1 = value acquired (capital + interest), A = original investment, v = interest rate, and n = number of years.

The growth of an amoeba colony. This simulation simulates the growth of a colony of amoebas (one-celled organisms) in a jar with a limited food supply. The reproduction rate will cause the colony population to double per unit time. The formula for geometric progressions is

$$S = a \times \frac{q^n - 1}{q - 1}$$

where S = sum, a = the first term (in this case = 1), q = the ratio for successive values (in this case = 2 because the colony doubles with each generation). However, pollution and limited food supply will decrease colony size at an increasing rate. Other-

wise, within one month's time, a single bacterium (about one tenth of a millimeter in diameter) dividing at a rate of five times a day would produce a volume of organisms equal to *one million times the volume of the sun*, provided food and space were available! A numerical listing or plot of the population versus time could be generated by the computer. Will the colony reach equilibrium (a stable state)? Along parallel lines, simulations of a large scale (for example, ecological balance in a forest) could be undertaken.

The laws of physics. The demonstration of some laws of physics could take the form of a graphical illustrations of planetary orbits, acceleration due to gravity, motion of a pendulum, and so on.

A popular physics demonstration program called "The Lunar Landing Simulation" is presented in Listing 5-2. In this simulation, the learner must control the flight of an Apollo moon lander under the influence of gravity. Limits on oxygen, food, and fuel supply must be contended with also. Similar programs have been written to graphically simulate the piloting of an airplane.

Listing 5-2: The Lunar Landing Simulation Program

```
10 CLS:KEY OFF
20 PRINT "LUNAR LANDING SIMULATION"
30 PRINT "------------------------"
40 PRINT
50 PRINT "DO YOU WANT INSTRUCTIONS (YES OR NO)"
60 INPUT A$
70 IF A$="NO" THEN 310
80 PRINT
90 PRINT "YOU ARE LANDING ON THE MOON AND HAVE TAKEN OVER MANUAL"
100 PRINT "CONTROL 500 FEET ABOVE A GOOD LANDING SPOT.  YOU HAVE A"
110 PRINT "DOWNWARD VELOCITY OF 50 FT/SEC."
120 PRINT "120 UNITS OF FUEL REMAIN."
130 PRINT:FOR X=1 TO 5000:NEXT
140 PRINT "HERE ARE THE RULES THAT GOVERN YOUR SPACE VEHICLE:"
150 PRINT "(1) AFTER EACH SECOND, THE HEIGHT, VELOCITY AND REMAINING"
160 PRINT "FUEL WILL BE REPORTED:"
170 PRINT "(2) AFTER THE REPORT, A '?' WILL APPEAR.  ENTER THE"
180 PRINT "NUMBER OF UNITS OF FUEL YOU WISH TO BURN DURING THE"
190 PRINT "NEXT SECOND. EACH UNIT OF FUEL WILL SLOW YOUR DESCENT"
200 PRINT "BY 1 FT/SEC."
```

```
210 PRINT "(3) THE MAXIMUM THRUST OF YOUR ENGINE IS 30 FT/SEC/SEC OR"
220 PRINT "30 UNITS OF FUEL PER SECOND."
230 PRINT "(4) WHEN YOU CONTACT THE LUNAR SURFACE, YOUR DESCENT"
240 PRINT "ENGINE WILL AUTOMATICALLY CUT OFF AND YOU WILL BE"
250 PRINT "GIVEN A REPORT OF YOUR LANDING SPEED AND REMAINING"
260 PRINT "FUEL."
270 PRINT "(5) IF YOU RUN OUT OF FUEL, THE '?' WILL NO LONGER APPEAR,"
280 PRINT "BUT YOUR SECOND BY SECOND REPORT WILL CONTINUE UNTIL"
290 PRINT "YOU CONTACT THE LUNAR SURFACE."
300 PRINT
310 PRINT "BEGIN LANDING PROCEDURE........."
320 PRINT "G O O D   L U C K "
330 PRINT
340 PRINT "SEC FEET    SPEED   FUEL","PLOT OF DISTANCE"
350 PRINT
360 T=0
370 H=500
380 V=50
390 F=120
400 IF B=0 THEN 430
410 PRINT T;TAB(4)H;TAB(12)V;TAB(20)F;TAB(29)"I";TAB(H/12+28);"**"
420 GOTO 440
430 PRINT T;TAB(4)H;TAB(12)V;TAB(20)F;TAB(29)"I";TAB(H/12+29)"**"
440 INPUT B
450 IF B<0 THEN 600
460 IF B>30 THEN 600
470 IF B>F THEN 490
480 GOTO 500
490 B=F
500 V1=V-B+5
510 F=F-B
520 H=H-.5*(V+V1)
530 IF H<=0 THEN 620
540 T=T+1
550 V=V1
560 IF F>0 THEN 400
570 IF B=0 THEN 590
580 PRINT "*** OUT OF FUEL ***"
590 PRINT T;TAB(4)H;TAB(12)V;TAB(20)F;TAB(29)"I";TAB(H/12+29)"**"
600 B=0
610 GOTO 500
620 PRINT "*** CONTACT ***"
630 H=H+.5*(V+V1)
640 IF B=5 THEN 670
650 D=(-V+SQR(V*V+H*(10-2*B)))/(5-B)
660 GOTO 680
670 D=H/V
680 V1=V+(5-B)*D
690 PRINT "TOUCHDOWN AT";T+D;"SECONDS."
700 PRINT "LANDING VELOCITY=";V1;"FT/SEC."
710 PRINT F;"UNITS OF FUEL REMAINING."
720 IF V1><0 THEN 750
```

```
730 PRINT "CONGRATULATIONS  A PERFECT LANDING"
740 PRINT "YOUR LICENSE WILL BE RENEWED...LATER"
750 IF ABS(V1)<5 THEN 780
760 PRINT "*** SORRY, BUT YOU BLEW IT ***"
770 PRINT "APPROPRIATE CONDOLENCES WILL BE SENT TO YOUR NEXT OF KIN."
780 PRINT "ANOTHER MISSION?"
790 INPUT A$
800 IF A$="YES" THEN 310
810 PRINT
820 PRINT "CONTROL OUT."
830 PRINT
840 END
```

Large Scale Simulations

Simulations on a large scale that require extensive preparation have also been accomplished on personal computer. These include the following.

The acoustics of a room. The acoustics of a room could be mathematically simulated if such parameters as the dampening effects of the walls, the shape of the room and its contents, the location of the sound source were provided; this could be useful to the architect or stereo-listening perfectionist. For example, in designing a small stereo listening room or studio, concentrations of standing waves cause unequal resonances in different spots within the room. To reduce the nonuniformity of standing waves at lower frequencies, room proportions must be carefully controlled to insure optimum diffusion of sound. Standing waves in a rectangular room are governed by a simple equation that could be modeled on your personal computer:

$$f(n_l, n_w, h_h) = (c/2) [(n_l/1)^2 + (n_w w)^2 + (n_h/h)^2]^{1/2}$$

where c=velocity of sound, and 1=ength, w=width, h=height of the room; the n's are the mode numbers; the lowest mode number (n=1) represents the lowest frequency resonance appearing, governed by the dimension, and higher n's represent higher frequency resonances. To calculate the frequency of a standing wave along one axis of the room, you set the n values for the other two axes equal to zero. For example, if n_l=1 and the others equal zero, the formula will give the lowest frequency standing wave along the length of the room. When two terms are non-zero, the standing waves are tangential. To obtain uniformity, the tangential waves are most desirable, the oblique waves are next, and the axial waves are least desirable. Thus, by using this equation, you can adjust room dimensions to provide the most even spacing of axial standing waves together with a preference for tangential waves, thereby allowing the greatest uniformity in frequency.

A simulation of world dynamics. This simulation, which is similar to Jay Forrester's Limits to Growth computer simulation, could be accomplished on a small scale. World dynamics involves the interaction of population, pollution, resources, and so on to predict future outcomes.

A simulation of astronomical and physical theories. This kind of simulation could possibly be accomplished with a personal computer system. Of course, the memory requirements would be very large, and simulation time could be hundreds of hours. See the article "Doing Physics with Microcomputers" in *Physics Today*, December 1983, pp. 25-28. The author describes a Monte Carlo simulation of the three dimensional Ising model for study of phase transitions.

A simulation of automotive fuel economy. This simulation could include such factors as fuel injection, fuel additives, pollution monitors, etc.

A simulation that stages your own World Series or Super Bowl. You could use statistical techniques to simulate a game or series of games using stars whose performances are based on their career averages.

ADDITIONAL CAI IDEAS

Examples of teaching programs for a variety of levels are listed below.

Elementary math flashcards. Programs designed to increase speed and efficiency in basic mathematics (for example, addition and multiplication) in which a time limit would be set for answering a question.

World problems. A program designed to output "random" word problems in mathematics for practice.

Rhymes and riddles. In this learning game, young children could try to unscramble words to form a line from a nursery rhyme or an answer to a riddle.

Fractions. A drill program in recognizing common denominators and adding and multiplying fractions.

Spell. A program that teaches the student to recognize commonly misspelled words.

Roots. A guessing/learning game in which the student must guess the square or cube root of a random number.

Kinema. A program in physics that helps the student learn to calculate the path of a projectile.

Gasvol. A plotting/calculating program that draws pressure/volume diagrams of a gas (chemistry and physics use).

Logic reasoning. This program tests the student on conditional statements, hypotheses, conclusions, deductions, fallacies, and definitions.

Balance. A drill program on balancing chemical equations.

Metric. An exercise in converting between the English and metric systems of units.

Bases. A demonstration program in teaching how to do conversions from one numerical base system to another.

Multiplication drill. The program in Listing 5-3 randomly generates single digit multiplication problems for practice in memorizing the multiplication tables. It has a variety of randomly selected responses to right and wrong answers and also keeps score. Problems that are answered incorrectly are stored and asked again at the end of the quiz.

Listing 5-3: The Multiplication Drill Program

```
10 V$=RIGHT$(TIME$,2): 'use PC clock to seed random number generator
20 V=VAL(V$)
30 RANDOMIZE V
40 REM MULTIPLICATION DRILL PROGRAM
50 INPUT "MULTIPLICATION DRILL--WOULD YOU LIKE INSTRUCTIONS";Z$
60 IF Z$="NO" THEN 110
70 PRINT "I'M GOING TO SEE HOW WELL YOU CAN MULTIPLY.  WHEN I SHOW YOU"
80 PRINT "A PROBLEM, TYPE IN THE ANSWER AND THEN PRESS THE 'ENTER' KEY."
90 PRINT "I'LL TELL YOU IF YOU ARE RIGHT AND WILL GIVE YOU A SCORE AFTER"
100 INPUT "TEN QUESTIONS. O.K.";Z$
110 A$="#########.":B$="########."
120 REM
130 FOR X=1 TO 10:X1=X1+1
140    A=INT(RND*10+1):B=INT(RND*10+1)
150    PRINT
160 E=0:PRINT "PROBLEM #";X1
170 GOSUB 190:NEXT X
180 GOTO 480
190 PRINT USING A$;A
200 PRINT "X";:PRINT USING B$;B
```

```
210 C=A*B
220 PRINT "-------------------------------"
230 INPUT "=        ";D
240 IF D=C THEN 360
250 E=E+1
260 IF E=2 THEN M=M+1:PRINT "THE ANSWER WAS:";C:GOTO 300
270 PRINT "YOU GOOFED...TRY AGAIN."
280 GOTO 190
290 GOTO 190
300 F=F+1
310 A(F)=A
320 B(F)=B
330 RETURN
340 REM
350 REM
360 X2=X2+1:R=INT(RND*5+1)
370 ON R GOTO 380,400,420,440,460
380 PRINT "RIGHT ON!!!"
390 RETURN
400 PRINT "FINE..."
410 RETURN
420 PRINT "GOOD WORK!!!"
430 RETURN
440 PRINT "KEEP IT UP!"
450 RETURN
460 PRINT "EXCELLENT!"
470 RETURN
480 PRINT "YOUR SCORE IS NOW";X2;"CORRECT AND ";M;"ERRORS.(";INT(100-(M/X1)*100)
;"%)"
490 INPUT "DO YOU WANT TO CONTINUE";Z$
500 IF Z$="YES" THEN 530
510 PRINT "THANKS FOR PLAYING WITH ME..."
520 END
530 G=0:FOR X=1 TO 10
540    IF (A(X)>0) OR (B(X)>0) THEN G=G+1
550 NEXT X
560 IF G=0 THEN 130
570 PRINT "I DIDN'T FORGET YOU MISSED THESE:"
580 FOR X=1 TO G
590    A=A(X):B=B(X)
600    GOSUB 190
610 NEXT X
620 GOTO 130
630 =0:PRINT "PROBLEM #";X1
```

Speed reading/tachistoscope. A program, helps such as the one in Listing 5-4, that helps you learn to read faster could be easily implemented by using a timing loop. Lines from a piece of literature could be stored in data statements and flashed momentarily on the screen; only one line at one time should be displayed. The timing loop is simply a BASIC FOR-NEXT loop that will require a specified amount of time to be executed (for example, FOR X=1 TO 500: NEXT X requires approxi-

```
Listing 5-4: The Speed Reading Program

5 CLS:KEY OFF
10 REM SPEED READING PROGRAM
20 N=500:REM SET N=INITIAL TIMING FACTOR
30 PRINT"THE THREE DAY BLOW, BY ERNEST HEMINGWAY"
40 GOSUB1000
50 PRINT"THE RAIN STOPPED AS NICK TURNED INTO THE ROAD "
60 GOSUB1000
70 PRINT"THAT WENT UP THROUGH THE ORCHARD. THE FRUIT HAD BEEN"
80 GOSUB1000
90 PRINT"PICKED AND THE FALL WIND BLEW THROUGH THE BARE TREES."
100 GOSUB 1000
110 PRINT"NICK STOPPED AND PICKED UP A WAGNER APPLE FROM "
120 GOSUB1000
130 PRINT"BESIDE THE ROAD, SHINY IN THE BROWN GRASS FROM THE"
140 GOSUB1000
150 PRINT"RAIN. HE PUT THE APPLE IN THE POCKET OF HIS MACKINAW"
160 GOSUB1000
170 PRINT"COAT.
180 GOSUB1000
190 REM CONTINUE TO INSERT LINES HERE IN THE FASHION ABOVE...
400 N=N-50:REM DECREASE TIMING FACTOR AFTER EACH READ-THROUGH
403 IFN<0THEN END
405 PRINT"TIMING FACTOR=";N:FORX=1TO500:NEXT X
410 GOTO 30:BEGIN ANEW WITH FASTER TIMING
1000 REM THIS SUBROUTINE INSERTS A DELAY BETWEEN EACH LINE
1010 REM DEPENDING ON THE VALUE OF THE TIMING FACTOR, N
1020 FOR X=1 TO N
1030 NEXT X
1040 REM EXPERIMENT WITH YOUR COMPUTER TO DETERMINE A
1050 REM REASONABLE VALUE FOR N IN LINE #20
1060 CLS:REM COMMAND TO CLEAR SCREEN
1070 PRINT:PRINT:PRINT:PRINT:PRINT
1080 RETURN
```

mately 1 second to execute with some forms of BASIC). The amount of time you have to read each line should be gradually decreased until a speed of several hundred words per minute is obtained.

A tachistoscope can be used to improve your perception and short-term memory. Psychologist G. Miller reports that anyone should be able to see from five to nine letters in any given brief exposure, whether 1/100 of a second long or ½ a second, which shows the limitation in our ability to perceive visual information in brief exposures. In addition, we are able to see many more letters displayed by the tachistoscope if they form a familiar word instead of an unfamiliar or foreign word. A tachistoscope program could be written for personal confirmation or as a science fair project. The program could offer adjustable speeds, familiar and unfamiliar words, and display of words for confirmation.

Chapter 6

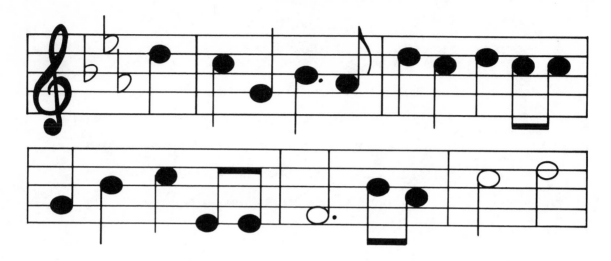

Hobby Applications

Your personal computer can make hobbies, from arts and crafts to photography easier, quicker, and more creative.

THE ARTS

It does not seem possible that a computer can create original art work until you consider the mathematical basis as well as randomness of some art forms. Art is an area in which the personal computer can be used in many different ways—and many of these ways are yet undiscovered.

The Visual Arts

The computer can serve both as a source of inspiration and as a tool for the artist or craftsperson. Below are some of the areas in which a computer can be used.

Mathematical Functions. Plotting or graphing a mathematical function can often produce interesting geometrical designs. Color terminals equipped to plot a grid in full color, each color indicative of the value of the function at each individual point, produce fantastic geometrics. The designs generated can be used in knitting or embroidering, or for producing a geometrical painting. A plotter or graphic pointer may be used for output. A standard printer may be used with the demonstration program in Listing 6-1, which creates plots with a three-dimensional appearance.

Listing 6-1: The Three Dimensional Plotter Program

```
5 KEY OFF:CLS
10 REM '3 DIMENSIONAL' PLOTTER
20 REM OTHER FUNCTIONS TO TRY INCLUD: S*(COS(Z/16))^2
```

```
30 REM THE SYMBOL ^ MEANS EXPONENTIATION
40 DEF FNA(Z)=S*EXP(Z*-Z/100)
50 INPUT "ENTER SCALE FACTOR (TRY '30')";S
55 INPUT "READ PRINTER; PRESS ENTER WHEN READY TO PROCEED";A$
60 FOR X=-S TO S STEP S/20:L=0
70 Y1=5*INT(SQR(S^2-X*X)/5)
80 FOR Y=Y1 TO -Y1 STEP -S/6
90 Z=INT(S-5+FNA(SQR(X*X+Y*Y))-.7*Y)
100 IF Z>L THEN L=Z:LPRINT TAB(Z)"+";
110 NEXT Y
120 LPRINT " ":NEXT X:END
```

Figure 6-1 shows some sample output from the three-dimensional plotter program.

Alteration of a design. A given design (for example, a drawing of a human face or an American flag,) transformed into a series of points on a grid can be manipulated using a mathematical algorithm to produce "modern art" effects. Additionally, one design may be gradually transformed into another, through a series of plots, producing a fascinating result reminiscent of animation.

Kaleidoscope. A kaleidoscopic pattern may be produced by plotting a continuous set of points that wander randomly horizontally and vertically in one of four corners on the screen. The other three corners are plotted by "reflecting" the wandering line, drawing in mirror-fashion. An example is shown in Fig. 6-2.

Random art patterns. For the ultimate in simplicity, a program could generate random numbers that in turn would cause graphics characters on the screen to turn on or off or would control a pen plotter in "random-walk" fashion. This, however, may exceed the confines of what is considered art. One hobbyist reports using his computer to randomly combine picture elements and then print "landscapes" using a plotter. Figure 6-3 shows an image produced using randomly determined elements.

A/D converters. Use of an analog/digital converter to digitize and transform real-world

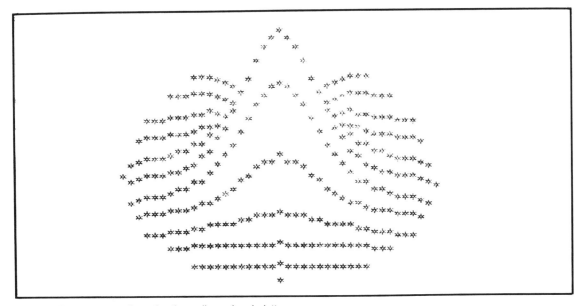

Fig. 6-1. Sample output from the three-dimensional plotter program.

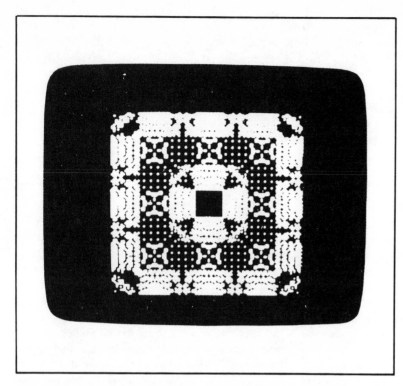

Fig. 6-2. A kaleidoscope pattern.

events can produce interesting results. For example, one hobbyist interfaced a human dancer to his computer by applying a dozen mercury switches to the dancer's body. The dancer's movements caused the switches to open and close, producing digital signals for the computer. The computer, in turn, created "choreographed music" from the signals.

Anamorphic art. Anamorphic images are those that appear distorted, but when viewed with a special device or from a unique perspective appear normal. An example of such a special device is a cylindrical mirror placed in the center of the image. The computer may be used to transform a set of points describing a "normal" image into an anamorphic equivalent. For examples of anamorphic art, see Leeman, Fred. *Hidden Images: Games of Perception, Anamorphic Art, Illusion.* New York: Harry N. Abrams, Inc., 1975. Figure 6-4 shows the results of such a program.

Crossword poetry. An interesting "crossword" of the words from a poem or piece of literature may be created by the computer. A program to create such "art" would scan each word and determine how that word could fit in crossword form with adjacent words:

138

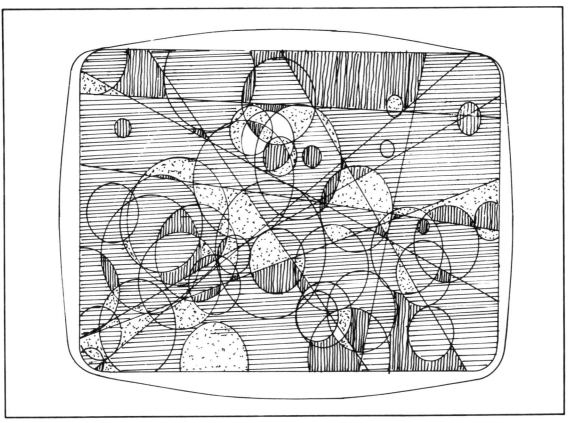

Fig. 6-3. A video image created by a program that randomly placed lines and circles of various sizes on the screen and filled in each area with a random color or texture.

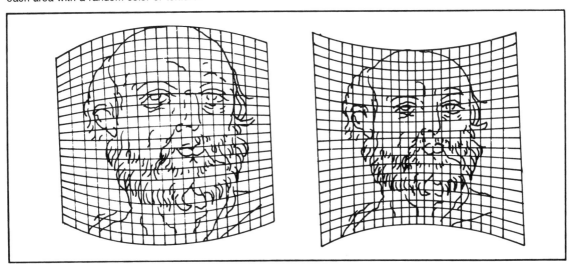

Fig. 6-4. "Computer Curvilinear Projection - Convex and Concave" by Ramon Masters. See *Computer Graphics and Art*, February, 1978, for a detailed explanation of how these and similar images can be created.

READ AS "Who has seen the wind?
　　　　　Neither I nor you.
　　　　　But when the leaves hang trembling,
　　　　　The wind is passing through."

Textile patterns. By combining the video graphics characters found on many personal computers into patterns, a textile appearance may be created. This may be considered art in itself or used as a model for a tapestry design. a simple program could select five graphics characters at random and then printout a full line of each graphic character. This pattern would then be repeated; surprisingly good results may be obtained. A more sophisticated program could combine different graphics characters within the line in symmetric fashion. Similarly, new quilting patterns could be designed mathematically. A sample textile pattern program is presented in Listing 6-2.

Perspective drawing aid. Given a set of points describing the (x, y, z) dimensions of objects in a picture, the computer could use matrix manipulations to produce a new set of points describing the picture from another perspective or viewpoint. Figure 6-5 shows an example. Additionally, if video graphics or plotting capabilities are available, the new picture could be plotted. Perspective transformations are useful in technical illustration and other art forms as well.

As an example of the perspective transformations that can be accomplished using a large array of points, let (x, y) be a coordinate pair under the "old"

Listing 6-2: The Textile Generator Program

```
10 V$=RIGHT$(TIME$,2): 'use PC clock to seed random number generator
20 V=VAL(V$)
30 RANDOMIZE V
40 PRINT "COMPUTER TEXTILE GENERATOR"
50 PRINT "CREATES RANDOM 'TEXTILE' PATTERNS"
60 PRINT "FOR OUTPUT ON A VIDEO SCREEN OR"
70 PRINT "GRAPHIC PRINTER.  REQUIRES A TVT"
80 PRINT "WHICH HAS GRAPHIC CHARACTER BLOCKS"
90 PRINT "ACCESSABLE USING 'CHR$(X)"
100 PRINT "CHOOSE THE AMOUNT OF COLOR YOU WANT IN THE DESIGN--"
110 PRINT "1) MONOCHROME"
120 PRINT "2) SIMPLE STRIPES"
130 PRINT "3) MULTI-COLOR STRIPES"
140 INPUT "4) CONFETTI DESIGNS",C
150 N=RND*9+1
160 FOR X=1 TO N
170   A$(X)=CHR$(INT(RND*49+174))
180 NEXT X
190 CLS
200 FOR M=1 TO 6
210   IF C>1 THEN COLOR INT(RND*14+1)
220   FOR X=1 TO N
230     IF C>2 THEN COLOR INT(RND*14+1)
240     FOR Y=1 TO 80
250       IF C>3 THEN COLOR INT(RND*14+1)
260         PRINT A$(X);
270       NEXT Y
280   NEXT X
290 NEXT M
300 GOTO 100
```

Fig. 6-5. Examples of the use of mathematical algorithms to alter drawings.

coordinate system. Let (x_θ, y_θ) be the center coordinates of the new system rotated through angle θ in relation to the old system. The new coordinates (x', y') may be calculated with these equations:

$$x' = (x - x_\theta) \cos\theta + (y - y_\theta) \sin\theta$$
$$y' = -(x - x_\theta) \sin\theta + (y - y_\theta) \cos\theta$$

A dimension scaling program would request the largest dimension of the object and the largest dimension of the drawing of the object; the scaling factor is the ratio of these values. The program would eliminate the headaches of creating a scale drawing by multiplying the input dimensions of the object by the scaling factor to arrive at the scaled down dimensions for the drawing.

Computer as sculptor. One hobbyist has created a computer-controlled router that can sculpt material in accordance with a set of programmed points (x, y, z). The computer controls the rotation of the sculpturing material (y axis) and the horizontal/vertical (x and z axes) motion of the router by means of servomechanisms. Eliminating one axis, the computer could also control a lathe to produce sculptured furniture legs of exacting proportions, for example.

Computer painting. A commercial computer-controlled airbrush system is being used to create murals from photos or other graphic images. The image is digitized (through the use of a TV camera and A/D converter) and then painted with much larger proportions by the use of a special x, y "plotting" system, which uses an airbrush in lieu of a pen. An enterprising hobbyist could construct such a system.

Computer posters. Everyone has seen the "computer portraits" popular at carnivals and shopping malls, in which a television picture of a subject is digitized and output on a line printer. One hobbyist has circumvented the expense of a television digitizer by taking an ordinary photograph and placing a fine grid over it; he assigns each square in the grid a brightness level and inputs this information. The computer prints dark characters or blocks for the squares with a low brightness level and vice versa for squares with a high brightness. Through this tedious and time-consuming process he creates computer posters and protraits without the expense of a television camera and video image digitizer.

A simple silhouette poster may be created by specifying the number of "X" and space characters to print on each line in DATA statements. For example, to print two spaces, one "X," one space, and one "X" on line number one, you could create a DATA statement that read DATA L1, S2, X1, S1, X1 and use the LEFT$ function to read the first character in each data item. The computer would then print the decoded representation and continue with the next line. The advantage to this method is that it requires less than the use of verbatim PRINT statements would.

The Verbal Arts

What usefulness could there be in creating poems by computer? Unlike humans, computers have the capability of being "completely" random. They are free from the "inspirational" selection of words when composing a poem; "composing a poem; "completely" is in quotes because there will always be some bias introduced by the programmer. A computer-generated poem can serve as a stimulus for the human poet. He can elaborate on the poem and extract inspirational clues in composing his own poetic works.

One crude method for generating computer poetry makes use of the following format in randomly selecting words from large lists of nouns, verbs, adjectives, definite articles, prepositions, conjunctions, and adverbs:

TITLE: Adjective + Noun

FIRST LINE: Adjective + Noun (plural) + Adverb + Verb (plural, present tense) + Adjective + Noun (plural)

SECOND LINE: Adjective + Noun (plural) + Verb (plural, present tense) + Adverb + Adjective + Noun (plural)

THIRD LINE: Article (definite, such as *the* + Noun (singular) + verb (singular, present tense) + Preposition + Article (definite) + Adjective + Noun (singular)

FOURTH LINE: Noun (plural) + Verb (plural, present tense) + Conjunction + Article (definite) + Noun (singular)

To ensure some continuity, the second adjective and noun of the first line may be repeated as the first adjective and noun of the second line. One computer-generated poem based on this structure read:

Clear Spirits
Warped trunks fraily dwell delicate leaves
Delicate leaves shudder cunningly intricate lines
The image vanishes to the sharp second
Bee fly against the cloud

Computers have poetic license too!

142

Listing 6-3: The Aphorism Generator Program

```
10 REM APHORISM GENERATOR
20 DIM A$(50):REM ADJUST THE DIMENSION EQUAL TO THE NUMBER OF WORDS
IN THE DATA STATEMENTS
30 FOR X=1 TO 50:READ A$(X):NEXT
40 PRINT A$(50*RND(1)); "IS THE ";A$(50*RND(1));" OF ";A$(50*RND
(1))
50 GOTO 40
60 REM ADD 40 NOUNS OF YOUR CHOICE TO THE DATA STATEMENTS BELOW
70 DATA SUCCESS, AGONY, MONEY, DEATH, LOVE
80 DATA REWARD, NAIVETE, FATHER, BEAUTY, SEX
```

Along similar lines, an aphorism generator could create aphorisms ad infinitum using the form "_____ is the _____ of _____," replacing each blank with a randomly selected noun. The underlying philosophical truism is up to the reader. The program in Listing 6-3 is an outline for an aphorism generator; you supply your own list of nouns.

The Musical Arts

Within the field of music, the personal computer can be used in a number of different areas. Some of these are listed below.

Music education. Possible music education applications include the following:

1. A graphic, flashcard style quiz that could display notes and other musical notation on the scale for identification as practice reading music.
2. A quiz on pronunciations and definitions of music terminology (for example, *andante, diatonic,* and *staccato*).
3. A musical staff drill. A graphic keyboard and staff could be presented, and the computer could select the note on the staff corresponding to the key that is "pressed." Key signature drills could be done in a similar manner.
4. A basic ear-training skills program. A computer capable of producing musical tones could quiz students on recognition of pitches, intervals, chords (major, augmented, diminished,

and minor), and scales (major, natural minor, harmonic minor, and melodic minor) and scales (major, natural minor, harmonic minor, melodic minor, whole tone, and chromatic).
5. A name the tune game. A computer-produced familiar tune can teach identification by sound of the degrees of the scale, using *solfeggio* syllables or scale degree numbers.
6. A wrong note program. Pitch error-detection can be practiced within various combinations of four-voiced chord types. Following the selection of a chord type, the computer can visually represent the chord and play the sound with one incorrect note. The student must identify the wrong voice and its corresponding pitch.
7. Harmony drills. Computer-produced aural diatonic chord progressions may be taught on various levels of difficulty.
8. Write that tune game. The computer plays a random or preprogrammed series of notes that the student must then reproduce on a video staff or on an interfaced musical keyboard.
9. Chord progressions practice. Students may predict chord progressions and receive feedback from the computer and subsequent visual and/or aural output.
10. Guitar chords practice. Students can practice finger placement required to produce guitar chords, with visual/aural feedback.
11. Famous composers and their music quiz. A quiz-style program could teach famous composer's names, pronunciations, and composi-

tions with the aural output of excerpts from those works.

12. Transposition practice. The student is presented with a short melody to transpose to a randomly-selected key. The computer verifies correct transposition.

13. Tuner program. Two computer-produced tones (separated by less than one half-step) are tuned to match each other by the student, who may select an increase or decrease in one of the tones.

14. Rhythm practice. The student could practice playing rhythm patterns on a keyboard. The computer can analyze them for accuracy, play the passage the way it should be played, and even demonstrate how the student's response differed from the expected response.

15. Composition packages. This program, given the notes of a composition, can display the piece in standard musical notation and actually play it. The student can experiment with tempo, timbre, and musical envelopes. Having control of timbre and musical envelope allows composition of a piece performed by three voices resembling the clarinet, flute, and oboe and demonstrates the interaction between voices.

Music composition. In the past, computer programs designed to compose music were based more upon random numbers than musical principles. Thus, the songs that were produced could only be compared to a child randomly hitting piano keys. Lately, progress has been made in developing more complex programs that adhere to the "rules of thumb" for composing particular types of music. One program, which used the following rules, was somewhat successful in composing "pop" music.

Basic melody requirements:

1. The first note must be other than a fourth, a flatted fifth, a minor second, or a ninth.

2. An ascending minor second progresses to a second, and a descending minor second progresses to the tonic; an ascending flatted fifth progresses to a fifth, and a descending fifth progresses to a fourth.

3. Not more than five notes in descension or ascension are allowed without a complementary movement.

4. The melody should consist of 35 to 60 notes.

5. The release begins on a subdominant major note.

6. Melodic leaps must not be larger than a major tenth.

7. A melodic leap may not be followed by another melodic leap larger than a major sixth.

8. No more than three consecutive melodic leaps are allowed.

9. No ascending or descending passage may contain more than one melodic leap.

One of the songs composed is represented as

/C/F*DA/G8C:8CF"G/C*AF8G8/G***/DEF"G/
ABC:B8C:8/C*B8C:8/D*C/F*DA/G8C:8C:F"G/
G*AF8G8/G***/DEF"G/ABC:B8C;8/C:*A*/F***
/A**C8CD/FE*/B**C:8EF"/G***

The corresponding music is shown in Fig. 6-6.

Rather than subjecting purely random notes to these compositional rules, a probability distribution used in conjunction with a random number generator could help to produce notes that would more likely fit the rules. The chart in Table 6-1 illustrates how this might be done. The name for each interval is given along with the corresponding number of notes on a keyboard. The next column gives a probability for selection of that interval, which may be changed according to the composer's wishes. The following two columns give the range of numbers, generated by a random number generator, that corresponds to the probability of selecting a given + or − interval. In this way a random number generator selecting numbers from 1-100 can provide a given probability distribution of notes.

To further ensure the choice of "good" notes, second or third-order probability distributions could be specified; that is, for each possible preceding interval (10), a probability distribution would exist for the purpose of choosing a particular

Fig. 6-6. An example of music generated by a computer.

value for the next interval. For instance, in traditional music, a tritone is usually followed by a stepwise interval (whole or half step); thus, the second-order probability distribution for a tritone would be heavily weighted toward a stepwise interval in selecting the next note of the composition.

Table 6-1. The Probability Distribution for the Random Selection of Notes.

INTERVALE	NO. OF NOTES AWAY FROM LAST NOTE	PROBABILITY OF SELECTION	RANDOM NUMBER RANGE	
			IN + DIRECTION	IN − DIRECTION
Unison	0	4%	49-52	49-52
Half Step	±1	14%	53-59	42-48
Whole Step	±2	12%	60-65	36-41
Minor Third	±3	10%	66-70	31-35
Major Third	±4	8%	71-74	27-30
Perfect Fourth	±5	12%	75-80	21-26
Tritone	±6	2%	81	20
Perfect Fifth	±7	14%	82-88	13-19
Minor Sixth	±8	6%	89-91	10-12
Major Sixth	±9	6%	92-94	7-9
Minor Seventh	±10	4%	95-96	5-6
Major Seventh	±11	2%	97	4
Octave	±12	6%	98-100	1-3

The music demonstration program in Listing 6-4 may be used to transpose from any key to any other key. It also serves to compose a four part harmony for any song written in the key of C. For the transposing subprogram, notes may be entered in the following format: C is C, C sharp is C#, C flat is C' and so on for A through G. For the harmonizer subroutine, notes are input in a numerical format; middle C is 0, the higher frequency notes D, E, F . . . are +1, +2, +3 . . ., and the lower frequency notes B, A, G . . . are −1, −2, −3 . . .. Because the song input must be in the key of C, sharps and flats are not absolutely necessary and are not provided for by the program. The addition of sharps and flats would be one improvement to experiment with. Of course, the transposing program may be adapted to use numerical notation instead of alphanumeric notation and then be used in conjunction with the transposing subprogram. Figure 6-7 shows the numerical system.

Listing 6-4: The Music Program

```
1 CLS:KEY OFF
10 PRINT "MUSIC PROGRAM:"
20 PRINT "HARMONIZES AND TRANSPOSES"
30 INPUT "SELECT: 1)TRANSPOSER  2) HARMONIZER";A
40 ON A GOTO 3000,100
100 REM HARMONY COMPOSING PROGRAM
110 REM A FOUR PART HARMONY IS PRODUCED FROM A GIVEN MELODY IN THE KEY OF C
120 DIM B(5,100),Y(6,6),V(100):RESTORE
130 J$=" ##  +##     +##      +##     +##"
140 FOR T1=1 TO 6:FOR T2=1 TO 6:READ Y(T1,T2)
150 NEXT T2,T1:R1=1
160 DATA 5,4,1,6,2,3,6,4,2,1,5,3,6,4,3,1,2,5,1,5,4,6,3,2,2,6,5
170 DATA 4,1,3,1,5,3,6,2,4,1,0,-3,-5,-7
180 INPUT "ENTER THE NUMBER OF NOTES IN THE MELODY ",W9
190 FOR E=0 TO 4:READ B(E,W9):NEXT E
195 REM INPUTTED MELODIES MUST BE IN THE KEY OF C
200 PRINT "ENTER NOTES INDIVIDUALLY IN THE FOLLOWING FORMAT:"
210 PRINT "MIDDLE C=0"
220 PRINT "NOTES ABOVE MIDDLE C ARE +1,+2,+3...CORRESPONDING"
230 PRINT "TO D,E,F..."
240 PRINT "NOTES BELOW MIDDLE C ARE -1,-2,-3...CORRESPONDING"
250 PRINT "TO B,A,G..."
260 FOR T1=1 TO W9:INPUT V(T1):NEXT T1
270 PRINT:PRINT "  #  SOPRANO  ALTO    TENOR   BASS"
280 L2=1
290 FOR W=W9 TO 1 STEP -1
300    IF W=W9 THEN 760 ELSE R1=1
310    FOR R=R1 TO 6
320      B=V(W):B(1,W)=B:L2=Y(L1,R):B(0,W)=L2
330      M=B(4,1+W):M(1)=L2-8:M(2)=L2-15
340      FOR S=1 TO 2
350        IF ABS(M(S)-M)<=5 THEN NEXT S ELSE A=M(3-S):GOTO 370
360        IF B>B(1,W+1) THEN A=M(2) ELSE A=M(1)
370        S=1:B(4,W)=A
380        FOR T=0 TO 4 STEP 2
390          G=B-(T+A):GOSUB 790:IF G=0 THEN 410
```

146

```
400          K(S)=A+T:S=S+1
410        NEXT T
420        IF S>3 THEN 690 ELSE  FOR U=0 TO 6
430          F(3,U)=K(1):F(0,U)=0:F(2,U)=K(2)
440          K=K(2):J=K(1):K(2)=J+7:K(1)=K
450        NEXT U
460        FOR U=0 TO 6
470          FOR E=2 TO 3
480            K=F(E,U)
490            IF (5-E*4>K) OR (17-E*4<K) OR (ABS(K-B(E,W+1))>5) THEN 610
500          B(E,W)=K:IF B(2*E-3,W)<=B(2*E-2,W) THEN 610 ELSE NEXT E
510          IF L1=L2 THEN  570 ELSE FOR E1=1 TO 4
520            FOR E2=E1+1 TO 4
530              M=B(E1,W+1)-B(E2,W+1)
540              G=M:GOSUB 790:IF (G=0) OR (G=4) THEN 550 ELSE 560
550              IF B(E2,W)-B(E2,W+1)=B(E1,W)-B(E1,W+1) THEN 610
560          NEXT E2,E1
570          FOR E=2 TO 3
580            M(E)=ABS(B(E,W)-B(E,W+1))
590          NEXT E
600          F(0,U)=M(2)+M(3):GOTO 620
610          F(0,U)=88
620        NEXT U
630        V=88:FOR U=0 TO 6
640          V1=F(X1,U)
650          IF V1>V THEN 660 ELSE V=V1:U9=U
660        NEXT U
670        IF V=88 THEN 690
680        B(3,W)=F(3,U9):B(2,W)=F(2,U9):GOTO 760
690      NEXT R
700      W=W+1:IF W9<>W THEN 710 ELSE PRINT "PROGRAM CANNOT CONTINUE":STOP
710      L1=B(0,W+1):L2=B(0,W)
720    FOR R=1 TO 6
730      IF L2=Y(L1,R) THEN 750
740    NEXT R
750    R1=R+1:GOTO 310
760    PRINT USING J$;W,B(1,W),B(2,W),B(3,W),B(4,W)
770 L1=L2:NEXT W
780 END
790 G=G-INT(G/7)*7:RETURN
3000 REM TRANSPOSER
3010 REM READ HARMONY PROG.DATA FIRST
3020 FOR X=1 TO 36
3030 READ A:NEXT X
3040 DIM A$(18,18),W$(100)
3050 FOR B=1 TO 17
3060   FOR C=1 TO 17
3070     READ A$(B,C)
3080 NEXT C,B
3090 INPUT "ENTER THE KEY THAT THE SONG IS IN (E.G.,C#)";B$
3100 FOR X=1 TO 17
3110   IF B$=A$(1,X) THEN 3120 ELSE NEXT X
```

```
3120    INPUT "ENTER THE KEY TO TRANSPOSE TO ",C$
3130    FOR T=1 TO 17
3140      IF C$=A$(1,T) THEN 3150 ELSE NEXT T
3150      PRINT "ENER THE NOTES OF THE SONG SEPARATELY"
3160      PRINT "ENTER 'END' TO END":R=1
3170      INPUT W$(R)
3180      IF W$(R)="END" THEN 3190 ELSE R=R+1:GOTO 3170
3190      R=R-1
3200      FOR Z=1 TO R
3210        FOR P=1 TO 17
3220          IF W$(Z)=A$(P,X) THEN 3230 ELSE NEXT P
3230          PRINT A$(P,T);" ";
3240    NEXT Z
3250 DATA C,C#,D-,D,D#,E-,E,F,F#,G-,G,G#,A-,A,A#,B-,B,C#,D
3260 DATA D,D#,E,E,F,G-,G,G,G#,A,A,A#,B,B,C,D-,D,D,D#,E,E,F
3270 DATA G-,G,G,G#,A,A,A#,B,B,C,D,D#,E-,E,F,F,F#,G,G#,A-,A,A#
3280 DATA B-,B,C,C,C#,D#,E,E,F,F#,G-,G,A-,A,A,A#,B,B,C,C#,D-,D
3290 DATA E-,E,E,F,F#,G-,G,A-,A,A,A#,B,B,C,C#,D-,D,E,F,F,F#,G,G
3300 DATA G#,A,A#,B-,B,C,C,C#,D,D,D#,F,F#,G-,G,G#,A-,A,B-,B,B,C
3310 DATA C#,D-,D,D#,E-,E,F#,G,G,G#,A,A,A#,B,C,C,C#,D,D,D#,E,E,F
3320 DATA G-,G,G,G#,A,A,A#,B,C,C,C#,D,D,D#,E,E,F,G,G#,A-,A,A#,B-
3330 DATA B,C,C#,D-,D,D#,E-,E,F,F,F#,G#,A,A,A#,B,B,C,D-,D,D,D#,E
3340 DATA E,F,F#,G-,G,A-,A,A,A#,B,B,C,D-,D,D,D#,E,E,F,F#,G-,G
3350 DATA A,A#,B-,B,C,C,C#,D,D#,E-,E,F,F,F#,G,G,G#,A#,B,B,C,C#,D-
3360 DATA D,E-,E,E,F,F#,G-,G,G#,A-,A,B-,B,B,C,C#,D-,D,E-,E,E,F,F#
3370 DATA G-,G,G#,A-,A,B,C,C,C#,D,D,D#,E,F,F,F#,G,G,G#,A,A,A#
```

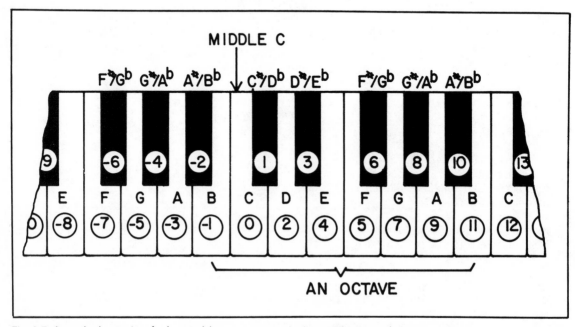

Fig. 6-7. A numbering system for harmonizing programs and other music-composing programs.

148

Additional possibilities for using your personal computer in music composition include the following:

1. Produce a stricter set of rules for composition than those given above; rely less upon randomness.
2. Develop programs to compose in assorted musical styles including classical, rock and roll, and children's music. Computer musicians have applied statistical analysis to various styles and composers to determine characteristic probability distributions. Random numbers subjected to these probability criteria can produce music reminiscent of the original style.
3. Develop programs to compose songs for given lyrics by using the timing of each syllable to time the duration of the notes accordingly. The ambitious programmer might try to link a lyric-producing program with a music composition program; some unusual results would undoubtedly be produced.
4. A popular melody could be mathematically transformed to produce a new melody, and this new melody would likely be more tuneful than compositions based on random number generators, fractals, or probability distributions. The original melody would be numerically encoded such that each note and note duration has a unique number. With the melody so coded, an algorithm could be applied to each note, translating that note into another. The simplest such algorithm could reflect each note around a central value, transforming high notes into low ones and vice versa. It could also be a mathematical formula, but extensive experimentation would be necessary.

The following formula is useful as a part of a musical tone generation program based upon the numbering notes according to octave (V), where middle C is in the fourth octave, and according to position within the octave where C=1, C#=2 . . . B=12.

$$\log_2\left(\frac{f}{55}\right) = V + \frac{P-22}{12}$$

where f = frequency in Hz.

A program that performs a simple song transformation is presented in Listing 6-5.

5. Given the score of a music piece written for a solo instrument (for example, the piano), the computer could transpose and analyze melodies, bass, and counter rhythms to pro-

Listing 6-5: The Simple Song Transformation Program

```
10 REM SIMPLE SONG TRANSFORMATION
20 REM REFLECTS NOTES AROUND A CENTRAL VALUE
30 READ N:REM SET N-NUMBER OF NOTES IN THE SONG
35 DIM M(N)
40 FOR X=1 TO N
50 READ M(X)
60 M(X)=10+(10-M(X)):REM REFLECT AROUND NOTE #10
70 NEXT X
80 FOR X=1 TO N
90 PRINT M(X);"  ";
100 NEXT X
110 END
120 REM FIRST DATA POINT IS # OF NOTES IN SONG
130 REM FOLLOWED BY NOTES OF SONG
140 DATA 10
150 DATA 4,2,5,7,5,5,13,1,12,3
```

duce sheet music versions for other instruments.

6. A microcomputer connected to a player piano via a solenoid interface could digitally record songs you play or song notes you input. The song could be stored on cassette or floppy disk and recalled to be played at normal speed, faster, slower, backwards, with staccato, and so on.

7. A microcomputer interfaced with a monophonic electronic synthesizer could theoretically produce a polyphonic effect, add a continuous bass or beat pattern, and perform a sequence of switching or mixing for live performances.

8. From a given composition, a simplified version could be extracted by the computer (the melody is usually carried by the highest notes, the bass by the lowest) and printed in standard musical notation. Also, a given piece could be arranged so that all chords are broken up into varying arpeggios.

9. Given a melody, the computer could be programmed to compose a bass counter-melody.

Computer controlled synthesizers. In 1982, a group of synthesizer manufacturers developed a standardized interface, called MIDI (Musical Instrument Digital Interface), to enable communication between synthesizers and computers. Each key is encoded in a fashion similar to a computer (ASCII) keyboard. For each key struck, a series of codes are sent: a NOTE ON signal, a PITCH signal, a VELOCITY signal, and (depending on the machine) other signals specifying pitch blends, patch changes, key release, after touch pressure, and front panel changes. This information can be sent to any other MIDI synthesizer so that two or more keyboards can perform in exact synchronization, although the patches are different on each machine. Special codes can indicate that only specified synthesizers are to respond to the following code. Through a serial interface, this information can also be sent to a computer, which may serve as a polyphonic sequencer or imitator of a multi-track tape machine. The computer may record, edit, store, and play back your music or play music entered through the ASCII keyboard. A composer can quickly change tempo, pitch, instruments, accents, and so on with the aid of such a system, which is capable of producing a flawless rendition.

The *Computer Music Journal* (P.O. Box E, Menlo Park, CA 94025) is a good source of information on composing, scoring, and playing music on computers, for the professional or amateur.

HOBBIES

The microcomputer can perform invaluable services for those involved in almost all hobbies.

Photography

The serious photographer should investigate the use of the computer to obtain more precise values for such things as development times, light exposures, and filters through the use of mathematical formulae. For example, the standard exposure meter assumes the following: 1) for any emulsion, the curve of the density versus the log of the exposure yields a straight line and is characterized by a single factor—speed, 2) time and intensity of light are interchangeable to provide a certain exposure (reciprocity). Actually, these assumptions are only approximations of true values. In extreme cases, reciprocity does not work; the density versus log of exposure curve is not linear, and emulsions have differing contrasts and latitudes. A reference manual describing the mathematical calculations of photography should describe the formulae used to take these factors into account.

Other ways in which photographers can use microcomputers include the following areas.

1. Exposure compensation is useful in the darkroom to calculate the exposure required to compensate for a change in photo enlargement magnification. Using the inverse square law, if you have data on a "perfect" print expressed as enlarger head height above the easel (H_0) and time of exposure (T_0), the formula for computing the new time of exposure (T_N) at the new height (H_N) with the same aperture is

$$T_N = \left(\frac{H_N}{H_O}\right)^2 \times T_O$$

A useful program could calculate exposure times for a range of specified heights at all available f-stops to permit easy enlargement of a negative to a given size.

2. Fill-in flash computation is used to determine the correct lens f-stop when a flash is used in the presence of strong ambient light to fill-in undesired shadows.
3. If you intended to do specialized photography requiring homebuilt equipment, the computer could be useful in optical and dimension calculations.
4. Automated control of darkroom equipment (including such features as temperature correction for chemicals, timer, development calculator) could expedite the development process. Alternatively, the computer could serve as a timer and reminder for steps to be taken in the development process.
5. An inventory of slides or photographs could be stored on disks or tapes, and topics could be indexed and cross-referenced. Thus, to create a slide show of a particular topic, you can use the computer to determine all relevant slides and output a listing of each along with its location and remarks.
6. A simple switching interface to a cassette recorder and slide projector could automate a complete audio-visual slide presentation. An exotic audio-visual light show could be controlled in a similar manner.
7. Focal length conversions from one camera to another, based on the diagonal or horizontal angle of view, could be done.
8. A program could be written to calculate film speed (ASA), flash ECPS value, or flash guide number, given the other two values. Once the flash guide number is known, the maximum f-stop for the distance from the flash to subject, may be calculated.

$$\text{f-stop} = \frac{\text{Guide number}}{\text{distance}}$$

The published flash guide number is for one speed of film only. If you use a different film with a different speed, the new guide number may be found using the formula

$$\text{New Guide No.} = \text{Old Guide No.} \times \frac{\text{New Film Speed}}{\text{Published Film Speed}}$$

9. Close-up photography values for subject distance, required lens focus setting, or field of coverage could be calculated given the other three values.
10. The depth of field indicates the distance from some point in front of the subject to some point in back of the subject for which a given photograph will be acceptably sharp. A computer program could mathematically determine how the desired near and far distances can be obtained, in terms of the f-stop and distance settings to use. The *hyperfocal* distance, or the nearest distance for which a lens can be focused to give satisfactory definition of infinity, is given by

$$H = \frac{F^2}{fxd}$$

where H = hyperfocal distance
       F = focal length of lens
       f = f/number
       d = diameter of circle of confusion.

11. A photograph of your video screen displaying alphanumerics or graphics could be used to title home slide shows or movies. A recommended procedure is to darken the room completely, use a tripod, and shoot with ASA 125 Plus −X at f/1.4, 1/8 second.

For serious hobbyists or professionals, a BASIC program for microcomputers to design and evaluate lenses was described in *Photonics Spectra*, December 1983, pp. 58-62.

Animated films. Although most microcomputers are not fast enough to display high-resolution real-time animation, a time-lapse film could be made with the end result being equivalent to real-time graphics. The graphic resolution should be a minimum of 200 by 200 individually definable blocks. Much better, although much more expensive, would be a system equipped with a plotter to draw all of the figures necessary to produce an animated film sequence. The three dimensional rotation of an object is a popular film subject due to the *relative* ease in programming.

Amateur Radio

The ham radio or citizen's band radio enthusiast could use a personal computer to assist with his hobby in these ways:

Morse code tutor. Computerists interested in passing the Morse code test to become amateur radio operators could use their machines to quiz themselves both visually and audibly. The visual representation of Morse code is, of course, a series of dots and dashes: --. -. ---.... Those of you who are using a TRS-80 without a built-in speaker can use one of the following methods to obtain the audible representation of the code.

1. Use an interfaced tone output speaker
2. Use timing loops to generate tones of a certain duration on an AM radio placed next to the CPU.

The standard method of learning Morse code is to first study the visual representations, and second, to transcribe an audio transmission at a gradually increasing rate. A program similar to the general CAI program described in Chapter 5 could be used to requiz you on the codes you have missed.

Message displayer. By using a Morse code decoder/sender interface between the radio and your computer, received and sent messages could be displayed on a video monitor in English, allowing the computer to "translate" Morse code (or some other code) to English and vice versa.

Message monitor. The computer could monitor a specified frequency for a particular audio signal or coded message. Transmissions immediately following this signal would be recorded digitally or on cassette tape. Thus, you need not attend to the radio constantly to receive a message. Received messages could also be forwarded automatically on another frequency to another station in a network.

Message relay. A stored message could be sent at the proper time if the station operator was unable to send it personally.

Controller. Add intelligence to your test equipment or radio with a controlling microprocessor. Test sequences could be done automatically.

Station log maintainer. Maintain your station log automatically—All entries could be stored, and classified, and special reports generated (for example, how many countries have been contacted? Have there been any repeat contacts?). If you hear someone and you're not sure whether or not you talked with him 6 months ago, you could type in his name or call letters and find out the last contact from a computer database of log entries.

Error correcting code senders. Error correcting codes could be automatically generated to improve communications.

Contest record keeper. Several ham radio contests have utilized small computers to keep track of all contacts.

Collections

Whether it be books, magazines, coins, stamps, antiques, or matchbook covers, most everyone collects something. The microcomputer can help you organize and present your collection

Collection inventory. If your collection involves many items, such as hundreds or even thousands of stamps, it is certainly a good idea to catalog each item. A computer database program, as described in the first chapter, is ideal for maintaining large collections of any kind.

In addition to storing an individual record specifying all pertinent information on each item, the computer would also be able to categorize, cross-index, and generate special lists of items. A special list could include all items that have a particular characteristic, for instance, a list of all British stamps or all stamps issued in 1979.

The fields to use in setting up a stamp collection database might look like this:

1. CATALOG NUMBER
2. NAME OR IDENTIFYING TITLE
3. DENOMINATION
4. SUBJECT
5. ORIGINAL COST
6. CONDITION
7. DATE ISSUED
8. QUALITY
9. CURRENT VALUE
10. COUNTRY OF ORIGIN
11. DESCRIPTIVE INFORMATION AND HISTORY
12. WHERE PURCHASED
13. MISCELLANEOUS COMMENTS

Using the database program, you could request the sum of field 5 or 9 for all records to determine the original cost and current value for the entire collection.

Collection management on your personal computer allows more time for the fun of collecting without the bother of record-keeping. Additionally, a cassette or floppy disk copy of the inventory could be stored in a safe location in the event an insured collection is destroyed.

Collection narrator. Hobbyists with collections will find that their personal computer with video display makes an excellent visual narrator of a collection. For example, a stamp collector created a file of his entire collection, with information on each item randomly accessible. His narrations were similar to this:

Decade of Space Achievement Issue
Issued: August 2, 1969 Purchased: September 1, 1969
Purchase price: .16 Value: .60

This stamp pair depicts the ascent of man upon the surface of the moon.

Interested persons can be instructed how to obtain information on a particular item, or else the computer can present a continuous display of each item in sequence; this technique can save you from monotonous repetition of information to visitors at an exhibition. Businessmen at expositions could put their personal computer to similar use in explaining products.

Astronomy

Potential applications for your personal computer in amateur astronomy include the following:
1. Locate and identify stars—Calculation of declination, sidereal hour angle from observed altitude, azimuth, and time.
2. Make records of observations efficiently in computer format for quick retrieval.
3. Interface telescope drive mechanics to a microprocessor controller for automatic photographic observations. For more information see *InfoWorld*, Volume 5, Number 47 (12/83) pp. 45-46 and *Sky and Telescope*, January 1981, p. 71.
4. Interconvert astronomical units, kilometers, light years, and parsecs.
5. Calculate and plot orbits of satellites and planets.

The astronomy demonstration program in Listing 6-6 calculates the relative position of Venus in degrees and hours from the sun for a given date.

A series of BASIC astronomical calculation programs for ephemeris of comets and minor planets, locations of celestial objects, and altitude

Listing 6-6: The Astronomy Demo Program

```
10 CLS:KEY OFF
20 PRINT "ASTRONOMY DEMO PROGRAM"
30 PRINT "CALCULATES THE RELATIVE POSITION OF VENUS AND THE SUN;"
40 PRINT "CALCULATES THE NUMBER OF DAYS SINCE 12/31/49"
50 INPUT "ENTER THIS YEAR AS TWO DIGITS (E.G. '84' FOR 1984)";Y
60 PRINT "ENTER NUMBER OF DAYS SINCE DECEMBER 31 OF LAST YEAR "
```

```
70 INPUT "FOR EXAMPLE, FEB. 5 WOULD BE 36 DAYS:",DA
80 CLS:LOCATE 11,25:PRINT "PLEASE WAIT--CALCULATING"
90 X=364*INT((Y-50)/4)+365*((Y-50)-INT((Y-50)/4))+DA
100 PI=3.141592:A=PI/180:C=A*.9856:B=180/PI:D=99.2*A:E=D+C*X
110 IF E<PI*2 THEN 130
120 E=E-PI*2:GOTO 110
130 E=SIN(E-A*105)*1.9*A+E:F=A*1.602:G=A*80.85:H=G+F*X
140 IF H<PI*2 THEN 150 ELSE H=H-PI*2:GOTO 140
150 H=H+SIN(H-A*135)*.8*A
160 J=SIN(H-A*232)*.0055+.7233
170 K=H-E:I=SIN(E-A*195)*.016+1:M=-PI/2
180 L=SQR(J*J+I*I-2*J*I*COS(K))
190 N=SIN(K)*(J/L)+SIN(M)
200 IF N<0 THEN M=PI/3600+M:GOTO 190:ELSE R=M*12/PI
210 CLS:PRINT "THE RELATIVE LOCATION OF VENUS IS";M*B;" DEGREES FROM THE SUN"
220 PRINT "=TO ";R;"HOURS FROM THE SUN";:END
```

and azimuth of the sun appeared in *80 Microcomputing*, October 1983.

Gardening

Writing a garden analysis program for one-time use would not be a practical idea, but your friends and neighbors could use such a program, and you may be able to sell the completed software to a local garden supply store. A complete analysis program is more complicated than it appears on the surface, no pun intended. These are some of the factors to consider:

1. pH, water, soil density, and sunshine levels of the plot.
2. Desired pH, water, soil density, and sunshine levels for the plants to be planted.
3. Nitrogen, phosphorus, and potassium contents in the soil compared to plant requirements.
4. The size of the garden.

Proper planning will allow you to position certain vegetables that ward off insects next to others that need this protection. The space needed between adjacent plants should also be considered. Specific plant requirements and the harvest times of the vegetables could be printed, along with a graphic presentation of the garden plot:

BEETS ....
CORN --

RADISHES ::
TOMATOES --

Additional outputs could explain how to form a compost heap and how to use fertilizer. One gardener uses his personal computer to track insecticide and herbicide application, precipitation dates and amounts, temperature, and chores to be done. Tables of times to plant, spray, and prune can also be stored for ready reference and to simplify planning.

Sports

A file of team and player statistics, player's names and numbers, and other sports information could be stored on the computer (preferably on floppy disk) for quick retrieval by the television sports fan. Sports statistics could be compiled, graphed, and analyzed. Probability forecasting of score and point spread based upon past performance of opposing teams could be accomplished. The computer could also "learn" from its mistakes, retaining the outcomes of many games in memory.

At local sporting events a microcomputer could be useful in maintaining scores, team records, and player records or statistics as the game progresses (for use by the announcer or for permanent records).

A series of elapsed-time computations could be accomplished efficiently with the proper pro-

154

gram. A programmable calculator could serve as a digital stopwatch as well.

Bowling, golf, and other sports involving the tedious calculation of averages and other statistics for a league are well-suited for computer bookkeeping. Sell such a computer service or offer it gratuitously to your local bowling alley or golf course.

Gambling

Your computer could become a helpful advisor for those who play poker and various other card games. All information available (for example the cards in your hand and the amount of the bet) would be input before each round, and an analysis based upon the laws of probability could determine your best move. (Perhaps your opponents would object to this advantage!). For example, these are the probabilities for obtaining particular poker and bridge hands:

Royal flush	649,739 to 1
Straight flush	72,192 to 1
Full house	693 to 1
Flush	508 to 1
One pair	1.37 to 1
Straight	254 to 1
13 card suit	158,753,389,899 to 1
12 card suit	367,484,698 to 1
Nine honors	104 to 1
Yarborough— no honors	1,827 to 1
Four aces/four of a kind	378 to 1
Three of a kind	47 to 1
Two Pair	21 to 1
One Pair	2 to 1
Nothing of Interest	2 to 1

These probabilities were in part computed by the use of the formulas for combinations and permutations. The number of combinations of n things taken four at a time is designated by

$$_nC_r = \frac{n!}{(n-r)!(r!)}$$

and the number of permutations of n objects taken r at a time, $_nP_r$ is

$$_nP_r = \frac{n!}{(n-r)!}$$

The mathematical concept of *expectation* is very useful in determining when to drop out of a poker hand or other gambling operation.

Expectation = probability times winnings

For example, suppose a poker player plans to call a bet of $2, which would increase the pot (potential winnings) to $14. If he can see from the exposed cards that his probability of winning is .4, his expectation is .4 × $14 = $5.60, for which he must pay $2. Since the expectation is worth more than the purchase price, he should call the bet. This is but one concept to incorporate with a betting analysis program.

Other forms of gambling (for example, football betting and jai-alai) may be computer-analyzed based upon past performances of the opponents and a confidence level established to conservatively pick the winner/point spread. Statistics to be incorporated in a database could include each team's win/loss record, the coach, the location (home or away), the playing surface, and each team's record against the point spread. A complete computer analysis of hundreds of games played from any one sport could yield a system for predicting future outcomes through the use of statistical cross-correlation between all variables.

Fishing

Potential applications for serious fishermen include the following:
1. The analysis of weather patterns and times in order to forecast the ideal time to fish.
2. The recording of weight and species of catch, locations fished, weather, tides, depth and temperature. Use this statistically correlated data for future reference. A portable microcomputer with an A/D converter could gather some of this data automatically. One

lobster fisherman has statistically analyzed his placement of lobster traps on his microcomputer to optimize his catch.

3. The computation of high and low tide times and time of sunrise/sunset.

The computation of times of sunrise/ sunset and high and low tides. Pilots as well as fishermen will find a sunrise/sunset calculating program useful. To keep such a program as simple as possible, tide or sunrise data from previous days could be entered to eliminate highly technical calculations. The times for future sunrises or sunsets may then be projected by linear regression or moving average calculation.

For those inclined to astronomical calculations, no pun intended, the time of sunrise/sunset may be more accurately calculated by consideration of the changing inclination to the sun and time of rotation for the earth.

Biorhythms, Astrology, and the Psychic

Those involved in exploring the more controversial aspects of human existence will also find the microcomputer useful.

Biorhythms. Biorhythms are supposedly the cycles in emotional, physical, and intellectual states governing everyone's behavior. Dozens of computer programs have been written to generate personalized biorhythm charts, yet interesting additions could be included. Potential innovations include the following:

1. Plotting or numerically comparing the biorhythms of two or more friends or a family.
2. Computing the average of all three biorhythmic cycles.
3. Generating a biorhythm chart in the form of a standard calendar.
4. Judging the reliability of biorhythms by objectively analyzing your three states at the end of each day and making a statistical comparison, and plotting this data versus your biorhythm.
5. Investigating the use of histograms and other means of presenting data to output biorhythms in a more favorable format, including artistic designs.
6. Comparing the reliability of your standard

biorhythm to one beginning with your estimated date of conception.

Astrology. The determination of the alignments of the planets and the sorting of astrological data are best done with a computer. Horoscopes, interpolation midpoints, aspects, and Placidus house and astropoints calculation may be done. Tarot, I-Ching, and Numerology may be accomplished in a similar manner.

The psychic. Purely for entertainment, "psychic" and "ESP" programs have been written using random number generators; can you predict the computer's choice of a card or number?

Additional Hobby Application

Hobbyists will find microcomputers useful in all the following areas:

Designing recreational vehicles. A hang glider or ultralight enthusiast considering designing a new aerofoil could find a detailed computer-simulated wind tunnel test beneficial. The proposed design could be mathematically described to the computer, and an aerodynamic simulation of this magnitude could only be done by someone with a good background in aerodynamics. Similar simultations could be applied to boats and other recreational vehicles.

Model building. A simple, time-saving program could calculate the scaling factor for model builders by dividing the length of the model by length of the object to be modeled. Next, each dimension of the object would be input, and the corresponding dimension for the model would be calculated by multiplying the original dimension by the scaling factor.

Model railroading. Model railroading enthusiasts with a large layout may wish to automate the trains, lights, switches, and so on with a controlling microprocessor. One hobbyist went so far as to print train schedules and tickets, and analyze freight business on his personal computer.

Scuba diving plan. A simple program could calculate one of these four parameters, given the other three:

1. Time underwater in minutes = TVW
2. Surface air consumption rate in cubic ft/min = S
3. Depth in feet = D
4. Total air volume of tank in cubic feet = TAV

$$\frac{33 \cdot TAV}{D \cdot S} = TUW$$

Geneological storehouse. A few hobbyists have obtained a sufficient amount of geneological information such that a personal computer is necessary to file and update the information. In addition, having specified characteristics of each family member instantly available eases the task of further geneological research.

Aquarium maintenance. One hobbyist uses his computer to compute amounts of chemicals necessary to maintain a seawater aquarium environment. Complex calculations are necessary to obtain exact values over a range of temperatures and conditions.

Chapter 7

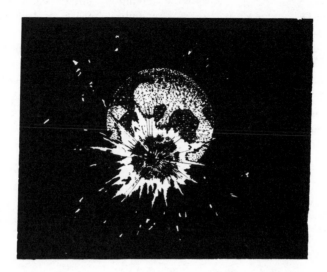

Games and Recreational Applications

According to polls, the most popular application of personal computers is games, with over 60 percent of owners claiming this to be their primary application. Although this percentage may decline with the advent of inexpensive, easy-to-use software for other purposes and the burgeoning computer networks, games will continue to be one of the most popular applications.

Games are not only fun, but they often have the added benefit of being educational. The child (or adult!) can hone his skills of eye-hand coordination and develop abilities to react creatively, solve problems logically, and make decisions. Games are often the best learn-to-program challenges for the beginner, yet the professional programmer may even find himself defeated in attempting to write complex game programs (for example, chess or Go). Games encourage imaginative and constructive programming and responses.

There are at least eight major categories of games that have been adapted to the computer:

1. Fantasy and adventure games: stemming from the popular college game, *Dungeons and Dragons*, fantasy and adventure games lead you step by step through an imaginary world to find a special treasure, to solve a mystery, or to outfox an evil wizard. However, you must figure out how to overcome or go through the many obstacles assigned to prevent your success in this elaborate puzzle. You can type simple commands, such as "go east" in English, and the computer will describe where you are and what the situation is after each command. The more elaborate adventure games may use vivid graphics to draw the scene and even use voice output. Another series of programs called interactive fiction allows you to interact with the characters and situations in a story.

2. "Video" games: games of this kind usually involve a live action, shoot-em-up approach, pitting you, for example, as the sole champion of a ship or planet versus the rest of the universe, which is invariably out to get you. If you begin to be successful, of course the battle conditions

deteriorate and the battlefield fills with increasingly difficult targets to hit. This genre is the most popular form of computer game and a challenge to your eye-hand coordination; all manner of competitions are available.

3. Strategy and battle games: for those who prefer a more enlightened approach to gaming, strategy games offer complex rules and tactics to employ in fighting battles against a computer or a human opponent. They often make use of excellent computer graphics displaying a battlefield and tokens representing forces on each side.

4. Card games: care to play bridge with three computerized opponents? The computer has also been programmed to play poker, gin, Kalah, Tripoli, solitaire and many other card games. Card tricks, bridge tutors, and poker betting systems have also been programmed.

5. Board and word games: included in this group are the old favorites of chess, backgammon, and checkers and the new-fangled Clue™, Monopoly™, Boggle™, and Scrabble™. Some of the word games may be equipped with vocabularies of up to 90,000 words. Chess, checkers, and backgammon programs can already compete at the master level, and it is only a matter of time before they become reigning world champions.

6. Gambling games: all the games in Vegas, from one-armed bandits to roulette, have been adapted to the personal computer. For those who take gambling seriously, programs are available to perform complex handicapping analysis for horse racing and football games and to do the calculations necessary for the prediction of other sporting events.

7. Sports games: football, baseball, auto racing, skiing, and numerous other sports have been computerized and often include live action with complex graphics.

8. Party games: many popular party games, from charades to spin the bottle, have been programmed. For those willing to take the advice of a computerized sex analyst, several commercial programs will ask you and your mate a series of questions and then determine the optimum "interlude," for which it provides explicit instructions.

BOARD AND STRATEGY GAMES YOU CAN PROGRAM

Although most of the popular live-action or real-time games on the market required hundreds to thousands of man-hours to develop, many nonanimated games can be written by the beginner and are sometimes just as entertaining as the more complex games. A sampling of game ideas to tackle in BASIC follows; some would require less than 30 program lines, and others are more difficult, possibly requiring hundreds of lines.

Board and Logic Games

Many popular board and logic games take on an added dimension when computerized, especially if the computer is programmed to be the opponent. Some of the many possibilities include the following games:

Tricolor. Tricolor is a game played on a hex board with hexagonal cells colored red, white, and blue (or different shades). An actual playing board should be used in the computerized version, because creating a board display on a video screen would be difficult.

Each player begins with 18 pieces. Those of one player are white; those of the other are black. At the start of the game, white places his pieces on hexes 1-18, and black on hexes 44-61 as shown in Fig. 7-1.

The pieces are called stacks because you can place more than one piece together to form a stack. The range of a stack, that is, the maximum number of cells it can traverse in any one direction is a single move, is determined by the number of pieces in the stack; one cell for a single piece, two cells for a stack of two pieces; and three cells for any larger stack.

The combat strength of a stack depends upon both the number of pieces it contains and the color (or shade) of the cell on which it rests. Taking the strength of a single white piece on a white cell as the unit, the strength of a stack of two pieces on a white cell is two units, and the strength of any larger stack on a white cell is three units. The

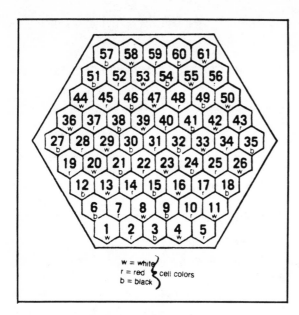

Fig. 7-1. The Tricolor game board.

strength of a stack on a black cell is twice what it would be on a white cell, and a stack on a red cell is worth three times as much as it would be on a white cell.

Players take alternate turns, each moving a single stack along a diagonal or horizontal line as far as he wishes, within the range of the stack. The entire stack or only a portion of it can be moved; the number of pieces in the part moved determines the strength of the stack. Occupied cells may not be jumped, but a player may move his stack to a cell occupied by another stack owned by himself or by the opponent. If the stack is his own, the stacks are merged. If the opponent owns the other stack, an "attack" has been initiated, and the disposition of pieces is as follows: a stack may attack an opposing stack only if it is stronger (contains more pieces). If it is more than twice as strong, the opposing stack is "killed," and all hostile pieces in the stack are removed from play; friendly pieces are added to the winning stack. If the attacking stack is not more than twice as strong, it "captures" the opposing stack by combining it with itself. If a capture or kill can be made in a player's turn, it must be made. The game ends with the capture or killing of all of one player's pieces.

Black Sheep. Black sheep is played on a chessboard between two players, one "white" and the other "black." White begins the game with four white checkers that are placed on the four black squares on one side of the chessboard. Black uses one black checker and places it on either of the middle black squares on the opposite side of the board. The white pieces may only move forward to the opposite side; black may move forward or backward. Both colors may only move one square at a time and only on the diagonal.

Black moves first and then moves alternate. The object for black is to reach the opposite side of the board without being "trapped" (surrounded by white pieces in such a way that there is no adjacent diagonal unoccupied square to move to). The objective for white is to trap black before it reaches the other side of the board. Apparently, no one has determined a winning strategy for this game; thus it would be challenging to develop a heuristic strategy for the computer to play either side.

Jam. In this simple, yet challenging game, the small circles in the diagram in Fig. 7-2 represent cities; the lines represent roads. Each road has a designated number. Players alternate turns choos-

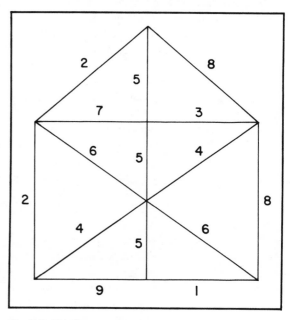

Fig. 7-2. The Jam game board.

ing one of the nine roads as their own property. The winner is the first to own three roads that connect directly with any one city. The game may be won with a mathematical strategy similar to that used in tic-tac-toe.

Hot. "Hot" is a clever variation of tic-tac-toe. The following words are listed on a computer screen: TANK, WOES, SHIP, WASP, HOT, BRIM, HEAR, FORM, TIED. Players take alternate turns picking one word from the list; words are removed from the list as they are chosen. The first player to pick three words that contain the same single letter is the winner.

The game may be analyzed by the computer in the same manner as tic-tac-toe, if the words are arranged on the board as in this diagram:

SHIP	BRIM	TIED
WASP	HEAR	TANK
WOES	FORM	HOT

By choosing three words in a row horizontally, vertically, or diagonally, a player can win the game. Thus, the strategy for play is the same as in tic-tac-toe, except the player that does not know these congruencies is at a disadvantage.

Bridge-it. In the game of Bridge-it, the first player is designated as 0 and the second player as X. Using the grid shown in Fig. 7-3, putting a connecting line between two horizontally or vertically adjacent markers of the player's symbol. The 0 player attempts to form a connected "bridge" from

	1	2	3	4	5	6	7	8	9	10	11
1		O		O		O		O		O	
2	X		X		X		X		X		X
3		O		O		O		O		O	
4	X		X		X		X		X		X
5		O		O		O		O		O	
6	X		X		X		X		X		X
7		O		O		O		O		O	
8	X		X		X		X		X		X
9		O		O		O		O		O	
10	X		X		X		X		X		X
11		O		O		O		O		O	

Fig. 7-3. The Bridge-it game board.

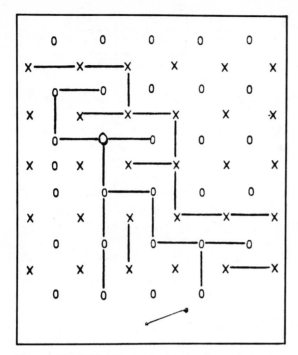

Fig. 7-4. The Bridge-it game board showing a win by X.

posed of hexagons, with eleven hexagons on each side (although other sizes have been used). Two opposite sides of the board are named black, while the other two are named white, as shown in Fig. 7-6. The hexes at the four junctions between sides are neutral. One player has black pieces, the other player has white. Alternate turns are taken, with each player placing one of his pieces on any unoccupied hexagon. The object for both players is to complete a continuous chain of his pieces between the two sides labeled by his color. The game is mathematically solvable on boards with certain dimensions. For an interesting discussion of winning strategy and Hex variants, the reader is referred to *The Journal of Recreational Mathematics*, Vol. 8(2), 1975-1976, p. 120.

Cross Capture. Cross Capture is played on a chess board. At the start of the game, a set of randomly distributed letters or numbers is put on the board (video display), with no more than one character per square. Most of the board remains empty. A sample board is shown in Fig. 7-7. Players take turns choosing one of the letters, and all other letters on the board that fall in a given category become property of that player. One category may be defined as all the letters in the

the top to bottom of the board, while the X player attempts to form a bridge from the left to right side of the board. The first to form a bridge wins the game.

A winning strategy exists for this game as illustrated in Fig. 7-4. For the 0 player to win, he should put his first line between the 0s at positions 9, 2, and 11, 2 as shown in Fig. 7-5. The game may be won by the 0 player if the following strategy is used. Whenever X joins a connecting line, the line will touch one of the dotted lines or semicircles in Fig. 7-5. 0 should draw a connecting line between two 0 markers such that the line will touch the end of the dotted line just touched by the line drawn by X following each X turn. In this manner, 0 will inevitably win.

Hex. Hex is a game similar to Bridge-it, but the game has not been solved such that a win is always certain. For this reason, hex would probably be more interesting to play against a computer. A heuristic strategy similar to that used in Bridge-it could be employed.

One game of Hex is played on a board com-

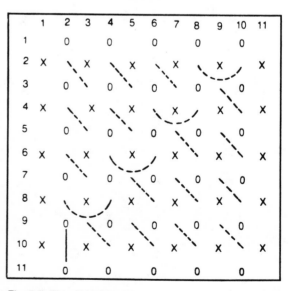

Fig. 7-5. The Bridge-it game board showing a winning strategy.

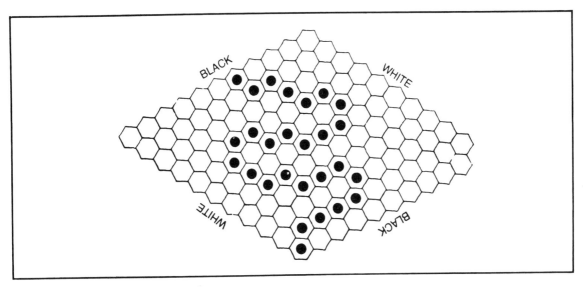

Fig. 7-6. The Hex game board.

same horizontal, diagonal, or vertical row as the chosen letter or as all the letters within a certain proximity to the chosen letter (for example, one space away). The player who possesses the most letters at the end of the game is declared the winner.

Tic-tac-toe variation. An interesting tic-tac-toe variation is played as follows. Each player puts his three pieces on a tic-tac-toe board such that piece ownership alternates around the periphery of the board. Following this setup, each player is allowed to move one of his pieces to an adjacent square. The winner of the game is the first to make three-in-a-row.

Tuknanavuhpi. Tuknanavuhpi is a Hopi Indian chase game played on a 4 × 4 board with diagonals drawn in each of the 16 squares. Pieces move on the points where lines meet on the board, not on the squares. There are two players; each one has 20 pieces placed on the board as indicated in the diagram in Fig. 7-8. The middle of the board is initially empty.

Players take alternate turns moving their pieces in any direction along the lines on the board, from one intersection to another adjacent intersection. As in checkers pieces are captured by jumping over any of the opponent's pieces. The winner is the

player who has captured all of his opponent's pieces.

Many other games popular in other cultures but undiscovered in the United States are well-suited to be computer games. These include Teekso, Hasami Shogi, Dreidel, Bell and Hammer, Asalto, Yofe, Ur, and Alquerque, which are referenced in game encyclopedias.

Nim. The game of Nim has become a very popular computer game. The rules are simple.

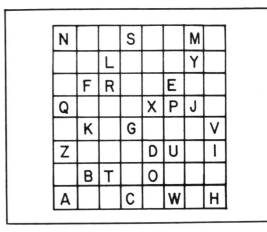

Fig. 7-7. A sample Cross Capture game board at the start of a game.

163

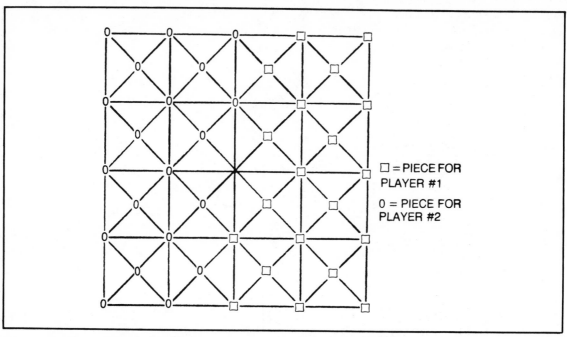

Fig. 7-8. The Tuknanavupi game board.

From a pile of any number of items (13 is the usual number), players take turns picking one, two, or three items. The player forced to pick up the last item loses the game. A winning strategy for the second player is to ensure that with every move you leave the pile with the number of objects equal to 9, 5, or 1. The program in Listing 2-1 plays and explains a variant of Nim. You can adapt it to play the Nim variations explained below.

Nim Variations. Here are a few games that

Listing 7-1: The Nim Program

```
10 KEY OFF:CLS
20 RAN$=RIGHT$(TIME$,2)
30 RAN=VAL(RAN$)
40 RANDOMIZE(RAN)
100 PRINT "THIS PROGRAM PLAYS THE GAME OF NIM.  ASSUME"
110 PRINT "THAT THERE ARE 25 STICKS IN A PILE.  THE PLAYERS TAKE"
120 PRINT "TURNS REMOVING 1,2,3,OR 4 STICKS FROM THE PILE.  THE"
130 PRINT "PLAYER WHO IS FORCED TO TAKE THE LAST STICK LOSES."
140 DIM C$(5),L$(5),W$(5)
150 FOR X=1 TO 5:READ C$(X):NEXT:FOR X=1 TO 5:READ L$(X):NEXT
160 FOR X=1 TO 5:READ W$(X):NEXT
170 PRINT
190 PRINT "DO YOU WANT TO GO FIRST";
200 INPUT Q$
210 PRINT
230 X=25
```

```
240 IF Q$>="Y" THEN 300
250 PRINT "I CHOOSE 4 STICKS."
260 PRINT "THERE ARE NOW 21 STICKS LEFT."
270 X=21
280 PRINT
300 FOR I=1 TO 10
310 GOSUB 380
320 IF X=1 THEN 650
330 IF X<1 THEN 760
340 GOSUB 490
350 IF X=1 THEN 760
360 NEXT I
370 REM---------------NUMBER OF STICKS OPPONENT TAKES------------
380 PRINT "HOW MANY STICKS DO YOU WANT";
390 INPUT N
400 IF N<>INT(N) THEN 450
410 IF N<1 THEN 450
420 IF N>4 THEN 450
430 X=X-N
440 RETURN
450 PRINT C$(INT(RND*5+1))
460 PRINT
470 GOTO 380
480 REM---------------NUMBER OF STICKS I TAKE--------------------

490 N=X-5*INT((X-1)/5)-1
500 IF INT((X-1)/5)<>(X-1)/5 THEN 520
510 N=INT(RND*4+1)
520 X=X-N
530 IF N>1 THEN 560
540 PRINT "I CHOOSE 1 STICK."
550 GOTO 600
560 PRINT "I CHOOSE";N;" STICKS."
570 IF X>1 THEN 600
580 PRINT "THERE IS 1 STICK LEFT."
590 GOTO 610
600 PRINT "THERE ARE NOW ";X;" STICKS LEFT."
610 PRINT
630 RETURN
640 REM---------------HE WINS-----------------------------------
650 PRINT L$(INT(RND*5+1))
660 PRINT
690 PRINT
700 PRINT "LET US PLAY ANOTHER GAME."
710 PRINT "SINCE YOU WENT FIRST LAST TIME, I WILL GO FIRST."
720 PRINT
740 GOTO 250
750 REM---------------I WIN---------------------------------
760 PRINT W$(INT(RND*5+1))
770 F=F+1
780 IF F>5 THEN 950
790 PRINT
```

```
810 PRINT "DO YOU WANT TO PLAY ANOTHER GAME";
820 INPUT R$
830 IF R$>="Y" THEN RESTORE:GOTO 160
840 REM--REMARKS IF OPPONENT TAKES ILLEGAL NUMBER OF STICKS---
850 DATA I THINK YOU ARE TRYING TO CHEAT!
860 DATA I CANNOT ALLOW THAT.,DID YOU READ THE DIRECTIONS?
870 DATA DO NOT TRY THAT AGAIN, WHY NOT GIVE UP?
880 REM-----------REMARKS IF OPPONENT WINS--------------------
890 DATA HOW LUCKY CAN YOU GET, YOU ARE BETTER THAN I EXPECTED
900 DATA I WAS NOT PAYING ATTENTION
910 DATA I CAN BEAT YOU--WATCH THIS,NOBODY IS PERFECT
920 REM--------------REMARKS IF I WIN---------------------------
930 DATA THE GOOD GUYS WIN AGAIN, I GUESS I WON,YOU LOSE
940 DATA I MUST BE SUPERIOR,NOW DO NOT GET ANGRY
950 END
```

can be mathematically analyzed in a manner similar to the way Nim has been analyzed

- Rectangular dominoes: players take turns placing dominoes on a chess-type board or a board of arbitrary size (8 × 8 is fine). The board is of a size such that a domino placed horizontally or vertically on it will cover up exactly two squares. The first player places his dominoes horizontally, the second player places his vertically; dominoes may not overlap. The winner of the game is the player who makes the last possible move. Figure 7-9 shows a sample game.

- Welter: the board for this game consists of an arbitrary number of squares in one line (usually about twenty). An arbitrary number of tokens are randomly placed in the squares, with only one token in each square (there are usually about five tokens). A sample game is shown in Fig. 7-10. Players take turns moving a single token to any unoccupied square to the left, jumping over other tokens if desired. The player who makes the last move wins the game.

- Traffic Jam: the game board in Fig. 7-11, repre-

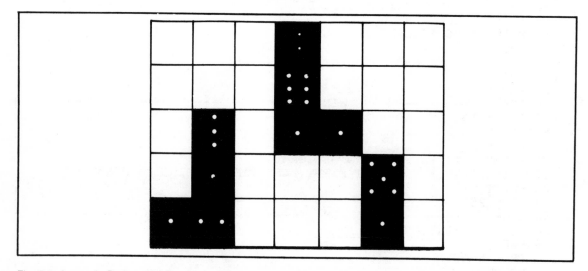

Fig. 7-9. A sample Rectangular Dominoes game.

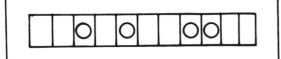

Fig. 7-10. A sample Welter game.

sents one-way roads between towns. An arbitrary number of vehicles are placed on the board to set-up the game. Players take turns moving one of the vehicles in the proper direction from one town to an adjacent town. The game continues until a traffic jam develops, in which no further moves are possible; the player who makes the final move is declared the winner.

• Innocent Marble game: in this game, either zero, two, or four markers may be placed in the circles on the game board shown in Fig. 7-12; only one marker may be in any one circle. Players take turns moving any one marker from one circle to an adjacent one, in the directions of the arrows. Whenever a marker is moved to a circle that is already occupied, both markers are removed from play. The winner is the player making the last possible move.

• Tsyanshidzi: this is the Chinese national game in which players may select from two piles of objects either an arbitrary number of objects from one pile or the same number of objects from each pile, but no fewer than one object from each

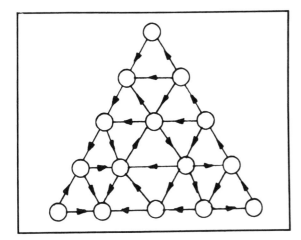

Fig. 7-11. The Traffic Jam game board.

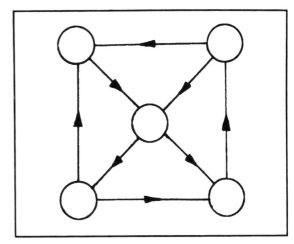

Fig. 7-12. The Innocent Marble game board.

pile. As always, the player taking all remaining objects wins. This game requires a more complex analysis than the simple game of Nim does.

• Acey-ducey: in this game the computer "shuffles" a card deck and deals two cards. The player then bets against the computer, wagering that the next card dealt will fill in between the first two cards in rank. Can you determine the mathematical strategy behind a winning program?

Neutron. Neutron is a two-player game played on a 5 × 5 grid, as shown in Fig. 7-13. At the start of the game, White owns the five pawns at the top, and Black the five pawns at the bottom. The neutron (n) begins at the center and is neutral. Each turn has two parts: first, the player must move the neutron in any one direction, and then the player must move one of his pawns in any direction. The winner is the first to maneuver the neutron to his back row, whether moved by himself or by forcing the opponent to do so. You can also win by stalemating an opponent—that is, by trapping him so that he can not complete his turn. For instance, if Black can completely surround the neutron with his pawns so that White can not complete his turn, Black wins. There is another thing to remember: any time a pawn or neutron is moved, it *must* be moved as far as it can go in a straight line (within the game board confines). A piece stops just before it reaches another piece of wall. Also, to even things

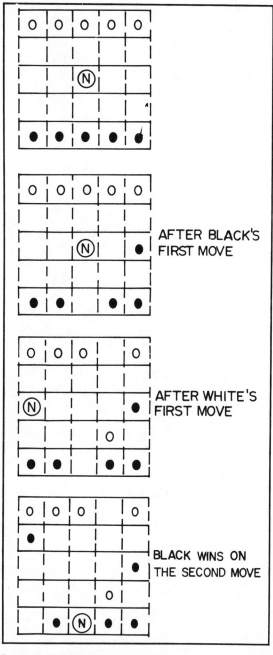

Fig. 7-13. The Neutron game board.

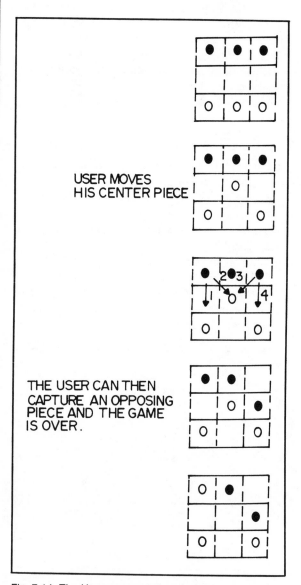

Fig. 7-14. The Hexpawn game board.

the *Etudes for Programmers* (Wetherell, Prentice-Hall, 1978). This would be an ideal prelude in programming for those interested in computer chess.

Hexpawn. This game was first introduced by Martin Gardener in *Scientific American* (Volume 200, No. 3). The game is played on a 3×3 grid as in tic-tac-toe. The two players each place their three pieces as shown in the first diagram in Fig. 7-14.

out, White moves first but does not move the neutron on this first turn. A program to play Neutron would be based on tree-searching principles, as described in most artificial intelligence books and in

The pieces move in a manner similar to the way pawns move in chess, that is, they move one space diagonally to capture and remove an opponent's piece. Players alternate turns, and the winner is the first player to reach the opponent's side of the board with a piece or the remaining player when the opponent has no legal move.

Hexpawn presents an excellent opportunity to write a program that learns as it plays, because the number of different ways to play is small. Consider the game shown in the third diagram in Fig. 7-14. The computer must choose between one of the four moves indicated. If number 4 is chosen and leads to defeat, this information is stored and the mistake is not repeated in the future. The computer continues to randomly select legal moves, provided these moves have not proven fatal in previous games, until it becomes a perfect player.

Countdown. How's your sense of timing? One or two players can test their skill with the computer serving as timekeeper and scorekeeper. First, the computer chooses and displays a random amount of time (say, from five to sixty seconds). Each player then presses a key when he or she thinks that amount of time has elapsed. The person who is closer is declared winner. Computers can execute a FOR-NEXT loop while the time is elapsing and from the number of executions multiplied by a time factor, determine the time elapsed. A variation of this game could test reaction time of two players; as soon as the word GO is displayed, the two players race to push their own keys, and the computer determines who reacted faster.

Mill. Mill is a two player game using the board shown in Fig. 7-15. Players alternate turns, placing one of their nine pieces on any of the corners or intersections of lines on the board. The moment one player gets three pieces in line, he may remove an opposing piece, provided that piece is not part of three in a row already.

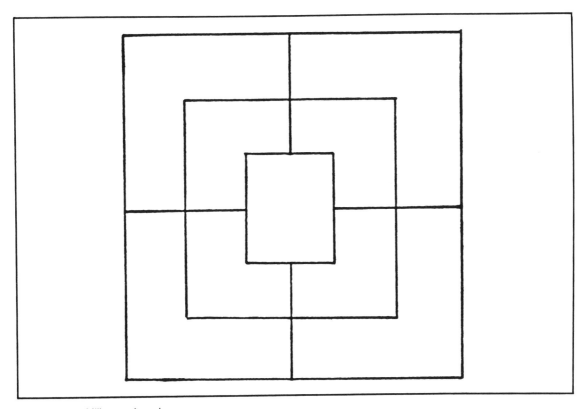

Fig. 7-15. The Mill game board.

After each player's nine pieces are placed, they may be moved one at a time to a vacant and adjacent corner or intersection. If any other lines of three are formed, another opposing piece may be removed. If a player has only three pieces on the board, he may move any one piece to any corner or intersection during his turn. The first player to be left with only two pieces is the loser.

Marked Square Game. In this simple game, the game board is a 9×9 grid. Players alternately mark one square with their initials. At the end of the game when all squares are filled, players receive 1, 2, or 3 points (respectively) for 3, 6, or 9 squares with their initials in a row; the player with the most points wins. The computer could serve as scorekeeper or opponent.

Star Fight

One of the earliest and most popular computer games is based upon the famous television series Star Trek. In this strategy game you are captain of the starship Enterprise, and you have been assigned the task of seeking and destroying a fleet of Klingon warships (usually around 20) that are menacing the United Federation of Planets. You are given a specified number of stardates to complete your mission, lest the empire be destroyed. Fortunately, you have a few star bases for resupplying your ship, although you must find them. You are assigned a random starting position in the galaxy, which is divided into an 8×8 quadrant grid. Each quadrant is subdivided into an 8×8 section grid. The program will explain the 12 command options, which include firing weapons, maneuvering, using clock devices, and heaven-forbid, self-destructing. The version in Listing 7-2 is one of the most complete in print and consumes about 20K of memory. Because it is written in BASIC, it can easily be modified until the universe is to your liking.

Listing 7-2: The Star Fight Program

```
1 CLS:KEY OFF:PRINT TAB(20)"--------------------STAR FIGHT----------------
"
2 V$=RIGHT$(TIME$,2): 'use PC clock to seed random number generator
3 V=VAL(V$)
4 RANDOMIZE V
5 REM
9 H1=0:F=0:R=0:D2=0:D3=0:B1=0:B2=0:C=0:C1=0:P=0:S=0
11 LET B$="PHASER BANKS"
13 LET C$="CLOAK ACTIVATED**"
15 LET K$="KLINGON "
17 LET E$="ENGINEERING REPORTS "
19 LET P$="PHOTON TORPEDOES "
21 LET D$=",DAMAGE REPORT-"
23 LET H$="HIGH ENERGY PLASMA BOLT"
25 LET G$="DAMAGED"
27 LET P3=1.5
29 LET R1=1
31 PRINT "SPACE--THE FINAL FRONTIER.  THESE ARE THE VOYAGES OF"
33 PRINT "THE STARSHIP ENTERPRIZE, HER FIVE YEAR MISSION--"
35 PRINT "TO EXPLORE STRANGE NEW WORLDS, TO SEEK OUT NEW LIFE AND NEW"
37 PRINT "CIVILIZATION, TO BOLDLY GO WHERE NO MAN HAS GONE BEFORE."
39 PRINT "(SWISH, TRUMPETS)":GOSUB 1111
41 PRINT
43 PRINT
```

```
45 LET Q=INT(10*RND)
47 PRINT "YOU ARE ON PATROL IN ARCTURUS SECTOR";Q;"WHEN YOU"
49 PRINT "PICK UP UNEXPECTED SENSOR READINGS, CONFIGURATION---"
51 PRINT "          KLINGON BATTLE CRUISERS"
53 PRINT "DO YOU NEED A SUMMARY OF YOUR SHIP'S CAPABILITIES";
55 INPUT A$
57 IF A$="NO" THEN 91
59 PRINT "CAPABILITIES OF THE USS ENTERPRIZE."
61 PRINT "AFTER THE QUESTION MARK TYPE TWO DIGITS SEPARATED BY COMMAS"
63 PRINT "EXAMPLE:0,0.  FIRST DIGIT IS THE OPTION."
65 PRINT "      SECOND DIGIT IS THE SHIP TO ATTACK."
67 PRINT "COMMAND OPTIONS:1) FIRES PHASER."
69 PRINT "            2) FIRES SECRET WEAPON."
71 PRINT "            3) FIRES FRONT PHOTON TORPEDOES."
73 PRINT "            4) FIRES REAR PHOTON TORPEDOES."
75 PRINT "            5) FIRES HIGH ENERGY PLASMA BOLT."
77 PRINT "            6) ACTIVATES SELF-DESTRUCT."
79 PRINT "            7) FOR CHANGE OF WARP SPEED."
81 PRINT "           11) ACTIVATES CLOAKING DEVICE"
83 PRINT "           12) DEACTIVATES CLOAKING DEVICE"
85 PRINT "           13) TURNS SHIP 180 DEGREES."
87 PRINT "          14) DIVERTS POWER TO REPAIRS."
89 PRINT "          15) DIVERTS POWER TO WEAPONS."
91 PRINT
93 PRINT
95 PRINT "HOW MANY KLINGONS DO YOU WANT TO TAKE ON";
97 INPUT N1
99 LET N1=INT(N1)
101 IF N1>0 THEN 107
103 PRINT "THE KLINGONS";
105 GOTO 111
107 IF N1<6 THEN 115
109 PRINT "THE KLINGONS ONLY"
111 PRINT "HAVE 5 BATTLE CRUISERS IN THIS QUADRANT"
113  GOTO 95
115  IF N1 = 1 THEN 125
117 IF N1>2 THEN 121
119 LET S=H(1)=H(2)=-1
121 PRINT N1;"KLINGONS";
123 GOTO 129
125 PRINT N1;K$;
127 LET S=H(1)=-3
129 PRINT "COMING INTO RANGE--SHIELDS ON"
131 PRINT
133 FOR I=1 TO N1
135   LET R(I)=400000!+(RND*200000!)
137   LET A(I)=360*(RND)
139   PRINT "RANGE OF ";K$;I;"=";R(I);"KM. AT";A(I);"DEGREES"
141 NEXT I
143 LET S=0
145 P3=1.5
147 R1=1
```

```
149 GOTO 363
151 LET M=D1=N2=0
153 PRINT "YOUR MOVE: DIRECTED AT ";K$;
155 INPUT M1,K:GOSUB 1127
157 LET K=INT(K)
159 LET M1=INT(M1)
161 IF M1>0 THEN 167
163 GOSUB 959
165 GOTO 521
167 IF M1>16 THEN 373
169 IF K>N1 THEN 373
171 IF M1<14 THEN 175
173 ON (M1-13) GOTO 349,357,145
175 ON M1 GOTO 217,217,177,183,217,219,219,217,219,219,219,327,335
177 IF F>=20 THEN 393
179 IF A(K)>180 THEN 373
181 GOTO 187
183 IF R>=10 THEN 403
185 IF A(K)<180 THEN 373
187 IF R(K)<200000! THEN 373
189 IF R(K)>600000! THEN 373
191 IF H1>=9 THEN 373
193 IF C(K)=1 THEN 373
195 IF N1<>1 THEN 201
197 LET N2=1
199 GOTO 219
201 PRINT "HOW MANY ";P$;" DO YOU WANT TO FIRE";
203 INPUT N2
205 LET N2=INT(N2)
207 IF N2>(N1*2)-1 THEN 381
209 IF N2<1 THEN 381
211 IF C=1 THEN 215
213 GOTO 217
215 IF N2>5 THEN 377
217 IF C(K)=1 THEN 373
219 ON M1 GOTO 221,237,243,253,259,859,897,949,945,295,319
221 IF R(K)>300000! THEN 373
223 IF A(K)>180 THEN 373
225 IF H1>=8 THEN 373
227 LET N3=2/M1
229 LET P=P+N3
231 GOSUB 959
233 LET N2=N3
235 GOTO 445
237 IF R(K)>300000! THEN 373
239 IF A(K)<180 THEN 373
241 GOTO 225
243 LET F=F+N2
245 IF F>20 THEN 387
247 LET P=P+N2
249 GOSUB 959
251 GOTO 445
```

```
253 LET R=R+N2
255 IF R>10 THEN 397
257 GOTO 247
259 IF H1>=8 THEN 373
261 IF C=1 THEN 373
263 IF R(K)<100000! THEN 373
265 IF R(K)>300000! THEN 373
267 LET B1=B1+1
269 IF B1>5 THEN 407
271 LET P=P+3
273 GOSUB 959
275 LET B=RND
277 IF B>.7 THEN 283
279 IF B>.2 THEN 289
281 GOTO 513
283 PRINT "DIRECT HIT ON ";K$;K:GOSUB 1135
285 LET H(K)=H(K)+4
287 GOTO 475
289 PRINT "HIT ON ";K$;K:GOSUB 1135
291 LET H(K)=H(K)+2
293 GOTO 475
295 IF H1>=7 THEN 373
297 IF H1<5 THEN 373
299 PRINT "HOW MANY MILLION STROMS DO YOU WANT TO USE ";
301 INPUT P1
303 LET P1=INT(P1)
305 IF P1<0 THEN 373
307 LET P=P+P1
309 GOSUB 959
311 LET H1=H1-(P1*.5)
313 IF H1>=5 THEN 521
315 PRINT "SHIELDS FIRMING UP"
317 GOTO 521
319 IF C=1 THEN 373
321 LET C=1
323 PRINT C$
325 GOTO 151
327 IF C=0 THEN 373
329 PRINT "CLOAK DEACTIVATED"
331 LET C=0
333 GOTO 153
335 IF C(K)=1 THEN 373
337 IF A(K)<180 THEN 343
339 LET A(K)=A(K)-180
341 GOTO 345
343 LET A(K)=A(K)+180
345 PRINT K$;K;"NOW AT";A(K);"DEGREES"
347 GOTO 153
349 LET R1=2
351 LET P3=.5
353 PRINT "POWER DIVERTED TO REPAIRS"
355 GOTO 151
```

```
357 LET P3=2.5
359 PRINT "POWER DIVERTED TO WEAPONS"
361 GOTO 151
363 IF C<>1 THEN 367
365 PRINT C$;
367 IF P3=2.5 THEN 359
369 IF P3=.5 THEN 353
371 GOTO 151
373 PRINT "MOVE IMPOSSIBLE, TRY AGAIN"
375 GOTO 153
377 PRINT "WITH THE CLOAK ACTIVATED ONLY 5 ";P$;" MAY"
379 GOTO 383
381 PRINT "WITH";N1;"KLINGONS ONLY";(N1*2)-1;P$" MAY"
383 PRINT "BE FIRED AT A TIME"
385 GOTO 151
387 LET F=F-N2
389 PRINT "ONLY";20-F;"FORWARD ";P$;" LEFT"
391 GOTO 151
393 PRINT "OUT OF FORWARD ";P$
395 GOTO 153
397 LET R=R-N2
399 PRINT "ONLY";10-R;"REAR ";P$;" LEFT"
401 GOTO 151
403 PRINT "OUT OF REAR ";P$
405 GOTO 153
407 PRINT "OUT OF ";H$;" S"
409 GOTO 153
411 PRINT "SECONDARY DILITHIUM CIRCUIT FUSED"
413 PRINT "IMPULSE POWER ONLY--LIMIT 2 MILLION STROMS"
415 PRINT "WARNING--IF CAPACITY OF IMPULSE ENGINE IS EXCEEDED, IT WILL IMPLODE"
417 LET C1=2
419 GOTO 427
421 PRINT "PRIMARY DILITHIUM CIRCUIT FUSED, SWITCHING TO SECONDARY"
423 PRINT "OVERLOAD CAPACITY FOR THIS CIRCUIT IS 10 MILLION STROMS"
425 LET C1=1
427 LET P=0
429 IF M1=5 THEN 441
431 IF M1=3 THEN 437
433 LET R=R-N2
435 GOTO 153
437 LET F=F-N2
439 GOTO 153
441 B1=B1-1
443 GOTO 153
445 FOR I=1 TO N2
447   B=RND
449   IF B>(R(K)*.0000005+.55) THEN 457
451   IF B>(R(K)*.0000005+.25) THEN 463
453   M=M+1
455   GOTO 467
457   H(K)=H(K)+2
459   PRINT "DIRECT HIT**";:GOSUB 1149
```

```
461    GOTO 467
463    H(K)=H(K)+1
465    PRINT "HIT**":GOSUB 1149
467    IF H(K)>=8 THEN 473
469 NEXT I
471 IF M=N2 THEN 513
473 PRINT
475 IF H(K)<6 THEN 479
477 F(K)=F(K)+1
479 PRINT "DAMAGE TO ";K$;K; "IN THIS ATTACK--";
481 IF H(K)>8 THEN 505
483 ON INT(H(K)) GOTO 485,485,489,489,493,497,501
485 PRINT "SHIELDS HOLDING, NO DAMAGE"
487 GOTO 515
489 PRINT "SHIELDS WEAKENING, MINOR DAMAGE"
491 GOTO 515
493 PRINT "ALL SHIELDS DESTROYED"
495 GOTO 515
497 PRINT B$;" DEACTIVATED"
499 GOTO 515
501 PRINT "ALL WEAPONS DEACTIVATED"
503 GOTO 515
505 PRINT
507 PRINT "*****";K$;K;"DESTROYED*******"
509 C(K)=1
511 GOTO 521
513 PRINT "NEAR MISS"
515 IF F(K)<>3 THEN 521
517 PRINT K$;K;"CAN NO LONGER REPAIR ITSELF"
519 F(K)=4
521 IF H1>=9 THEN 527
523 P=P-P3
525 GOTO 529
527 P=P-P3-.5
529 IF D>4 THEN 589
531 IF P3=2.5 THEN 589
533 FOR I=1 TO R1
535    Z1=H1-.5
537    IF Z1>-1 THEN 543
539    H1=-1
541    GOTO 545
543    H1=H1-.5
545    IF H1=9.5 THEN 549
547    GOTO 551
549    IF C1<>2 THEN 561
551    IF H1=8.5 THEN 565
553    IF H1=7.5 THEN 577
555    IF H1=6.5 THEN 581
557    IF H1=4.5 THEN 585
559    GOTO 587
561    PRINT "E$;" WARP ENGINES REPAIRED"
563    GOTO 587
```

```
565    IF F<20 THEN 569
567    IF R>=10 THEN 573
569    PRINT E$;P$;" PROJECTORS REPAIRED"
571    GOTO 587
573    PRINT E$;" NORMAL POWER LEVELS RESTORED"
575    GOTO 587
577    PRINT E$;B$;" REPAIRED"
579    GOTO 587
581    PRINT E$;" SHIELDS RESTORED AT A LOW POWER LEVEL"
583    GOTO 587
585    PRINT E$;" SHIELDS FIRMING UP"
587 NEXT I
589 FOR K=1 TO N1
591    IF C(K)=1 THEN 707
593    IF C=0 THEN 601
595    IF M1=0 THEN 631
597    IF H(K)>5 THEN 635
599    IF F(K)>2 THEN 635
601    IF R(K)<=500000! THEN 605
603    IF H(K)<7 THEN 621
605    IF R(K)>=1000000! THEN 609
607    IF H(K)>=7 THEN 635
609    IF R(K)>=200000! THEN 613
611    IF H(K)>6 THEN 635
613    IF R(K)>=300000! THEN 617
615    IF H(K)<6 THEN 653
617    IF R(K)>=200000! THEN 621
619    IF T(K)<10 THEN 691
621    IF H(K)<6 THEN 625
623    IF T(K)=10 THEN 635
625    R(K)=R(K)/2
627    PRINT K$;K;"APPROACHING"
629    GOTO 709
631    PRINT K$;K;"DOING NOTHING"
633    GOTO 717
635    IF H(K)>=7 THEN 641
637    R(K)=R(K)+200000!+RND*100000!
639    GOTO 643
641    R(K)=R(K)+100000!+RND*50000!
643    PRINT K$;K;"ATTEMPTING TO BREAK CONTACT"
645    IF R(K)<1000000! THEN 709
647    PRINT K$;K;"OUT OF SENSOR RANGE--CONTACT BROKEN"
649    C(K)=D(K)=1
651    GOTO 707
653    IF N1>2 THEN 657
655    IF RND<.7 THEN 661
657    PRINT K$;K;"FIRES PHASERS AT ENTERPRIZE"
659    GOTO 787
661    IF B2=10 THEN 657
663    IF R(K)<100000! THEN 657
665    B2=B2+1
667    IF B2=10 THEN 673
```

```
669    PRINT K$;K;"LAUNCHES ";H$
671    GOTO 675
673    PRINT K$;K;" LAUNCHES ITS LAST ";H$
675    B=RND
677    IF B>.7+C*.3 THEN 687
679    IF B>.2+C*.4 THEN 683
681    GOTO 795
683    H1=H1+1
685    GOTO 805
687    H1=H1+2
689    GOTO 799
691    IF N1>2 THEN 695
693    IF RND>.4 THEN 621
695    T(K)=T(K)+1
697    IF T(K)=10 THEN 703
699    PRINT K$;K;"FIRES ";P$
701    GOTO 787
703    PRINT K$;K;FIRES ITS LAST ";P$
705    GOTO 787
707    D1=D1+1
709    IF D<4 THEN 717
711    IF D>9 THEN 717
713    PRINT E$;" FURTHER MAJOR REPAIRS IMPOSSIBLE"
715    D=10
717 NEXT K
719 IF D1>=N1 THEN 977
721 PRINT
723 FOR J=1 TO N1
725    IF C(J)=1 THEN 741
727    R(J)=R(J)-RND*1000
729    IF R(J)>1000 THEN 733
731    R(J)=R(J)+RND*10000
733    A(J)=A(J)-(5*RND)
735    IF A(J)>10 THEN 739
737    A(J)=A(J)+(RND*20)
739    PRINT "RANGE OF ";K$;J;"=";R(J);"KM. AT";A(J);"DEGREES"
741 NEXT J
743 FOR I=1 TO N1
745    IF C(I)=1 THEN 781
747    IF F(I)>=3 THEN 781
749    H(I)=H(I)-.5
751    IF H(I)>S THEN 755
753    H(I)=S
755    IF H(I)<>6.5 THEN 759
757    IF T(I)<10 THEN 767
759    IF H(I)=5.5 THEN 771
761    IF H(I)=4.5 THEN 775
763    IF H(I)=2.5 THEN 779
765    GOTO 781
767    PRINT K$;I; "HAS REPAIRED ITS PHOTON TORPEDO PROJECTORS'
769    GOTO 781
771    PRINT K$;I;"HAS REPAIRED ITS ";B$
```

```
773    GOTO 781
775    PRINT K$;I;"HAS RESTORED ITS SHIELDS AT LOW POWER"
777    GOTO 781
779    PRINT K$;I;"HAS RESTORED ITS SHIELDS TO FULL POWER"
781 NEXT I
783 PRINT "YOUR CURRENT POWER OVERLOAD IS";P;"MILLION STROMS":GOSUB 1117
785 GOTO 363
787 B=RND
789 IF B>(R(K)*.0000005+.6+C*4) THEN 799
791 IF B>(R(K)*.0000005+.3+C*.2) THEN 805
793 IF B>.3 THEN 811
795 PRINT "NEAR MISS"
797 GOTO 709
799 PRINT "DIRECT HIT ON USS ENTERPRIZE ";D$;
801 H1=H1+2
803 GOTO 817
805 PRINT "HIT ON USS INTERPRIZE ";D$;
807 H1=H1+1
809 GOTO 817
811 IF M1<=0 THEN 795
813 PRINT "YOU OUT MANEUVERED HIM, A MISS"
815 GOTO 709
817 IF H1<8 THEN 821
819 D=D+1
821 IF H1>=11 THEN 853
823 IF H1<5 THEN 827
825 ON INT(H1-4) GOTO 831,831,835,839,843,849,853
827 PRINT "SHIELDS HOLDING, NO DAMAGE"
829 GOTO 709
831 PRINT "SHIELDS WEAKENING"
833 GOTO 709
835 PRINT "ALL SHIELDS DESTROYED"
837 GOTO 709
839 PRINT B$;" DEACTIVATED, "
841 GOTO 835
843 PRINT
845 PRINT "ALL WEAPONS, SHIELDS DEACTIVATED, POWER DROPPING":GOSUB 1149
847 GOTO 709
849 PRINT "WARP POWER GONE,"
851 GOTO 845
853 PRINT "USS ENTERPRIZE DESTROYED":GOSUB 1145
855 D2=1
857 GOTO 977
859 PRINT TAB(15)"A C T I V A T E D"
861 R1=9800*RND+200
863 PRINT "RADIUS OF EXPLOSION=";R1;"KM."
865 FOR I=1 TO N1
867    IF C(I)=1 THEN 889
869    IF R(I)>R1 THEN 889
871    IF R(I)>R1*.8 THEN 879
873    PRINT K$;I;"DESTROYED";:GOSUB 1113
875    C(I)=1
```

```
877    GOTO 887
879    H(I)=H(I)+6
881    IF H(I)>=8 THEN 873
883    F(I)=F(I)+1
885    PRINT K$;I;"HEAVILY ";G$;
887    PRINT " BY THE BLAST"
889 NEXT I
891 GOTO 855
893 PRINT "IMPULSE ENGINE OVERLOAD"
895 GOTO 861
897 IF C1=2 THEN 373
899 IF H1>=10 THEN 373
901 PRINT "HOW FAST DO YOU WANT TO GO, WARP 1-8";
903 INPUT W
905 IF W<0 THEN 373
907 IF W>8 THEN 373
909 P=P+W
911 GOSUB 959
913 IF M1<>9 THEN 917
915 W=2
917 FOR I=1 TO N1
919    IF C(I)=1 THEN 941
921    R(I)=R(I)+W*100000!-RND*50000!
923    IF R(I)>1000000! THEN 931
925    IF A(I)>180 THEN 941
927    A(I)=A(I)+180
929    GOTO 941
931    C(I)=1
933    D(I)=2
935    IF H(I)<7 THEN 939
937    D(I)=1
939    PRINT "LOST CONTACT WITH ";K$;I
941 NEXT I
943 GOTO 521
945 W=1
947 GOTO 909
949 P=P+1
951 GOSUB 959
953 R(K)=R(K)/2
955 A(K)=A(K)/2
957 GOTO 521
959 IF C<>1 THEN 963
961 P=P+3
963 IF P<=20 THEN 967
965 IF C1=0 THEN 421
967 IF P<=10 THEN 971
969 IF C1=1 THEN 411
971 IF P<=2 THEN 975
973 IF C1=2 THEN 893
975 RETURN
977 PRINT
979 PRINT
```

```
 981 PRINT "RESULTS OF THIS BATTLE:"
 983 PRINT
 985 FOR I=1 TO N1
 987    IF C(I)<>1 THEN 991
 989    IF D(I)=1 THEN 1015
 991    IF C(I)<>1 THEN 995
 993    IF D(I)=2 THEN 1019
 995    IF C(I)=1 THEN 1005
 997    IF H(I)>=6 THEN 1011
 999    IF H(I)>=3 THEN 1027
1001    PRINT K$;I;"NOT ";G$
1003    GOTO 1029
1005    PRINT K$;I;"DESTROYED"
1007    LET D3=D3+1
1009    GOTO 1029
1011    PRINT K$;I;"HEAVILY";G$
1013    GOTO 1021
1015    PRINT K$;I;"FORCED TO RETIRE"
1017    GOTO 1007
1019    PRINT "CONTACT LOST WITH ";K$;I
1021    IF H(I)<6 THEN 1025
1023    IF F(I)>=3 THEN 1007
1025    GOTO 1029
1027    PRINT K$;I;"LIGHTLY";G$
1029 NEXT I
1031 PRINT "USS ENTERPRIZE ";
1033 IF D2=1 THEN 1055
1035 IF C1=2 THEN 1051
1037 IF H1<5 THEN 1041
1039 ON INT(H1-4) GOTO 1047,1047,1051,1051,1051,1051,1051
1041 IF C1=1 THEN 1047
1043 PRINT "NOT ";G$
1045 GOTO 1057
1047 PRINT "LIGHTLY ";G$
1049 GOTO 1057
1051 PRINT "HEAVILY ";G$
1053 GOTO 1057
1055 PRINT "LOST"
1057 IF D3<N1/2 THEN 1061
1059 IF D2=0 THEN 1071
1061 IF D3>=N1/2 THEN 1075
1063 IF D2<>0 THEN 1067
1065 IF D3>=1 THEN 1075
1067 PRINT "THIS BATTLE AWARDED TO THE KLINGONS":GOSUB 1145
1069 GOTO 1089
1071 PRINT "CONGRATULATIONS--YOU HAVE WON A MAJOR VICTORY"
1073 GOTO 1077
1075 PRINT "CONGRATULATIONS--YOU HAVE WON A TACTICAL VICTORY"
1077 PRINT
1079 PRINT "DO YOU WANT ANOTHER BATTLE";
1081 INPUT Z$
1083 IF Z$="NO" THEN 1107
```

```
1085 PRINT "REPAIRS COMPLETED"
1087 GOTO 9
1089 PRINT
1091 PRINT "DO YOU WANT ANOTHER BATTLE";
1093 INPUT Z$
1095 IF Z$="NO" THEN 1107
1097 PRINT "HERE'S ANOTHER STARSHIP---BE MORE CAREFUL THIS TIME"
1099 GOTO 9
1101 P3=1.5
1103 GOTO 9
1105 IF D2=1 THEN 1109
1107 PRINT "REPORT TO STARBASE";INT(RND*12+1)
1109 END
1111 REM space music
1113 PLAY "t100o218g.o3l16c14f.18e19co2ao3dl2g."
1115 RETURN
1117 FOR K=1 TO 3: 'OVERLOAD NOISE
1119 SOUND 130,5
1121 SOUND 180,5
1123 NEXT K
1125 RETURN
1127 FOR S=800 TO 1046 STEP 20: 'PHASER FIRE NOISE
1129 SOUND S,1
1131 NEXT S
1133 RETURN
1135 FOR K=1 TO 5: 'PHASER HIT NOISE
1137 SOUND 32767,2
1139 SOUND 1046,1
1141 NEXT K
1143 RETURN
1145 PLAY "O1F+C": 'FAILURE NOISE
1147 RETURN
1149 FOR T=1 TO 4: 'BATTLE STATIONS NOISE
1151 FOR S=800 TO 1046 STEP 20
1153 SOUND S,1
1155 NEXT S
1157 NEXT T
1159 RETURN
```

COMPUTER QUIZZES

Computer quiz games can be instructive as well as fun, if clever programming techniques are used. Examples of these techniques include the following:

- Having a large data base of questions from which a few are randomly selected to produce a new set of questions for each quiz
- Automatically recording the score and rewarding the player with graphic or musical interludes for good scores; new scores may be compared with old scores or with those of other players
- Providing explanations of missed answers
- Allowing for the selection of questions according to the player's level of ability or providing for an automatically-adjusting level of difficulty based upon performance.

Assorted suggestions concerning topics for quiz games include the following:

- Names and capitols of states or countries, possi-

bly using computer graphics to draw maps
- Vocabulary words
- I.Q. tests
- Personality and aptitude tests
- Foreign language vocabulary or grammar
- Preschool skills including comparing and counting random shapes, words, and numbers, and copying letters, words, and numbers
- Practice questions for examinations such as the SAT, GMAT, MCAT, LSAT, and ACT.
- Analogies
- Spelling bees
- Verses from literature or the Bible
- Trivia questions for trivia lovers, on science fiction, movies, and history
- Basic math skills
- Chemical equation balancing

- English grammar
- History of the United States, the Renaissance period, or World War I
- Constellations or planets

GAMES THAT USE WORDS

You can program a wide variety of games and activities based on words including the following:

- *Cryptograms*, or coded messages, could be displayed for you to decode; simple clues could be provided.
- *Anagrams*, or jumbled words, are a popular recreation. The program in Listing 7-3 randomly chooses one of many words stored in the DATA statements beginning with line 500. The program scrambles the letters in the word and prints it on the video screen for you to unscramble and input.

Listing 7-3: the Anagram Creator Program

```
10 V$=RIGHT$(TIME$,2): 'use PC clock to seed random number generator
20 V=VAL(V$)
30 RANDOMIZE V
40 CLS:KEY OFF:PRINT "ANAGRAM CREATOR"
50 PRINT "SCRAMBLES WORDS FOR ENTERTAINMENT"
60 N=6   'NUMBER OF WORDS IN DATA STATEMENTS
70 DIM M(N),W$(N),A(20)
80 FOR I=1 TO N
90    M(I)=I
100 NEXT I
110 FOR I=1 TO N-1
120    R=(N+1-I)*RND
130    R=INT(R)+I
140    T=M(R)
150    M(R)=M(I)
160    M(I)=T
170 NEXT I
180 FOR I=1 TO N
190    READ W$(M(I))
200 NEXT I
210 FOR I=1 TO N
220    A$=" "
230    A=LEN(W$(I))
240       FOR B=1 TO A
250          A(B)=B
260       NEXT B
270       FOR B=1 TO N-1
280          S=(A+1-B)*RND
```

```
290     S=INT(S)+B
300     C=A(S):A(S)=A(B):A(B)=C
310   NEXT B
320   FOR B=1 TO A
330     A$=A$+MID$(W$(I),A(B),1)
340   NEXT B
350   PRINT A$
360   INPUT C$
370   IF C$=W$(I) THEN PRINT "RIGHT!" ELSE PRINT "WRONG, THE ANSWER WAS:";W$(I)
380 NEXT I
390 END
400 REM DATA STATEMENTS CONTAIN WORDS HERE...
410 DATA COMPUTER,TELEVISION,GAME,INSTRUMENT,WRITE,BASIC
```

- The game of hangman, in which one has ten guesses to determine the letters in a randomly chosen word, serves to familiarize the player with vocabulary terms.

- Word search puzzles ad infinitum may be computer generated, either from a word list or as a random matrix similar to the popular Boggle™ game. A program to determine the locations of all words in the puzzle could also be implemented. You could also have the computer assist in creation of a crossword puzzle. Choose a topic and enter words; the computer will automatically fit the common letters together to form a crossword grid. Next, enter an obscure or humorous clue for each word. The completed crossword can be saved for later use or printed and sent to friends.

- Word guessing games, similar to twenty questions, can be computerized. In these games, the player asks the computer questions to determine what word has been randomly selected. Replies for the many possible questions a human could pose must be stored; thus there are difficult programming challenges. The dialogue with one such program went like this:

> (c=computer, h=human)
> h: Does it grow?
> c: To answer that question might be misleading.
> h: Can I eat it?
> c: Only as food for thought.
> h: Do computers have it?
> c: Strictly speaking, no.
> c: The word is "Knowledge."

- A word game similar to the popular Mastermind™ game would involve the computer's selecting a three-letter word from a large list. The player would guess by entering a three-letter word and would be told whether or not the computer's word contained any of the letters in the word the player guessed and whether or not those letters were in the correct position. The object is to guess the computer's word in the least number of tries.

- In the game of Confound, the computer outputs 15 letters (consonants and vowels). The players must form the longest word possible using these letters. The computer serves to keep score and check to ensure that no letters were used improperly, that is, used more often than they appear in the list.

Story Writer

Using the combination of a random number generator, a list of words, and simple rules for English grammar, a microcomputer can compose original stories ad infinitum; the results are often amusing. Here are some story writing suggestions:

- Use a standard story line in which blanks are left to be filled in with inputted words. The inputted words could consist of personalized information, or arbitrary nouns, adjectives, and adverbs, as done in the Mad Libs™ party games. For example, a story could begin

Space, the *(adjective)* frontier.
These are the voyages of the starship *(noun)*,
It's five-year mission:
To seek out new *(noun)* and new *(noun)* . . .

The operator is requested to provide one adjective and three nouns to fill in the four blanks above, but is unaware of the story line until later when these words are incorporated and the story is printed out. Here is a sample result.

Space, the *nauseating* frontier.
These are the voyages of the starship *lemon*
Its five-year mission:
To seek out new *games* and new *computers…*

Also included in this category are "Me Books" for young children. The computer fills the blanks in a story with a child's name, address, and other personalized information. The resultant personalized story often increases a child's interest in reading.

• A much more difficult approach to story writing involves the random selection of words or phrases to compose a series of sentences that follow standard rules of grammar. A program written in 1960 (before high-level languages were in widespread use) called SAGA was designed to produce short scripts for movie westerns. Here's a sample of the output:

Sheriff:
    The Sheriff is at the window
    Sheriff sees robber
    Robber sees Sheriff
    go to door
    wait
    open door
    Sheriff sees robber
    go through door
    robber sees Sheriff
    go to window
Robber:
    take gun from holster with right hand
    aim
    fire
    Sheriff nicked

Sheriff:
    take gun from holster with right hand
    aim
    fire
    robber hit
    blow out barrel
    put gun down at door
    go to table
    pick up glass with right hand . . .

Writing a program to accomplish the above is more complex than it would seem on first impression; the program was considered quite an achievement in 1960. Random numbers were used to determine the sequence of events; the events were selected from a wide range of preprogrammed possibilities. The program had to guard against a character firing a gun without first withdrawing it from his holster and similar situations. Also, a routine was necessary to compose "sentences" using the rules of grammar (for example, "gun takes robber from holster with right hand" would not be allowed, but "robber takes gun from holster with right hand" would be allowed). The use of programmed phrases instead of individual words to select from would simplify this task considerably. In like manner, a science fiction spoof or soap opera dialogue could be written. A professional software house sells a program to produce random, technical double-talk to "fill out business reports that are too short." A sample line produced by the program reads, "The product configuration requires considerable analysis and trade-off studies to arrive at the total system rational."

MAGIC

Magic tricks performed by your computer would make an interesting demonstration for your guests. Here are some suggestions:

Micro mentalist. The computer becomes a mind reader in this trick. The performer, who is the computer operator, is given an item from the audience. The performer enters a question such as, "What is the item given to me by the audience?" After a brief delay, the computer displays the name of the item.

The trick is based on a code programmed into the computer that allows the performer to indicate inconspicuously to the computer which of approximately 20 items he has been given. The code is contained within the inputted sentence; different sentences stand for different objects. For example, "What do I have now?" could indicate a watch, and "What am I holding?" could indicate a match folder. The computer merely matches the inputted question to the item list stored in its memory.

Age determination. The performer hands a member of the audience a pocket calculator and tells him to enter his age and then subtract his favorite one-digit number. Next, the guest multiplies this result by nine and adds his age to the product. The final result is called out and is inputted to the computer. The determination of the guest's age is accomplished by adding the first two digits in the result to the last digit (for example, if the result were 176, adding 17 and 6 gives you 23, the guest's age).

The break in the chain. This trick is performed with a complete set of dominoes (usually 28 pieces). Beforehand, the performer removes one of the dominoes (it may not be a double) and inputs the two numbers on the domino to be stored in the computer. The guests are given the remaining set and are asked to complete a single domino chain as in regular play. Once completed, the numbers on the two ends of the chain are noted, and the performer inputs a question such as, "What are the two numbers?" The computer replies correctly by displaying the two previously stored numbers. The trick is automatic and will work with any domino chosen, excluding doubles.

COMPUTER-INTELLIGENCE GAMES

Programs can be written to make a computer "learn" from its mistakes, entering the realm of artificial intelligence. A checker-playing program that stores the results of all previous moves has been written. Although the time necessary to decide on a move increases as the game progresses, the computer's moves are much better than they were at the beginning of the game. Here are some games that the computer can "learn" to play.

- Nim as described earlier in this chapter, is a popular computer game in which a player may take 1, 2, or 3 items from a pile of 20 in an attempt to force an opponent to take the last item. Although this game is completely solvable, a Nim program could be written as a demonstration of computer "learning."
- A BASIC game called *Animal*, in which the computer plays the game of twenty questions with a human, has been written. The computer asks such questions as "Does it swim?" to try to determine what animal the human is thinking of. If that animal is not in the computer's file, the human is requested to provide information so that a file on the new animal can be created. Thus, the computer "learns." Of course, it may be interesting to use a subject other than animals; for example, you could use places instead of animals to help young people learn geography.
- A crude "mind reading" program based upon probability could be created. The human would be instructed to choose one of two words. Then the computer will output the word it "believes" was chosen. After a number of trials, the computer should be able to formulate a strategy for guessing which word will be chosen next, because humans can never be random and tend to guess in patterns; theoretically, the computer should be able to achieve better than 50% correct responses.

Other applications of personal computers in the area of artificial intelligence include programs that can tutor humans to play complex games such as chess, in which moves can be analyzed and changed, and suggestions or tips given.

PROGRAMS FOR YOUNG CHILDREN

Programs that make liberal use of graphics and are designed to be foolproof may serve as educational tools for young children. They can familiarize children with using a keyboard, cursors, and computer graphics, and can provide learning experiences. Suggestions include the following:

- Matching Games: children can match letters, words, and shapes.
- Drawing Machine: a joystick controller or arrow

keys permit drawing on a video screen. A library of shapes including squares, triangles, and circles can also be used to construct pictures.

- Face Maker: children can create their own funny face on a video screen by selecting eyes, ears, a nose, hair, and a mouth from a collection of possibilities.
- Storybook: using the keyboard, children can write their own stories, which the computer then interprets and animates on the screen. Stories can involve stored images such as houses, trees, people, and cars, which may then be animated to illustrate a sentence such as "The girls walked from home to school."

THE COMPUTER AS BOARD DISPLAY DEVICE, BOOKKEEPER, AND GAME ADVISOR

Certain games are designed in such a way that the computer cannot be programmed to be a formidable opponent. You can use the computer with these games in other ways, including the following:

- Board display and bookkeeping for complex board games such as Risk™, Stratego™, Go, Metagames, and Avalon-Hill games can be accomplished with high-resolution graphics. In addition to displaying the board, the computer could
  - —generate random numbers to replace spinners, dice, cards
  - —record each move for later review
  - —compute the game status at the end of each turn
  - —compute energy, arsenal, moves, positions, money and statistics for each player.
- Advising and bookkeeping for such games as checkers and chess can be accomplished. The computer could store each move, advise against potential checks, skewers, and forks, alert the players to discoveries, and print a listing of the game, move by move, at the finish. Advising for gambling games such as blackjack could take the form of the creation of an odds table for the high cards remaining in the deck, the computation of whether to stay or hit, and the calculation of the safest amount to bet.

DRAWING AND KALEIDOSCOPE PROGRAMS

Most picture drawing programs utilize the arrow (cursor positioning) keys on the video terminal keyboard to direct a cursor point that leaves a line. Several additions could be made to these programs, including animation routines, special standard designs that may be called to the screen, provisions for storing a design on cassette or floppy disk, and for using light pens and joysticks. The *kaleidoscope effect* refers to a computer algorithm used to alter a design in kaleidoscope fashion (that is, the design is multiply reflected as its mirror image) in real time. Fascinating "modern art" designs can be made with programs that use random numbers with the DRAW, LINE, CIRCLE, FULL, and PAINT commands found in some BASIC interpreters. Random lines and circles of various sizes fill the screen, and each area defined by lines is filled in with various colors.

SIMULATION AND ADVENTURE GAMES

Simulations of real-world situations need not be outputted as complex numerical listings; they may be transformed into games suited for people young and old. Some of the many possibilities include the following:

Pool Table. A pool playing game displayed using video graphics could serve to teach the principles of elastic collisions and angular geometry.

Motorcycle Jump. A simulation in which a motorcycle must leap a certain distance to land safely could illustrate projectile motion. The ramp angle and initial motorcycle velocity would be determined by the person playing the game.

Projectile motion formulae are provided below for those with faint recollections of high school physics:

1. Position relative to point of projection after time t

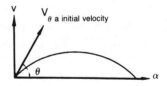

$$x = v_0 t \cos \theta$$

$$y = v_0 t \sin \theta - \frac{gt^2}{2}$$

2. Range, maximum height and time of flight

$$T = \frac{2v_0}{g} \sin \theta$$

$$R = \frac{2v_0^2}{g} \sin \theta \cos \theta$$

$$H = \frac{v_0^2}{2g} \sin^2 \theta$$

3. Necessary angle of projection for given range with given speed of projection

$\sin 2\alpha = \dfrac{Rg}{v^2}$ giving two possible angles α, and α_1, and aα_2.

Navigation. A simulation in which the participant must find his way to an island, using a radio direction finder in his sailboat, could teach principles of geometry as well as sailboat handling for example.

Detective. The participant would assume the role of a detective in this simulation. A valuable gem has been stolen from a museum and five persons are suspected. The use of deductive reasoning is the only way the detective can solve this crime.

MX Missile. In this grid search game, one player hides MX missiles among several possible silos and may shuffle missiles while the other player shoots at them trying to hit silos containing missiles.

World Race. Using a combination of race and rally tactics, players compete to be the first to motor from England to New York and back to New York, navigating their way through Europe, Asia, the Far East, and South America. Strategy plays a large part as players have to motor through towns in every country in order to pick up points. Out of the way towns score higher than those along main routes. The winner is the player who reaches New York in the least time and with the most points. Rabies in Europe, tropical rains in South America, drought in Africa, and so on deter everyone's progress. The game serves to teach geography.

Wall Street. A stock market simulation, preferably multiplayer, would allow players to buy and sell stocks according to market conditions. A computer determines the outcome of each round and the price for each stock and serves as bookkeeper.

World Conflict. This multiplayer simulation would place each player as the head of a nation. Players must decide whether they should go to war, form cartels, or make concessions and compromises. The computer could select the conflicting situations (for example, oil embargoes, assassinations, nuclear threats, Communist expansion).

Decision. A simulation of corporate management and big business could place each player as a top level executive. Each executive has the authority to produce the product of his choice and sell the product at the best market price. Throughout the game, prices fluctuate according to the law of supply and demand.

Fire. The object of this simulation is to subdue a raging forest fire with chemicals, backfires, and other fire-fighting methods. The success of the player depends upon quick decisions concerning how to control a geometrically increasing fire.

Atomic Fission. This simulation demonstrates geometric progressions by simulating a nuclear reaction in which each split atom releases enough energy to split two or more other atoms, and so on.

Auction. Principles of bidding at an auction could be simulated in a one or more player game involving the auction of art. Players must be careful of forgeries.

Adventure. The object of this simulation is survival in a desperate attempt to locate buried treasure on an island. How does one obtain fresh water on an island surrounded by salt water?

Ethics. This simulation, involving the conflict

between morals and greed, uses the computer as the judge of ethics. Conflicting situations in which players must decide the outcome are provided. If a preprogrammed decision does not match with a player's, that player accumulates "morality deductions." The winner is the player with the most money and fewest deductions.

Careers. This simulation game places the player in new occupations to enable him or her to experience decision making, conflicts, opportunities, and financial stress from different viewpoints in a variety of careers.

Artillery. This is a simulation in which a gun in a fixed emplacement must fire a projectile at such a velocity and angle that it will hit a target. The distance the projectile lands from the target could be displayed as the integer of the log to the base 2 of the absolute value of the distance; several other possibilities exist for teaching mathematical principles.

Grid Search Simulations. A search game, for example, one that pitted a destroyer against a submarine, could be programmed. The game would use a 10×10 grid that must be selectively searched by the ship or the submarine in its efforts to find and attack the other vessel. Similarly, a game played on the same grid could involve a spy searching for hidden documents with hidden enemy agents to watch for as well.

Rat Race. A video graphics program that draws a maze and animates a mouse could be created. The programming involved in enabling the mouse to "learn" to solve the maze could demonstrate rudimentary artificial intelligence principles.

Computer. Based on a large scale computing system, the object of this simulation is to process two complete programs before your opponents can. Players who make the best decisions can avoid the jeopardies of power failures, restricted use of I/O channels, bugs, and priority interrupts.

Laser Tank. The player and the opponent (the computer) each have a laser-firing tank and a base. The object is to be the first to destroy the opponent's base while avoiding his fire. Obstacles litter the battlefield, and laser fire is destructive

only at a limited range.

Robotwar. The purpose of this simulation is to teach computer programming. Two opposing players are instructed to secretly design programs, written in a custom language, that would create and control robots designed to annihilate any other robots. The programs would be entered, and a video display of the combat field would be updated in real-time. The objective could be to hit the opposing robot five times to win.

Robot War II. The program in Listing 7-4, Robotwar II is a challenging game to play against your computer. In the game, you are represented by an *, while the computer controls annihilating robots represented by +. An electrified, lethal fence defines the playing field.

The computer's robots will destroy you if they come close. However, the robots will destroy themselves if they run into the fence. Your objective is to evade the robots until all have been destroyed by the fence. To move in a desired direction, use the chart in Fig. 7-16, which indicates the number to input.

VIDEO GAMES

A personal computer with a memory-mapped video display and high-resolution graphics could emulate the popular video games. Although programs written in BASIC do not execute as fast as the real video games do, programs written in assembly language do run as fast. Here are some ideas you might want to try:

Maxwell's Demon. Semifloating molecules are trapped in one chamber of a two-chamber box. A

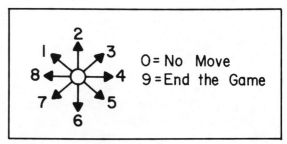

Fig. 7-16. The numbers corresponding to the directions in the Robot II game.

Listing 7-4: The Robotwar II Program

```
100 V$=RIGHT$(TIME$,2): 'use PC clock to seed random number generator
110 V=VAL(V$)
120 RANDOMIZE V
150 CLS:KEY OFF
160 PRINT TAB(20)"-------------ROBOTWAR II-----------------"
170 PRINT
180 INPUT "INSTRUCTIONS (Y/N)";Y$:IF Y$="Y" THEN GOSUB 1800
185 CLS
190 REM SET UP THE GAME
200 DIM A(10,20),E(21),F(21)
210 G=0:Z7=1
220 FOR B=1 TO 10
230   FOR C=1 TO 20
240     A(B,C)=0
250     IF B<>1 THEN 260
251   A(B,C)=1
260     IF B<>10 THEN 270
261   A(B,C)=1
270     IF C<>1 THEN 280
271   A(B,C)=1
280     IF C<>20 THEN 290
281     A(B,C)=1
290   NEXT C
300 NEXT B
310 FOR D=1 TO 21
320   B=INT(RND*8+2)
330   C=INT(RND*8+2)
340   IF A(B,C)<>0 THEN 320
350   A(B,C)=1
360   IF D>=6 THEN 370
361 A(B,C)=2
370   IF D<>6 THEN 380
371 A(B,C)=3
380   E(D)=B
390   F(D)=C
400 NEXT D
490 GOSUB 1900
499 REM PRINT PATTERN
500 FOR B=1 TO 10
510   FOR C=1 TO 20
520     IF A(B,C)<>0 THEN 530
521 PRINT " ";
530     IF A(B,C)<>1 THEN 540
531 PRINT "X";
540     IF A(B,C)<>2 THEN 550
541 PRINT "+";
550     IF A(B,C)<>3 THEN 560
551 PRINT "*";
560   NEXT C
```

```
570    PRINT
580 NEXT B
590 REM MAKE MOVE
600 B=E(6)
610 C=F(6)
620 A(B,C)=0
630 INPUT Y
640 IF Y=0 THEN 800
650 ON Y GOTO 660,660,660,690,680,680,680,690,1400
660 B=B-1
670 GOTO 690
680 B=B+1
690 ON Y GOTO 700,800,720,720,720,800,700,700
700 C=C-1
710 GOTO 800
720 C=C+1
790 REM CALCULATE THE RESULTS
800 IF A(B,C)=1 THEN 1500
810 IF A(B,C)=2 THEN 1600
820 A(B,C)=3
830 E(6)=B
840 F(6)=C
850 FOR D=1 TO 5
860    IF A(E(D),F(D))<>2 THEN 960
870    A(E(D),F(D))=0
880    IF E(D)>=B THEN 890
881    E(D)=E(D)+1
890    IF E(D)<=B THEN 900
891    E(D)=E(D)-1
900    IF F(D)>=C THEN 910
901    F(D)=F(D)+1
910    IF F(D)<=C THEN 920
911    F(D)=F(D)-1
920    IF A(E(D),F(D))=3 THEN 1600
930    IF A(E(D),F(D))=0 THEN 940
931    G=G+1
940    IF A(E(D),F(D))<>0 THEN 950
941    A(E(D),F(D))=2
950    IF G=5 THEN 1700
960 NEXT D
970 PRINT "MAP";
980 INPUT Y$
990 IF Y$="Y" THEN CLS:GOTO 490
1000 GOTO 600
1400 PRINT "SORRY TO SEE YOU QUIT"
1401 Z9=Z9+1
1410 GOTO 1710
1500 PRINT "YOU TOUCHED THE FENCE"
1501 Z9=Z9+1
1510 GOTO 1710
1600 PRINT "YOU HAVE BEEN DESTROYED BY A LUCKY COMPUTER"
1601 Z9=Z9+1
```

```
1610 GOTO 1710
1700 PRINT " ** YOU DESTROYED THE ENEMY **"
1701 Z8=Z8+1
1710 PRINT "DO YOU WANT TO PLAY AGAIN (TYPE Y OR N)";
1720 INPUT Y$
1730 IF Y$="Y" THEN Z7=Z7+1:CLS:GOTO 210
1731 PRINT "COMPUTER WON:";Z9" ","THE HUMAN WON:";Z8
1732 PRINT "COMPUTER'S AVERAGE:";100*(Z9/(Z8+Z9));"%; THE HUMAN'S AVERAGE:";100*
(Z8/(Z8+Z9));"%"
1733 PRINT
1740 PRINT "HOPE YOU DON'T FEEL FENCED IN"
1750 PRINT "TRY AGAIN SOMETIME."
1760 END
1800 PRINT "YOU--'*'; ROBOTS--'+'"
1810 PRINT "FENCE--'X'.  FENCE IS LETHAL!"
1820 PRINT "ROBOTS WILL DESTROY YOU IF THEY COME CLOSE.  THE FENCE WILL DESTROY"

1830 PRINT "ANYTHING THAT TOUCHES IT--INCLUDING YOU.  EVADE THE ROBOTS UNTIL"
1840 PRINT "THE FENCE HAS DESTROYED THEM ALL.  TO MOVE, INPUT A NUMBER FROM"
1850 PRINT "THE CHART WHICH APPEARS NEXT TO THE GAME GRID."
1860 INPUT "PRESS ENTER TO START";Y$:CLS:RETURN
1900 REM MOVES CHART
1910 LOCATE 1,1
1920 LOCATE 1,20:PRINT TAB(50)"2"
1930 LOCATE 2,1:PRINT TAB(50)"!"
1940 LOCATE 3,1:PRINT TAB(45)"1";TAB(50)"!";TAB(55)"3"
1950 LOCATE 4,1:PRINT TAB(46)"!";TAB(54)"!";TAB(65)"0=NO MOVE"
1960 LOCATE 5,1:PRINT TAB(47)"!";TAB(53)"!"
1970 LOCATE 6,1:PRINT TAB(40)"8----";TAB(50)"0";TAB(56)"----4"
1980 LOCATE 7,1:PRINT TAB(47)"!";TAB(53)"!"
1990 LOCATE 8,1:PRINT TAB(46)"!";TAB(54)"!";TAB(65)"9=END GAME"
2000 LOCATE 9,1:PRINT TAB(45)"7";TAB(50)"!";TAB(55)"5"
2010 LOCATE 10,1:PRINT TAB(50)"!"
2020 LOCATE 11,1:PRINT TAB(50)"6"
2030 RETURN
```

gate connects the two compartments. The molecules are constantly bombarding each other and bouncing off walls; the object is to open and close the gate at the right times so that all molecules will be trapped in the other compartment.

Hockey and Tennis type games. These computer games could be controlled with joysticks, simple potentiometers, or keyboard switches just as their video game counterparts are.

Tanks. In a projectile-shooting battle between two tanks, the computer could act as the opponent. Similarly, a battle could be designed for jet fighters, biplanes, or ships instead of tanks.

Pinball. A moving set of paddles could replay a "ball" to hit targets and score points.

Lunar Lander. This game involves a lunar-landing module that is governed by rocket propulsion, fuel supply, and gravity. It must land at a low velocity so that no damage is done and must land on a plateau, avoiding lunar mountains and craters. The lunar lander program could be made more complex by requiring that you take-off from the lunar surface, navigate over an obstacle of random size, and land again accurately.

Football, Baseball, and Basketball. An animated display of players, ball positions, and the playing field could be used to display the action in these sports.

Racetrack. The object of this game is to finish the race in the least time. Hazards include attaining too much speed to slow down before a curve, oil slicks, and other cars. Hazards cause you to lose time.

Skydiver. The player in this game must control chute opening and jump time for a parachutist who must land at a precise point. A wind of randomly selected direction and velocity presents a challenge to overcome.

Robot Bowl. The player controls a bowling robot in an attempt to knock down as many pins as possible. The time of release, angle of approach, and weight of the ball are selected by the player.

Shooting Gallery. Several moving targets of different point values and a directional "gun" could comprise a video version of the popular shooting gallery.

Golf. A golf game with a set of graphical holes (or design-your-own-hole provisions) would let the players choose the clubs they will use for each shot and the angle at which the ball will be hit. Hazards include sand traps, water, "dog-legs," and strong winds.

RECREATIONS INVOLVING THE COMPUTER ITSELF

A hobby computer magazine once listed some suggestions on "busting your computer" to determine the limitations of your BASIC (or other high-level language). The results may suprise you. Here are a few ideas:

- Determine the maximum number of parentheses that can be used in one statement. (Don't be surprised if over 100 are allowed!)
- Determine the maximum dimension allowed for an array.
- Determine the maximum number of nested FOR-NEXT loops allowed.

Other challenges include writing a "self-duplicating" program that is not simply composed of verbatim PRINT statements, yet prints a duplicate of itself. If you are ambitious, you might attempt to break the record for carrying out Pi to the most decimal places (500,000).

COMPUTERS AND CHESS

Chess is one of the most popular computer recreations for several reasons. First, it requires an advanced level of computer programming, described by some as "artificial intelligence," that enables a computer to emulate human thought. Second, it may be difficult to find chess opponents at your level of ability. The computer, as your opponent, solves that problem by having adjustable skill levels, making it possible to find an opponent of your own strength. Third, many chess programs can serve as chess tutors by suggesting moves, demonstrating piece movements, allowing the rearrangement of boards, and even stepping you through a collection of games from masters-level tournaments. Many of today's chess programs are rated in the middle 1200s or above and can serve as a formidable opponent for novice to intermediate level players.

Chess playing programs are almost always written in assembly language for the purpose of speed; they may analyze from a few thousand to over one million possibilities before making a move. A large scale computer chess program is described below for those interested in the inner workings of the game. The discussion can, perhaps, provide added insights for your game and can assist those who are interested in writing their own chess programs. A warning, however: most credible chess programs have required thousands of man-hours in development time and are truly a programmer's ultimate challenge.

The program described here is named OS-TRICH; it competed in the First World Computer Chess Tournament. The OSTRICH program is composed of three modules: BOOK, which provides standard book opening moves for up to the first five moves, CHESS, which is the main program used during most of the game, and END GAME, which takes over in rook/king or queen and king/king end games. CHESS, the main module, is comprised of approximately 9000 instructions, which are divided into five subprograms:

1. A subroutine for the control of input and output and for the control of the size of the search tree. The *search tree* refers to the branching search for all move possibilities that the computer performs before making each move. The size of the tree indicates the depth or number of moves ahead that will be considered for each move.
2. A subprogram to generate all move possibilities or search the tree.
3. A subprogram to arrange each possible move on a hierarchy scale according to its plausibility (each move is given a plausibility score). Following this initial ordering, another set of routines is called upon to improve the ordering.
4. A subprogram to calculate a terminal score or to evaluate the chess board at each terminal or branching point in the tree.
5. A subroutine to update all arrays, lists, and pointers used by the remainder of the program.

The Reference Arrays Used by Chess

1. The lists of the locations of each chess piece: an 8 × 8 array holds an identification number for each of the pieces on the board, in a corresponding memory location. The white pieces are identified as follows: King = 6, Queen = 5, Rook = 4, *Bishop* = 3, Knight = 2, and Pawn = 1. The black pieces are identified as the negative of the corresponding white piece number. The boards position array is updated after each move.
2. The piece location arrays: two separate arrays are generated at the beginning of each tree search. The list contains the names and corresponding locations of the white pieces; the other does the same for the black pieces.
3. The possible moves list: a list of possible moves for *ply* 1 (ply refers to the depth searched), ply 2, and ply 3, corresponding to each initial move, is generated. Additionally, memory is reserved to indicate which moves will result in a capture.
4. The control piece array: this array stores the

squares that each piece "controls" as well as the pieces that control a particular square. Thus, it is possible to determine the power of each piece along with what pieces are in control of the specific square in question.
5. The change array: all changes made at a node in the search tree are stored in this array when control advances to a new node. The purpose of the list is to expedite the restoring of positions.
6. The pinned pieces list: a listing of all pinned pieces is maintained in this array.
7. The en prise pieces list: a separate list of en prise pieces at each search node is maintained.
8. The Alpha and Beta cut-offs lists: two lists, one of the last eight moves resulting in alpha refutations and the other of beta refutations, are maintained.
9. The ply 3 plausibility list: CHESS maintains a list of the best ply 3 move for each possible ply 2 opponent's move for each ply 1 move investigated.
10. The principal variations list: each principal variation originating in the tree search is stored in this list.
11. The position records list: this listing of all moves since a recent capture or pawn move is used to determine whether a draw should be made because of repetition.

Tree Size

Tree size is automatically controlled by the program so that decisions will not exceed a predetermined time limit. Conditions that warrant an extension of the tree size include potential checks, captures. Pawn promotions, Pawns on the seventh rank, and the presence of en prise pieces.

The flowchart in Fig. 7-17 illustrates the processing that occurs each time a new node is reached. The node is determined to be either "terminal" or "nonterminal." A terminal node can be declared by a subroutine known as the gamma algorithm, by the fact that the node is past the tree length or by the fact that the node is past the minimum ply, but the board has no special features. All other nodes are classified as nonterminal.

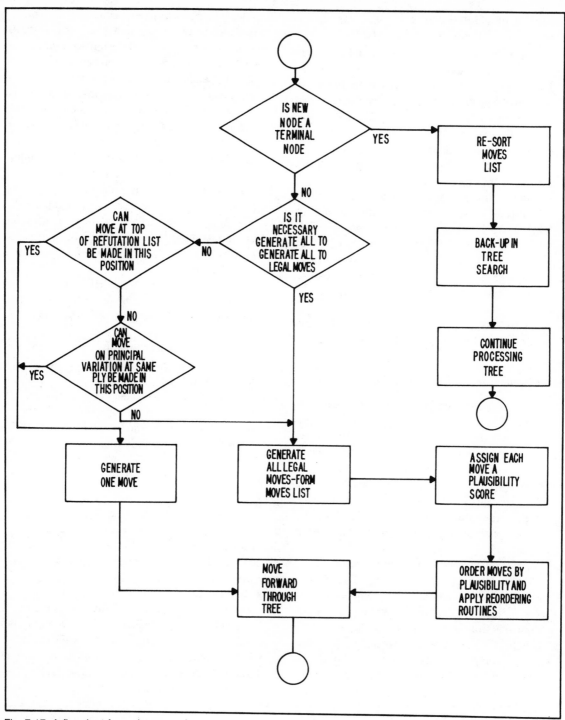

Fig. 7-17. A flowchart for node processing.

Nonterminal Node Processing

The One Move Generator subroutine is the first processing done at a nonterminal node. This subroutine determines whether one move is sufficient or all legal moves must be generated; if the first move could cause a refutation, the program continues; otherwise, the Move Generator determines all legal moves. Following move generation, a plausibility score is assigned to each move, and moves are sorted according to decreasing plausibility. The list is then resorted by special routines.

Plausibility Scoring

All possible moves are assigned a plausibility score that is based on the following parameters:

1. Captures: the score given for each capture is 2400 points plus the results of this formula:
   additional points=(point value of captures— piece point value of capturing piece)/10
   where the points for the chess pieces are Pawn = 600, Knight = Bishop = 1800, Rook = 3000, Queen = 5400, King = 300,000.
2. Castling: the point value for castling is 10,000 points.
3. Randomizer: this routine adds a random number of points to each move such that no piece will have excessive moves on the moves list. Up to ten points may be added.
4. Advance: any move which retreats a Queen, Knight, or Bishop receives a penalty of twenty points.
5. Pawn attack: any move which places a Queen, Rook, Bishop, or Knight where it can be captured on the next move by a Pawn receives a penalty of 200 point.
6. Pawn scoring: a Pawn move past the fourth rank is awarded 300 additional points, and a move past the sixth rank is given 1000 additional points. A move of the King's or Queen's Pawn is awarded 21 additional points, and a move of the Bishop's Pawn is given 15 additional points.
7. Rook scoring: moves for Rooks past the sixth rank are given 200 additional points. Moves for Rooks on the first rank to another square on the first rank that has no Pawns on the second and third ranks is awarded 40 points.
8. Refutation moves: any move on either the alpha or beta refutation lists is given an additional 300 points.
9. En prise moves: any move that defends an en prise piece is given a bonus of 300 points. Moves of en prise pieces are awarded 300 points if the move is to a safe square and are penalized 20 points if the move is an unsafe square.
10. Attack moves: if a move will place a piece where it can attack more pieces than before the move, additional points are awarded according to the pieces which may be attacked (and other factors).

Reordering the Moves List

Following the plausibility score analysis, special reordering routines are used to generate a final listing of moves in the order of their advantages. The three reordering routines used by OSTRICH are as follows:

1. Capture reordering: the plausibility analysis arbitrarily places capturing moves at the top of the moves list; however, a capture is usually not the best move in most positions. This routine generally places captures by non-Pawns on the opponent's side behind the non-capturing moves next on the list. No capture is moved to a point on the list where it will not be considered in the final analysis, however. Captures of pieces moved at the last ply are ilaced at the top of other captures, except at ply one, where this is done only under the condition that the following move will be a recapture.
2. Special reordering: a move called "Second Best" is generated after each move; it is the second to the last move that the search evaluated as it searched the first ply move list. This move is matched with the same move on the moves list, if it is there. Any such move is

195

placed on the top of the moves list, if it is legal.

3. Midsearch reordering: a midsearch reorder is done to the ply one moves list when the third move at ply one is to be considered. A match is sought between the moves remaining on the ply one list, and the move at the third ply is retrieved from the present principal continuation. If a match is found, that move is placed at the top of the moves list; if no match is found, matches are sought between this move and the most recent refutations.

Processing at Terminal Nodes

A scoring routine is applied to each terminal node, once it has been determined to be a terminal node. The seventeen scoring functions are as follows:

1. Board material: credit is awarded for the number and types of pieces that will remain on the board. The values given to each piece are Pawn=1, Bishop=Knight=3, Rook=5, Queen=9 King=300.

2. Material ratio: the material ratio routine scores favorably for trading pieces when you are ahead in material and penalizes for trading when you are behind: 100 points are awarded to the side that is ahead.

3. Castling: a King side castling is given 600 points, while a Queen side castling is given 300 points.

4. Board control: points are awarded in the following manner for control (ability to capture) of certain squares on the board: 12 points for each of the four center squares, 7 points for control of any square in the ring surrounding the four center squares, and 12 points for squares surrounding the opponent's King.

5. Tempo: 200 points are deducted from the score of either side for wasting time in one of the following ways: moving one piece twice in the opening, moving King or Rook prior to castling, moving a piece to its last previous position, using more than one move to move a piece to a position it could have reached in one move.

6. Opening Queen moves: moves of the Queen before the eighth move are penalized 400 points.

7. Blocking unadvanced Pawns: 470 points are deducted for moves that block unadvanced King or Queen Pawns.

8. Minor piece development: a penalty of 140 points is given for each unmoved center Pawn, Bishop, or Knight.

9. Center Pawns: an additional 50 points are awarded for all Pawns on K4 or Q4; 70 points are awarded for a Pawn on K5 or Q5.

10. Pawn structure: Isolated pawns are penalized 400 points; doubled Pawns are penalized 20 points; advancing Pawns are awarded 10 points.

11. Passed Pawns: passed Pawns on the seventh rank are worth 700 point, on the sixth 400 points, on the fifth 340 points, on the fourth 40 points, on the third 100 points, on the second 40 points. If Pawns and Kings are the only pieces left, the point values are doubled.

12. Kind defense: if there are more non-Pawn opposing pieces in the King's sector than defending pieces, a penalty of 75 points is assessed.

13. Doubled Rooks, Bishop pairs: if the two rooks are on the same column, 150 points are awarded; if one side has two Bishops and the other side does not, 150 points are awarded.

14. Trades: if the piece that moved at the last ply is under attack, the score is adjusted as follows: the score is reduced by the value of the attacked piece if the number of defenders is zero. Otherwise, a sequence of trades is performed on the square, and the score is changed based on the pieces exchanged.

15. King vs Pawns: if, after move thirty, the King is within one square of an opposing Pawn, 200 points are awarded.

16. Knight position: any Knight on column 9 or 7 is penalized 40 points.

17. Attacks: ply one moves that place an opposing piece en prise are awarded 40 points.

The Gamma Algorithm

The gamma algorithm was mentioned earlier

during the discussion concerning how to determine whether a node is terminal or nonterminal. Although the algorithm is complex, the logic behind its decision-making is that "if the situation is becoming progressively worse and better moves are available, classify this node as terminal."

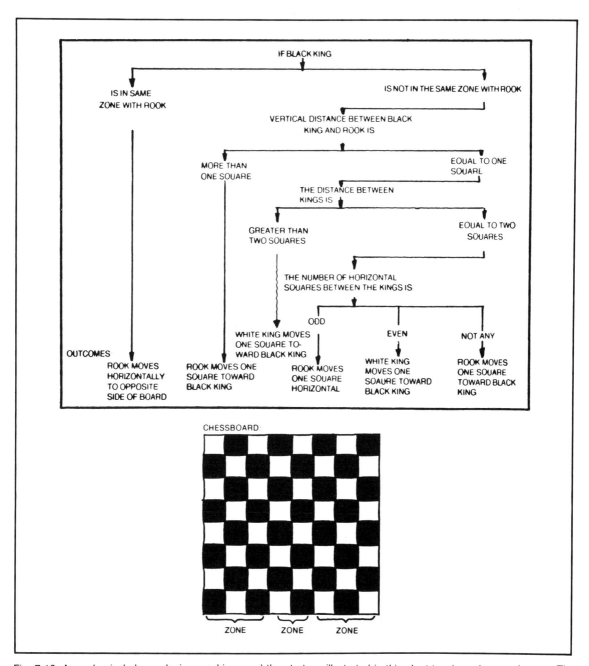

Fig. 7-18. A mechanical chess playing machine used the strategy illustrated in this chart to win a chess end game. The machine possessed a white King and Rook while the human opponent possessed only a King.

Possibilities for Chess-Related Programs

1. Chess end game program: of course, computer analysis becomes much simpler at the end of a chess game, when only a few pieces are left. The beginning programmer might wish to write a chess program to play end games between a few selected pieces only. The program would provide any initial set-up of pieces before the game. The strategy is shown in Fig. 7-18.

2. Chess variations: perhaps computers would be able to compete better in playing one of these chess variations:

   - Marseille game—each player moves two pieces in succession.
   - Legal game—white uses eight extra Pawns instead of a Queen.
   - Marked Pawn—the first player to make a capture wins this chess variation.
   - Chancellor—the Knight and Rook have the same combined move capabilities as each one has individually.
   - Grasshopper—pieces may leap over others; captures are as usual.

3. Advisor: a computer program updated with each move you make could advise you of situations you might miss. It would be interesting to compare the move you intend to make with the computer's suggestion.

4. Check: write a program that will determine whether Black or White is in check given a particular board set up.

5. Take the Queen: write a program that can determine whether a black Rook can take the white Queen in no more than four moves if neither white pieces nor any other black pieces are allowed to move in between the successive moves of the black Rook.

6. Eight Queens: this chess recreation was devised in the seventeenth century. The challenge is to discover how many ways it is possible to place eight Queens on a chessboard in such a manner that no one Queen can be taken by another? There are 92 solutions to the problem, which may be found by a computer program using this strategy: place a Queen in the first column and row of the board and a second Queen in an uncapturable or conflict—free row of column 2, and so on until a solution is generated or a conflict arises. When a conflict arises, backtrack to the column immediately before and place the queen in a new conflict-free position, and then continue on. If no other conflict-free position exists, backtrack to the next previous column and place that Queen in a new conflict-free position, and so on.

7. Five Queens: write a program to determine how five Queens may be placed on the board in such a manner that every square is dominated by at least one of the Queens.

8. Twelve Knights or eight Bishops: write a program to place 12 Knights or 8 Bishops on the board in such a manner that all other squares are dominated.

9. Knight's Tour: this program would find the path a Knight must take if he is placed on any square, and in 64 moves, he must land on each square once and only once. This problem may be solved by use of the heuristic strategy: For any square x on the chessboard, let $p_i(x)$ (i=1, 2, 3 . . .) be the number of squares accessible from x in i moves, not counting squares already visited. The knight always moves to a square x for which $p_i(x)$ exist, choose an x such that $p_2(x)$ is also as small as possible.

Listing 7-5: The Card Shufling Routine.

```
10 V$=RIGHT$(TIME$,2):REM use PC clock to seed random number generator
20 V=VAL(V$)
30 RANDOMIZE V
```

```
100 KEY OFF:CLS:PRINT"CARD SHUFFLING ROUTINE"
110 DIM M(52)
120 N=52:FOR I=1 TO N
130 M(I)=I:NEXT I
140 FOR I=1 TO N-1
150    R=(N+1-I)*RND
160    R=INT(R)+I
170    T=M(R)
180    M(R)=M(I)
190    M(I)=T
200 NEXT I
210 FOR I=1 TO N
220     PRINT M(I);
230 NEXT I
240 END
```

ADDITIONAL GAME PROGRAMS

Below are three listings that you can type into your computer and use.

Card Shuffler

You can incorporate the handy shuffling routine in Listing 7-5 into computer card games. The cards of the deck are numbered from 1 to 52 and are stored in the array M(x). A separate subroutine would convert these numbers into corresponding spot or face cards and suits.

William Tell Game

The program in Listing 7-6 presents a puzzle that will challenge those of all ages. The program describes "William Tell," and it's your job to determine what else characterizes William Tell. The solution is encoded so that typing in the program does not reveal the secret.

Listing 7-6: The William Tell Program

```
100 REM WILLIAM TELL
110 KEY OFF:CLS
120 V$=RIGHT$(TIME$,2):V=VAL(V$)
130 RANDOMIZE(V)
140 PRINT TAB(10)"WILLIAM TELL"
170 DIM A$(20),B$(20)
190 PRINT "WILLIAM TELL IS A GAME OF LOGIC IN WHICH THE COMPUTER"
200 PRINT "GIVES YOU EXAMPLES OF WHAT WILLIAM TELL IS AND YOU HAVE"
210 PRINT "TO GUESS THE SECRET BEHIND THE WORDS THAT CHARACTERIZE"
220 PRINT "WILLIAM TELL.  THE COMPUTER WILL PROVIDE YOU WITH EXAMPLES"
230 PRINT "AS A HINT.  YOU MUST THEN GUESS WHAT WILLIAM TELL IS AND"
240 PRINT "IS NOT BY TYPING IN NEW WORDS YOU THINK MAY CHARACTERIZE"
250 PRINT "WILLIAM TELL.  IF YOU HAVEN'T FIGURED IT OUT AFTER 20"
260 PRINT "TRIES YOU CAN ASK FOR THE ANSWER OR TRY THE SAME SET"
270 PRINT "AGAIN.  HERE IS YOUR FIRST EXAMPLE AND CHANCE TO GUESS:"
290 PRINT:FOR X=1 TO 20
300 READ A$(X),B$(X)
310 NEXT
330 REM THIS LIST OF EXAMPLES MAY BE EXPANDED
340 DATA BRILLIANCE,GLORY,GLASSES,SPECTACLES,MELLOW,INTOXICATED
```

```
350 DATA DULL,STUPID,COMMODITY,OBJECT,SHEEN,BRIGHT,UNDRESSED
360 DATA NUDE,MISSION,OBJECTIVE,SPEECH,PROSE,PASSIVE,INERT
370 DATA SUGGESTION,ADVICE,SYMMETRICAL,REGULAR,JITTERY,NERVOUS
380 DATA IMPRESSIVE,MAGNIFICENT,ERRONEOUS,FAULTY,FEEBLE,LAME
390 DATA CALLOUS,INSENSITIVE,SOOTHING,SERENE,SHALLOW
400 DATA SUPERFICIAL,NAMELESS,ANONYMOUS
410 FOR Y=1 TO 20
420 PRINT "WILLIAM TELL IS ";A$(Y);" BUT NOT ";B$(Y)
430 INPUT "WILLIAM TELL IS...";C$
440 GOSUB 730
470 IF F=1 THEN 560
480 INPUT "BUT, WILLIAM TELL IS NOT...";C$
490 GOSUB 780
500 IF F=1 THEN PRINT "WILLIAM TELL IS ";C$;"!!!"
510 GOSUB 790
530 PRINT
540 NEXT Y
550 GOTO 640
560 INPUT "BUT, WILLIAM TELL IS NOT";C$
570 GOSUB 730
580 IF (F=1)AND(G=1) THEN PRINT "WHOOPS, I THOUGHT YOU GOT IT":PRINT "LETS
    TRY SOME MORE...":G=0:PRINT
590 IF (F=0)AND(G=1) THEN 630
600 IF (F=0) THEN PRINT:PRINT "BY GOLLY, MAYBE YOU HAVE IT!":PRINT "LETS TRY
    ONCE MORE...":PRINT:G=1
610 IF F=1 THEN PRINT "WILLIAM TELL IS ";C$;"!!!!":PRINT
620 GOTO 540
630 PRINT "RIGHT!!!!!"
640 INPUT "WOULD YOU LIKE TO TRY AGAIN (A) OR HEAR THE ANSWER(H)";A$
650 IF A$="H" THEN 670 ELSE 370
660 REM ENCODED ANSWER FOR WILLIAM TELL
670 PRINT "THE SECRET IS:"
680 A$="UGJJ?K/RCJJ/GQ/?LW/UMPB/AMLR?GLGLE/RUM/AMLQCASRGTC*/GBCLRGA?J/JCRRCPQ,"
710 NEXT X
720 END
730 F=0:REM ANSWER EVALUATION
750 FOR X=1 TO LEN(C$)
760 IF MID$(C$,X,1)=MID$(C$,X+1,1) THEN F=1:ELSE NEXT X
770 RETURN
780 REM WRONG ANSWER CHOICES
790 ON INT(RND*5+1) GOTO 800,810,820,830,840
800 PRINT "NOPE...GIVE IT ANOTHER TRY:":RETURN
810 PRINT "SORRY, NOT EVEN CLOSE.":RETURN
820 PRINT "THAT DOES NOT COMPUTE (IT'S WRONG)":RETURN
830 PRINT "YOU'RE STILL COLD...TRY AGAIN:":RETURN
840 PRINT "THAT ONE ALMOST BLEW MY CIRCUITE...HERE'S ANOTHER HINT:"RETURN
```

Listing 7-7: The Personality Test Program

```
10 CLS:KEY OFF
```

```
20 REM PERSONALITY TEST--BASED ON PSYCHOLOGICAL RESEARCH
30 PRINT "THE FOLLOWING PERSONALITY TEST IS NOT COMPREHENSIVE, BUT HAS"
40 PRINT "BEEN USED TO DETERMINE GENERAL CHARACTERISTICS."
50 PRINT
60 PRINT "INSTRUCTIONS: THREE VERSES WILL BE PRINTED.  FOLLOWING"
70 PRINT "EACH VERSE WILL BE A LIST OF INTERPRETATIONS.  INPUT"
80 PRINT "THE CORRESPONDING NUMBER FOR THE INTERPRETATION YOU"
90 INPUT "BELIEVE IS THE BEST.  PRESS 'ENTER' WHEN READY.",A$
100 CLS
110 PRINT "A BOOK OF VERSES UNDERNEATH THE BOUGH,"
120 PRINT "A JUG OF WINE, A LOAF OF BREAD--AND THOU"
130 PRINT "BESIDE ME SINGING IN THE WILDERNESS--"
140 PRINT "OH, WILDERNESS WERE PARADISE ENOW!"
150 PRINT
160 PRINT "1) HAPPINESS OR CONTENTMENT CAN BE FOUND WITHOUT MUCH PLANNING"
170 PRINT "2) HAPPINESS IS IN ACCEPTING AND ENJOYING SIMPLE THINGS"
180 PRINT "3) HAPPINESS IS ALWAYS PRESENT IF WE TAKE THE TIME TO LOOK"
190 PRINT "4) IF YOU SET YOUR MIND TO IT, HAPPINESS CAN BE FOUND"
200 PRINT "5) HAPPINESS IS WHERE WE FIND IT"
210 INPUT X1
220 CLS
230 PRINT "THERE IS A TIDE IN THE AFFAIRS OF MEN,"
240 PRINT "WHICH, TAKEN AT THE FLOOD, LEADS ON TO FORTUNE;"
250 PRINT "OMITTED, ALL THE VOYAGE OF THEIR LIFE"
260 PRINT "IS BOUND IN SHALLOWS AND IN MISERIES."
270 PRINT ""
280 PRINT "1) MAKE THE MOST OF YOUR CHANCE WHEN YOU GET IT"
290 PRINT "2) IN MANY CASES OF FAILURE, PEOPLE WERE AFFECTED BY CIRCUMSTANCES"
300 PRINT "3) OVER WHICH THEY HAD LITTLE CONTROL."
310 PRINT "3) ONE WHO PLANS WELL WILL SURVIVE WELL UNDER THE LAWS OF NATURE"
320 PRINT "4) LIFE IS SUCH THAT IT PAYS TO WATCH WHAT YOU DO BEFORE YOU RUN INTO
 TROUBLE"
330 PRINT "5) ONE SHOULD BE ON THE WATCH FOR OPPORTUNITY TO KNOCK, OTHERWISE HE"

340 PRINT "   WILL MISS OUT ON GOING PLACES."
350 INPUT X2
360 CLS
370 PRINT "NO MAN IS AN ISLAND, ENTIRE OF ITSELF."
380 PRINT
390 PRINT "1) EVERYONE SHOULD CONSIDER THE NEEDS AND WANTS OF OTHERS"
400 PRINT "2) USE OTHER'S INFLUENCE TO HELP YOU PLAN YOUR LIFE."
410 PRINT "3) ONE WHO ACTS WITHOUT REGARD FOR OTHERS DOES NOT REALIZE THAT"
420 PRINT "   HE IS A SOCIAL ANIMAL."
430 PRINT "4) TO GET WHERE YOU WANT TO BE IN LIFE YOU MUST REALIZE THE NEED"
440 PRINT "   FOR HELP FROM OTHERS."
450 PRINT "5) ALTHOUGH I AM THE CAPTAIN OF MY SOUL, I MUST MAKE MY WAY"
460 PRINT "   IN LIFE AMONG MANY OTHER CAPTAINS."
470 INPUT X3
480 CLS
490 PRINT "THE TEST INDICATES THAT YOU POSSESS THESE TRAITS:"
500 IF X1=1 THEN PRINT "IRRESPONSIBLE" ELSE IF X1=2 THEN PRINT "CONVENTIONAL AND
 MORALISTIC" ELSE IF X1=3 THEN PRINT "MORALISTIC" ELSE IF X1=4 THEN PRINT "FORMA
```

```
L" ELSE PRINT "PRACTICAL"
510 IF X2=1 THEN PRINT "PRACTICAL AND LOGICAL" ELSE IF X2=2 THEN PRINT "MORALIST
IC" ELSE IF X2=3 THEN PRINT "CONVENTIONAL" ELSE IF X2=4 THEN PRINT "HUMOROUS AND
 SENSIBLE" ELSE PRINT "EGO-CENTRIC"
520 IF X3=1 THEN PRINT "CONVENTIONAL" ELSE IF X3=2 THEN PRINT "PRACTICAL AND LOG
ICAL" ELSE IF X3=3 THEN PRINT "OBJECTIVE" ELSE IF X3=4 THEN PRINT "EGO-CENTRIC"
ELSE PRINT "MORALISTIC"
530 PRINT "IF THE SAME TRAIT IS LISTED TWICE THEN IT IS ALL THE"
540 PRINT "MORE INDICATIVE OF YOU."
550 END
```

Personality Test

The program in Listing 7-7 will be interesting to guests. A series of verses is printed, and the player is asked to provide an interpretation. Although this program is based upon psychological research, don't take it too seriously. However, it is interesting to note that the day of the computer psychologist is near; computers have already been used to question patients and provide an overall psychological analysis on the basis of standard psychological tests.

Chapter 8

Control and Peripheral Applications

The potentials for computer control and monitoring of the home are endless; only a few of the possible applications have been put into practice with the incorporation of microprocessors in household appliances. Several industry demonstration homes have been built to exhibit microprocessor control of the home. The following suggestions have been included in these homes or have been suggested by leading industry forecasters and futurists:

- Climate control is just one of the many functions provided by the home computer system. The rate of temperature change and humidity is noted, and the air conditioner or heater is turned off before the house is at a preset level; the temperature will "coast" to the desired level. The system also times the thermostat. In winter it turns down the temperature at night, turns it up again in the morning, and then turns it back down while you go off to work; in the summer it controls the air conditioner in the same manner. To conserve energy, the hot water heater is also turned down during certain hours when hot water isn't needed.

- A vocal input interface to the home computer is continuously active, waiting for a command by one of the occupants. All appliances and lights controlled by the system can be switched on and off by voice command or can be programmed to start and stop at selected times.

- An intelligent alarm system will turn off all electricity and gas and call the fire department in case of fire. A burglar detection system calls the police if an intruder is detected ultrasonically or by other sensors.

- Interfaces to stereo, televisions, and telephones are also interesting. The telephone controller acts as a phone message recorder with additional features. If a message is taken, the unit can be instructed to call someone at another number and deliver the message. A telephone call to the machine itself can allow you to change the recorded message, play back messages, or control any of the devices connected with the home computer. A telephone file of commonly used numbers is stored in the computer. Additionally, you can dial numbers by simply calling them out vocally; if a busy signal is encountered the computer continually redials the number until the line is free.

- The stereo interface transforms an ordinary stereo into a "jukebox" from which recordings may be selected and played at the touch of a button. A special device can monitor radio broadcasts and record all music; commercials and news are not recorded (voice patterns can be distinguished from music). You can preprogram the volume level and the type of music you want to have recorded for special purposes such as musical interludes and background music for dinner. A given song can be played a selected number of times, or the computer may bé programmed to skip to the next song on a record or cassette.

- The television interface will turn on the set at selected times or record shows on video tape; a directional antenna or satellite dish is automatically turned for the best reception.

- Even the bar is automated. Drinks of your choice are mixed automatically (bottles of ingredients are connected by hoses to the special machine).

- You can use a voice synthesizer to audibly awake you in the morning with "Good Morning Mr. T. It's 8 A.M. ," and then summarize your itinerary for the day.

- An automatic system can release fresh food and water for pets left at home for a long period, can sense when the animal has not eaten the food, and can notify the veterinarian to check the home.

Some other applications currently being used by hobbyists include the following:

- Voice or sound synthesizers are incorporated into games to provide dialogue or sound effects.

- Voice input computers are used for recording information called out by an operator. One hobbyist uses such a system to make simple calculations in his home workshop while his hands are full. Although such systems are usually limited to a vocabulary of about thirty words, some hobbyists have managed to develop automatic "dictation-taking" typewriters for limited purposes (a word capacity of 100 is considered maximum).

- A hobbyist has used his small computer to replace over 7000 mechanical relays necessary to control a pipe organ in his home. Similarly, computers could be used to light the keys on an organ to help you learn to play a song. Although a commercial piano player has been developed to digitally record music played and play it back later, the cost is high. If you were to implement such a system with your computer, additional features could be added; speed, sustain, attack, and other features could all be varied.

- One hobbyist is using a microprocessor to create intelligent test equipment that can automatically perform a set of test routines on a given circuit. This is an interesting application for amateur radio operators. A calculating oscilloscope is able to compute exact items for rises, perform integrals, and differentials, compute peak areas, RMS values, and peak to peak distances, and do n-point averaging; all data can be stored.

- With the addition of silver contacts and a small amplifier, your computer could serve as a biofeedback monitor or lie detector. Galvanic skin resistance, temperature, or heartbeat could all be measured with the use of the proper instruments. This information could be sent through a joystick port or other J/D port and analyzed or displayed by the computer. An article describing the construction and operation of a computer biofeedback monitor appeared in *80 Microcomputing,* October 1983, pp. 176-192.

The capabilities of a computer allow sophisticated analysis and conversion of waveforms not obtainable with standard biofeedback equipment. An assembly language program could be written to convert alpha brain wave signals, which are in the range of 8-12 Hz, to audible sound by raising all the frequency components of the brain wave signal to the audible range while preserving the ratios between frequencies. Such a program could be used for a variety of unique applications—for example, for converting your voice from a very deep level to a "Mickey Mouse" level or for dealing with any situation requiring the conversion of analogue signals. You can envision future digital music players that have the added capability of altering songs through the use of hardwired computer circuits.

- A New Hampshire resident uses his home computer to control his wood stove; he reports a 10 to 30 percent improvement in efficiency.
- A digital/audio file in which a standard cassette interface is used to record digital information between songs (audio) could be used to index songs, prompt a vocal announcement by a voice synthesizer, or control volumes, speakers, times, or mixing.
- Hobbyists have connected computers to exercise equipment, such as jogging pads or exercise bikes, to keep track of energy expended, speed, or time. These special input devices could also be used as controllers for special video games.
- Special software and hardware configurations could permit two or more opposing players to use separate but interconnected computers in such a manner that they cannot see each other's gamefield. Games of this type (*multiplayer* games) are gaining in popularity on computer networks.
- Chess fanatics who also happen to be gadget fanatics would take delight in a computer-interfaced chessboard capable of sensing the movement of pieces. A robotic arm, of course, would move pieces for the computer.
- Personal computers can be used to generate titles for home video or film movies that can involve animated color graphics. Titles for slide shows could also be made by photographing the screen.
- Along similar lines, your computer could flash subliminal messages over television programs for behavior modification. These would last 1/30 of a second and assail your subconscious with messages to help you control your weight, deal with stress, smoking, or alcoholism, or become motivated toward success. Messages such as "I exercise" and "I am successful" could be repeated every minute.
- Radio scanner buffs can interface their computer

to a scanner via CompuScan™, a Bearcat product, allowing them to monitor up to 200 channels. The computer can display the frequency and the description of the channel received on a video monitor.
- Weather sensors such as electronic anemometers, thermometers and barometers can be interfaced with a computer to provide automatic weather monitoring.

HOUSEHOLD CONTROL DEVICES

The interfaces that allow a personal computer to help you out around the house are now commercially available from the firms listed below. For those with a hardware bent, schematics for a simple control latch system and A/D converter are included at the end of this chapter.

The firms have been divided into two groups, depending upon the type of product they offer: those listed under "Personal-Computer Systems" offer products that are designed to work with one or more popular brands of personal computers; those listed under "Dedicated Systems" offer products that are made specifically for home control applications but can be interfaced to computers by electronic geniuses.

Personal Computer Systems

Circuit Science, 4 Townsend West, Nashua, NH 03063; (603) 880-4066. Circuit Science manufactures the CSI-1200, a controller interface that plugs into an RS-232 port. This system eliminates the BSR control box, but uses the BSR remote modules for each appliance controlled.

Compu-Home Systems, 3333 East Florida Ave., Denver, CO 80210; (303) 777-6600. This firm manufactures the Tomorrowhouse system for the Apple II, which controls lights, appliances, solar-heating systems, sprinklers, hot tubs, indoor heat, and air-conditioning. It guards against burglars and reminds you of appointments and important dates.

Cyberlynx Computer Products, 4828 Sterling Dr., Boulder, CO 80301 (303) 444-7733.

Cyberlynx offers the Smarthome I system for connection to your Apple RS-232 port. It can be attached to an infrared detector to sense heat or movement in a room and cause lights and appliances to turn on and off to scare off an intruder. The system is also configured to control appliances for convenience and energy saving.

HyperTek, P.O. Box 137, Route 22 East, Salem Industrial Park, Whitehouse, NJ 08888; (201) 874-4773. HyperTek manufactures the HomeBrain, a dedicated microprocessor for home control that uses sensor for heat, temperature, and motion. It uses Leviton wireless controllers and hardwired relays to integrate and schedule many home appliances. It can be connected with any personal computer via an RS-232 port.

Intelectron, 1275 A St., Hayward, CA 94543; (415) 581-4490. This firm offers The Control Center, a system operating on the same principle as the BSR system.

Infield Software, 2422 Alvin St., Suite 100, Mountain View, CA 94043. Infield sells the Home Controller for connection to your Apple II Plus or *II*e; it incorporates the BSR home control unit to run appliances, lights, sprinklers, spa, and so on.

Dedicated Systems and Hardware

Anova Electronics, Three Waters Park Drive, San Mateo, CA 94403; (415) 572-9686. Anova sells three dedicated microprocessor-based systems for home control. These systems can be used for control via telephone; and offer timed or instant remote control of appliances, and protection against fire, burglary, and utility failure.

Audio Command Systems, 46 Merrick Road, Rockville Center, New York, NY 11570; (516) 766-2627. This firm offers remote control devices including low-voltage lighting-control systems, motorized drapery controllers, stereo components, and robots.

BSR, Route 303, Blauvelt, NY 10913; (914) 358-6060. This firm is the granddaddy of home control systems; their BSR System is used by a variety of other manufacturers as a component of their system. The BSR controller encodes a signal on the 60-cycle alternating current of the house's electrical system, eliminating the need for special wiring throughout the house. Each controlled appliance is plugged into a remote unit that may be turned on and off the the main control box of the BSR system.

Leviton, 59-25 Little Neck Parkway, Little Neck, NY; 11362 (212) 229-4040. Levition manufactures electronic control devices that allow computer control of lighting and appliances.

Technicom International, 23 Old Kings Highway South, Darien, CT 06820; (202) 655-1299. This firm offers the Energy Control System (ECS), which can control up to eight devices in the home using BSR remote modules.

The Use of Home Control Systems

Users of these control systems report applications as diverse as energy conservation through keeping various rooms at desired temperatures for different times of day, sprinkling the lawn according to the amount of ground moisture, securing doors, signaling a baby's movements in a crib, making and logging phone calls, detecting the seepage of water into a basement, opening and shutting drapes and starting the roast by a phone call from the office.

The control system can be arranged in such a manner that one computer controls the entire house, or a network of computers (one in each area of the house) can be interconnected via RS-232 communications channels as shown in the diagram in Fig. 8-11

MUSIC

A few music/voice synthesizers are now on the market as personal computer peripherals. Possible uses for these include the following:

- Use them with games for special sound effects.
- Use them with a music composing program to generate and play original music continuously.
- Use a music synthesizer as programmable drummer to accompany other instruments. Various drum sounds, speeds, and patterns including Latin, swing, jazz, waltz, and march, could be programmed. The metronome, cymbals, and other percussion devices could also be imitated.
- Use a voice synthesizer to "sing" the vocals of a music piece, producing a unique composition.

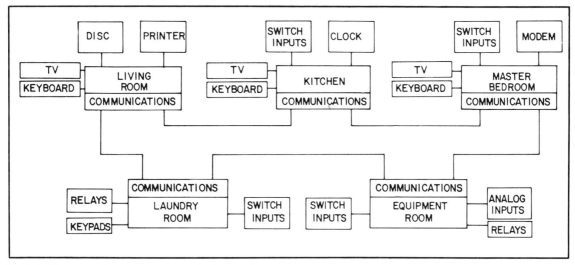

Fig. 8-1. Five areas of a computer-controlled house. Separate microprocessor-based nodes communicate via an intelligent communications processor and an advanced data link controller.

- Use the standardized MIDI (Musical Instrument Digital Interface) to connect a home computer to one or more electronic musical synthesizers to play or digitally record your compositions on a standard electronic keyboard. Comprehensive reformation on MIDI is available from: MIDI Users Group, P.O. Box 593, Los Altos, CA 94022, phone (408) 253-4684.

Additional applications in the area of music include the following:

- If you have a plotter or a graphic printer or terminal, your musical compositions or those of the computer could be displayed in standard musical notation.
- Loops of the proper speed and duration will generate a specific audible frequency on an AM radio placed next to a CPU. A machine language or BASIC program to make use of this effect could produce sounds that resemble music.
- If music is dignitized with the use of an A/D converter, it can be altered in various ways. Here are some examples:
  —Selected voices or instruments could be removed/added after an analysis of frequency content.
  —The music could be played at any selected rate

without a change in pitch, or could be played backwards for special effect. You could transform a given composition into another style of your choice.
- Today's color organs, which produce a pulsating light in response to music, rely upon analog circuits and often do not produce good results. A dedicated microprocessor could be used to control the lights instead, resulting in a more favorable response.

AN EXTERNAL DEVICE CONTROLLER FOR YOUR COMPUTER

The project described below will allow the electronic enthusiast to economically interface his or her computer with external devices. For those not electronically inclined, controlling interface circuit boards are commercially available for under $200.

The controller described here will allow you to economically interface your computer with virtually any external electrical device; up to sixteen devices (channels) can be controlled simultaneously.

This interface switches on and off a small amount of current to control relays that in turn can control larger electrical loads (see Fig. 8-2). Prac-

207

tically all eight-bit computers can drive the interface, and a four-bit microprocessor could drive a modified interface for specialized control purposes.

The interface consists of three modules: a sixteen-channel demultiplexer, a sixteen-bit "memory," and sixteen single transistor driver amplifiers (see Fig. 8-3); the construction cost should not exceed $30. The interface is designed to be connected directly with a parallel output port.

The four low-order bits of data coming from the parallel output port are inputted to the demultiplexer. The demultiplexer selects the appropriate output pin and pulls it low (for example, if the four bits are 0000, channel zero will be selected and pin one pulled low). Since only sixteen individual signals are possible with four bits, sixteen is the maximum number of channels that can be selected. Each output signal switches the state of one of the sixteen flip-flop chips. Thus, the flip-flops act as a sixteen-bit memory to maintain the status of each channel continuously, Signals sent to one flip-flop will alternatively toggle the corresponding channel on and off. The fifth bit of the data byte is first buffered and then connected to the reset pin of each flip-flop. Thus, all channels may be reset (turned off) simultaneously through the use of the fifth bit.

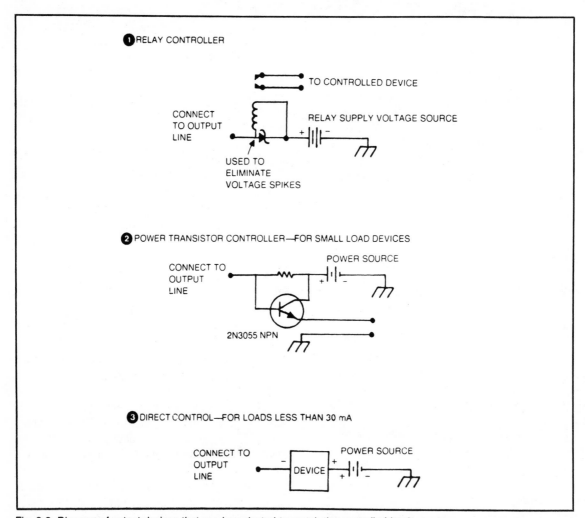

Fig. 8-2. Diagram of output devices that can be selected to match the controlled load.

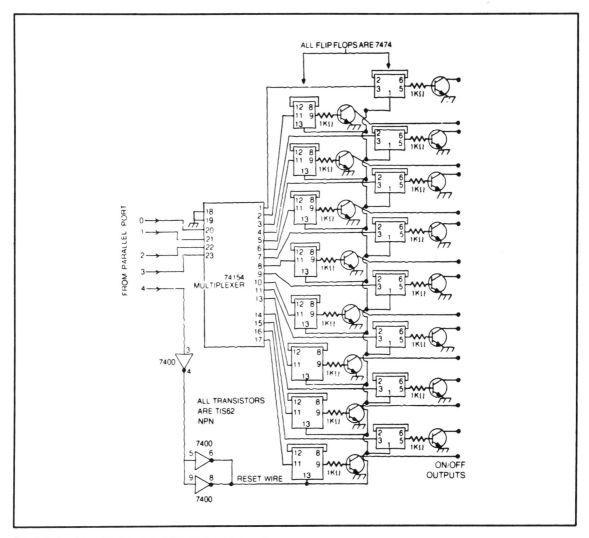

Fig. 8-3. A schematic diagram of the control latch system.

The software must output the signal corresponding to the correct channel to control devices connected to the interface. However, channel cannot be switched on and off continuously by selecting that channel over and over again. This restriction is due to the fact that the flip-flops only switch on rising edges from the demultiplexer, which occur only if the multiplexer has been changed to select a different channel. Therefore, to switch a given flip-flop on and then off, follow these steps: 1) select the channel with the proper data byte, 2) select any other channel (for example an unused channel), 3) wait for the first channel to toggle on 4) reselect the first channel to turn it off.

AN A/D CONVERTER FOR YOUR COMPUTER

The A/D (analog to digital) converter has many applications for use with personal computers. It will allow you to interface joysticks or potentiometers with computers for use during editing, video drawing, or game playing. Automation of test equipment and control over robots or machines are among the many other possible applications.

The eight-channel interface described here is

209

designed for use in converting signals in the range of about 0.1 Hz to 100 Hz, which is sufficient for the applications listed above (see Fig. 8-4). The "sample-and-hold" principle is used in the design to store an analog signal as a capacitor charge until it is processed. The two power supplies necessary should fall between 4.5 to 6.5 V and 12 to 15 V respectively.

An assembly language software description is provided below; you should supply the op codes for your microprocessor.

1. Initialize the pointer
2. Load the next byte for output
3. Output the byte
4. Set the accumulator equal to the pointer
5. Select the next channel and enable the sample and hold process
6. Turn off the sample and hold strobe
7. Turn off the selected sample and hold
8. Decrement the value of the pointer
9. If the pointer is greater than or equal to zero, loop back to step 2; otherwise return to the main program.

As you can see, the program sequentially addresses a channel, outputs the voltage that is to be held, disables that channel, repeats the process for the other channels, and then returns to the main program. You could arrange the program to act as an

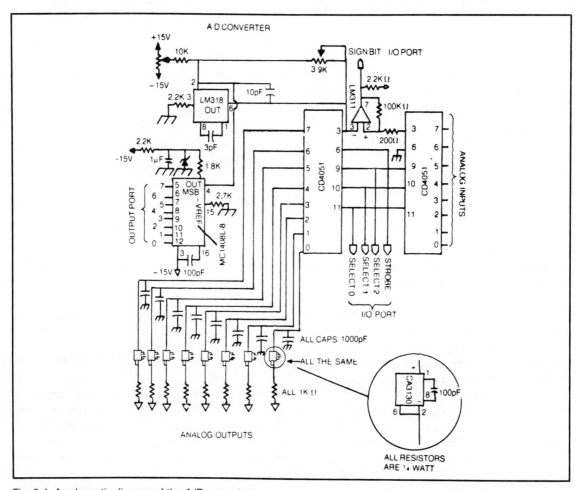

Fig. 8-4. A schematic diagram of the A/D converter.

interrupt handler signaled by a clock strobe on an interrupt line.

A D/A (digital to analog) converter can also be built or purchased and used to produce speech, music, or sound effects or to control the speed of a motor, among many other applications.

PERSONAL ROBOTS

Today the development of personal robotics is at the stage personal computers development was in the early 1970s. It's a young field with great potential and much remaining to be explored. Personal robotics is discussed here as a control application for your personal computer, considering that many robots available on the market rely upon external microcomputers for partial or complete control over their actions.

The state of the art personal robot can locomote, talk, and perhaps perform crude manipulator functions or chores such as vacuuming the house or automatically finding the battery recharge unit when necessary. Capabilities such as setting the table like a maid, fetching a beer, or mowing the lawn like a loyal son are currently out of the question. As of this date, none of the available products even come close to replacing appliances or offspring. In fact, most of the robots for sale do not have functional arms, and few are self-contained; most communicate with their host computer by means of a cord or via radio transmissions. At present, personal robots serve little purpose other than entertainment and as an educational tool. However, advances are being made to allow more practical use of personal robots, and you could be part of that frontier!

Manufacturers of Personal Robots include:

Androbot, Inc.
101 E. Daggett Dr.
San Jose, CA 95134

Heath Co.
Benton Harbor, MI 49022

Microbot, Inc.
453-H Ravendale Dr.
Mountain View, CA 94043

RB Robot Corp.
14618 W. 6th Ave., Suite 201
Golden, CO 80401

Robotics International Corp.
2335 E. High
Jackson, MI 49203

Sandhu Machine Design, Inc.
308 S. State St.
Champaign, IL 61820

Technical Micro Systems, Inc.
366 Cloverdale
Box 7227
Ann Arbor, MI 48107

Terrapin, Inc.
380 Green St.
Cambridge, MA 02139

Chapter 9

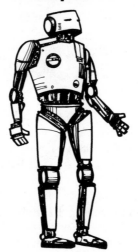

Artificial Intelligence, the Future Personal Computer, and Networking

In his book *Future Shock,* Alvin Toffler describes a future home computer system named OLIVER, the primary purpose of which is to help the owner deal with decision overload.

"In its simplest form, OLIVER would merely be a personal computer programmed to provide the individual with information and to make minor decisions for him. At this level, it could store information about his friends' preferences for Manhattans or martinis, and data about traffic routes, the weather, stock prices, and so on. The device could be set to remind him of his wife's birthday or to order flowers automatically. It could renew his magazine subscriptions, pay the rent on time, order razor blades and the like. As computerized information systems expand, they would tap into a worldwide pool of data stored in libraries, corporate files, hospitals, retail stores, banks, government agencies, and universities. OLIVER would thus become a kind of universal question answered for him. However, some computer scientists see much beyond this. It is theoretically possible to construct an OLIVER that would analyze the content of an owner's words, scrutinize his choices, deduce his value system, update its own program to reflect changes in his values, and ultimately handle larger and larger decisions for him."

FUTURISTIC APPLICATIONS THAT ARE FEASIBLE NOW

Although many of these applications will probably not be feasible within the coming decade, some ideas being put into practice include the following:

Medical monitoring. A specially designed microcomputer could be programmed to make checks of your bodily functions. Information such as nutritional and caloric intake, pulse rate, blood pressure, and weight loss or gain could be entered into a program especially tailored for your metabolism. Specific conditions that warrant a visit to the doctor could be computed and outputted.

With a telephone modem, the computer could transmit such information to a larger data bank for processing. Additionally, answers to common medical questions could be provided by the data bank.

Information research. The facilities to tap computerized information banks (for example, the information banks of the New York Times and the World Trade Center) are already available via telephone modems connected to such service companies as The Source[SM]. Such services are especially useful to businessmen, authors, and educators who need to locate specialized information. In addition, a home computer interfaced to a standard modem could tap the Library of Congress's computerized card catalog as well as numerous other data banks.

Personalized news service. A home computer on-line with a news service could select news items by category and store them for review later by the home owner. The United Press International wire service provides all major national and world news; news items are coded by category, and thus, a computer on-line could select items of interest.

Travel information. A travel service data bank, filled with information regarding flights, schedules, prices, availability, reservations, and so on could supply all the information necessary for you to plan a vacation or an outing, via a telephone modem.

Stock market quotes. A continual Dow Jones listing service could supply stock market quotes to the home computer via a telephone modem. Such a service would be a boon to those attempting stock market analyses with their computer.

Educational programs. Quality, comprehensive educational programs are being developed for the growing home computer video tape player can be used in conjunction with the computer to provide television images that cannot be provided with conventional computer grpahics. In addition, the computer can randomly access video images from a video disk to provide interactive education.

Business extensions. Computer programmers, professional investors, and other professionals who do most of their work with a computer system are beginning to install home terminals; soon traveling to an office will be unnecessary.

Computer networks. Numerous amateur and professional computer networks have been formed for the exchange of programs, ideas, tips, and other information. Commercially available "bulletin board" software allows anyone with a computer and auto-answer modem to form their own network. Consult Appendix A for a listing of computer bulletin board systems available in your area.

Intelligent devices. A home computer interfaced with household devices could create a complete home management system. Climate control, solar energy system control, television set timing, cooking device control, and so on could all be done simultaneously by a properly equipped home computer. With falling costs for microcomputers, such control applications are becoming economical.

Other possibilities include a complete, computer-controlled diagnostic system for your automobile.

Artificial intelligence? A popularly quoted assessment of computers and people goes like this: "Computers are fast, accurate, and stupid. People are slow, inaccurate, and brilliant. Together they can perform incredible feats beyond the imagination." With the advent of artificial intelligence, computers have begun to enter the "brilliant" category. So-called *expert systems* are capable of making informed decisions on the basis of hundreds of thousands of rules and relationships much as a human expert can. Although most artificial intelligence programs are intended for large computer systems, some of this technology will be available in the near future for the personal computer. Numerous applications in medicine, business, science, and education are foreseen. For further information and experimental programs for use on your personal computer, see *Artificial Intelligence,* by Neil Graham, TAB Books, Inc., Blue Ridge Summit, PA 17214.

FUTURISTIC APPLICATIONS THAT ARE NOT YET FEASIBLE

However, not all applications suggested by the media are practical, and in some cases may not be possible to accomplish with current technology.

The examples of impractical applications described below will serve to define the limits of personal computer control/peripheral applications.

Personal security system. By determining heights, weights, and diameters of all who come to your doorstep, your computer will be able to recognize whether or not that person is an acquaintance (based on previously stored information).

The problems associated with this application are obvious; the equipment to determine heights and diameters of a person in motion would be difficult to interface with the computer, and no purpose is given for spending hundreds of dollars to accomplish such a feat.

Robot maid. Some authors have claimed that domestic androids will be available within a few years to do such chores as vacuuming a home, walking the dog, washing dishes, preparing food, and so on and will have the capability of carrying on a natural conversation with the owner.

Although several robots are commercially available for home use, the application of these as useful household servants has not passed the point of tedious control of their every movement by humans. Some robots are available with sensors that enable them to avoid collisions with people and objects such as furniture. These robots can even vacuum a floor in a semirandom fashion, but further applications are limited by inadequate mechanics and the problem computers have in recognizing "universals." Dennis Gabor described this problem in his book *Innovations*.

"One can say that it is incomparably easier to design a computer for solving a wave equation beyond the reach of the best analyst than to design one that will pick up and empty ashtrays, because ashtrays come in so many shapes."

Presumably, the use of the television camera is the only way to give a robot "sight." Computer analysis of the thousands of individual pixels, or dots, in a television picture to determine what objects are in the picture is not yet practical for personal computers.

The problems of speech input are also numerous. A very large memory capacity and a high processing speed are necessary for "understanding"

anything even approaching normal conversation.

However, hobbyists show considerable interest in robotics, and over the next few years they will produce increasingly sophisticated robots.

Controlling an automobile. The problems associated with the computerized control (driving) of an automobile are much the same as those associated with the control of domestic androids.

NETWORKING

The world is your neighbor via your microcomputer. Within the past few years there has been a tremendous growth in *networking,* the connection of computers to other computers through the use of modems and phone lines. Many experts predict that networking will be one of the primary uses of personal computers in the future.

What services are available from networks, now and in the near future? One important application will be the creation of an electronic banking system. With this system, you will be able to make and receive payments via your home computer terminal, which would be the main computer system in your bank or supermarket. The so-called *cashless society* will become a reality.

Another important aspect of networking is that you will have access to vast amounts of information instantly—everything from stock market quotations to major newswires to journal and encyclopedia articles. You will also be able to exchange information, programs, and other forms of *electronic mail* with one or all of the thousands of users on a typical network. The applications of networking services for personal computer users is in its embryonic stage, and many new applications are forthcoming.

Modems

Modems are electronic devices that allow communication between your computer and another computer. They translate the electronic signals from a computer into audio tones that may be sent through an ordinary phone line and translate the incoming audio signals into digital signals. The cost for a modem ranges from $50 to over $600 depending upon its capabilities, but most personal computer users can find a modem to suit their needs for under $200.

A *direct-connect* modem patches into your phone line directly and is the simplest to use. An *acoustic-coupled* modem which cradles an ordinary telephone handset, is often less reliable, but it has the advantage of being usable at public phones. If you're willing to spend extra, a direct-connect modem can be equipped with a feature that will answer the telephone automatically and can dial numbers stored in the computer and then initiate data transmission; these features are called *auto-answer* and *auto-dial*.

The other consideration in buying a modem is the speed at which it can send and receive data. The normal telephone line is capable of sending 300 bits of information per second, or 300 *baud*. This rate is most commonly used by computer hobbyists, although higher speeds of data transmission can be had for a price.

Terminal Programs

As a final requirement, you must write or purchase software to communicate with the modem and the outside world; the required software is commonly called a *terminal* or *communications* program. Modems are often sold with these communication programs as a package designed for your brand of personal computer. This software will allow you to send messages or programs to the main network computer and display or store incoming data. Again, a wide price range exists, depending upon the capabilities you need; these factors should be reviewed with your salesman before purchase.

Available Networks

There are two principle networks of broad interest—CompuServe and The Source. Both of these services offer an extensive variety of information sources, which are outlined below:

CompuServe
5000 Arlington Centre Blvd.
P.O. Box 20212
Columbus, Ohio 43220

COMPUSERVE INFORMATION SERVICE SUBJECT INDEX

AAMSI Medical Forum	Asian weather	Billing, general	Canning, home	General news
AID calculations	Assoc. Press Access	Billing, reviewing	Car care	Metals news
AMEX prices (MQUOTE)	Assoc. Viewdata Wire	Biorhythms	Cars, comparison	Weather
ASCMD SIG	Astrology Game	Blackjack game	Cattle prices	Commodore newsletter
ASI Monitor	Astronautics	Bliss language	Central Trade Bank	Commodore VIC (SIG)
AVSIG	Atari Forum	Book, ordering:	Changing password	Comm. Industry Forum
Academic American Ency	Athletic equipment	Fifth Avenue Shopper	Changing terminal type	CompuServe command
Access	Athletic's Outfitter	Howard Sams Books	Charges, monthly	
Access phone numbers	Atlas, shopping service	Book, reviews:	Checking, banking	Comp-U-Store
Adult education	Attorneys	AAMSI, medical journals	Child care	Computer, books
Adventure game	Author's (SIG)	Rainbo's Reviews	Children, education	Computer club news:
Advertisers, TODAY	Auto Information:	Boston, Shawmut Bank	Children's games	Computers & Electronics
Advertising:	Gov't publications	Bridge game	Cinema news	The Micro Advisor
For sale	Investors Diversified	Brokerage	Clarke School for Deaf	Computer Magazine Index
Notices	Popular Science	Budgeting, home:	Classified Ads:	Computers & Electronics
TODAY Magazine	AutoNet	CompuServe	St. Louis Post-Dispatch	Concentration game
Want ads	Autos, buying:	Gov't publication	Clothing, fashion	Consumer items for sale
Advertising, classified:	AutoNet	Bulletin Board	Clothing, sport	Consumer news:
St. Louis Post-Dispatch	St. Louis Post-Dispatch	Business, farming	Cocoa news	Software
Advice:	Aviation:	Business Information Wire	Coffee news	Continuing education
Aunt Nettie	ASI Monitor	Business news:	College cost program	Cooking (SIG)
African weather	EMI Flight Planning	AP Viewdata Wire:	Color computer (SIG)	Corporate news release
Agribusiness	NSW Aviation Weather	Business Wire	Color graphics	Copper futures prices
Agricultural news	Official Airline Guide	Canadian, U.S., Int'l	Columbus area:	Copper news
Air travel:	Peak Delay Guide	CompuServe	Banks	Cotton futures prices
Firstworld Travel Club	Aviation Rules & Reg	Middlesex Daily	Chamber of Commerce	Cotton news
Official Airline Guide	Aviation Safety Inst	St. Louis Post-Dispatch	Education	Court cases, aircraft
Pan Am	Aviation (SIG)	Washington Post	SIG	Cross Assemblers
Travel Fax	Aviation weather	CB Interest Group	Command level	Cruise line
Air travel delays	Bacchus Data Services	CB Radio simulation:	Commentaries:	Current rates
Aircraft	Banking, electronic	Access to	Investment	Database, how to use
Airline guide	Banks:	Instructions	Video	Database searches
Airport delay guide	Central Trade Bank	Introduction	Commodities calendar	dataFamiliae
Amateur Radio	First Tennessee Bank	CB Society	Commodities future	Decwars game
Analogies test	Huntington National Bank	CEMSIG	Commodities glossary	Decwars (SIG)
Annual reports	Shawmut Bank of Boston	CP/M user's group	Commodity News Service:	DEFALTS, setting
Apple, programs for	Banshi game	Cameras for sale	Agricultural news	Department of State
Apple User's Group	Baseball (AP wire)	Canadian:	Commodity prices	Disk area
Appliances for sale	Basic CompuServe	Business news	Economic news	Document delivery
Arcade (SIG)	Beef prices	Currency exchange	Futures industry news	Document retrieval
Art Gallery	Belmont Golf Association	Stocks	Futures market prices	Documentation ordering
Articles, computer	Belmont's golf (SIG)			Dress

THE SOURCE

McLean, Virginia 22102
(800) 336-3366
(800) 572-2070 (in Virginia)
(703) 734-7500 (outside the U.S.)
Abbreviated listing

Source Telecomputing Corporation
The Reader's Digest Association, Inc.
1616 Anderson Road

Silver Coins
Silver Prices
Silver News
MONEY MARKET NEWS AND COMMENTS
Afternoon Lead
Futures
Markets at a Glance
Night Lead
Noon Lead
NYSE Trends
Opening Lead
Stock Pulse
What the Market Did
FINANCIAL MODELING
  FOR BUSINESS PLANNING
FINANCIAL NEWS
GAMES
Adventure
Backgammon
Blackdragon
Cards
  Blackjack
  Super Blackjack
  Bridge
  Poker
  Tricks
Checkers
Chess
Children's Programs
Civil War
Craps
Draw
Farmer
Fill in Letters
Football
Golf
Govern Sumeria
Guess Computer's Number
Hangman
Horse Race
I-Ching
IQ Test
Life
Lunar Landing
Market A Product
Mastermind

Maze Generation
Mind Reading
NIM
Patrol Streets (game)
Poster
Puzzles
Rule Sumeria
Score Four
Sinners
Slalom
Slot Machine
Sonnets
Statistics
Star-Trek
Super Adventure
Target Practice
Tic Tac Toe

Toro
Tricks
Vegas
Wumpus Hunt
INFORMATION ON DEMAND
INFORMATION ON UPDATES TO THE SOURCE
MANAGEMENT CONTENTS
  Overview
  Instructions
  The List of Journals:
    On the following Journals:
      Across the Board
      Administrative Management
      American Demographics
      The Banker
      Business and Society Review
      Business Week
      Cash Flow Magazine
      Dun's Review
      Federal Reserve Bulletin
      Financial Executive
      Forbes
      Fortune
      Futurist
      Harvard Business Review
MEDIA GENERAL STOCK ANALYSES
  Overview
  Instructions

INC
Institutional Investor
Journal of Retailing
Medical Economics
Mergers & Acquisitions
Monthly Labor Review
Office, The
Practical Accountant
Sloan Management Review
Taxes
Venture
Vital Speeches
Wharton Magazine

Categories of Stock Comparison
Definitions of Data Items
Industry Groups Numbers List
Creating Portfolio Files
Stock Analysis and Tables
MEDICAL ADVICE
MENU TO MANY DATA BASES ON THE SOURCE
MOVIE REVIEWS BY JAY A. BROWN
NEWS
PERSONAL CALENDAR & NOTEBOOK
PERSONAL FINANCE
POLITICAL ACTION REPORT
PORTFOLIO MANAGEMENT
PROFESSIONAL BOOK CENTER
PUBLISHERS WEEKLY
  BESTSELLERS LIST
RADIO PROGRAMS TO ORDER
RAYLUX FINANCIAL SERVICES
SCIENCE & ENGINEERING
SELF-PERCEPTION
SMITHSONIAN EXHIBITS
  AND TOURING EXHIBITS
SPECIAL APPLICATIONS
STUDENT AID
TAXES
  Assets
  Calculation of Income Statement
  Computing Taxes
  Contributions
  Credits
  Debts
  Deductions
  Dependents
  Depreciation Schedule
  Donations
  Expenses
  Income Statement, Pro Forms
  Income Tax
  Taxes
TRAVEL CLUB
UNISTOX
UNITED PRESS
  INTERNATIONAL (UPI)
USER PUBLISHING
VOICEGRAM
WEATHER
WINE
WISDOM OF THE AGES

Local networks. A comprehensive listing of local networks or "bulletin board systems" (BBS), the computer era's answer to old-fashioned corkboards, for personal computerists follows. To post a notice, you dial the service and add your message to a list of notices that will appear on your screen. If any message interests you, you can reply—on your computer, of course. Usually, your only cost is the phone charges.

The codes printed next to each BBS phone number are explained here:

*24   denotes 24-hour
       operation
#1   denotes original system
       of that type
—rb   denotes call, let ring
       once and call back
—so   sexually oriented
       messages
—rl   religious orientation
!   new system or new number

for existing system
1   Supports VADIC 1200 baud
       operation
&   Supports 212A 1200 baud
       operation

Start dialing and explore!

A-C-C-E-S-S Olympia, WA	(206) 866-9043*24
Dial-Your-Match #16	(206) 256-6624-so
FORUM-80 Seattle, WA	(206) 723 3282
JCTS Redmond, WA	(206) 883-0403*24
MSG-80 Everett, WA	(206) 334-7394
Mail Board-82 Seattle, WA	(206) 527-0897*24
Mini-Bin Seattle, WA	(206) 762-5141*24
PMS - Software Unltd, Kenmore, WA	(206) 486-2368*24
RCP/M RBBS Yelm, WA	(206) 458-3086-rb
Seacomm-80 Seattle, WA	(206) 763-8879*24
DIAL-YOUR-MATCH #26, Clovis, CA	(209) 298-1328-so
ABBS (?) Queens, NY	(212) 896-0519
Bronx BBS, NY	(212) 933-9459
BULLET-80 New York, NY	(212) 740-5680*24
COMM-80 Queens, NY	(212) 897-3392*24
CONNECTION-80 Woodhaven, NY	(212) 441-3755*24
Leigh's Computer World, NY, NY (7PM)	!(212) 879-6257
NET-WORKS New York, NY	(212) 410-0949
Nybbles-80 NY	(212) 626-0375
Pat-100 System New York, NY	(212) 991-1664*24
PEOPLE-LINK	#1!(212) 877-7703*24
PMS - McGraw-Hill Books, New York, NY	(212) 997-2488
STUART-200 BBA Howard Beach, NY	(212) 835-5962*24
TCBBS AstroCom, New York, NY	#1!(212) 799-4649
TCBBS B.A.M.S. New York, NY	(212) 362-1040*24
TCBBS Leigh's Computer World, NY	(212) 897-7698
VTUGS NY, NY (VIC-20)	#1(212) 534-3149*24
All Night BBS	(213) 564-7636
ABBs Computer Conspiracy, Santa Monica, CA	(213) 829-1140
ABBS Pacific Palasades, Los Angeles, CA	(213) 459-6400
BBS B.R., Los Angeles, CA	(213)394-5950*24
Computer Connection	(213) 657-1799
CONFERENCE-TREE #4, Santa Monica, CA	(213) 394 1505
CONFERENCE-TREE Kelp Bed, Los Angeles, CA	(213) 372-4800
Datamate, Conoga Park, CA	#1(213) 998-7992-so
DIAL-YOUR-MATCH #1	(213) 842-3322-so
DIAL-YOUR-MATCH #11	(213) 242-1882-so
DIAL-YOUR-MATCH #22	(213) 990-6830-so
DIAL-YOUR-MATCH #4	(213) 783-2305-so
DIAL-YOUR-MATCH #9	(213) 345-1047-so
Dragons Game System (pass-DRAGON)	(213) 428-5206
Electric Line Connection, Sherman Oaks, CA	(213) 789-9512
Greene Machine Fricaseed Chicken, Arcadia, CA	(213) 445-3591*24
Greene Machine, Los Alamitos, CA	!(213) 431-1443
Greene Machine, Temple City, CA	!(213) 287-1363
Kluge Computer	$&(213) 947-8128*24
L.A. Interchange, Los Angeles, CA	(213) 631-3186*24
Long Beach Community Computer	(213) 591-7239*24
NET-WORKS Coin Games, Los Angeles, CA	(213) 336-5535
NET-WORKS Computer World, Los Angeles, CA	(213) 859-0894*24
NET-WORKS Softworx, West Los Angeles, CA	(213) 473-2754
Novation CO., Los Angeles, CA [pass-CAT]	(213) 881-6880
Oracle North Hollywood, CA	(213) 980-5643-so
PASBBS Torrance, CA	#1(213) 516 708
PMS - Los Angeles, CA	(213) 334-7614*24
PMS - O.A.C., Woodland Hills, CA	(213) 1849*24
RCP/M CBBS Pasadena, CA	(213) 799-1632*24
RCP/M RBBA BBA Valley	!(213) 360-5053
RCP/M RBBA GRRN Dta Exch. Palos Verdes, CA	$&(213) 541-2503*24
RCP/M RBBS Sofwaire Store, Los Angeles, CA	(213) 296-5927*24
ABBS Dallas Info Board	(214) 248-4539
ABBS Teledunjon II, Dallas, TX	(214) 530-0858
ABBS Teledunjon III, Dallas, TX	(214) 960-7654
ABBS The Moon, Dallas, TX	(214) 931-3437*24
BBS-80 DALTRUB, Dallas, TX	(214) 235-8784*24
BULLET-80 Hawkins, TX	(214) 769-3036
NET-WORKS Apple Grove, Dallas, TX	(214) 644 5197
NET-WORKS Apple Shack, Dallas, TX	(214) 644 4781*24
NET-WORKS Eclectic Computer, Dallas, TX	(214) 239 5842
NET-WORKS Hacker-net, Dallas, TX	(214) 824 7160
NET-WORKS Winesap, Dallas, TX	(214) 824 7455
RCP/M CBBS Dallas, TX	(214) 931-8274
BULLET-80 Langhorne, PA	(215) 364-2180
COMNET-80 North Wales, PA	(215) 855-3809
Hermes-80 Allentown, PA	(215) 434-3998
Lehigh Press BB, PA	#1(215) 435-3388
RCP/M RBBA Allentown, PA	(215) 398-3937*24
ABBS Akron Digital Group, Akron, OH	(216) 745-7855*24
BBS Computer Applications Co., Poland, OH	(216)757-3711
BULLET-80 Chesterland, OH	(216) 729-2769
COMNET-80 Akron, OH	&(216) 645-0827*24
FORUM-80 Cleveland, OH	&(216) 486-4176
INFOEX-80 Akron, OH	!(216) 724-2125*24
PMS - Massillon, OH	(216) 832-8392*24
PMS - RAUG, Akron, OH	(216) 867-7463*24
BULLET-80 Springfield, IL	(217) 529-1113
NET-WORKS C.A.M.S., Decatur, IL	(217) 429-5541
A-C-C-E-S-S Annapolis, MD	(301) 267-7666*24
ABBS Computer Crossroads, Columbia, MD	(301) 730-0922
ARMUDIC Computer Age, Baltimore, MD	(301) 587-2132
BBS IBM PC Beltsville, MD	!(301) 937-4339*24
BBS IBM PC Bethesda, MD	!(301) 460-0538*24
BBS IBM PC Gaithersburg, MD	!(301) 251-6293*24
BBS IBM PC Rockbille, MD	!(301) 949-8848*24
CBBS CPEUG/ICST Gaithersburg, MD	(301) 948-5717
CONNECTION-80 Gaithersburg, MD	(301) 840-8588*24
HEX Silver Spring, MD	%(301) 593-7033*24
NET-WORKS COMM Center, Laurel, MD	(301) 953-3341
PMS - Baltimore, MD	(301) 764-1995*24
PMS - Ellicott City, MD	(301) 465-3176
PMS - Pikesville, MD	(301) 653-3413
PSBBS Baltimore, MD	(301) 994-0399*24
RCP/M RBBA Bethesda, MD	(301) 229-3196
RCP/M RBBA Laurel, MD	(301) 953-3753*24
Remote Northstar NASA, Greenbelt, MD	(301) 344-9156
ABBS Denver, CO	(303) 759-2625
BBA IBM PC Denver, CO	!(303) 773-2699*24
CONNECTION-80 Denver, CO	(303) 690-4566*24
FORUM-80 #2, Denver, CO	(303) 399-8858*24
HBBS Denver, CO	(303) 343-8401*24
RCP/M CUG-NOTE, Denver, CO	(303) 781-4937*24
RCP/M RBBS Arvada Elect., Colorado Springs, CO	(303) 634-1158*24
RCP/M RBBS Boulder, CO	(303) 499-9169
Remote Northstar Denver, CO	(303) 444-7231
NET-WORKS Charleston, WV	(304) 345-8280
ABBS Byte Shop, Ft. Lauderdale, FL	(305) 486-2983
ABBT Byte Shop, Miami, FL	(305) 261-3639
ABBS West Palm Beach, FL	(305) 848-3802
AMIS APOGEE Miami, FL	(305) 238-1231-rb
BBS Homestead, FL	(305) 246-1111
CONNECTION-80 Orlando FL	(305) 644-8327*24
CONNECTION-80 Winter Garden, FL	(305) 894-1886*24
FORUM-80 Ft. Lauderdale, FL	(305) 772-4444*24
Greene Machine Corsair, WPB, FL	!(305) 968-8653
Greene Machine, WPB, FL	(305) 965-4388-so
INFOEX-80 West Palm Beach, FL	(305) 683-6044*24
MOUSE-NET Orlando, FL	(305) 277-0473*24
Micro-80 West Palm Beach, FL	(305) 686-3695
NET-WORKS Big Apple, Miami, FL	(305) 948-8000
Personal Msg. System-80 Deerfield Bch, FL	&(305) 427-6300*24
TRADE-80 Ft. Lauderdale, FL	#1(305) 525-1192
PET BBS SE Wyoming PUG	(307) 637-6045*24
ABBS Peoria, IL	(309) 692-6502
NET-WORKS MAGIE, Galesburgh, IL	(309) 342-7178
RCP/M Geneseo, IL	(309) 944-5455
ABBS CODE, Glen Ellny IL	(312) 537-7063*24
ABBS Gamemaster, Chicago, IL	(312) 475-4884*24
ABBS Illini Microcomputer, Naperville, IL	(312) 420-7995
ABBS Rogers Park, Chicago, IL	(312) 973-2227
AMIS Chicago, IL	(312) 789-3610*24
ANESSY Chicago, IL	+1(312) 773-3308
BBS IBM PC Modem Chicago, IL	!(312) 259-8086*24
CBBS Chicago, IL	#1(312) 545-8086*24
MCMS C.A.M.S. Chicago, IL	#1&(312) 927-1020*24
MCMS L.A.M.S. Round Lake, IL	(312) 740-9128
MCMS Metro West Database, Chicago, IL	&(312) 260-0640*24
MCMS P.C.M.A. Wheaton, IL	!&(312) 462-7560*24
MCMS WACO Hot Line, Schaumburg, IL [pvt]	(312)4374*24
NET-WORKS Chipmunk, Hinsdale, IL	(312) 323-3741*24
NET-WORKS North Parks, Chicago, IL	(312) 745-0924
NET-WORKS Pirate's Ship, Chicago, IL	(312) 935-2933*24
PBBA Co-operative Comp Svc, Palatine, IL	(312) 359-9450*24
PET BBA Commodore, Chicago, IL	(312) 397-0871*24
PMS - Chicago, IL	(312) 373 8057*24
PMS - Downers Grove/SRT, Downers Grove, IL	(312) 964-6513
PMS - I.A.C., Lake Forest, IL	(312) 295-6926*24
RATS Homewood, IL	(312) 957-3924
RCP/M A.B. Dick Co., Niles, Il	&(312) 647-7636*24
RCP/M AIMS Hinsdale, IL	(312) 789-0499*24
RCP/M IBM PC, Niles, IL	(312) 259-8086
RCP/M Logan Square, Chicago, IL	(312) 252-2136
RCP/M NEI, Chicago, IL	(312)949-6189
RCP/M Palatine, IL	&(312) 359-8080*24
Scream Machine	(312) 680-9613-so
ABBS Detroit, MI	(313) 477-4471
ABBS Michigan Apple-Fone, Southfield, MI	(313) 357-1422
AMIS A.R.C.A.D.E. Sterling Heights, MI	(313) 978-8087*24
AMIS M.A.C.E. Detroit, MI	#1(313) 868-2064*24
Apple-Gram	)313) 295-0783*24
BBS Metro Detroit, MI	!(313) 455-4227-so
BULLET-80 Waterford, MI	(313) 683-5076*24
COMNET-80 Mt. Clemens, MI	&(313) 465-9531
Davy Jones Locket	(313) 764-1837
RCP/M Detroit, MI	(313) 584-1044-rb

RCP/M MCBBS Keith Petersen, Royal Oak, MI	(313) 759-6569-rb
RCP/M MCBBS TCBBS Dearborn, MI	(313) 846-6127*24
RCP/M RBBS Pontiac, MI	(313) 338-85?5
RCP/M RBBS Southfield, MI	(313) 559-5326*24
RCP/M RBBS Westland, MI	(313) 729-1905-rb
Treasure Island	(313) 547-7903
Twilight Phone	(313)775-1649*24
Westside Download, Detroit, MI	(313) 533-0254
ABBS Century Next Computers, St. Louis, MO	(314) 442-6502
ABBS St. Louis, MO	(314) 838-7784*24
Midwest, St. Louis, MO	(314) 227-4312-so
NET-WORKS Computer Station, St. Louis, MO	(314) 432-7120
PET BBS Commodore Comm., Lake St. Louis, MO	(314) 625-4576*24
Greene Machine, Rome, NY	!(315) 337-7720
FORUM-80 Wichita, KA	&(316) 682-2113*24
NET-WORKS Greenfield, IN	(317) 326-3833*24
ONLINE Indianapolis, IN. [ID#-GUES, pswd-pass].	(317) 787-9881*24
PET BBA AVC Comline, Indianapolis, IN	(317) 255-5435*24
PMS - Indianapolis, IN	(317)787-5486*24
FORUM-80 Shreveport, LA	(318) 631-7107*24
ABBS Apple-Med, Iowa City, IA	(319) 353-6528
CBBS Cedar Rapids, IA	(319) 364-0811
NET-WORKS Computer City, Providence, RI	(401) 331-8450*24
ABBS Omaha, NE	(402) 339-7809
DIAL-YOUR-MATCH #23, Omaha, NE	(402) 571-8942-so
TRADE-80 Omaha, NE	(402) 292-6184
Lethbridge Gaming system, Lethbridge, Alta	(403) 320-6923
RCP/M RBBS Computron, Edmonton, Alta., Canada	(403) 482-6854*24
RCP/M RBBS Edmonton, Alberta, Canada	&(403) 454-6093*24
ABBS #X, Atlanta, GA	(404) 256-1549
ABBS AGS, Atlanta, GA	(404) 733-3461*24
ABBS Baileys Computer Store, Augusta, GA	(404) 790-8614
BBS IBM Hostcomm Atlanta, GA	!(404) 252-4146
BBS IBM PC Atlanta, GA	!(404) 252-9438*24
BBS IBM PC Atlanta, GA	!(404) 294-6879
BULLET-80 Fayetteville, GA	(404) 461-9686
CBBS Atlanta, GA	(404) 394-4220*24
Remote Northstar Atlanta, GA	#1(404) 926-4318*24
Telemassage-80, Altanta, GA	(404) 962-0616
HBBS Oklahoma City, OK	(405) 848-9329*24
BBS IBM PC Billing, MT	(406) 656-9624
AMIS GRAFEX Cupertino, CA	(408) 253-5216
AMIS IBBBS San Jose, CA	(408) 298-6930
AMIS T.A.B.B.S., Sunnyvale, CA	(408) 942-6975
BULLET-80 San Jose, CA	(408) 241-0769
NET-WORKS Computer Emprium, San Jose, CA	(408) 227-0227
PMS - Campbell, CA	(408) 370-0873*24
PMS - Santa Cruz, Aptos, CA	(408) 688-9629*24
RCP/M Collossal Oxgate, San Jose, CA	(408) 263-2588
RCP/M RBBS DataTech 004, Sunnyvale, CA	(408) 732-2433
RCP/M RBBS San Jose Exgate, San Jose, CA	(408) 287-5901*24
RCP/M Silicon Valley, CA	(408) 246-5014*24
? (Western Massachusetts)	(413) 637-3515
CBBS PACC, Pittsburgh, PA	(412) 822-7176*24
ABBS Colortron Computer, WI	(414) 637-9990*24
Big Top Games System, Milwaukee, WI	(414) 259-9475
CBBS MAUDE Milwaukee, WI	(414)241-8364*24
RCP/M RBBS Mike's, Milwaukee, WI	!(414) 647-0903
TBBS Canopus, Milwaukee, WI	!(414) 281-0545*24
Vanmil, Milwaukee, WI	!(414) 271-7580*24
ABBS Computerland, Fremont, CA	(415) 794-9314
ABBS Hayward, CA	(415) 881-5662
ABBS PCnet, San Francisco, CA	(415) 863-4703*24
ABBS South of Market, San Francisco, CA	(415) 469-8111-so
BBS Living Videotext, Menlo Park, CA	(415) 327-8876*24
Blue BOSS IBM PC, Berkeley, CA	(415) 845-9462*24
CBBS Lambda, Berkeley, CA	(415) 658-2919-so
CBBS Promima, Berkeley, CA	(415) 357-1130
CONFERENCE-TREE #3, Hayward, CA	(415) 538-3580
CONNECTION-80 Fremont, CA	(415) 651-4147*24
DIAL-YOUR-MATCH #17	(415) 991-4911
Drummer	(415) 552-7671-so
PMS - Pleasanton, CA	(415) 462-7419*24
PMS - Portola Valley, CA	(415) 851-3453*24
RCP/M RBBS DataTech 001, San Carlos, CA	#1$&(415) 595-0541*24
RCP/M RBBS DataTech 006, San Francisco, CA	(415) 563-4953
RCP/M RBBS Larkspur, CA	(415) 461-7726*24
RCP/M RBBS Marin County, CA	(415) 383-0473*24
RCP/M RBBS Piconet Oxgate, Mountain View, CA	(415) 965-4097*24
Sunrise System Oakland, CA	(415) 452-0350
System/80 San Leandro, CA	(415) 895-0699
BBS IBM Hostcomm Toronto, Ontario, CA	!(416) 499-7023*24
BBS NET Toronto, Ontario, CN	(416) 445-6696*24
KPri, Toronto, Ont., CN	#1(416) 624-5431*24
PET BBS TPUG, Toronto, Ontario, CN	(416) 223-2625*24
RPC/M HAPN Hamilton, Ontario, CN	(416) 335-6620*24
RCP/M Mississauga HUG, Toronto, Ont., CN	$&(416) 826-5394*24
ABBS ABACUS II, Toledo, OH	(419) 865-1594
ABBS Computer Store, Toledo, OH	(419) 531-3845
CONNECTION-80 Little Rock, AS	(501) 372-0576
PMS - Ft. Smith Comp. Club, Ft. Smith, AK	(501) 646-0197
CBBS NW, Portland, OR	(503) 646-5510*24
OARCS Portland, Oregon	(503) 641-2798
FORUM-80 Medford, OR	(503) 535 6883*24
PMS - Computer Solutions, Eugene, OR	(593) 689-2655*24
PMS - Portland, OR	!(503) 245-2536
ABBS Baton Rouge, LA	(504) 291-1360
CBBS Baton Rouge, LA	(504) 273-3116*24
NET-WORKS Crescent City, Baton Rouge, LA	(504) 454-6688
Baton Rouge Data System, Baton Rouge, LA	(504) 926-0181
ABBS Electro-Mart, Spokane, WA	(509) 534-2419*24
ABBS Rob Roy Computer, Yakima, WA	(509) 575-7704
CBBS Corpus Christi, TX	(512) 855-1512
CONFERENCE-TREE Victoria, TX	(512) 578-5833
FORUM-80 San Antonio, TX	!(512) 655-8143
NET-WORKS Sparklin' City, Corpus Christi, TX	(512) 882-6569
Bathroom Wall BBS, San Antonio, TX	(512) 655-8143
SATUG BBS, San Antonio, TX	(512) 494-0285
XBBS Hamilton, OH	(513) 863-7681*24
NET-WORKS Dayton, OH	(513) 223-3672
PMS - Cincinnati, OH	(513) 671-2753
CONNECTION-80 Laval BELE, Laval, Quebec, CN	(514) 622-1274*24
ONLINE Computerland, Montreal, Quebec, CN	(514) 931-0458*24
NET-WORKS Computer Emporium, Des Moines, IA	(515) 279-8863
ABBS Pirates Cove, Long Island, NY	(516) 698-4008
CBBS LICA LIMBS, Long Island, NY	(516) 561-6590*24
CBBS Long Island, NY	(516) 334-3134*24
CONNECTION-80 Centereach, NY	(516) 588-5836
CONNECTION-80 Great Neck, NY	(516) 8491*24
NET-WORKS Pirate's Trek	(516) 627-9048
Adventure BBS	(516) 621-9296
CONNECTION-80 Lansing, MI	(517) 339-3367
Capital City BBS, Albany, NY	(518) 346-3596*24
Remote Apple Jackson, MS	(601) 992-1918*24
A-C-C-E-S-S Phoenix, AZ	#1(602) 996-9709*24
A-C-C-E-S-S Phoenix, AZ	&(602) 957-4428*24
A-C-C-E-S-S Phoenix, AZ	(602) 274-5964
A-C-C-E-S-S Scotsdale,AZ	(602) 998-9411*24
ABBS Phoenix [AZ	(602) 898-0891
CBBS TSG, Tucson, AZ	(602) 746-3956*24
FORUM-80 Sierra Vista, AZ	(602) 458-3850*24
BBS Apollo, Phoenix, AS	!(602) 246-1432*24
CONNECTION-80 Peterborough, NH	(603) 924-7920
FORUM-80 Nashua, NH	(603) 882-5041
NET-WORKS Portsmouth, NH	(603) 436-3461
Software Referral Service	(603) 625-1919
ABBS Vancouver, B.C.	(604) 437-7001
CBBS Prince George, B.C., Canada	(604) 562-9515
RCP/M CBBS Frog Hollow, Vancouver, BC, CN	(604) 873-4007*24
RCP/M Terry O'Brien, Vancouver, BC, Canada	(604) 584-2543
RCP/M SJBBS Johnson City, NY	(607) 797-6416
AMIS Magic Lantern, Madison, WI	(608) 251-8538
BBS IBM PC Madison, WI	!(608) 262-4939*24
RATS Wenonah, NJ #2	(609) 468-3844
RATS Wenonah, NJ	(609) 468-5293
ABBS Calvary Mission Church, Mnpls, MN	(612) 471-0252-rl
CONFERENCE-TREE Minneapolis, MN	(612) 854-9691
MCMS NC Software, Minneapolis, MN	(612) 533-1957*24
PMS - Minneapolis, MN	(612) 929-6699*24
PMS - Twin Cities, Minneapolis, MN	!(612) 929-8966
ABBS Compumart, Ottawa, Ontario, Canada	(613) 725 2243
BULLET-80 Ironton, OH	(614) 532-6920
Applecrackers, Columbus, OH	(614) 475-9791*24
Ohio Valley BBS	(614) 423-4422
RCP/M CBBS Columbus, OH	(614) 272-2227*24
ABBS Computer Room, Kalamazoo, MI	(616) 382-0101
AMIS G.R.A.S.S. Grand Rapids, MI	(616) 241-1971*24
CONNECTIONS-80 W. Mich. Micro Group, MI	(616) 457-1840*24
AMIS Starbase 12 Philadelphia, PA	(617) 876-4885
BULLET-80 Boston, MA	&(617) 266-7789*24
CBBS Boston, MA	(617) 646-3610*24
CBBS Lawrence General Hospital, Boston, MA	(617) 683-2119
DIAL-YOUR-MATCH #18	(617) 334-6369-so
PMS - Apple Guild, Weymouth, MA	(617) 767-1303*24
Computer City, Danvers, MA	(617) 774-7516
New England COmp. Soc., Maynard, MA	(617) 897-0346
RCP/M MCBBS Superbrain, Lexington, MA	$&(617) 862-0781*24
Visiboard, Wellesley, MA	!(617) 235-5082
NET-WORKS Granite City, IL	(618) 877-2904
NET-WORKS Warlock's Castle St. Louis, MO	(618) 345-6638
CONNECTION-80 Escondido, CA	(619) 746-6265
ONLINE CDC, San Diego, CA	(619) 452-6011
ONLINE Saba, San Diego, CA	(619) 692-1961*24
ONLINE Santee, CA [ID#GUEST, pswd-PASS]	(619) 561-7271*24

PMS - Computer Merchant, San Diego, CA ....(619) 582-9557
PMS - Datel Systems Inc., San Diego, CA ....!(619) 271-8613*24
RCP/M RBBS San Diego, CA ....$&(619) 273-4354*24
PMS - El Cajon, CA ....(619) 579-0553
PMS - Lakeside, CA (type PMS to activate) ....(619) 561-7271*24
PMS - Santee, CA ....#!(619) 561-7277*24
NET-WORKS Armadillo, ND ....(701) 746-4959
FORUM-80 Las Vegas, NV...............................(702) 362-3609*24
SIGNON Reno, NV ....[pswd-FREE].....(702) 826-7234
ABBS Software Sorcery, Herndon, VA ....(703) 471-0610
BBS IBM Hostcomm Fairfax, VA ....!(703) 425-9452*24
BBS IBM Hostcomm Fairfax, VA ....!(703) 591-5120*24
BBS IBM Hostcomm Fairfax, VA ....!(703) 978-0921*24
BBS IBM Hostcomm Fairfax, VA ....!(703) 978-9592*24
BBS IBM Hosteomm Springfield, VA.......................!(703) 425-7229*24
C-HUG Bulletin Board, Fairfax, VA ....(703) 360-3812*24
Carrier 2 Alexandria, VA ....(703) 823-5210
Potomac Micro Magic Inc., Falls Church, VA ....(703) 379-0303*24
RCP/M CBBS RLP, MacLean, VA ....(703) 524-2549*24
Switchboard, Alexandria, VA ....(703) 765-2161*24
TCUG BBS, Washington, DC ....(703) 836-0384*24
RCP/M RBBS Napa Valley, CA ....(707) 253-1523??
Armadillo Media Services, Houston, TX ....(713) 444-7098
Compuque-80, Houston, TX ....(713) 444-7041*24
PMBBS ....(713) 441-4032
RCP/M RBBS Houston, TX ....(713) 497-5433
Weekender, Houston, TX ....(713) 492-8700
Zachary *Net, Houston, TX ....(713) 933-7353*24
IDBN Info-Net, Costa Mesa, CA ....(714) 545-7359
North Orange County Computer Club ....(714) 633-5240
OCTUG Orange County, Garden Grove, CA ....(714) 530-8226
Orange County Dta Exchange, Garden Grove, CA ....(714) 537-7931

DATABASES

Would you like to know about the latest advances that doctors have made against arthritis? Or find out how long it takes to fly to Chicago? What about the addresses of all your competitors' offices in California? To get the answers to these and other obscure questions, it's not necessary to live or work near a large reference library.

All this information and more is available through computerized databases that are accessible through computers with modems, which allow communication across the country via phone lines. Indeed, just about everything that is available in print is also available on a database. There are now 1300 public databases, available to anyone willing to pay to use them, and at least 6000 private databases maintained by colleges, trade associations, and companies.

Most databases provide abstracts of materials that have already been published elsewhere, usually in a journal, magazine, newspaper, or conference proceeding. A few provide only citations, that is, the names of authors, the titles, and the publications in which the articles appeared. However, it has become increasingly popular for databases to contain the entire text of all articles.

The greatest advantage to the use of databases, aside from their ready availability, is

their indexing and cross-referencing features. These features enable you to conduct a rapid search through thousands of periodicals and other information sources, spanning whatever years you specify, and give you the capability of finding an article based solely on the date of publication or the author's name. You can often search through "free text"—every word in an abstract or article—to determine whether or not they contain the words you specify. These features provide information-gathering capabilities transcending those possible or reasonable using a traditional approach.

One disadvantage of databases is a lack of common indexing terms (each system has its idiosyncracies). Another disadvantage is that they may only be searched one at a time.

For a comprehensive review of over 1000 public database systems, consult the *OMNI Online Database Directory*, by Mike Edelhart and Owen Davies, MacMillian Publishing Co., 1983, and read the sampler of databases below.

A Sampler of Information Utilities.

BRS/After Dark
BRS, 1200 Rt. 7, Latham, NY 12110; (800) 833-4707. This service offers electronic mail, abstracts of books and magazine articles in science, finance, education, energy, and general reference. Hours: 6 P.M. to midnight Monday through Friday, and all day Saturday and Sunday. Rates: $6 to $15 per hour, plus $50 subscription fee.

CompuServe
CompuServe, Consumer Information Service, 5000 Arlington Center Blvd., P.O.Box 20212, Columbus, Ohio 43220; (800) 848-8199 or (614) 457-0802 in Ohio. This service offers hundreds of data bases for both the consumer and business markets, including news, entertainment, electronic mail, programming languages, and user groups. Hours: 24 hours, 7 days. Rates $6 to $12.50 per hour, plus a subscription fee of $19.95 to $49.95, depending on where purchased.

Delphi
General Videotex Corp., 3 Blackstone St., Cam-

bridge, MA 02139; (617) 491-3393. This consumer-oriented utility offers services and information similar to those offered by The Source and CompuServe. Hours: 24 hours, 7 days. Rates: $6 to $17 per hour, and a subscription fee of $49.95.

Dialog Information Retrieval Service
Dialog Information Services, Inc., 3460 Hillview Ave., Palo Alto, CA 94304; (800) 227-1927, or (800) 982-5838. This service offers a large collection of databases about business, government, current affairs, and the environment, among others. Hours: 22 hours, Monday through Saturday. Rates: $15 to $300 per hour, with no minimum.

Dow Jones News/Retrieval
Dow Jones and Company, P.O. Box 300, Princeton, NJ 08540; (800) 257-5114. This business-oriented service provides detailed financial information, including current and historical quotations from major stock exchanges, commodities prices, media general reports, and financial disclosure details on thousands of American corporations. Hours: 22 hours, 7 days. Rates: $6 to $72 per hour, plus subscription fees ranging from a one-time $50 to $50 per month.

ITT Dialcom
ITT Dialcom Inc., 1109 Spring St., Silver Spring, MD 20910; (301) 588-1572. This service offers a variety of data bases with information about medicine, government, energy, and travel, as well as electronic mail. Hours: 24 hours, 7 days. Rates: $11 to $15 per hour, with a $100 per month minimum.

Knowledge Index
Dialog Information Services Inc., 3460 Hillview Ave., Palo Alto. CA 94304; (800) 528-6050, ext. 415 or (800) 227-1927. This service offers a subset of Dialog's more consumer-oriented databases, including business, engineering, psychology, magazines and computer information. Hours: 6 P.M. to 5 A.M. Monday through Thursday; 6 P.M. to midnight Friday; 8 A.M. to midnight Saturday; and 3 P.M. to midnight Sunday. Rates: $24 per hour, $35 subscription fee.

NewsNet
NewsNet, 945 Haverford Rd., Bryn Mawr, PA 19010; (800) 345-1301 or (215) 527-8030. This service offers the full text of over 100 newsletters on a variety of subjects, plus electronic mail connections with the newsletter publishers. Hours: 24 hours, 7 days. Rates: $18 to $24 per hour, with a $15 per month minimum.

Nite-Line
National Computer Network, 1929 Harlem Ave., Chicago, IL 60635; (312) 622-6666. This service offers financial and business databases. Hours: 24 hours, 7 days a week. Rates: $9 to $20 per hour.

Orbit Information Retrieval System
SDC Information Services, 2500 Colorado Ave., Santa Monica, CA 90406; (800) 421-7229 or (800) 352-6689. This service offers reference databases covering business, chemistry, engineering, electronics, and other fields. Hours: 22 hours, Monday through Friday. Rates: $40 to $125 per hour, with a start-up fee of $125 to $400, depending on the training requested.

The Source
Source Telecomputing Corp., 1616 Anderson Road, McLean, VA 22102; (800) 336-3366. This service is a large general-interest utility offering consumer information, electronic mail and conferencing, programming languages, and other services. Hours: 22 hours, 7 days. Rates: $5.75 to $22.75 per hour, plus a $100 subscription fee and a $10 per month minimum.

Chapter 10

Askey Louis

Auman Glen

Avey Mana

Baer Egar

Bard Ellis

Barlup Helen

Basorea Edwina

Cosey Sid

Covalt Mark

Freena Merla

Gsel Tim

Hamilton Angela

Kerman Ed

Loche Ron

Lundio P. Ron

Utility Programs

Although your computer system may not offer many of the useful features of larger systems, software can often be written to simulate many of these features. Such software is often referred to as *utility programs*. The category of *utility programs* also includes commonly-used routines or subprograms that can be incorporated in a larger program. Through the use of utility programs, your personal computer can emulate its big brothers.

MULTIPURPOSE PROGRAMS

Although some computer systems provide the features found below, others don't. The person who develops programs to perform these and other utility functions will often have a readily salable product.

- Diagnostic programs: programs that test all of the statements and commands found in given BASIC are useful in determining whether or not BASIC has loaded properly for execution. Programs to test memory by filling and reading all locations are also helpful.

- Memory-map programs: a machine-language program to output a memory map would be valuable.

- Menu selection programs: a machine-language routine to automatically find and execute any programs that are on line would make life easier for some operators.

- Routines for improved data file handling for floppy disks or cassettes are needed for some computers.

- Machine language programs that automatically convert one cassette/floppy disk standard to another are needed by a number of people.

- Variable list programs: a program to output the current value and location for all variables used in a program would be useful in large-program debugging.

- Renumber or resequence programs: a program to remember the statements in an assembly language program or BASIC program would be a convenient tool for programmers.

- Base conversion programs: this kind of program is useful in assembly language programming.

- BASIC patches that allow commands such as INKEY$ or GET, which permit program inputs without the pressing of the ENTER or RETURN key and can limit the time allowed for a response.
- Vector graphic assembly language routines could be useful.
- Cross-assemblers or conversion programs between languages such as BASIC, FORTRAN, and APL would be a boon for programmers.
- Routines for handling fractions instead of decimals for greater precision in certain applications could be created.
- Specialized compilers for BASIC: although writing a complete BASIC compiler would be difficult, specialized compilers could be written to handle string, mathematical, or sorting functions. The advantage is the tenfold or more increase in execution speed.
- BASIC patches to provide increased debugging power could include error simulation routines to test a program (ERROR(code) and ON ERROR GOTO commands), TRACE commands to output a listing of each line number as it is executed, and powerful editing functions.
- Memory routines: relocating memory loaders, which could be written in extended BASIC, could combine two programs, add machine language calls, and so on. A memory dump program could be provided to output programs in a variety of formats (decimal, hexadecimal, octal, and so on). A memory search program could be used to identify all occurrences of a specific byte value between any starting and ending addresses; such a program would be useful in disassembling and debugging.
- AUTO command: the AUTO command automatically provides line numbers when a program is being typed in.
- PLOT command: the PLOT command is useful in automatically displaying the values of a function or given set of data in graphical form.
- Multiple-precision routines: the scientific user of small computers (and some business users) needs multiple-precision capability.

In addition, a useful reference manual that included commonly used BASIC or assembly-language routines would simplify programming for the beginner.

UTILITY SUBROUTINES

Below are some practical routines that deal with matrices and string manipulation

Matrix and String Utility Routines

```
100 REM MATRIX ADDITION 3-D
110 FOR I=1 TO N1
120    FOR J=1 TO N2
130       FOR K=1 TO N3
140          C(K,J,I)=A(K,J,I)+B(K,J,I)
150       NEXT K
160    NEXT J
170 NEXT I
180 RETURN


100 REM MATRIX TRANSPOSITION 2-D
110 FOR I=1 TO N1
120    FOR J=1 TO N2
130       B(J,I)=A(I,J)
140    NEXT J
150 NEXT I
160 RETURN


100 REM MATRIX MULTIPLICATION BY ONE
VARIABLE 3-D
110 FOR I=1 TO N3
120    FOR J=1 TO N2
130       FOR K=1 TO N1
140          B(K,J,I)=A(K,J,I)*X
150       NEXT K
160    NEXT J
170 NEXT I
180 RETURN


1000 REM INSTRUING SUBROUTINE
1010 FOR I=1 TO LEN(X$)-LEN(Y$)+1
1020    IF Y$=MID$(X$,I,LEN(Y$)) THEN
RETURN
1030 NEXT I
1040 RETURN


100 REM MATRIX INPUT ROUTINE 3-D
110 FOR I=1 TO N1
120    PRINT "PAGE";I
```

```
130    FOR J=1 TO N2
140      PRINT "INPUT ROW";J
150      FOR K=1 TO N3
160        INPUT X(J,K,I)
170      NEXT K
180    NEXT J
190    PRINT
200 NEXT I
210 RETURN


100 REM MATRIX INPUT SUBROUTINE (TWO
DIMENTION)
110 FOR H=1 TO N
120    PRINT "ENTER ROW";H
130    FOR I=1 TO N1
140      INPUT X(H,I)
150 NEXT I,H
160 RETURN


100 REM MATRIX PRINT SUBROUTINE 3-D
110 FOR I=1 TO N1
120    FOR J=1 TO N2
130      FOR K=1 TO N3
140        PRINT X(J,K,I),
150      NEXT K
160      PRINT
170    NEXT J
180    PRINT
190 NEXT I
200 PRINT
210 RETURN


200 REM MATRIX READ FROM DATA STATEMENTS
IN 3-D
210 FOR I=1 TO N1
220    FOR J=1 TO N2
230      FOR K=1 TO N2
240        READ X(J,K,I)
250 NEXT K,J,I
260 RETURN
270 REM DATA INSERTED HERE


100 REM MAT=ZER MATRIX SET TO ZERO
SUBROUTINE 3-D
110 FOR I=1 TO N1
120    FOR J=1 TO N2
130      FOR K=1 TO N3
140        X(K,J,I)=0
150 NEXT K,J,I
160 RETURN
```

Sorting Routines

Among the different sorting routines listed here, the Quicksort is the most efficient although it requires more BASIC program lines than some of the other sorts require. The Bubble sort is the least efficient:

```
100 REM BUBBLE SORTING ROUTINE
110 FOR I=1 TO N-1
120    FOR J=I+1 TO N
130      IF A(I)<=A(J) THEN 170
140      T=A(I)
150      A(I)=A(J)
160      A(J)=T
170    NEXT J
180 NEXT I


50 REM ALPHABETIZING PROGRAM
60 REM OUTPUTS LISTING ONLY (DOESN'T
REARRANGE MEMORY)
100 CLEAR 5000
110 DIM A$(100),N$(100)
120 FOR N=1 TO 1000
130    INPUT "WORD";N$(N)
140    IF N$(N)="STOP" THEN 160
150 NEXT N
160 REM
170 FOR I=1 TO N
180    A$(I)=N$(I)
190 NEXT I
195 K=0
200 I=1
210 FOR J=2 TO N
220    IF A$(I)<A$(J) THEN GOTO 230 ELSE
I=J
230 NEXT J
240 IF N$(I)="STOP" THEN 250 ELSE PRINT
N$(I)
250 A$(I)="ZZZ"
260 K=K+1
270 IF K=N THEN 280 ELSE 200
280 PRINT:PRINT
290 END


100 REM IMPROVED RIPPLE SORT ROUTINE
110 C=0:N=N-1
120 IF N=0 THEN GOTO 200
```

```
130 FOR I=1 TO N
140    IF A(I)<=A(I+1) THEN 180
150    T=A(I)
160    A(I)=A(I+1)
170    A(I+1)=T
180    C=1
190 NEXT I
200 IF C=1 THEN 110



5 REM SHELL-METZNER SORT
10 P=N:REM N=NUMBER OF DATA ELEMENTS IN
D( )
20 P=INT(P/2)
30 IF P=0 THEN RETURN:REM ARRAY NOW
SORTED; RETURN TO MAIN PROGRAM
40 K=N-P:J=1
50 I=J
60 L=I+P
70 IF D(I)<D(L) THEN 100
80 T=D(I):D(I)=D(L):D(L)=T:I=I-P
90 IF I>=1 THEN 60
100 J=J+1
110 IF J<=K THEN 50 ELSE 20
```

```
2 CLS
5 REM QUICKSORT
6 REM N=NUMBER OF DATA ELEMENTS IN
D( )
10 X=0:I=X+X:S(I+1)=1:S(I+2)=N:X=X+1
20 IF X=0 THEN RETURN
25 IF X=0 THEN 1020
30 X=X-1:I=X+X:A=S(I+1):B=S(I+2)
40 Z=D(A):TP=A:BT=B+1
50 BT=BT-1
60 IF BT<=TP THEN 110
70 IF Z<=D(BT) THEN 50 ELSE D(TP)=D
(BT)
80 TP=TP+1
90 IF BT=TP THEN 110
100 IF Z>=D(TP) THEN 80 ELSE D(BT) =D
(TP):GOTO 50
110 D(TP)=Z
120 IF B-TP>=2 THEN I=X+X:S(I+1)=TP+1
:X=X+1:S(I+2)=B
130 IF BT-A>=2 THEN I=X+X:S(I+1)=A:X=
X+1:S(I+2)=BT-1
140 P=P+1:GOTO 25
1000 FOR X=1 TO 9:D(X)=X*-1:NEXT
1010 GOSUB 5
1020 FOR X=1 TO 9:PRINT D(X);:NEXT
```

Chapter 11

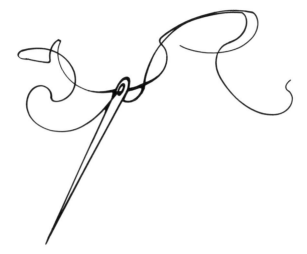

Miscellaneous Applications

There are a number of applications that don't fit easily in the categories already covered. These applications will be discussed in this final chapter.

COMPUTERS AND THE HUMANITIES

Amateur as well as professional scholars of history, language, literature, anthropology, archeology, and other fields of the humanities may find personal computers useful in storing, organizing, analyzing, and indexing data.

History

The historian may wish to encode information of the following types for use with computers:

1. Census records.
2. Congressional voting records.
3. Election statistics.
4. Court records and decisions.
5. Ship sailing records—historical, geneological, and economic significance.
6. Diplomatic records.
7. Journalism statistics. A school of journalism has used a personal computer to record and plot the ratios of column inches devoted to various political parties or candidates in fifteen major national newspapers, under the assumption that the amount of text space allotted to a candidate or party reflects the paper's views. You or your organization may wish to pursue similar lines of research.

Language

The microcomputer can be used to deal with languages in at least two ways.

Translations. It is possible to program a personal computer to act as a crude translating machine, capable of recognizing foreign vocabulary words and providing the English equivalent. Sentence structure and overall meaning are much more difficult to program, however, and are a current area of research in computer science. The pocket translating machines and spelling-checker programs available today may serve as models for such a program, which may provide an interpretable English equivalent to a given foreign phrase. For example, if provided with the Spanish phrase, "Mucho gusto en conocerlo" (Pleased to meet you), the literal computer translation may read, "Very much in to meet you." A more sophisticated program could check for idiomatic expressions such as this and provide a better translation. A translating program may prove to be educational and useful to those with a minimum of familiarity with a language.

Compilation of dictionaries. The dialects and languages of a speech community can be entered into a computer database for ease in compiling a dictionary.

Literature and Writing

There are a number of ways in which you can use your personal computer to help you in your writing and in analyzing literature.

Auto-editor. A personal computer program capable of performing basic editing functions has been developed. The program balks at overly long sentences, or stilted, cumbersome expressions and suggests alternatives. For instance, it will suggest "absolutely" for "categorically," and "by" or "under" instead of "in accordance with." It proposes "now" instead of "at this point in time." It can detect spelling errors, improper punctuation, split infinitives, and other common grammatical errors.

Thesaurus. An on-line thesaurus can provide rapid, time-saving access to alternative word choices. This feature, in conjunction with a word processor, can serve as a powerful writing tool.

Automatic table of contents/index generation. In preparing a text on a word processor, the author need only flag with a special code the keywords to be indexed or the chapter headings for the table of contents. The computer will compile and alphabetize these entries in desired form.

Writer's outline utility. A specialized word processor with database capabilities could assist the writer in preparing outlines.

Spelling checker. Numerous spelling checker programs are available for personal computers. These are capable of checking documents for errors on the basis of 30,000-90,000 stored words. The user has the option of adding or deleting words, and special dictionaries are available (for example, medical terms).

Analysis of literature. Computers can be used to prepare statistical analyses of literature that you have typed using your word processor. Such a program would calculate the number of lines, number of sentences, number of words, number of syllables, average word length, average sentence length, and the reading level based upon any of the standard formulas developed by Flesch, Fry, Raygor, Dale Chall, or Spache. For instance, the Fog index (F1) is given by

$$FI = \left[\frac{\text{total no. words}}{\text{total no. sentences}} + \frac{\text{no. "hard"}}{\text{words} \times 100} \right] \times 4$$

where "hard" words are considered to be those words with three or more syllables, except proper names, compounds of short words (for example, down-and-out), and words in which the third syllable ends in es or ed (for example, arrested). If the value of FI is 20 or more, you should consider the reading level advanced or difficult. To ensure that your message gets across to the masses, aim for a FI of around 10. A concordance table, listing all words used and their absolute or relative frequency of use can also be constructed; the list can be sorted alphabetically or by frequency. See *Microcomputing,* page 60, June 1981 for a sample BASIC program. Word-class distribution statistics, measures of redundancy of vocabulary (averages, medians, and so on), numbers of modifiers, adverb/verb and auxiliary verb/verb ratios, clause length statistics, distribution of clause types (simple, compound subject, and so on), distribution of sentence openers (prepositional phrase, subordinated clause, and so on), and style of sentence structure could also be analyzed by a more complex program.

Along similar lines, computers have been used to statistically determine whether works of indefinite authorship are typical of a given writer (for example works by Bacon and Shakespeare are compared), since the above statistical parameters tend to remain constant for one writer and may be compared with the figures for other writers.

Literature database. A specialized database could store important manuscripts and be used to index, cross reference, and find given keywords or phrases quickly. QWIK-Indexes™ may also be generated.

AID TO THE HANDICAPPED

Use of microcomputers as aids to the handicapped is a very important and useful application; only the forefront has been explored, and the potential is tremendous. Examples of this application include the following:

The computer can act as a "robot" for the handicapped. One system was used by a paraplegic to communicate with others; the computer scanned the alphabet and once a particular letter was reached, the patient would make a certain movement to signal that that letter was to be typed out. In this manner, words and sentences were produced.

Voice synthesizers and decoders are especially helpful for those who cannot interact with a computer through a video terminal.

A computer with a printer (either dot matrix or daisy-wheel type) could be used to convert inputted text into braille. Each line of text would be reversed in computer memory and the braille equivalent (composed of periods or dots) printed in its mirror image. By turning over the output, the impressions left by the printer will form braille text.

The personal computer could be used to monitor people who are chronically ill, are predisposed to suffer heart attacks, or are in other life threatening situations. Twice a day the patient would be required to input something into their computer; if they don't, medical personnel would be alerted by telephone dialing and vocal output peripherals.

Other areas in which the microcomputer can help the handicap include the following:

- Sensory enhancement or translation: clarification of audio or visual information or translation of video information to and from audio information.
- Manipulator controls: powered prostheses or robots for individuals with severe motor impairment.
- Information amplification for the motion impaired: increase the amount of information that can be relayed with a given number of keystrokes, for example a shorthand translator, as described in the first chapter.
- Recreation and development aids: games and educational programs allowing handicapped persons a reliable means to control, explore, and manipulate objects or learn about them.
- Communication aids: telephone dialers, computer-aided writing and filing systems, and phone communication through the use of speech synthesizers, for example.
- Security/monitoring systems: mechanisms for controlling locks and windows, emergency call systems, medication reminders, and monitoring systems that will periodically demand a response and signal if the individual fails to answer its queries.
- Information resource/management: inability to quickly manipulate and scan materials may prevent the handicapped from making effective use of dictionaries, phone lists, calendars, filing systems, and books. These functions can be paralleled through the use of specifically designed microcomputer-based interfaces that work with residual physical and sensory capabilities.

TEST YOUR TYPING SPEED

Those learning to type will appreciate a measurement of their progress in speed. A program to test typing speed would have to be written in assembly language if your BASIC doesn't provide INKEY$, GET, ENTER (or RETURN) or WAIT type commands.

MAINTENANCE OF ORGANIZATION RECORDS

Clubs and other organizations may find it worthwhile to purchase or use a member's small computer to ease paperwork. Anyone who develops software for this application may be able to sell it to local organizations or charge for computing services done on his own computer.

CO-OP SCHEDULING AND FINANCES

A computer analysis of costs and duties could help divide these responsibilities fairly between members of communal residence or cooperative organizations. A duty roster in calendar form as well as a financial summary of amounts owed could then be printed out.

TAILOR'S CALCULATIONS

Alterations to dress, suit, and other patterns for "tailor-made" clothing could be mathematically determined by your computer. If you have a printer with a line length large enough, the altered pattern could be printed in actual size.

PHONE CODE

A relatively simple program could be written to produce a listing of all the possible letter combinations on the phone dial for a given phone number. Businessmen may use this listing to find an appropriate, easy-to-remember word representing their phone number (for example, a computer store number was 266-7883 and COMPUTE was the corresponding telephone word). An interesting word may appear for you to use with your home phone.

BRAINSTORMER

A few years ago, a large sphere containing thousands of plastic squares with a different word printed on each was sold as a "brainstormer." The idea behind the device was to rotate the sphere, mix up the words, and then peek through a window at whatever words appeared. From this combination of adjectives and nouns, the user was to come up with a new invention or idea. The "brainstormer" could be useful in stimulating ideas; for instance, if the words *television* and *game* appeared, a properly prepared mind could have made the intuitive leap to invent video games. You could create your own computerized "brainstormer" by programming a large array of nouns and adjectives with a random number generator that calls them to the video screen 5-10 at a time.

A similar program could be called an "idea stimulator." Instead of miscellaneous words randomly appearing, a special set of adjectives or phrases describing possible improvements to an invention would appear individually and in random order on the screen. For instance, if you were trying to invent a new type of cooking pot and the word *slower* appeared, the brainstormed idea might be a slow crockpot cooker. The list of brainstorming questions below could be randomly arranged by your computer and individually called to the screen.

Brainstormer programs needn't be limited to products and inventions. Choreographer Merce Cunningham, Mozart, Oscar Wilde, and cartoonist Sergio Alverez, among others in the arts, have reported using similar random methods as an approach to artistic creation. One cartoonist reports use of a computer program to randomly mix cliches, locations, props, and various character types for possible cartoon ideas.

Brainstorm Chart for Products, Processes, or Services

In what other way can it be made more effective?
Is there a surer way to do it?
Is there a cleaner, neater way to do it?
Is there a more comfortable way to do it?
Is there a more healthful way to do it?
Is there a safer way to do it?
Is there a more durable form?
Is there a more pleasant way to do it?
Is there a quicker way to do it?
Is there an easier way to do it?
In what other way can it be improved?
Can the package be improved?
Can the distribution methods be improved?
Can it be made disposable or portable?
Can a combination with other devices be devised.
Can something be added to enhance its value?
Can it be adapted to some other use?

Is there a way to increase its usefulness; can it become multipurposed?

Can it be made more attractive?

Is there a cheaper way to do it?

Can a similar result be obtained in any other way?

Inventor's Idea Stimulator

The program in Listing 11-1 can be very useful to those who have a creative and intuitive mind. A large list of "idea words" are shuffled and displayed three at one time. The object is to apply your thinking to these words in relation to another idea. For example, if you had to design a new product, such as a cigarette lighter, and the word *disposable* appeared, the idea of a disposable lighter would come to you.

SOURCE INDEX

Addresses of manufacturers, institutions, or-

Listing 11-1: The Inventor's Idea Stimulator Program

```
10 CLS:KEY OFF
20 PRINT "INVENTOR'S IDEA STIMULATOR
30 DIM A$(98),M(98)
40 PRINT "THE PURPOSE OF THIS PROGRAM IS TO STIMULATE YOUR CREATIVE"
50 PRINT "THINKING WHEN WORKING ON AN INVENTION OR PRODUCT.  A SERIES"
60 PRINT "OF THREE WORDS WILL BE PRINTED.  THINK ABOUT EACH CAREFULLY"
70 PRINT "AND TRY TO APPLY THEM TO YOUR INVENTIVE PROCESS.  FOR EXAMPLE"
80 PRINT "IF YOU WERE TRYING TO DEVELOP A PRODUCT TO IMPROVE OFFICE"
90 PRINT "COMMUNICATION AND THE WORD 'EFFICIENT' APPEARED, YOU MIGHT"
100 PRINT "THINK OF A DICTATING MACHINE, ETC."
110 INPUT "PRESS 'ENTER' WHEN READY",A$
120 FOR X=1 TO 98:READ A$(X):NEXT X
130 N=98:FOR I=1 TO N
140 M(I)=I:NEXT I
150 FOR I=1 TO N-1
160    R=(N+1-I)*RND
170    R=INT(R)+I
180    T=M(R)
190    M(R)=M(I)
200    M(I)=T
210 NEXT I
220 PRINT "PRESS 'ENTER' WHEN FINISHED WITH EACH WORD SET"
230 FOR X=1 TO 33 STEP 3
240    PRINT A$(M(X))
250    PRINT A$(M(X+1))
260    PRINT A$(M(X+2))
270    INPUT B$
280 NEXT X
290 END
300 DATA LARGER,SMALLER,LONGER,SHORTER,THICKER,THINNER,DEEPER,SHALLOWER,STAND VE
RTICALLY/HORIZONTALLY,MAKE SLANTED OR PARALLEL
310 DATA STRATIFY,INVERT,CONVERGE,ENCIRCLE,INTERVENE,DELINEATE,BORDER,MORE,LESS,
CHANGE PROPORTIONS,FRACTIONATE,JOIN SOMETHING
320 DATA ADD SOMETHING,COMBINE,COMPLETE,CHANGE ARRANGEMENT,FASTER,SLOWER,LAST LO
NGER,CHRONOLOGIZE,MAKE PERPETUAL,SYNCHRONIZE
330 DATA RENEWABLE,ALTERNATING,STIMULATED,ENERGIZED,STRENGTHENED,LOUDER,LESS NOI
```

```
SE,COUNTERACTING,STRONGER,WEAKER,ALTERED
340 DATA CONVERTABLE,SUBSTITUTED,INTERCHANGED,STABILIZED,REVERSED,RESILIENT,UNIF
ORM,CHEAPER,ADD/CHANGE COLOR,IRREGULAR DESIGN
350 DATA CURVED DESIGN,MODERN DESIGN,HARDER,SOFTER,SYMMETRICAL,NOTCHED,ROUGHER,S
MOOTHER,DAMAGE AVOIDED,DELAYS AVOIDED
360 DATA THEFT AVOIDED, ACCIDENTS PREVENTED,CONFORMABILITY,ANIMATED,STILLED,DIRE
CTED MOTION,ATTRACTED/REPELLED MOTION,LOWERED
370 DATA BARRED,OCILLATED,AGITATED,HOTTER,COLDER,OPENABLE,PREFORMED,DISPOSEABLE,
INCORPORATED,SOLIDIFIED,LIQUEFIED,VAPORIZED
380 DATA PULVERIZED,ABRADED,LUBRICATED,WETTER,DRYER,INSULATED,EFFERVESCED,COAGUL
ATED,ELASTICIZED,RESISTANT,LIGHTER,HEAVIER
390 DATA FOR MEN/WOMEN/CHILDREN,FOR ELDERLY/HANDICAPPED,FOREIGN MARKETING
```

ganizations, and other sources of information or products can be stored in computer form and indexed for future reference. Any source of information or materials that you don't have use for at present, yet know you may need in the future, should be stored (for example, manufacturers and suppliers of peripherals for your system). These sources can be indexed under the material they can provide.

PEOPLE MATCHING

At a party or other social gathering it is often best to make arrangements so that those who are most similar will meet each other. Recently at a convention, a microcomputer was used to create special name cards for each guest. Everyone who attended had previously filled out a questionnaire indicating his or her occupation, hobbies, age, sex, likes and dislikes, and so on. This data was input to the computer, which subsequently produced a special name card with differently colored dots on it for each individual. Each color indicated a specific characteristic of that person, and thus, the guests could instantly find others who had the same color dots and thus the characteristics as themselves.

Computers have prepared seating charts for dinners, arranged blind dates, matched carpools, and paired athletes according to individual characteristics (partner or opponent matching). A bulletin board service for modem owners called Dial-Your-Match (213) 842-3322 allows computer dating for the would-be romantic.

An interesting people matching game would ask participants to rank their ideals. The list of common ideals below could be used for that purpose.

1. Active and satisfying life
2. Active and satisfying athletic life
3. Power over things (for example, automobiles, boats, and computers)
4. Socially significant activity
5. Good health
6. Opportunities for risk and adventure
7. Resilience (ability to "bounce-back")
8. Prestigious family life
9. Artistic ability
10. Ability to initiate and maintain friendships
11. Intellectual ability
12. Ability to draw love from others
13. Ability to influence others with your ideas
14. Ability to be a caring person
15. Ability to give love
16. Close and supportive relationships
17. Intellectual stimulation
18. Approval by opposite sex
19. Wealth
20. Ability to be self-sufficient
21. Physical attractiveness

Each participant could rank each item in terms of its importance to him or her. Next, everyone would be allotted a certain number of tokens to use in bidding for the items of the most importance to themselves. Participants will realize what is of the most significance in their life and that of others.

Similarly two or more players could rank 1) what I think I am, 2) what the other player thinks I am, and 3) what the other player thinks I think I am (and 2 and 3 for the other player) for these characteristics: aggressive, dependent, enthusiastic, intelligent, honest, humorous, jealous, kind, rude, sensitive, sensual, and sociable. The personal computer would then compare and correlate responses in a useful, insightful way.

On a more personal basis, programs have been written to first determine the "personality" makeup of a couple and then suggest an appropriate "interlude." This is *not* a children's game and is an application to be used at your own risk.

Along similar lines, your local organization or business could use a computer car-pool matching program if there are many people involved.

GREETING CARD PRODUCER

Some clever hobbyists have written programs to produce assorted types of greeting cards, announcements, and invitations on their printers. One example is shown in Fig. 11-1. The cards can be personalized and can make use of computer art. One hobbyist uses his computer and printer to produce Christmas gift wrapping paper by printing designs of Christmas trees, snowflakes, and other patterns.

CONTESTS

For those who take sweepstakes seriously, a personal computer can be used to fill out multiple contest entry forms with name, address, and additional information required. One group of computerists entered a large national contest a few years ago, using a computer to print 10,000 entry forms; they won over 90% of the prizes. As a result, many contests now require hand-printed entry forms. However, peripherals are now available that can duplicate your handwriting or signature using a programmable "mechanical writing arm." Technology marches onward.

HANDWRITING ANALYSIS

Many major corporations are now using handwriting analysis as one instrument to evaluate

```
                          M
                        MERRY
                      MERRYCHRI
                    MERRYCHRISTMA
                  MERRYCHRISTMASMER
                MERRYCHRISTMASMERRYCH
                  MERRYCHRISTMA
                MERRYCHRISTMASMER
              MERRYCHRISTMASMERRYCH
            MERRYCHRISTMASMERRYCHRIST
          MERRYCHRISTMASMERRYCHRISTMASM
        MERRYCHRISTMASMERRYCHRISTMASMERRY
                MERRYCHRISTMASMER
              MERRYCHRISTMASMERRCH
            MERRYCHRISTMASMERRYCHRIST
          MERRYCHRSITMASMERRYCHRISTMASM
        MERRYCHRISTMASMERRYCHRISTMASMERRY
      MERRYCHRISTMASMERRYCHRISTMASMERRYCHRIS
    MERRYCHRISTMASMERRYCHRISTMASMERRYCHRISTMA
  MERRYCHRISTMASMERRYCHRISTMASMERRYCHRISTMASMER
                        MERRY
                        MERRY
                        MERRY
                        MERRY
```

Fig. 11-1. A computer generated greeting card.

prospective employees, although its usefulness remains controversial. The gaudy carnival "handwriting analysis computers" do litte more than printout a random evaluation, as handwriting analysis is still on the cutting edge of computer science. However, a relatively simple program could printout the standard interpretations for handwriting characteristics after these have been encoded by an expert. Such a program could eliminate the drudgery of writing an explanation for each characteristic and could check for conflicting or concording results.

FIFTY MISCELLANEOUS APPLICATIONS

To further exemplify the scope of applications of personal computers in all walks of life, I have listed some of the more unusual uses readers have contributed:

- Design and animation of marching band patterns.
- Maintenance and inventory of equipment and instruments in small laboratories.
- Membership tracking for small organizations with the addition of dues accounting, questionnaire analysis, and mailing list capabilities.
- TV pattern generator for electronic technicians.
- Artistic pacifier for toddlers based on random graphical patterns, as a form of the stimulation necessary for the development of a normal IQ.
- Banner and sign generator to prominently display your message, created on ordinary lineprinters.
- Posters and calendars from lineprinter output.
- Translations of foreign words done by portable computers for travelers (or for educational purposes).
- Analysis of the cost-saving benefits of various solar collector designs.
- Calculation of home improvement costs by determining gallons of paint, rolls of wallpaper, or square yards of carpeting for a given job.
- Car maintenance reminder for routine tuneups and parts replacement according to miles driven.
- Car pool record keeping program which records car usage by driver, destination, and date with the ability to print schedules for each member.

- Bendo Kagawa, a Zen priest in Japan, uses his personal computer to help people meditate.
- Bob Waltz's personal computer at Smithers-Oasis can tell you all you ever wanted to know about germanium growing.
- Three Harvard professors writing a physiology text use their personal computers to exchange chapters by phone.
- Edward Adler arranged for his computer to rock his baby's cradle every time she cried.
- Architects can sketch new designs on personal computers that rival design systems formerly costing in the millions.
- For training purposes, companies are now using personal computers to instruct employees in everything from advanced optics to photocopier repair.
- A psychologist is using his computer to teach people self-relaxation techniques and self-hypnosis.
- Earth, Wind, and Fire use a computer to set off flash pots and explode small bombs on stage during their pyrotechnic rock performances.
- A German firm is using a personal computer to create new sweater patterns.
- Daryl Faud's personal computer sifts through hundreds of bacterial strains to assist in recombinant DNA experiments.
- Dr. Terry Pundiak uses a voice interface with his computer to give antismoking lectures.
- Experimental systems that are being developed to read ordinary text to the blind are based on personal computers.
- Boy Scouts across the nation are using personal computers for help in earning the Computer merit badge.
- Dr. Michael Lamb has adapted his personal computer for anesthesia monitoring during surgery.
- Colossal Pictures Corporation used a personal computer to create the title sequences for *The Black Stallion* and *One From The Heart.*
- Psychologist John McPhee developed a program to analyze Rorschach Inkblot Tests on his personal computer.
- The Sports Car Club of America, San Francisco

office uses a PC personal computer to track race results instantly.

- David Curtis turned his personal computer into a lie-detector and analysis machine.
- One hobbyist creates personalized Christmas letters by using a word processor, cutting the time required in half.
- A bar-code reader allows a hobbyist to rapidly input information concerning supermarket items purchased. A pantry inventory can easily be created.
- One thrifty personal computer owner devised a program to randomly match each person in his extended family for exchange of gifts.
- One family uses their system as a message board to store, word-process, and display messages to other family members.
- Traveling salesmen use their portable computers to maintain expense accounts.
- One hobbyist created a "drunkometer" program to evaluate residual cognitive function in those smashed by alcohol.
- A nighttime and vacation check-off program to remind the hobbyist that nights and vacations exist for a purpose and to ensure that all necessary duties have been taken care of could be a godsend to obsessive programmers.
- A citrus grower uses his personal computer to continuously monitor temperature and soil conditions to alert him of changes and automatically control heaters and sprinklers.
- An instrumentalist uses his personal computer to accompany him on the flute.
- A wrestling coach no longer tussles with the problem of pairing 500 boys by age and weight; he uses his personal computer.
- A personal computer owner about to marry created a database to map out chapel seating for 100 wedding guests and table arrangements for 220 lunch guests and to do tabulations on no-shows. He is also keeping a record of those who give gifts and what they send.
- A new minister was given information concerning the personal and familial problems of his flock stored in a database created by the retiring minister.
- Chicago Alderman Lawrence Bloom keeps a database of 6,000 voters on his computer. Precinct workers can make personalized calls and say "Alderman Bloom helped you get rid of that abandoned car. Now he needs your help."
- Carter Scholz used his personal computer to compute the lengths of a set of tuned wind chimes.
- The Osvoz family of New York, use their personal computer to maintain database of family medical information, including blood types, allergies, dates of checkups, poison antidotes, eyeglass prescriptions, insurance policies, check-up reminders, height, and weight.
- Professionally-prepared programs are available to plan a vacation trip for you, given the starting point and the destination; miles, costs, routes, and itinerary can be computed automatically.
- Dave Adams, a businessman, uses his personal computer with a modem to access on-line airline schedules and make reservations. The Source and CompuServe, among other networks, offer this service.
- Automotive expense records, including the following information, may be tracked using your personal computer: loan or lease payment records, accumulated gasoline costs, MPG average, maintenance and repair records, insurance records, depreciation, automotive tax deductables, and accumulated cost per mile to operate.
- Bill Strozier uses his personal computer to operate a passive solar heating system in his home. The computer controls the opening and closing of movable partitions and shades and an air circulation system. Other personal computer owners have controlled active solar heating collectors, directed air or liquid to areas where it was needed, and analyzed the performance of the system.
- One hobbyist uses a program to organize his elaborate home workshop; he maintains a tool and equipment inventory and lists of parts and supplies, projects completed, and future projects (with tentative starting dates).

- Bird watcher Edward Mair uses a personal computer to store his lifetime, year, state, property, and feeder lists and for exchanging information with other birdwatchers across the nation via a network.

- Several executives, computer programmers, and writers can now do their work at home, rather than traveling to the office, thanks to personal computers linked with their company's computer via modems.

Appendix
Software Source Books

The books and magazines listed below are the most popular guides to microcomputer software available for popular brands of home computers. For many of the applications discussed in this book, there is a professionally designed program available and listed in the guides below.

The Addison-Wesley Book of Apple Software $19.95
   Addison-Wesley
The Addison-Wesley Book of ATARI Software $19.95
   Addison-Wesley
Big Blue Book for the Apple
   Scribner
Big Blue Book for the ATARI
   Scribner
Big Blue Book for the Commodore
   WIDL Video
Big Blue Book for the IBM PC
   WIDL Video
The Buyer's Guide to Software for the IBM PC
   Byte/McGraw-Hill
Commodore Software Encyclopedia
   Howard Sams and Co.
CP/M Software Finder $14.95
   Que Corporation
IBM PC Expansion and Software Guide
   Que Corporation

VanLoves Apple II/III Software Directory $24.95
   VanLoves

PUBLISHER'S ADDRESSES

Addison-Wesley Publishing Co.
Jacob Way
Reading, MA 01867

Byte/McGraw-Hill
1221 Avenue of the Americas
New York, NY 10020

Howard Sames & Co.
4300 W. 63rd St.
Indianapolis, IN 46268

Que Corporation
7960 Castleway Dr.
Indianapolis, IN 46250

Charles Scribner's Sons
597 Fifth Ave.
New York, NY 10017

WIDL Video
5245 W. Diversey Ave.
Chicago, IL 60639

MICROCOMPUTER MANUFACTURERS

Access Matrix Corp.
2159 Bering Drive
San Jose, CA 95131

Albert Computers
3170 Los Feliz Drive
Unit C
Thousand Oaks, CA 91362

Alspa Computer
300 Harvey West Blvd
Santa Cruz, CA 95060

Altos Computer Systems,
2641 Orchard Park Way
San Jose, CA 95134

Apple Computer
20525 Mariani Drive
Cupertino, CA 95014

Atari Products
Box 50047
San Jose, CA 95150

Athena Computer
31952 Camino Capistrano
San Juan Capistrano, CA 92675

Basis, Inc.
5435 Scotts Valley Drive
Scotts Valley, CA 95066

Canon USA
One Canon Plaza
Lake Success, NY 11042

Casio, Inc.
15 Gardner Rd.
Fairfield, NJ 07006

Coleco Industries
945 Asylum Ave.
Hartford, CT 06105

Columbia Data Products
8990 Route 108
Columbia, MD 21045

Commodore Business Mach.
1200 Wilson Drive
West Chester, PA 19380

Compaq Computer Corp.
20333 FM 149
Houston, TX 77070

CompuPro
Box 2355
Oakland Airport, CA 94614

Computer Devices, Inc.
25 North Ave.
Burlington, MA 01803

Cromemco, Inc.
280 Bernado Ave.
Box 7400
Mountain View, CA 94039

Digital Equipment Corp.
2 Mount Royal Ave.
Box 1008
Maynard, MA 01752

Docutel/Olivetti Corp.
155 White Plains Rd.
Tarrytown, NY 10591

Durango Systens
3003 North First St.
San Jose, CA 95134

Dynalogic Info-Tech Corp.
8 Colonnade Road
Ottawa, CANADA, K2E 7M6

Eagle Computer, Inc.
983 University Ave.
Los Gatos, CA 95030

Epson America
3415 Kashiwa St.
Torrance, CA 90505

Formula International
12603 Crenshaw Blvd.
Hawthorne, CA 90250

Franklin Computer Corp.
2138 Route 38
Cherry Hill, NJ 08002

Fujitsu Microelectronics
3320 Scott Blvd.
Santa Clara, CA 95051

Gavilan Computer Corp.
240 Hacienda Ave.
Campbell, CA 95008

Gifford Systems
1922 Republic Ave.
San Leandro, CA 94577

Heath Company
Benton Harbor, MI 49022

Hewlett-Packard
1000 NE Circle Blvd.
Corvallis, OR 97330

Hitachi Sales Corp.
West Artesia
Compton, CA 90220

Honeywell, Inc.
200 Smith St.
Waltham, MA 02154

IBC
21592 Marilla St.
Chatsworth, CA 91311

IBM
Box 1328
Boca Raton, FL 33432

IMS International
2800 Lockheed Way
Carson City, NV 89701

Intertec Data Systems
2300 Broad River Rd.
Columbia, SC 29210

Ithaca Intersystems
200 E. Buffalo, Box 91
Ithaca, NY 14851

Kaypro Division
PO Box N
Del Mar, CA 92014

LNW Research Corp.
2620 Walnut
Tustin, CA 92680

Mattel Electronics
5150 Rosecrans Ave
Hawthorne, CA 90250

Morrow Designs
600 McCormick St.
San Leandro, CA 94577

Multitech Electronics
195 West El Camino Real
Sunnyvale, CA 94086

NEC Home Electronics
1401 Estes Ave.
Elk Grove Village, IL 60007

NEC Information Syst.
5 Militia Drive
Lexington, MA 02173

Netronics Research
333 Litchfield Rd.
New Milford, CT 06776

North Star Computers
14440 Catalina St.
San Leandro, CA 94577

Osborne Computer Corp.
26538 Danti Court
Hayward, CA 94545

Panasonic Co.
One Panasonic Way
Secaucus, NJ 07094

Radio Shack
One Tandy Center
Fort Worth, TX 76102

Sage Computer Tech.
35 North Edison Way, Suite 4
Reno, NV 89502

Sanyo
51 Joseph St.
Moonachie, NJ 07074

Seequa Computer Corp.
209 West St.
Annapolis, MD 21401

Sharp Electronics
10 Sharp Plaza
Paramus, NJ 07652

Sony
Sony Drive
Park Ridge, NJ 07656

Sord Computer
200 Park Ave
New York, NY 10166

Spectravideo
39 W. 37th St.
New York, NY 10018

Sumicom Inc.
17862 East 17 St.
Tustin, CA 92680

TeleVideo Systems
1170 Morse Ave
Sunnyvale, CA 94086

Texas Instruments
Box 53
Lubbock, TX 79408

Timex Computer
Box 1700
Waterbury, CT 06721

Toshiba America
2441 Michelle Dr.
Tustin, CA 92680

Unitronics
401 Grand Ave.
Suite 350
Oakland, CA 94610

Vector Graphic, Inc.
500 North Ventu Park Rd.
Thousand Oaks, CA 91320-2798

Video Technology
2633 Greenleaf Ave.
Elk Grove, IL 60007

Wang Laboratories
One Industrial Ave.
Lowell, MA 01851

Xerox Corp.
1341 West Mockingbird Lane
Dallas, TX 75247

Zenith Data Systems
1000 North Milwaukee Ave
Glenview, IL 60025

Glossary

address—The location in memory where a given binary bit or word of information is stored.

alphanumeric—The set of punctuation, letters of the alphabet, and numerical characters used for computer input.

analog/digital (A/D) conversion—An A/D converter measures incoming voltages and outputs a corresponding digital number for each voltage.

ASCII—The American Standard Code for Information Interchange.

assembly language—A low level symbolic programming language that comes closest to programming a computer in its internal machine language. Instead, machine language code is represented by mneumonics.

binary—The number system of base two, which has two symbols, 1 and 0, representing the on and off states of a circuit.

bit—One binary digit.

byte—An assembly of eight bits representing a computer word. The memory capacity of a computer is usually measured in terms of bytes.

chip—An integrated circuit.

compiler—A program that converts the program statements of a high-level language into machine codes for execution.

CPU (Central Processing Unit)—The major operations center of the computer where decisions and calculations are made.

data—Computer-coded information.

data rate—The amount of information (data) transmitted through a communication line per unit of time.

debug—Remove program errors (bugs) from a program.

digital—A circuit that has only two states, on and off, and is usually represented by the binary number system.

disk—A memory storage device that makes use of a magnetic disk.

DOS—Disk operating system; allows the use of general commands to manipulate data stored on a disk.

firmware—Software permanently stored in a

computer using a read-only-memory (ROM) device.

floppy disk—See disk.

flowchart—A diagram of the various steps to be taken by the computer in running a program.

hardware—The manufactured equipment of a computer system, as opposed to the programs for a computer.

hexadecimal—A base sixteen number system often used in programming in assembly language.

input—Information (data) fed into the computer.

input/output (I/O) devices—Peripheral hardware devices that communicate with or receive communications from the computer.

interface—A device that converts electronic signals to enable two devices to communicate with each other; also called a port.

interpreter—A program that accepts one statement of a high-level language at a time, converts that statement to machine language, and proceeds to the next statement. BASIC is a high-level language that is usually an interpreter rather than compiled.

keyboard—A series of switches, usually in the form of a typewriter keyboard, which a computer operator uses to communicate with the computer.

languages—The sets of words/commands that are understood by the computer and used in writing a program.

loop—A portion of a program that is to be repeated (looped) several times.

machine language—The internal low-level language of the computer.

mainframe—Referring to the hardware of the central processing unit (CPU).

memory—Data (information) stored for future reference by the computer in a series of bytes.

microcomputer—A miniaturized small computer containing all the circuitry of a "minicomputer"

on a single integrated circuit chip.

microprocessor—The single integrated circuit chip that forms the basis of a computer (the CPU).

mnemonic—An abbreviation or word that stands for another word or phrase.

modem—A peripheral device that converts digital signals to audio and vice-versa.

MPU—See CPU.

octal—A base eight number system often used in machine langauge programming.

opcode—An operation code signifying a particular task to be done by the computer.

parallel port—A data communication channel that uses one wire for each bit in a single byte.

peripherals—Input/output devices such as printers, mass storage devices, and terminals.

program—A set of instructions for accomplishing a task that the computer understands.

RAM (random access memory)—Memory devices from which data can be procured or in which data can be stored by the computer.

ROM (read only memory)—Memory devices from which data may be procured only; the memory contents may not be changed.

RS232—A standard form for serial computer interfaces.

serial communication—A method of data communication in which bits of information are sent consecutively through one wire.

software—Computer programs, instructions, and languages.

statement—A single computer instruction.

subroutine—A smaller program (routine) within a larger program.

terminal—An input/output device using a keyboard and video or printer display.

TVT—A television typewriter, or computer terminal.

word—A basic unit of computer memory usually expressed in terms of a byte.

Index

Index

1001 Things to do
with Your IBM PC®

If you are intrigued with the possibilities of the programs included in *1001 Things to do with Your IBM PC®* (TAB Book No. 1826), you should definitely consider having the ready-to-run disk containing the software applications. This software is guaranteed free of manufacturer's defects. (If you have any problems, return the disk within 30 days, and we'll send you a new one.) Not only will you save the time and effort of typing the programs, the disk eliminates the possibility of errors that can prevent the programs from functioning. Interested?

Available on disk at $24.95 for each disk plus $1.00 shipping and handling.